Cambridge International GCSE
Biology

Cambridge International GCSE Biology is tricky, but this lovingly-made CGP book explains everything you need to know — facts, theory, practical skills... the lot.

What's more, we've included lots of exam-style questions to put your knowledge to the test. There's even a set of realistic practice papers in the back. Amazing!

It's great for both the Core and Extended courses — the supplement content for the Extended course is clearly marked up throughout the book.

Complete
Revision & Practice
Everything you need to pass the exams!

Contents

Some of the content in the specification is 'Supplemental'. This content will only be assessed if you're taking the Extended version of the Cambridge International GCSE. We've marked up all the content that's only for the Extended course with purple brackets, like the ones on this box, or the example below:

Information or questions with a bracket like this are for the Extended course only.

Supplement

Supplement

Published by CGP

From original material by Paddy Gannon.

Editors:
Luke Bennett, Ellen Burton, Emily Forsberg, Claire Plowman, Joe Shaw, Camilla Sheridan, Hayley Thompson.

With thanks to Janet Cruse-Sawyer, Sarah Pattison and Glenn Rogers for the proofreading.

ISBN: 978 1 78908 702 4
With thanks to Emily Smith for the copyright research.

DDT diagram on page 134 from Biological Science Combined Volume Hardback, 1990, Soper, Green, Stout, Taylor. © Cambridge University Press 1984, 1990. Reproduced with permission of the Licensor through PLSclear.

Page 199 contains public sector information licensed under the Open Government Licence v 3.0. http://www.nationalarchives.gov.uk/doc/open-government-licence/version/3/

Printed by Elanders Ltd, Newcastle upon Tyne.

Clipart from Corel®

Illustrations by: Sandy Gardner Artist, email sandy@sandygardner.co.uk

Based on the classic CGP style created by Richard Parsons.

Characteristics of Living Organisms

Welcome to the wonderful world of Biology. It's wonderful because it's all about living organisms — which includes you. And all living organisms share the same seven basic characteristics...

The **Seven Basic Characteristics** Are...

The table below shows the seven characteristics in the left-hand column, with their description in the right-hand column. You need to make sure you know them all:

KEY TERM

Characteristic	Description
Movement	An action made by an organism or parts of an organism which results in a change of place or position. This could be to move towards things like water and food, or away from things like predators and poisons. Even plants can move a bit.
Respiration	The chemical reactions that happen in cells to break down nutrient molecules and release the energy needed for metabolism (see p.72). Metabolism is all of the chemical reactions that happen in cells, including respiration. Respiration is what transfers energy for other metabolic reactions.
Sensitivity	The ability of an organism to detect and respond to changes in its internal or external environment (see p.80). E.g. a plant's ability to detect and grow towards light (p.90) or your body's ability to detect a high internal body temperature and sweat (p.87).
Growth	The process by which the size and dry mass of an organism increases permanently. Dry mass is the mass excluding any water in the tissues.
Reproduction	The processes that produce more of the same type of organism (see p.96).
Excretion	The removal of metabolic waste products and of substances that are in excess of what the organism needs (see p.77).
Nutrition	The taking in of substances used for energy, growth and development in organisms.

Remember "Mrs Gren"

REVISION TIP

It's important you learn all seven characteristics and their descriptions. Use the first letter of each characteristic to help you remember them — they spell out "Mrs Gren".

Classification

I hope you like organising things, because it's time to put millions of organisms into groups...

Classification is Organising Living Organisms into Groups

1) There are millions of different organisms living on Earth and they come in a huge range of shapes and sizes — from small and simple (like bacteria) to large and complex (like blue whales). They also have a wide variety of physical features — e.g. wings, beaks, claws, teeth, leaves, branches, etc.

2) All of these organisms can be organised into groups. For example:

- Plants can be divided into two major groups — flowering plants (e.g. daisies) and non-flowering plants (such as ferns and mosses).
- Animals can also be divided into two major groups — invertebrates (which lack a backbone, e.g. insects) and vertebrates (which have a backbone, e.g. mammals).

3) There are different ways of classifying organisms (see next page).

4) One way of classifying organisms is the five kingdom system. In this system, living things are first divided into five groups, called kingdoms:

- Animals — fish, mammals, reptiles, etc.
- Plants — grasses, trees, etc.
- Fungi — mushrooms and toadstools, yeasts, mould.
- Prokaryotes — single-celled organisms without a nucleus.
- Protoctists — eukaryotic (p.5) single-celled or simple multicellular organisms, e.g. algae.

5) These are then subdivided into smaller and smaller groups that have common features.

6) The smallest group in this system is called a species.

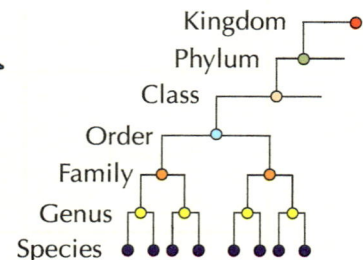

KEY TERM A species is a group of similar organisms that can reproduce to give fertile offspring.

Kingdom
Phylum
Class
Order
Family
Genus
Species

Each Organism has its Own Two-Part Scientific Name in Latin

Organisms are named according to the binomial system.

KEY TERM The binomial system is an internationally agreed system to scientifically name organisms using their genus and species.

1) The first part of a binomial name refers to the genus that the organism belongs to. This gives you information on the organism's ancestry. The second part refers to the species. E.g. humans are known as *Homo sapiens*. 'Homo' is the genus and 'sapiens' is the species.

2) The binomial system is used worldwide and means that scientists in different countries or who speak different languages all refer to a particular species by the same name — avoiding potential confusion.

Classification

Here's some more information about classification systems, and a diagram of an odd-looking tree.

You Can **Classify Organisms** by Their **Features**

1) Organisms can be arranged into different groups based on the internal and external features they share. (This is the way classification was traditionally done.)

2) This means that you can look at an organism and classify it (work out which group it belongs to) by identifying its defining features (see pages 4-8).

DNA Sequencing is Also Used for **Classification**

1) Scientists are now able to determine the sequence (order) of DNA bases in different organisms' genes and compare them.

There's more on DNA on pages 26 and 112.

2) The more similar the base sequences of a gene are, the more closely related the organisms are.

Classification Systems Reflect **Evolutionary Relationships**

1) Evolutionary trees show how scientists think different species are related to each other.

2) They show common ancestors and relationships between species. The more recent the common ancestor, the more closely related the two species — and the more characteristics they're likely to share.

3) Scientists analyse lots of different types of data to work out evolutionary relationships. For living organisms, they use the current classification data (e.g. DNA analysis and structural similarities).

4) Groups of organisms which share a more recent ancestor also have more similar DNA base sequences than groups of organisms that only share a distant ancestor.

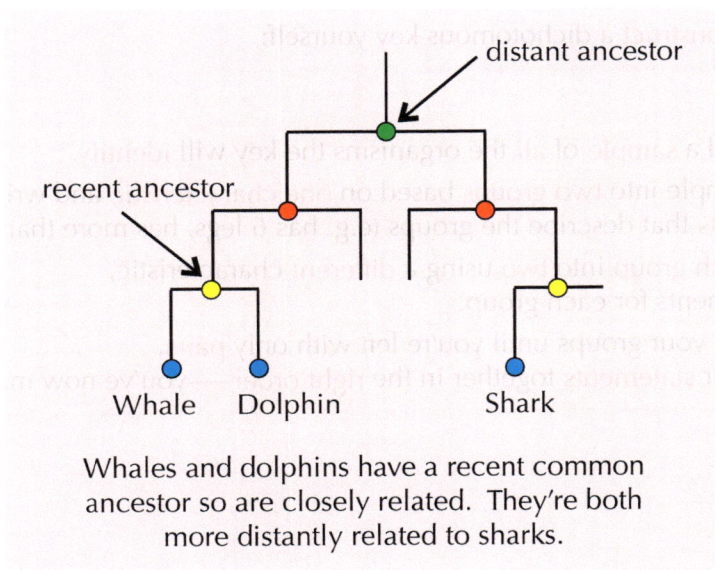

distant ancestor

recent ancestor

Whale   Dolphin   Shark

Whales and dolphins have a recent common ancestor so are closely related. They're both more distantly related to sharks.

Classification systems group together closely related organisms

Classification systems aim to show the evolutionary relationships between organisms by grouping them with their closest relatives. New technology such as DNA sequencing has made this task a lot easier.

Dichotomous Keys

You might need to identify some organisms based on their features. Keys are a useful way of doing that.

Dichotomous Keys are Used to Identify Organisms

1) A key is a written tool that you can use to figure out what an unknown organism is.

2) A dichotomous key is a specific type of key that repeatedly divides groups of organisms into two categories.

3) To use a key you start at question 1, and the answer to that question (which you know by looking at your mystery organism) is used to narrow down your options of what it could be.

4) Sometimes keys will just have statements, rather than questions.

5) As you answer more and more questions you narrow down your options further until eventually you're just left with one possible species your organism could be.

Part of a dichotomous key is shown on the right. It can be used to identify ladybird species.

5)	Black spots on wings	go to 6
	No spots on wings	go to 11
6)	Rings around wing spots	Eyed ladybird
	No rings around wing spots	go to 9

6) You can even construct a dichotomous key yourself:

1) First you need a sample of all the organisms the key will identify.
2) Split your sample into two groups based on one characteristic and write down two statements that describe the groups (e.g. has 6 legs, has more than 6 legs).
3) Then split each group into two using a different characteristic, writing statements for each group.
4) Keep splitting your groups until you're left with only pairs. Then link your statements together in the right order — you've now made a key.

EXAM TIP

Dichotomous keys — unlocking the door of classification...

Dichotomous keys aren't too tricky but you need to make sure you know how to use them and how to construct one yourself. If you're asked to make one in the exam, remember that each question or statement should have only two options.

Features of Organisms

As you saw on page 2, living organisms can be arranged into groups called kingdoms, according to the features they have in common. Here are some of the kingdoms you need to know...

Plants and Animals are Eukaryotic Organisms

Eukaryotic cells have their genetic material in a structure called a nucleus. Plants and animals are eukaryotic organisms — they are made up of eukaryotic cells.

All plants share similar features. So do all animals. Read on to find out more...

For more on the structure of plant and animal cells, see page 11.

Plants

1) Plants are multicellular.
2) They have chloroplasts (see p.11), which means they can photosynthesise and so produce their own food (see p.34).
3) Their cells have cell walls (see p.11), which are made of cellulose.
4) Plants store carbohydrates as sucrose or starch.
5) Plants can reproduce sexually or asexually (see p.96).

Animals

1) Animals are also multicellular.
2) They don't have chloroplasts and they can't photosynthesise — they have to eat other organisms to get food.
3) Their cells don't have cell walls.
4) Most have some kind of nervous coordination (see p.80). This means that they can respond rapidly to changes in their environment.
5) They can usually move around from one place to another.
6) They often store carbohydrate in the form of glycogen.
7) Most animals reproduce sexually.

Fungi are Also Eukaryotic Organisms

1) Some are single-celled, but others have a structure called a mycelium. The mycelium is made up of hyphae (thread-like structures) which contain lots of nuclei.
2) They can't photosynthesise, so they feed off other organisms.
3) Their cells have cell walls made of chitin.
4) They can store carbohydrate as glycogen.
5) They reproduce using spores.

'Nuclei' is the plural of 'nucleus'.

Supplement

Supplement

Features of Organisms

Here are two more kingdoms you need to know about, and a group that isn't a kingdom at all...

Protoctists are Eukaryotic Organisms

1) These are mostly single-celled and microscopic (really tiny).
Some are multicellular and quite big (e.g. seaweed).

2) Some have chloroplasts and are similar to plant cells.
Others are more like animal cells or fungal cells.

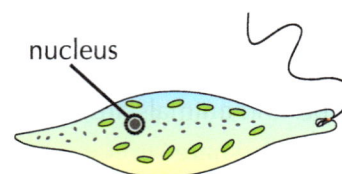

nucleus

Prokaryotes Include Bacteria

1) Prokaryotes are single-celled and microscopic.

2) They don't have a nucleus but they do have a cell wall.

3) They have a circular chromosome of DNA.

4) Some can photosynthesise. Most bacteria feed off other organisms — both living and dead. Some are pathogens — they cause disease (see p.63).

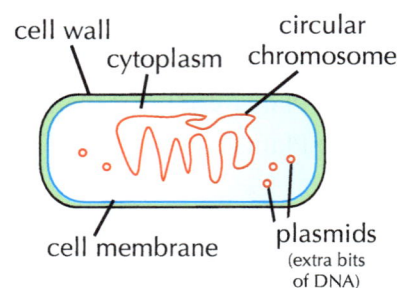

cell wall
cytoplasm
circular chromosome
cell membrane
plasmids (extra bits of DNA)

Prokaryotes are prokaryotic cells.

Viruses are Not One of the Kingdoms

1) Viruses are particles, rather than cells, and are smaller than bacteria.

2) They don't have a cellular structure (e.g. a cell membrane or cytoplasm) — instead they have a protein coat around some genetic material (either DNA or RNA).

3) They can only reproduce inside other living cells — they are parasites. They're also all pathogens.

There's more on DNA on p.26. RNA is a similar type of molecule to DNA.

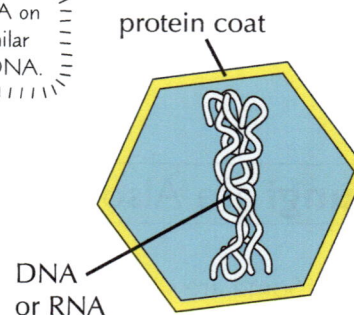

protein coat

DNA or RNA

The organisms within each kingdom have common features

Viruses are not living organisms — they rely on other organisms to reproduce. If you're studying the Extended course, you still need to know a few of their features, as well as the features for the five kingdoms.

More on Features of Organisms

The organisms in different kingdoms can be divided into different groups. You need to know about the main features that are used to classify the organisms in the animal kingdom.

Animals are Divided into Vertebrates and Invertebrates

1) Vertebrates are all species of animals with a backbone and an internal skeleton.
2) Invertebrates do not have these structures, although some have an external skeleton (exoskeleton).
3) Vertebrates are divided into five main groups:

Mammals

- Have hair or fur somewhere on their bodies. Also have sweat glands.
- Have lungs for breathing and external ears.
- Are warm-blooded (able to maintain a constant body temperature).
- Most give birth to their young, though a few species lay eggs.
- Females produce milk from mammary glands to feed their young.

The embryos of mammals that give birth to their young develop inside the female's body. Females develop a placenta during pregnancy (p.104).

Birds

- Have feathers and wings (which help most birds to fly) and scaly feet.
- Have beaks for feeding and lungs for breathing.
- Are warm-blooded.
- Lay eggs to produce offspring.

Reptiles

- Most live on land.
- Have dry scaly skin which stops them from losing too much water.
- Have lungs for breathing.
- Are cold-blooded (unable to maintain a constant body temperature).
- Most lay soft-shelled eggs to produce offspring, but some have live births.

Fish

- Live in water and have fins to swim with.
- Have skeletons made of bone or cartilage. Most fish have scales.
- Have gills for breathing.
- Are cold-blooded.
- Most lay eggs, which are fertilised externally, but some have live births.

Amphibians

- Live on land and in water.
- Have smooth, moist and permeable skin, through which they can breathe. Adults usually have lungs. Some young amphibians have gills.
- Are cold-blooded.
- Most lay their eggs in water to be fertilised externally.

More on Features of Organisms

It's not just vertebrates that you need to know how to classify. Arthropods are a type of invertebrate that have their own features for classification — watch out, there are lot of legs coming up...

There are Four Types of Arthropods

1) Arthropods are invertebrates with exoskeletons and segmented bodies (bodies made of repeating parts).
2) There are four main groups of arthropods:

> 1) Myriapods — have lots of legs. They have one pair of antennae. Centipedes and millipedes are myriapods.

Antennae look a bit like legs attached to the head. Arthropods use them to sense their surroundings.

> 2) Insects — have three pairs of legs and a body that is divided into three parts (a head, a thorax and an abdomen). They have one pair of antennae. They usually have wings. Beetles, ants, bees and butterflies are all insects.

> 3) Arachnids — have four pairs of legs and a body that is divided into two parts (a combined head/thorax and an abdomen). They do not have antennae or wings. Spiders, scorpions and mites are all arachnids.

> 4) Crustaceans — most live in water. They have jointed legs and some have limbs that branch into two at the ends. They have two pairs of antennae but no wings. Crabs, lobsters, shrimps and woodlice are all crustaceans.

Plants are Either Flowering or Non-Flowering

1) Most flowering plants reproduce using flowers and seeds.
2) A lot of non-flowering plants, such as ferns, reproduce with spores, though some use seeds.
3) Flowering plants can be divided into two groups. These groups are based on a structure in plant embryos called a cotyledon. The cotyledon usually forms the first leaf.

> Monocotyledons — these only have one cotyledon. Their petals usually come in multiples of three and the veins in their leaves run parallel to each other.

This lily is a monocotyledon. It has six petals.

> Dicotyledons — these have two cotyledons. They usually have multiples of four or five petals in each flower and the veins in their leaves form a branching network.

This buttercup is a dicotyledon. It has five petals.

Supplement

Four groups of arthropods and I don't like any of them...

Some of the features of the different organisms might seem obvious — but make sure you know the differences between them so that you don't get confused between your cats, catfish and caterpillars.

Warm-Up & Exam Questions

That's it — the first section is finished. Have a go at these questions to see how much you know.
If there's anything you've forgotten, have a look back over the last few pages to remind yourself.

Warm-Up Questions

1) Describe what is meant by nutrition.
2) What is a species?
3) What are arthropods?

Exam Questions

1   Sam is using a dichotomous key to identify some butterflies based on their wing markings.
    Part of the key is shown.

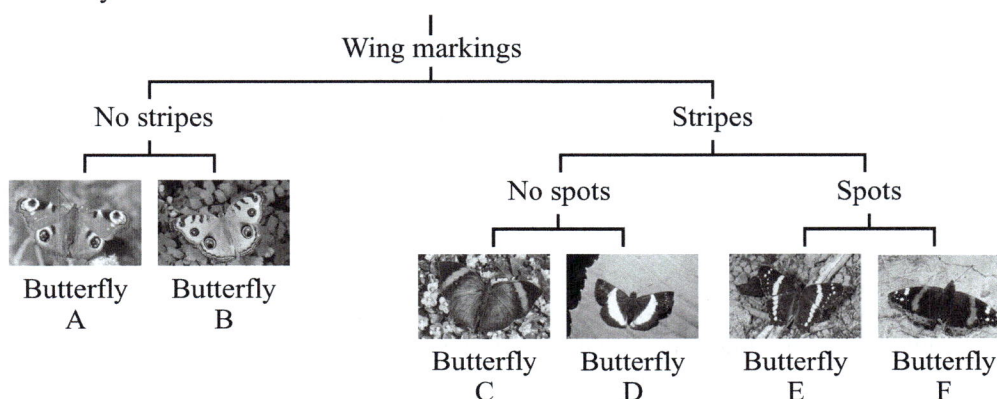

Sam is given the photograph shown below.

(a)   Using the key, describe the wing markings shown on the butterfly in the photograph.

[1]

(b)   Sam uses the key and an information sheet to identify the butterfly species in the photograph.
      It is a Red Admiral butterfly. Which of the butterflies in the key is a Red Admiral butterfly?

[1]

(c)   (i)   Identify which group of arthropods the butterfly belongs to.

[1]

      (ii) Give **one** feature, shown in the photograph, that only this group of arthropods have.

[1]

[Total 4 marks]

Exam Questions

2 The picture on the right shows an adult starfish. Starfish are found in oceans around the world. On the undersides of their arms they have small structures called 'tube feet', which are very sensitive to chemicals in the water, helping them to detect food. When they detect food, they move their arms to travel in the right direction. To reproduce, their arms contain glands which release eggs or sperm into the water.

(a) Give **three** pieces of evidence from the passage that show starfish are living organisms.

[3]

(b) Name the process by which starfish release energy from the food they eat.

[1]

(c) Starfish carry out the process of excretion. Describe what this means.

[1]

(d) Suggest how a very young starfish may differ from the adult starfish above.

[1]

The common starfish has the binomial name *Asterias rubens*.

(e) What genus does it belong to?

[1]

[Total 7 marks]

3 Classification involves arranging living organisms into groups. In one system of classification, organisms are first arranged into five groups called kingdoms.

(a) List the five kingdoms in this classification system.

[1]

Viruses are not living organisms and are not classified into their own kingdom.

(b) Give **two** features of viruses.

[2]

[Total 3 marks]

4 Scientists can carry out DNA analysis to determine the evolutionary relationships between organisms.

(a) Explain how DNA sequencing can be used to determine relationships between organisms.

[2]

The table below shows the percentage similarities between the DNA sequences of humans and four other organisms.

Organism	A	B	C	D
% DNA sequence similarity to humans	18	44	92	54

(b) Suggest which of the organisms, A-D, is most closely related to humans. Explain your answer.

[2]

[Total 4 marks]

Supplement

Cells

Cells are the microscopic building blocks of all life. They have their own building blocks as well.

Plant and Animal Cells have Similarities and Differences

Animal Cells

One of the big differences between plant and animal cells is the structures in the cells. Most animal cells have the following structures — make sure you know them all:

1) Nucleus — contains genetic material that controls the activities of the cell.

2) Cell membrane — holds the cell together and controls what goes in and out.

3) Ribosomes — these are where proteins are made in the cell.

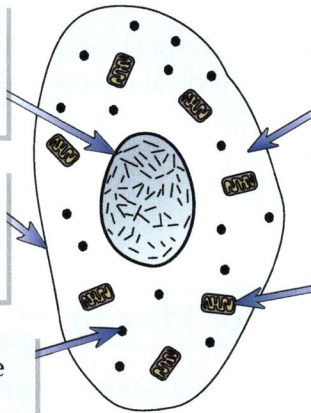

4) Cytoplasm — gel-like substance where most of the chemical reactions happen. It contains enzymes (see page 29) that control these chemical reactions. It also contains other cell structures.

5) Mitochondria — these are where most of the reactions for aerobic respiration take place (see page 72).

Plant Cells

Plant cells usually have all the structures that animal cells have, plus a few extra things that animal cells don't have:

1) Rigid cell wall — made of cellulose. It supports the cell and strengthens it.

2) Vacuole — contains cell sap, a weak solution of sugar and salts. It helps to keep the cell plump and swollen.

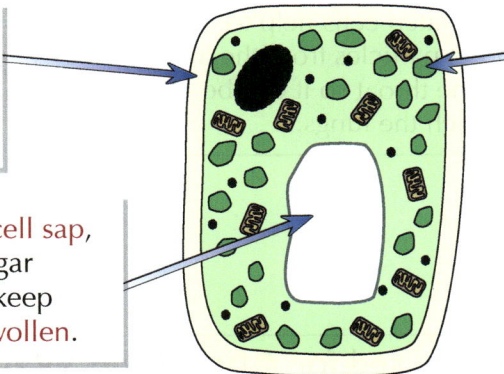

3) Chloroplasts — these are where photosynthesis occurs, which makes food for the plant (see page 34). They contain a green substance called chlorophyll, which absorbs the light needed for photosynthesis.

Bacterial Cells Have No Nucleus

Bacterial cells are a lot smaller than plant or animal cells. Here's what a bacterial cell might look like:

1) Circular DNA — controls the cell's activities and replication. It floats free in the cytoplasm (not in a nucleus).

2) Plasmids — small loops of extra DNA that aren't part of the circular DNA. Plasmids contain genes for things like drug resistance (see p.94), and can be passed between bacteria.

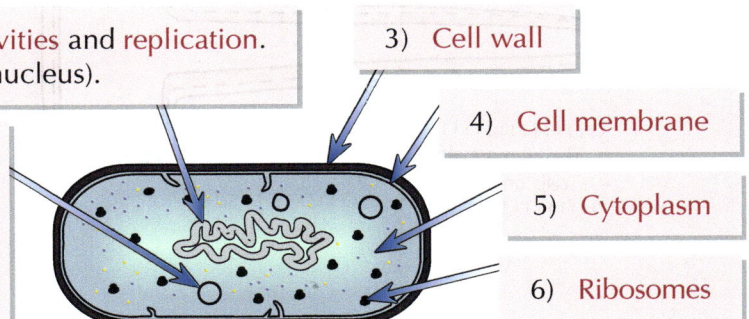

3) Cell wall

4) Cell membrane

5) Cytoplasm

6) Ribosomes

Specialised Cells

The previous page shows the structure of some typical cells.
However, most cells are specialised for a particular function, so their structure can vary...

Different Cells Have Different Functions

1) Multicellular organisms are organisms that contain lots of different types of cells (i.e. cells with different structures).
2) Cells that have a structure which makes them adapted to their function are called specialised cells.
3) You need to know examples of how some specialised cells are adapted to their functions. Let's take a look at ciliated cells first...

Ciliated Cells Are Specialised for Moving Materials

1) Ciliated cells line the inner surfaces of some animal organs.
2) They have cilia (hair-like structures) on the top surface of the cell.
3) The function of these ciliated cells is to move substances — the cilia beat to move substances in one direction, along the surface of the tissue.

In the trachea and bronchi (tubes that carry air to and from your lungs), ciliated cells help to move mucus (and all of the particles from the air that it has trapped) up to the throat so it can be swallowed and doesn't reach the lungs.

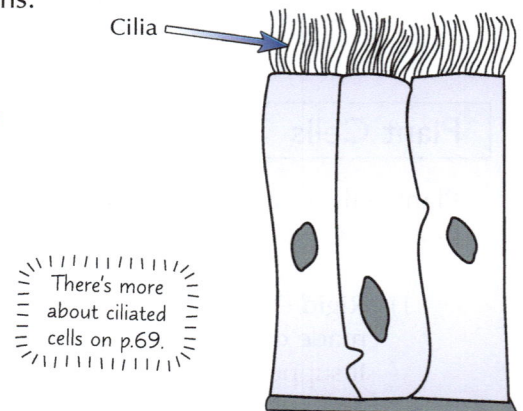

Cilia

There's more about ciliated cells on p.69.

Root Hair Cells are Specialised for Absorbing Water and Minerals

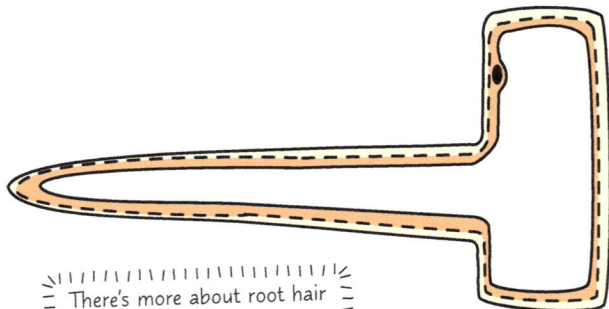

1) Root hair cells are cells on the surface of plant roots, which grow into long "hairs" that stick out into the soil.
2) This gives the plant a big surface area for absorbing water and mineral ions from the soil.

There's more about root hair cells on pages 24 and 49.

Specialised Cells

Sperm and Egg Cells are Specialised for Reproduction

1) The main functions of an egg are to carry the female DNA and to nourish the developing embryo in the early stages of its development.

2) An egg cell is adapted to nourish the embryo because it is large and contains nutrients in the cytoplasm to feed the embryo.

Sperm and egg cells are sex cells (gametes). There's more about sperm and egg cells on page 103.

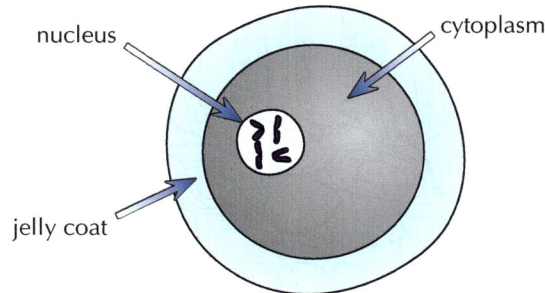

nucleus   cytoplasm

jelly coat

3) The function of a sperm is to transport the male's DNA to the female's egg. This is how it's adapted to its function:

Flagellum   Middle section   Nucleus   Head

Acrosome

1) A sperm cell has a long flagellum (tail) and a streamlined head to help it swim to the egg.

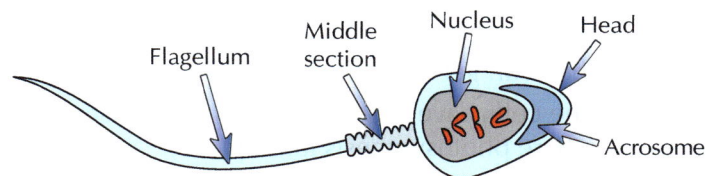

2) It has enzymes in its 'head', which are needed to digest through the membrane of the egg cell. These enzymes are stored in the acrosome.

3) It has lots of mitochondria (p.11) in the middle section to provide the energy (from respiration) needed to swim this distance.

Neurones are Specialised for Impulse Conduction

1) The function of neurones (nerve cells) is to conduct (carry) electrical impulses (signals) from one part of the body to another.

2) These cells are long (to cover more distance) and have branched connections at their ends to connect to other neurones and form a network throughout the body.

There's more about neurones on p.80.

Specialised Cells

Palisade Mesophyll Cells are Specialised for Photosynthesis

1) Palisade mesophyll cells are where most of the photosynthesis happens in a plant leaf.

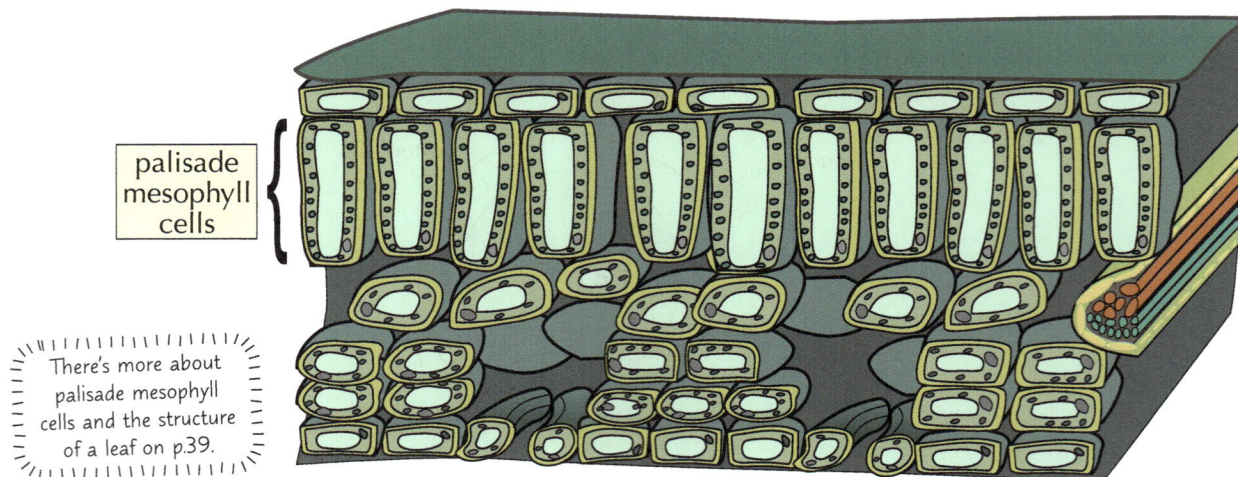

palisade mesophyll cells

There's more about palisade mesophyll cells and the structure of a leaf on p.39.

2) Palisade mesophyll cells are found in a layer near the top of the leaf. Being near the top means they can get the most light for photosynthesis.

The upper layers of the leaf are transparent so that light can pass through it to the palisade mesophyll layer.

3) The cells have lots of chloroplasts (the structures where photosynthesis takes place).

4) They're also long and thin, so more of them can be packed into the same space.

Red Blood Cells are Specialised to Transport Oxygen

1) The job of red blood cells is to transport oxygen from the lungs to all the cells in the body.

2) Their shape is a biconcave disc (a disc that's squashed in the centre) — this gives a large surface area for absorbing oxygen.

3) They contain a red pigment called haemoglobin. This substance allows red blood cells to carry oxygen.

4) They don't have a nucleus — this allows more room to carry oxygen.

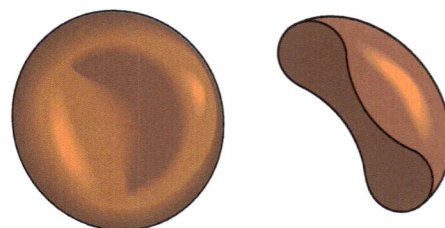

There's more about red blood cells on p.58.

REVISION TIP

Cells have the same basic structures but are often specialised

Make sure you know the structures of a typical animal, plant and bacterial cell. Try copying out the diagrams and see if you can remember all the labels. And remember, specialised cells might look different from these typical cells and not all of them will contain all of the structures.

Levels of Organisation

Multicellular organisms contain lots of cells. These need some form of organisation.

Cells are the Most Basic Level of Organisation

1) All living things are made up of cells.
2) The structure of a cell depends on the type of organism (see p.11) and the function of the cell (see p.12-14).
3) To make new cells, existing cells needs to undergo cell division (see p.113).
4) Multicellular organisms organise these cells into increasingly more complex levels.

Single-celled organisms consist of a single cell and include yeast and bacteria. Multicellular organisms include plants and animals.

Similar Cells are Organised into Tissues

1) A tissue is a group of similar cells that work together to carry out a shared function.
2) A tissue can include more than one type of cell.

In mammals (like humans) an example of a tissue is muscular tissue. This contracts (shortens) to move whatever it's attached to. E.g. when you breathe in, intercostal muscles between the ribs contract to move the ribs upwards (see page 68).

Muscular tissue

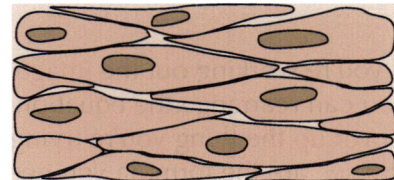

Tissues are Organised into Organs

An organ is a group of different tissues that work together to perform specific functions.

Lungs in mammals and leaves on plants are two examples of organs — they're both made up of several different tissue types. The function of the lungs is gas exchange. Leaves have several functions, including carrying out most photosynthesis.

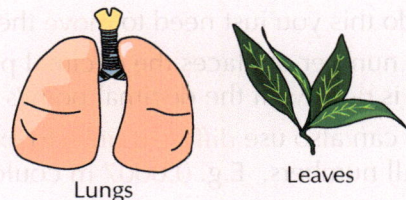

Lungs

Leaves

Organs Make Up Organ Systems

1) An organ system is a group of organs working together to perform body functions.

For example, in mammals, the urinary system is made up of organs including the kidneys, ureters, bladder and urethra. Its function is the removal of waste from the body.

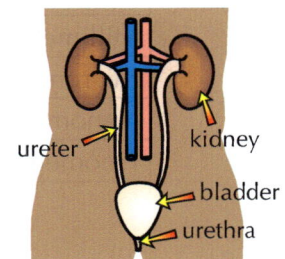

2) Organ systems work together to make entire organisms.

ureter

kidney

bladder

urethra

The Urinary System

Remember — cells, tissues, organs, organ systems, organisms

It's important to understand the levels of organisation in organisms. Read the page again if you need to.

Magnification

You can use microscopes to look at cells. Sometimes you need to do a bit of maths with microscope images.

Magnification is **How Many Times Bigger** the Image is

1) Microscopes use lenses to magnify images (make them look bigger).

2) If you know the actual size of a specimen and have measured the size of the microscope image, you can work out the magnification of the image. This is the formula you need:

$$\text{magnification} = \frac{\text{image size}}{\text{actual size}}$$

Both measurements should have the same units. If they don't, you'll need to convert them first (see below).

EXAMPLE:
A magnified image is 2 mm wide, and the specimen is 0.02 mm wide. What is the magnification?

$$\text{magnification} = \frac{\text{image size}}{\text{actual size}} = \frac{2}{0.02} = \times\ 100$$

3) If you're working out the image size or the actual size of the object, you can rearrange the equation using this formula triangle. Cover up the thing you're trying to find. The parts you can still see are the formula you need to use.

$$\frac{\text{image size}}{\text{magnification} \times \text{actual size}}$$

You Might Need to **Convert Units** or Use **Standard Form**

1) Because microscopes can see such tiny objects, sometimes it's useful to write figures in standard form.

2) This is where you change very big or small numbers with lots of zeros into something more manageable, e.g. 0.017 can be written 1.7×10^{-2}.

3) To do this you just need to move the decimal point left or right.

4) The number of places the decimal point moves is then represented by a power of 10 — this is positive if the decimal point's moved to the left, and negative if it's moved to the right.

5) You can also use different units to express very big or very small numbers. E.g. 0.0007 m could be written as 0.7 mm.

6) The table shows you how to convert between different units. The right hand column of the table shows you how each unit can be expressed as a metre in standard form.

To convert	Unit	To convert	In standard form:
× 1000	Millimetre (mm)	÷ 1000	$\times\ 10^{-3}$ m
× 1000	Micrometre (μm)	÷ 1000	$\times\ 10^{-6}$ m
× 1000	Nanometre (nm)	÷ 1000	$\times\ 10^{-9}$ m
	Picometre (pm)		$\times\ 10^{-12}$ m

So 1 pm = 0.000000000001 m.

If you're taking the Core exams, you only need to be able to use millimetres in magnification calculations. If you're taking the Extended exams, you need to be able to convert between millimetres and micrometres in magnification calculations.

7) These conversions work for lots of other units too, e.g. 1 milligram (mg) = 1000 micrograms (μg).

REVISION TIP

Learn the formula for calculating magnification

You might need to use that formula triangle in the exam, so make sure you know it off by heart. If you can remember that image size goes at the top of the triangle, you can easily fill the rest of the formula in at the bottom — just remember 'image' begins with i and goes high in the triangle.

Warm-Up & Exam Questions

It's easy to think you've learnt everything in the section until you try the questions.
Don't panic if there's a bit you've forgotten, just go back over that bit until you know you really remember it.

Warm-Up Questions

1) Give two similarities and two differences between the
   structure of an animal cell and the structure of a plant cell.
2) Give one cellular structure found in animal cells but not in bacterial cells.
3) Name the structure in a plant cell that contains the genetic material that controls
   the activities of the cell.

Exam Questions

1   The diagram on the right shows a typical plant cell.

   (a)   Which label points to a chloroplast? Tick **one** box.

   ☐ **A**   ☐ **B**   ☐ **C**   ☐ **D**

[1]

   (b)   What is the function of a chloroplast?

[1]

   (c)   The diagram also shows a cell wall.
         What is the function of a cell wall?

[1]
[Total 3 marks]

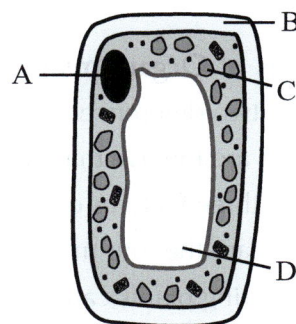

2   The diagram on the right shows a root hair cell.
     Explain how a root hair cell is specialised for its function.

[Total 2 marks]

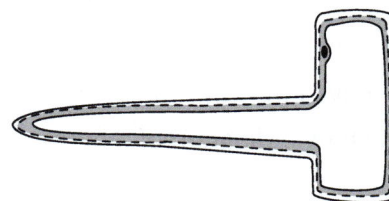

3   A microscope is used to observe a layer of onion cells on a slide.

   (a)   When the onion cell is viewed with × 100 magnification, the image of the cell is 7.5 mm wide.
         Calculate the actual width of the onion cell using the formula:

   $$\text{magnification} = \frac{\text{image size}}{\text{actual size}}$$

   Give your answer in mm.

[2]

   (b)   Convert your answer from **part (a)** into μm.

[1]
[Total 3 marks]

Revision Summary for Sections 1 & 2

That's the end of Sections 1 & 2 — time to put yourself to the test and find out how much you really know.
* Try these questions and tick off each one when you get it right.
* When you've done all the questions for a topic and are completely happy with it, tick off the topic.

Characteristics of Living Organisms (p.1) ☑

1) Define movement.
2) Why is respiration important?
3) True or false? Growth is the temporary increase in the dry mass of an organism.

Classification and Dichotomous Keys (p.2-4) ☑

4) How does the binomial system name organisms?
5) True or false? Organisms can be classified based on their features.
6) True or false? The more closely related two organisms are, the less recent their common ancestor.
7) What is a dichotomous key?

Features of Organisms (p.5-8) ☑

8) Give two differences between animals and plants.
9) What are the five main groups of vertebrates?
10) Give three features of birds.
11) What are the four main groups of arthropods?
12) Flowering plants can be divided into two main groups — what are they?

Cells and Specialised Cells (p.11-14) ☑

13) Name three structures that are found in the cytoplasm of an animal cell.
14) What is the function of the cell membrane?
15) What is the purpose of the ciliated cells that line the bronchi and trachea?
16) Give one way that a sperm cell is adapted for swimming to an egg cell.
17) Draw a diagram of a neurone. Why is it this shape?

Levels of Organisation (p.15) ☑

18) What is a tissue?
19) What name is given to a group of different tissues working together to perform specific functions?
20) Give one example of an organ and one example of an organ system.

Magnification (p.16) ☑

21) What is the formula for calculating magnification?
22) How would you write 0.017 using standard form?
23) What number do you multiply by to convert from millimetres to micrometres?

Diffusion

Diffusion is really important in living organisms — it's how a lot of substances get in and out of cells. In diffusion, particles move about randomly until they end up evenly spaced.

Diffusion is Just Particles Spreading Out

1) Diffusion is simple. It's just the gradual movement of particles from places where there are lots of them to places where there are fewer of them.

KEY TERM — Diffusion is the net movement of particles from an area of higher concentration to an area of lower concentration as a result of their random movement.

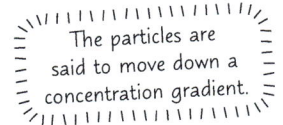

The particles are said to move down a concentration gradient.

2) Diffusion happens in both solutions and gases — that's because the particles in these substances (solutes or gas molecules) are free to move about randomly.

3) The simplest type is when different gases diffuse through each other. This is what's happening when the smell of perfume diffuses through a room:

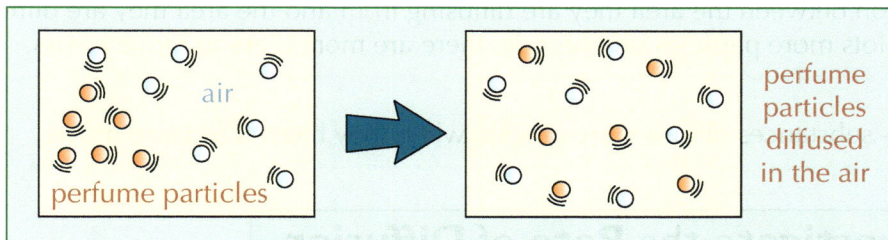

perfume particles

air

perfume particles diffused in the air

4) Diffusion is due to the molecules and ions moving about randomly because of their kinetic energy. It doesn't require any additional energy from cells to make it happen.

Cell Membranes are Pretty Clever...

1) They're clever because they hold the cell together but they let stuff in and out as well.

2) Only small molecules can diffuse through cell membranes though — things like glucose, amino acids, water and oxygen. Big molecules like starch and proteins can't fit through the membrane.

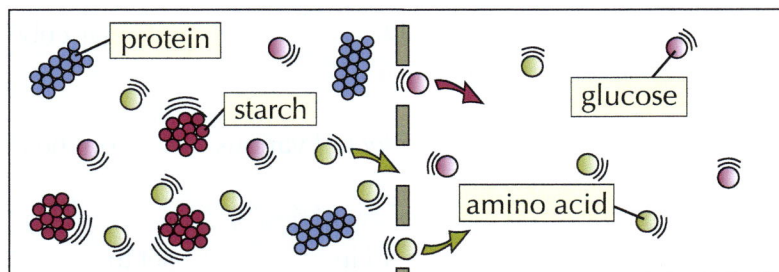

protein

starch

glucose

amino acid

- Just like with diffusion in air, particles flow through the cell membrane from where there's a higher concentration (more of them) to where there's a lower concentration (fewer of them).
- They're only moving about randomly of course, so they go both ways — but if there are a lot more particles on one side of the membrane, there's a net (overall) movement from that side.

3) Diffusion allows cells to obtain substances they need to survive (such as oxygen and nutrients). It also allows them to get rid of waste products (like carbon dioxide).

Investigating Diffusion

You need to know about the four different factors that affect diffusion, and how you can investigate them.

The **Rate of Diffusion** Depends on **Four Main Things**

1) Surface area — the more surface there is for molecules to move across, the faster they can get from one side to the other. This means that the bigger the surface area to volume ratio of an object, the faster particles will diffuse in or out of it.

Have a look at this example using cubes. The smaller cube has a larger surface area to volume ratio.

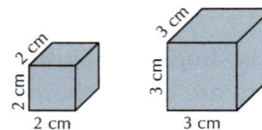

Surface area / cm²	$2 \times 2 \times 6 = 24$	$3 \times 3 \times 6 = 54$
Volume / cm³	$2 \times 2 \times 2 = 8$	$3 \times 3 \times 3 = 27$
Surface area to volume ratio	$24 : 8 = \underline{3 : 1}$	$54 : 27 = \underline{2 : 1}$

2) Temperature — the higher the temperature, the greater the kinetic energy of the molecules and therefore the faster their movement.

3) Concentration gradient — substances diffuse faster if there's a big difference in concentration between the area they are diffusing from and the area they are diffusing to. If there are lots more particles on one side, there are more there to move across.

4) Distance — substances diffuse more quickly when they haven't as far to move.

You Can **Investigate** the **Rate** of **Diffusion**

Phenolphthalein is a pH indicator — it's pink in alkaline solutions and colourless in acidic solutions. You can use it to investigate diffusion in agar jelly:

1) First, make up some agar jelly with phenolphthalein and dilute sodium hydroxide. This will make the jelly pink.
2) Put some dilute hydrochloric acid in a beaker.
3) Cut out a few cubes from the jelly and put them in the beaker of acid.
4) The cubes turn colourless as the acid diffuses into the jelly and neutralises the sodium hydroxide.
5) Time how long it takes for the colour to change.

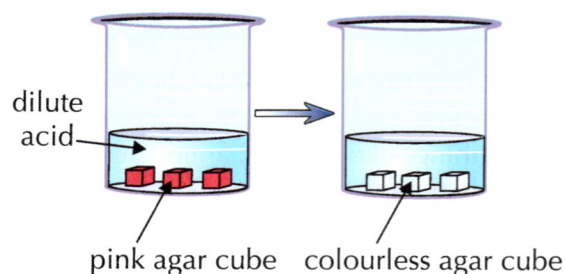

dilute acid

pink agar cube   colourless agar cube

You can modify this experiment to investigate the effect of various factors on the rate of diffusion:

- Surface area — use different sized cubes of agar jelly.
- Temperature — put the beakers of dilute acid in water baths set to different temperatures.
- Concentration gradient — use different concentrations of dilute acid.

To investigate the effect of distance on rate, you'll need to carry out a slightly different experiment:

1) Fill two identical beakers with different volumes of water, e.g. 100 cm³ and 250 cm³.
2) Once the water is still, add a couple of drops of ink to each beaker.
3) Time how long it takes for the ink to spread out completely in each beaker.

Water and Osmosis

Water is needed by all living organisms to stay alive. It travels into and out of cells by osmosis.

Water is Important as a Solvent

Water is a major component of living organisms. It is a solvent, which means that some substances dissolve in it to form a solution. Most chemical reactions take place in solution. Water is important as a solvent in:

1) TRANSPORT — for example, water allows soluble molecules, such as urea (a waste product produced from the breakdown of proteins), glucose and amino acids, to be transported around the body in the blood. Water also transports soluble mineral ions from the roots to the leaves in plants.

2) DIGESTION — digestive enzymes need to be in solution to work properly. Water helps animals to digest food by acting as a solvent for the enzymes. Water also acts as a solvent for the products of digestion, which allows them to diffuse into the bloodstream.

3) EXCRETION — all living organisms need to get rid of metabolic waste products such as urea and other toxins. These toxins are often dissolved in water, e.g. urea is removed in both sweat and urine (wee).

Osmosis is a Special Case of Diffusion

1) Water diffuses through partially permeable membranes by osmosis.

2) A partially permeable membrane is just one with very small holes in it. So small, in fact, only tiny molecules (like water) can pass through them, and bigger molecules (e.g. sucrose) can't.

3) A cell membrane is a partially permeable membrane.

4) The water molecules actually pass both ways through the membrane during osmosis. This happens because water molecules move about randomly all the time.

5) But because there are more water molecules on one side than on the other, there's a steady net flow of water into the region with fewer water molecules, e.g. into the sucrose solution.

6) This means the sucrose solution gets more dilute. The water acts like it's trying to "even up" the concentration either side of the membrane.

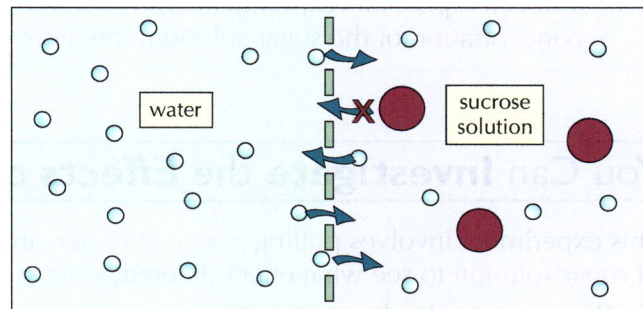

Net movement of water molecules

When water molecules diffuse, their net movement is from an area of higher concentration to an area of lower concentration — like all diffusing particles.

Water Potential Tells You How Concentrated a Solution is

1) You can talk about osmosis in terms of water potential — water potential is the potential (likelihood) of water molecules to diffuse out of or into a solution.

2) If a solution has a high water potential, then it has a high concentration of water molecules. If it has a low water potential, then it has a low concentration of water molecules.

Pure water has the highest water potential. All solutions have a lower water potential than pure water.

3) So, you can say that:

KEY TERM

Osmosis is the net movement of water molecules from an area of higher water potential to an area of lower water potential, across a partially permeable membrane.

4) You could also describe osmosis as the net movement of water molecules from a dilute solution to a concentrated solution, across a partially permeable membrane.

Supplement

Investigating Osmosis

You need to know some different ways to investigate osmosis.

You Can Investigate Osmosis Using Dialysis Tubing

1) Fix some dialysis tubing over the end of a thistle funnel. Then pour some sugar solution down the glass tube into the thistle funnel.

2) Put the thistle funnel into a beaker of pure water — measure where the sugar solution comes up to on the glass tube.

3) Leave the apparatus overnight, then measure where the solution is in the glass tube. Water should be drawn through the dialysis tubing by osmosis and this will force the solution up the glass tube.

Dialysis tubing is a partially permeable membrane.

Glass tube

Dialysis tubing covering the open end of thistle funnel

Pure water

4) You can repeat this experiment with different concentrations of sugar solution. The higher the concentration of the sugar solution, the more water should be drawn into the glass tube.

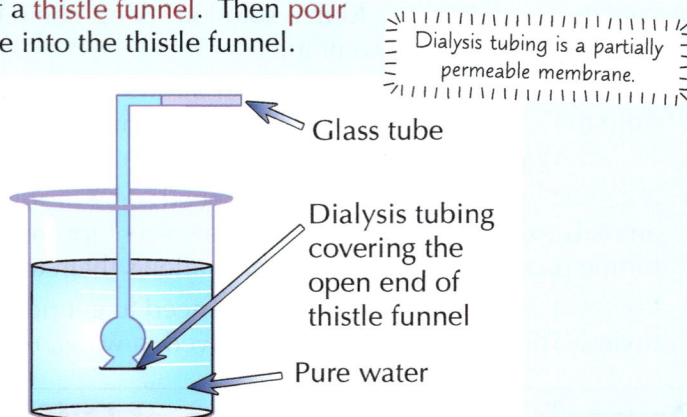

You Can Investigate the Effects of Osmosis in Plant Tissues

This experiment involves putting potato cylinders into different concentrations of sugar solution to see what effect different water concentrations have on them.

1) Prepare some beakers with different sugar solutions in them. One should be pure water and another should be a very concentrated sugar solution. Then you can have a few others with concentrations in between.

The higher the concentration of the sugar solution, the lower the water concentration.

2) Peel a potato to remove the skin, then use a cork borer to cut the potato into identical cylinders.

3) Weigh each cylinder to find its mass.

4) Leave one cylinder in each beaker for thirty minutes (make sure they all get the same amount of time).

The only thing that you should change in each beaker is the concentration of the sugar solution. Everything else (e.g. the volume of solution and the time the cylinder is left for) must be kept the same in each case or the experiment won't be a fair test.

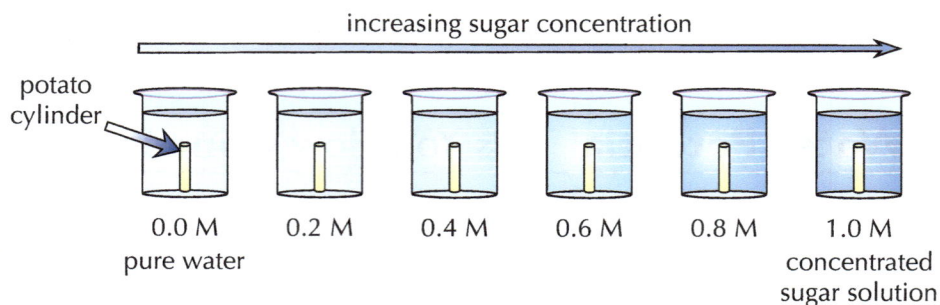

increasing sugar concentration

potato cylinder

| 0.0 M pure water | 0.2 M | 0.4 M | 0.6 M | 0.8 M | 1.0 M concentrated sugar solution |

5) Remove the cylinders and pat dry gently with a paper towel. This removes excess water from the surface of the cylinders.

6) Weigh each cylinder again and record the mass.

7) If the cylinders were placed in a solution with a higher concentration of water molecules than the solution inside the potato cells, they will have drawn in water by osmosis. This means they'll have increased in mass.

8) If the cylinders were placed in a solution with a lower concentration of water molecules than the solution inside the potato cells, water will have been drawn out by osmosis. This means they'll have decreased in mass.

This experiment uses sugar as a solute, but you could also do it with different solutes (e.g. salt). You could even do it with a different root vegetable, e.g. a carrot or swede (rutabaga).

Osmosis and Cells

You need to know more specifically about how osmosis affects plant cells.

Osmosis Affects **Plant Cells**

1) As you saw in the investigation on the previous page, water can be drawn into or out of plant cells by osmosis.

2) If a plant cell is placed in a solution with a higher concentration of water molecules than the solution inside the plant cell, water will move into the cell by osmosis. This will make the cell become plump and swollen.

3) A plump and swollen cell is called a turgid cell.

4) When the plant cell is full of water, the pressure of the water presses outwards on the cell wall. This helps to support the cell. When all its cells are full of water, the plant as a whole is supported.

5) The pressure of the water against the inelastic (rigid) cell wall is called turgor pressure.

6) If a plant cell is placed in a solution with a lower concentration of water molecules than the solution inside the plant cell, water will move out of the cell by osmosis. This will make the cell become limp and wilted.

7) A limp and wilted cell is called a flaccid cell.

8) If the plant's really short of water, the cytoplasm inside its cells starts to shrink and the membrane pulls away from the cell wall. This process is called plasmolysis.

Plants absorb water from the soil through their root hair cells (see p.12).
The water potential of the soil always tends to be higher than that of the solution inside root hair cells, which allows the plant to constantly draw in water by osmosis.

Osmosis Affects the Cells of **Other Organisms** too

1) Animal cells don't have cell walls so they're more affected by their surroundings than plant cells.

2) Tissue fluid surrounds the cells and tissues in the body — it's basically just water with oxygen and glucose dissolved in it. It's squeezed out of the capillaries to supply cells and tissues with everything they need.

3) The tissue fluid will usually have a different water potential to the fluid inside a cell or tissue. This means that water will either move into the cell or tissue from the tissue fluid, or out of the cell or tissue, by osmosis.

4) The lack of cell walls means that animal cells can burst if they're surrounded by a solution with a higher water potential than them. If the water potential of the solution surrounding a cell is lower than the cell, the cell can shrivel up and die.

Water always moves into the more concentrated solution

That's why it's bad to drink sea-water. The high salt content means you end up with a much lower water potential in your blood and tissue fluid than in your cells. All the water is sucked out of your cells by osmosis and they shrivel and die. So next time you're stranded at sea, remember this...

Active Transport

Sometimes substances need to be absorbed against a concentration gradient, i.e. from a lower to a higher concentration. This is done by a process called active transport.

Active Transport Works Against a Concentration Gradient

1) Active transport is different from diffusion because particles are moved against a concentration gradient rather than down a concentration gradient.

2) Unlike diffusion, active transport also requires energy in addition to kinetic energy to make it work.

KEY TERM

Active transport is the movement of particles across a cell membrane from an area of lower concentration to an area of higher concentration using energy from respiration.

Respiration is a series of chemical reactions in cells that releases energy for the cells — see p.72 for more.

3) Active transport uses proteins called carriers to move molecules and ions across cell membranes. These proteins are embedded (permanently stuck) in the membranes.

Root Hairs Take in Minerals Using Active Transport

Active transport is an important process. It's used to move molecules and ions into and out of cells when diffusion would mean that they'd move in the wrong direction. Here's an example:

1) Plants need mineral ions for healthy growth.

Water is taken into root hair cells by osmosis (see page 23).

2) The concentration of minerals is usually higher in a plant's root hair cells (see p.12) than in the soil around them.

3) This means plants can't use diffusion to take up mineral ions from the soil. If they followed the rules of diffusion, minerals would move out of the root hair cells.

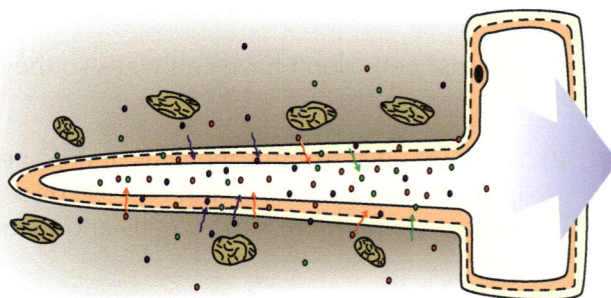

4) Instead, the cells use active transport to move minerals across their cell membranes. This allows the plant to absorb minerals from a very dilute solution, against a concentration gradient.

Supplement

REVISION TIP

Active transport is an active process — it requires energy

Active transport involves moving substances against the concentration gradient, so it needs additional energy from respiration to make it work. Think of it like this: if you're trying to walk along a crowded street, it's hard to walk in the opposite direction to the one most people are travelling in. You have to push your way through — and that requires energy.

Warm-Up & Exam Questions

Question time again — Warm-Up first, then Exam (or the other way round if you want to be different).

Warm-Up Questions

1) What is the definition of osmosis? Use the term 'water potential' in your answer.
2) Give one difference between diffusion and active transport.

Exam Questions

1 In an experiment, four identical cylinders were cut from a fresh potato.
The cylinders were then placed in different sugar solutions, as shown below.
After 30 minutes the potato cylinders were removed and their masses measured.

| Tube A | Tube B | Tube C | Tube D |

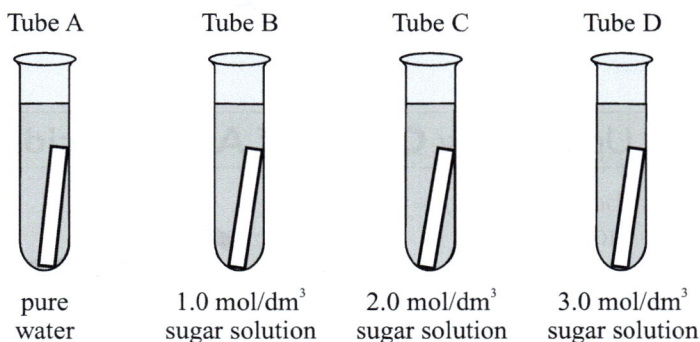

| pure water | 1.0 mol/dm³ sugar solution | 2.0 mol/dm³ sugar solution | 3.0 mol/dm³ sugar solution |

(a) Which potato cylinder would you expect to have the lowest mass after 30 minutes?
Explain your answer.

[2]

(b) The potato cylinder in tube A increased in mass during the 30 minutes. Explain why.

[2]

[Total 4 marks]

2 A student made up some agar jelly with cresol red solution and dilute ammonium hydroxide.
Cresol red solution is a pH indicator that is red in alkaline solutions and yellow in acidic solutions.
He cut the agar jelly into cubes of different sizes, and placed the cubes in a beaker of dilute
hydrochloric acid. He measured how long it took for the cubes to change from red to yellow as the
acid moved into the agar jelly and neutralised the ammonium hydroxide. His results are shown.

Size / mm	Time taken for cube to become yellow / s			
	Trial 1	Trial 2	Trial 3	Trial 4
5 × 5 × 5	174	167	177	182
7 × 7 × 7	274	290	284	292
10 × 10 × 10	835	825	842	838

(a) Name the process by which hydrochloric acid moves into the cubes in this experiment.

[1]

(b) Explain the relationship between the size of the cube and the time taken for it to become yellow.

[2]

[Total 3 marks]

Biological Molecules

Biological molecules (molecules found in living organisms) are things like carbohydrates, proteins, fats and DNA. They're generally long, complex molecules made up from smaller basic units.

Learn the Structure of Carbohydrates, Proteins and Fats

Carbohydrates are Made Up of Simple Sugars

- Carbohydrate molecules contain the elements carbon, hydrogen and oxygen.
- Starch (in plants) and glycogen (in animals) are used as short-term energy stores. Cellulose is the main component of plant cell walls.
- They are all large, complex carbohydrates, which are made up of many smaller molecules of glucose (a simple sugar) joined together in a long chain.

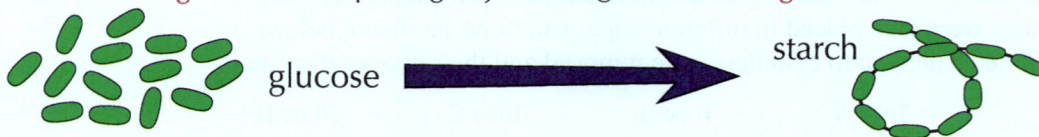

glucose ⟶ starch

Proteins are Made Up of Long Chains of Amino Acids

- Proteins all contain carbon, nitrogen, hydrogen and oxygen atoms.
- Some proteins also contain sulfur atoms.

amino acids ⟶ proteins

Fats and Oils are Made Up of Fatty Acids and Glycerol

- Fats contain carbon, hydrogen and oxygen atoms.

glycerol & fatty acids ⟶ fat

DNA is a Double Helix

1) A DNA molecule has two strands coiled together in the shape of a double helix (two spirals).

2) Each strand is made up of chemicals known as bases. There are four different bases (shown in the diagram as different colours) — A, C, G and T.

3) The two strands are held together by bonds that are formed between pairs of bases.

4) A always pairs with T, and C always pairs with G.

base pairings

A ⟶ T
C ⟶ G

Supplement

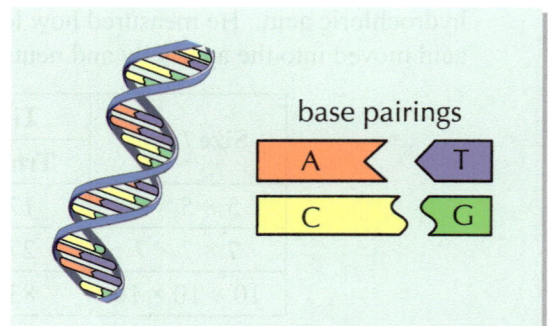

Biological molecules are the basic units of Biology

EXAM TIP Since all living organisms are made up of carbohydrates, proteins and fats, you'll come across all of these molecules again during your course. This makes them very likely to come up somewhere in your exams — so make sure you learn everything you need to here before you move on.

Testing for Biological Molecules

You need to know how you can test for biological molecules using different chemicals.

You Can Test for Sugars Using Benedict's Solution

There are lots of different types of sugar molecules. Due to their chemical properties, many sugars (e.g. glucose) are called reducing sugars. You don't need to know exactly what reducing sugars are, but you do need to know how to test for them:

1) Add Benedict's solution (which is blue) to a sample and heat it in a water bath that's set to 80 °C.

2) If the test's positive it will form a coloured precipitate (solid particles suspended in the solution).

3) The higher the concentration of reducing sugar, the further the colour change goes — you can use this to compare the amount of reducing sugar in different solutions.

The colour of the precipitate changes from:

blue ⇒ green ⇒ yellow ⇒ orange ⇒ brick red

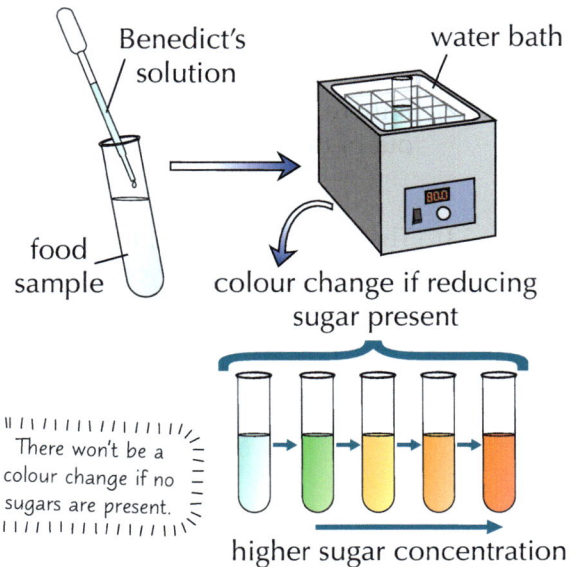

Benedict's solution

water bath

food sample

colour change if reducing sugar present

There won't be a colour change if no sugars are present.

higher sugar concentration

The Biuret Test is Used for Proteins

If you needed to find out if a substance contained protein you'd use the biuret test.

1) First, add a few drops of potassium hydroxide solution to make the solution alkaline.

2) Then add some copper(II) sulfate solution (which is bright blue).

3) If there's no protein, the solution will stay blue.

4) If protein is present, the solution will turn purple.

Negative result

Positive result

test solution, potassium hydroxide and copper(II) sulfate solution

solution staying blue indicates no protein

purple colour indicates protein

You could use biuret solution instead, which is just a mixture of potassium hydroxide and copper(II) sulfate solutions.

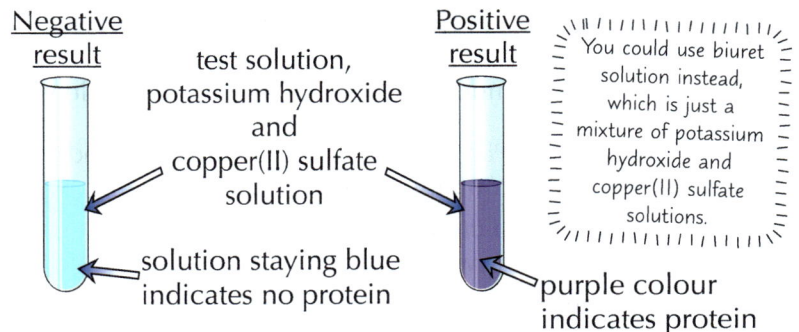

Starch is Tested for with Iodine Solution

Just add iodine solution to the test sample.

1) If starch is present, the sample changes from brown to a dark, blue-black colour.

2) If there's no starch, it stays brown.

Make sure you say iodine solution and not just iodine in the exam.

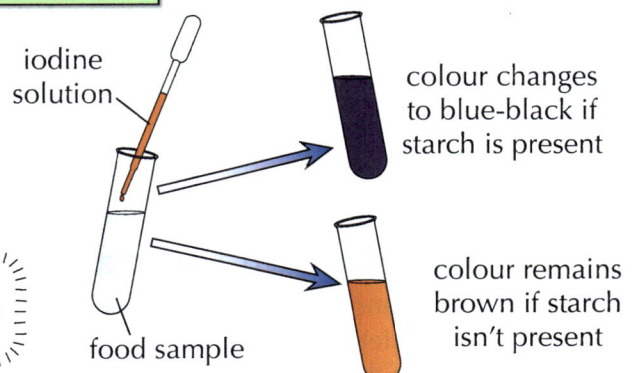

iodine solution

colour changes to blue-black if starch is present

colour remains brown if starch isn't present

food sample

Testing for Biological Molecules

There are a couple more tests coming up on this page — for fats and oils, and vitamin C.

Use the **Ethanol Emulsion Test** for **Fats** and **Oils**

To find out if there are any fats or oils in a sample:

1) Shake the test substance with ethanol for about a minute until it dissolves, then pour the solution into water.

2) If there are any fats or oils present, they will precipitate out of the liquid and show up as a milky emulsion.

An emulsion is when one liquid doesn't dissolve in another — it just forms little droplets.

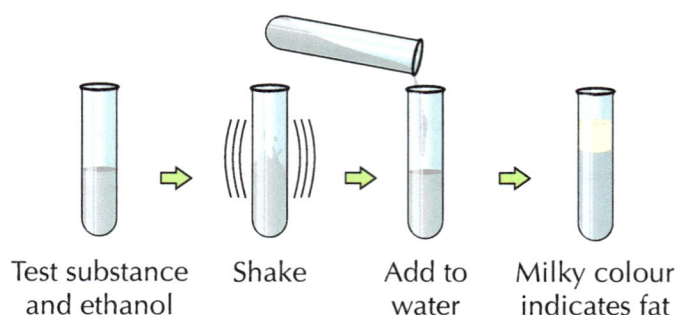

3) The more fat there is, the more noticeable the milky colour will be.

| Test substance and ethanol | Shake | Add to water | Milky colour indicates fat |

Use the **DCPIP Test** for **Vitamin C**

To find out how much vitamin C is in a food sample you'd use DCPIP solution.

1) Add DCPIP solution drop by drop to a food sample containing vitamin C (e.g. juice).
2) DCPIP solution changes from blue to colourless when vitamin C is present.
3) Keep adding DCPIP until the blue colour no longer disappears when it's mixed with the sample. (Vitamin C reacts with DCPIP solution, making it colourless. The colour stops changing when all the vitamin C has been used up.)
4) The higher the volume of DCPIP solution added before the blue colour stops disappearing, the more vitamin C the food sample contains.

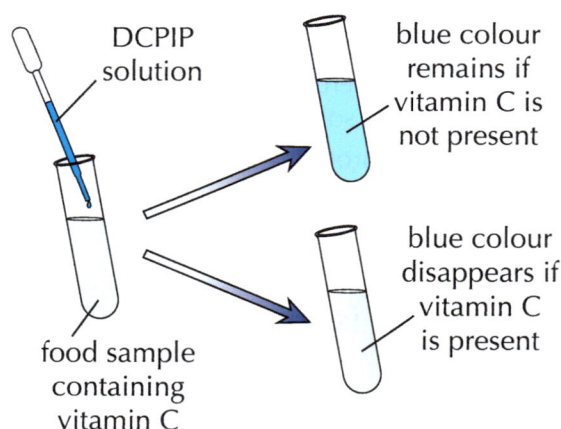

DCPIP solution

food sample containing vitamin C

blue colour remains if vitamin C is not present

blue colour disappears if vitamin C is present

Make sure you think about all of the hazards...

PRACTICAL TIP

Iodine solution is an irritant to the eyes, and the chemicals used in the biuret test are dangerous, so wear safety goggles when carrying out these tests. If you spill any of the chemicals on your skin, wash them off straight away. Be careful around the water bath in the Benedict's test, too.

Enzymes

Life would not be possible without chemical reactions. And enzymes are essential for chemical reactions.

Enzymes are **Proteins** that Act as **Catalysts**

1) Living things have thousands of different chemical reactions going on inside them all the time. These reactions need to be carefully controlled — to get the right amounts of substances in the cells.

2) You can usually make a reaction happen more quickly by raising the temperature. This would speed up the useful reactions but also the unwanted ones too... not good. There's also a limit to how far you can raise the temperature inside a living creature before its cells start getting damaged.

3) Catalysts allow reactions to take place faster without needing to increase the temperature.

> **KEY TERM**
> A catalyst is a substance which increases the rate of a reaction, without being changed or used up in the reaction.

4) So living things produce enzymes:

> **KEY TERM**
> Enzymes are proteins that act as a biological catalysts in all metabolic reactions.

5) Enzymes reduce the need for high temperatures and we only have enzymes to increase the rate of the useful chemical reactions in the body. These reactions are called metabolic reactions. Without enzymes, metabolic reactions would not be fast enough to sustain life.

An **Enzyme's Shape** Lets it **Catalyse Reactions**

1) Chemical reactions usually involve things either being split apart or joined together.

2) A substrate is a molecule that is changed in a reaction.

3) The part of an enzyme where the substrate binds is known as the active site.

4) The active site has a shape that is complementary to (matches) the shape of the substrate molecule that binds to it.

5) When the substrate molecule binds to the active site, it is changed to a product and then released.

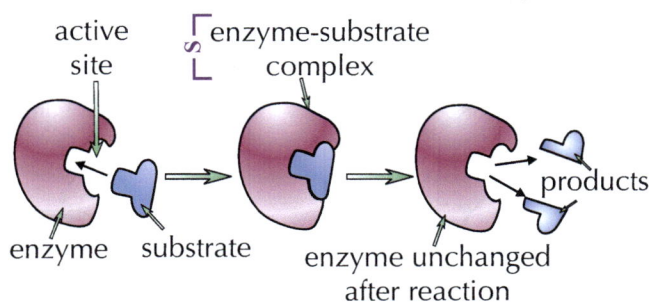

active site — enzyme-substrate complex — products — enzyme — substrate — enzyme unchanged after reaction

If the shape of an enzyme's active site changes so that it is no longer complementary to its substrate molecule, it is said to be denatured. Denaturation occurs if the temperature is too high or if the pH is too high or low — enzymes need to be kept at their optimum temperature and pH (see next page).

(see next page).

Supplement

1) Since the active site has to be complementary in shape to its substrate for the substrate to bind, it means that enzymes are specific — they usually only work for one substrate and speed up one reaction.

2) When a substrate binds to an enzyme, a temporary enzyme-substrate complex forms.

3) The substrate is then converted to products.

Enzymes speed up chemical reactions

A substrate fits into an enzyme just like a key fits into a lock. You've got to have the correct key for a lock and the right substrate for an enzyme. If the substrate doesn't fit, the enzyme won't catalyse the reaction.

More on Enzymes

Enzymes need just the right conditions if they're going to work properly.

Enzymes Like it Warm but Not Too Hot

Supplement

1) Like with any reaction, a higher temperature increases the rate at first, up to an optimum temperature where the enzyme is most active.

2) After the optimum temperature, the rate of reaction decreases.

3) As the temperature increases, the enzymes and substrate have more kinetic (movement) energy, so they move about more and there are more effective collisions forming enzyme-substrate complexes.

4) But if it gets too hot, some of the bonds holding the enzyme together break. This changes the shape of the enzyme's active site, so the substrate won't fit any more.

5) When this happens the enzyme is said to be denatured.

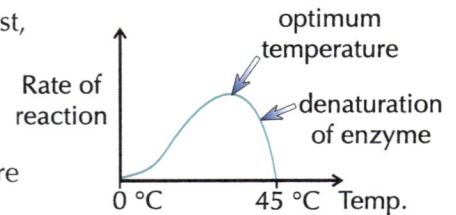

Enzymes Also Need the Right pH

Supplement

1) Enzymes have an optimum pH that they work best at. If the pH is above or below the optimum, the rate of reaction decreases.

2) When the pH is too high or too low, the pH affects the bonds holding the enzyme together. This changes the shape of the active site and denatures the enzyme.

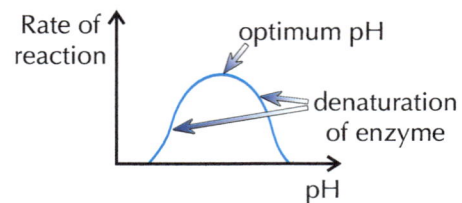

You can Investigate Factors that Affect Enzyme Activity

One way of investigating how temperature affects enzyme activity is by measuring the rate at which starch is broken down by the enzyme amylase (p.45). Here's how to do it using iodine solution (p.27) and the apparatus shown below:

1) Put a drop of iodine solution into each well on the spotting tile.

2) Every ten seconds, drop a sample of the starch and amylase mixture into a well using a pipette. When the iodine solution remains brown (i.e. starch is no longer present) record the total time taken.

3) Repeat with the water bath at different temperatures to see how it affects the time taken for the starch to be broken down. Remember to control all of the variables each time.

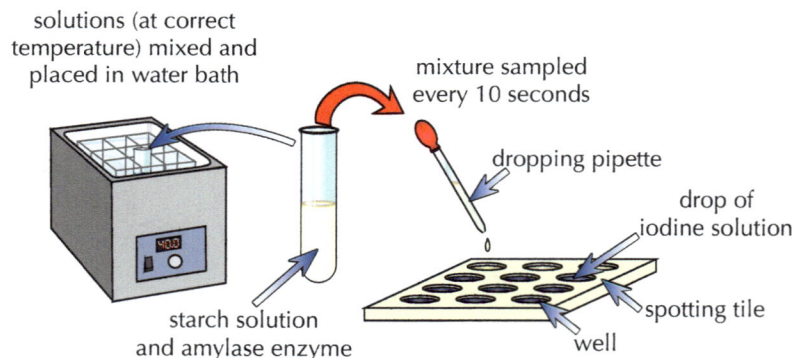

You can adapt this experiment to investigate the effect of pH on enzyme activity. Follow the same method but instead of changing the temperature, add different buffer solutions (solutions with constant pH) with different pH levels to different tubes containing the starch-amylase mixture.

If only enzymes could speed up revision...

Make sure you can describe the effect of changes in temperature and pH on enzyme activity. If the temperature or pH is too high or too low, the enzyme will stop working and no product will appear.

Warm-Up & Exam Questions

The best way to check whether you've learnt something is to test yourself. Have a go at these questions.

Warm-Up Questions

1) Which smaller molecule is cellulose made from?
2) Name the smaller basic units that make up the following molecules: a) a fat, b) a protein.
3) What solution is used to test for reducing sugars?
4) Some iodine solution is added to a sample and the colour changes from brown to blue-black. What does this indicate?
5) What are enzymes?
6) What is the name for the part of an enzyme that a substrate joins onto?
7) Why does an enzyme usually only catalyse one reaction?
8) Why don't enzymes work well when the temperature is too hot?

Exam Questions

1   The elements below make up different biological molecules.
   1. carbon
   2. hydrogen
   3. nitrogen
   4. oxygen

   Which of these elements make up proteins?

   ☐ **A**   1, 2, 3 and 4

   ☐ **B**   1, 2 and 4 only

   ☐ **C**   1 and 4 only

   ☐ **D**   1 and 3 only

   [Total 1 mark]

2   Which row in the following table best describes enzymes?

		are affected by pH	speed up reactions	get used up during reactions	all have the same shape
☐	**A**	✓	✓		
☐	**B**			✓	
☐	**C**	✓	✓		✓
☐	**D**		✓	✓	✓

   [Total 1 mark]

Exam Questions

3 A student is analysing the nutrient content of egg whites.

Describe a test the student could do to find out if fat is present in a sample of the egg whites.

[Total 4 marks]

4 The enzyme amylase is involved in the breakdown of starch into simple sugars.

A student investigated the effect of temperature on the activity of amylase in starch solution.
The student used the following method:

1. Amylase and starch solution were added to test tubes **X**, **Y** and **Z**.
2. The test tubes were placed in water baths of different temperatures, as shown in the table below.

Test tube	Temp / °C
X	45
Y	60
Z	75

3. Spotting tiles were prepared with a drop of iodine solution in each well.
    Iodine solution is brown but it turns blue-black in the presence of starch.
4. Every 30 seconds, a drop of the solution from each of the test tubes was
    added to a separate well on a spotting tile.
5. The resulting colour of the solution in the well was recorded in the table below.

Time / s	30	60	90	120	150
Tube **X**	Blue-black	Blue-black	Blue-black	Brown	Brown
Tube **Y**	Blue-black	Brown	Brown	Brown	Brown
Tube **Z**	Blue-black	Blue-black	Blue-black	Blue-black	Blue-black

(a) Name **one** piece of equipment that could be used to add iodine solution to each well.

[1]

(b) State the temperature at which the rate of reaction was greatest. Explain your answer.

[2]

(c) Suggest an explanation for the results in tube **Z**.

[1]

(d) Suggest **two** variables that should be controlled in this experiment.

[2]

[Total 6 marks]

5 Describe the structure of a DNA molecule.

[Total 4 marks]

Revision Summary for Sections 3 & 4

That's nearly all for Sections 3 & 4 — try these summary questions to put your knowledge to the test.
- Try these questions and tick off each one when you get it right.
- When you've done all the questions for a topic and are completely happy with it, tick off the topic.

Movement In and Out of Cells (p.19-24) ☐

1) What is diffusion? ☐
2) Describe how surface area affects the movement of substances in and out of cells. ☐
3) Describe an experiment that shows diffusion taking place. ☐
4) How is osmosis similar to diffusion? ☐
5) A solution of pure water is separated from a concentrated sucrose solution by a partially permeable membrane. In which direction will molecules flow, and what substance will these molecules be? ☐
6) Describe how to set up an experiment using dialysis tubing that shows osmosis taking place. ☐
7) Describe an experiment using plant tissue that shows osmosis taking place. ☐
8) What is turgor pressure? ☐
9) What is plasmolysis? ☐
10) What happens when animal cells are placed in a solution with a higher water potential than theirs? ☐
11) How is active transport different from diffusion in terms of:
   a) energy requirements,
   b) concentration gradients? ☐
12) Give one example of when active transport is used by organisms. ☐

Biological Molecules (p.26-28) ☐

13) Name the three main chemical elements that are found in carbohydrates. ☐
14) Name one biological molecule made up of glucose molecules. ☐
15) What type of biological molecules are made up of fatty acids and glycerol? ☐
16) What are the four bases in a DNA molecule? ☐
17) How do the bases in a DNA molecule pair up? ☐
18) Describe how you could use biuret solution to test for proteins. ☐

Enzymes (p.29-30) ☐

19) What does a biological catalyst do? ☐
20) Do enzymes and substrate molecules have more or less kinetic energy when the temperature increases? ☐
21) What happens to the frequency of effective collisions between enzyme and substrate molecules when the temperature increases? ☐
22) What does it mean when an enzyme has been 'denatured'? ☐
23) What happens to an enzyme's rate of reaction when the pH is too high or too low? ☐
24) Briefly describe an experiment to show how temperature can affect enzyme activity. ☐

Photosynthesis

Plants can make their own food — which sounds easier than going out to the shops. Here's how they do it...

Photosynthesis Needs Sunlight

1) Basically, photosynthesis is the process that produces 'food' in plants. The 'food' it produces is glucose.

2) You need to learn the proper definition for photosynthesis though:

> **KEY TERM**
>
> Photosynthesis is the process that plants use to synthesise carbohydrates (glucose) from raw materials (carbon dioxide and water) using energy from light.

3) Photosynthesis happens in the leaves of all green plants — this is largely what the leaves are for.

4) More specifically, it happens inside the chloroplasts, which are found in leaf cells and in other green parts of a plant. Chloroplasts contain a green pigment called chlorophyll, which absorbs sunlight.

5) Chlorophyll transfers light energy from the Sun into chemical energy in molecules, such as glucose.

6) The word equation for photosynthesis is shown below:

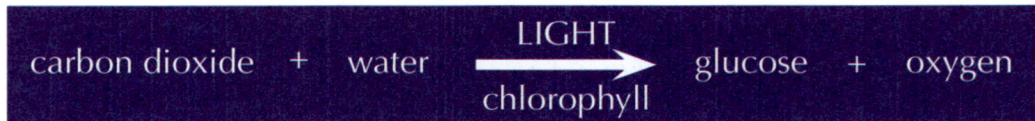

$$\text{carbon dioxide} + \text{water} \xrightarrow[\text{chlorophyll}]{\text{LIGHT}} \text{glucose} + \text{oxygen}$$

Supplement

7) If you're taking the Extended course, you also need to learn the balanced chemical equation:

$$6CO_2 + 6H_2O \longrightarrow C_6H_{12}O_6 + 6O_2$$

Supplement

Plants Use Glucose in Several Ways...

For respiration — This transfers energy from glucose (see p.72) which enables the plants to convert the rest of the glucose into various other useful substances, and provides energy for other processes, e.g. active transport.

Storing as starch — Glucose is turned into starch and stored in roots, stems and leaves. The starch acts as an energy store ready for use when photosynthesis is happening less, like in the winter.

Making cellulose — Glucose is converted into cellulose for making strong plant cell walls (see p.11).

Converting to sucrose — Glucose is converted into sucrose for transport around the plant in the phloem (see p.48).

Making nectar — Glucose is used to create a sweet sugary liquid called nectar, which is used to attract pollinating insects to flowers (see p.98).

REVISION TIP

Make sure you really know the photosynthesis equation

Keep trying to write it out from memory (without peeking at the book) until you can do it by heart.

Rate of Photosynthesis

Photosynthesis can happen at different rates (speeds) depending on the environmental conditions.

Limiting Factors Affect the Rate of Photosynthesis

1) The rate of photosynthesis varies. It all depends on what the limiting factor is at that moment in time.

2) A limiting factor is something present in the environment in such short supply that it restricts life processes.

3) Limiting factors that affect photosynthesis include light intensity, temperature and CO_2 concentration.

4) The limiting factor depends on the environmental conditions. E.g. in winter, low temperatures might be the limiting factor. At night, light is likely to be the limiting factor.

Not Enough Light Slows Down the Rate of Photosynthesis

Chlorophyll uses light energy to carry out photosynthesis. It can only photosynthesise as quickly as the light energy is arriving.

1) If the light intensity is increased, the rate of photosynthesis will increase steadily, but only up to a certain point.

2) Beyond that, it won't make any difference.

3) Then it'll be the temperature or the CO_2 level which is the limiting factor.

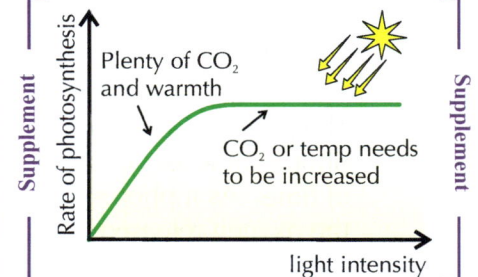
Rate of photosynthesis vs light intensity — Plenty of CO_2 and warmth; CO_2 or temp needs to be increased

Too Little CO₂ Slows Down the Rate of Photosynthesis

CO_2 is one of the raw materials needed for photosynthesis — only 0.04% of the air is CO_2, so it's limited as far as plants are concerned.

1) As with light intensity, increasing the concentration of CO_2 will only increase the rate of photosynthesis up to a point. After this, it won't make any difference.

2) This shows that CO_2 is no longer the limiting factor.

3) As long as light and CO_2 are in plentiful supply then the factor limiting photosynthesis must be temperature.

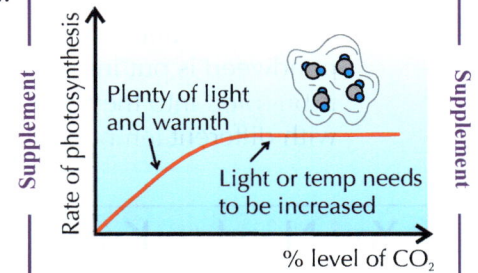
Rate of photosynthesis vs % level of CO_2 — Plenty of light and warmth; Light or temp needs to be increased

The Temperature Has to be Just Right

As temperature increases, the rate of photosynthesis increases up to a point — then it rapidly decreases.

1) Temperature affects the rate of photosynthesis — because it affects the enzymes involved.

2) If the temperature is too high (over about 45 °C), the plant's enzymes will be denatured (destroyed), causing the rapid decrease in the rate of photosynthesis.

3) Usually though, if the temperature is the limiting factor it's because it's too low, and things need warming up a bit.

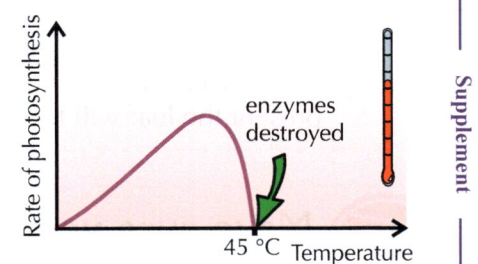
Rate of photosynthesis vs Temperature — enzymes destroyed at 45 °C

Investigating Photosynthesis

Oxygen and glucose are products of photosynthesis (see p.34). Glucose can be stored by plants as starch. You can test for oxygen and starch to investigate photosynthesis.

Oxygen Production Shows the Rate of Photosynthesis

Canadian pondweed can be used to measure the effect of light intensity on the rate of photosynthesis. The rate at which the pondweed produces oxygen corresponds to the rate at which it's photosynthesising — the faster the rate of oxygen production, the faster the rate of photosynthesis.

Here's how the experiment works:

1) The apparatus is set up according to the diagram. The gas syringe should be empty to start with. Sodium hydrogencarbonate may be added to the water to make sure the plant has enough carbon dioxide (it releases CO_2 in solution).

2) A source of white light is placed at a specific distance from the pondweed.

3) The pondweed is left to photosynthesise for a set amount of time. As it photosynthesises, the oxygen released will collect in the capillary tube.

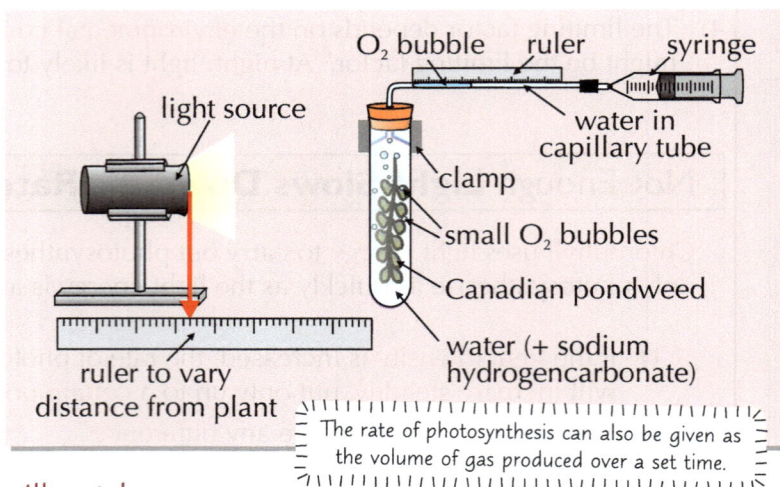

Labels: O_2 bubble; ruler; syringe; light source; water in capillary tube; clamp; small O_2 bubbles; Canadian pondweed; water (+ sodium hydrogencarbonate); ruler to vary distance from plant

The rate of photosynthesis can also be given as the volume of gas produced over a set time.

4) At the end of the experiment, the syringe is used to move the gas bubble in the tube up alongside a ruler and the length of the gas bubble is measured. This is proportional to the volume of O_2 produced.

5) For this experiment, any variables that could affect the results should be controlled, e.g. the temperature the pondweed is left to photosynthesise at and the length of time it's left for.

6) The experiment is then repeated with the light source placed at different distances from the pondweed.

The apparatus above can be altered to measure the effect of temperature and CO_2 on photosynthesis, e.g. the test tube of pondweed is put into a water-bath at a set temperature and CO_2 is bubbled into the test tube (then the experiment's repeated with different temperatures of water or concentrations of CO_2).

You should find that as you move the light source closer to the plant, increase the temperature, or increase the CO_2 concentration, that the rate of photosynthesis increases (up to a point).

You Need to Know How to Test a Leaf for Starch

1) Start by holding the leaf in boiling water (hold it with tweezers or forceps). This stops any chemical reactions happening inside the leaf.

2) Now put the leaf in a boiling tube with some ethanol and heat it in an electric water-bath until it boils — this gets rid of any chlorophyll and makes the leaf an almost white colour.

3) Finally, rinse the leaf in cold water and add a few drops of iodine solution — if starch is present the leaf will turn blue-black.

Iodine solution can also be used to test for starch in biological molecules — see page 27.

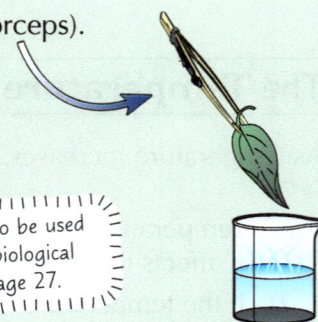

Make sure you stay safe during these investigations

For example, ethanol is highly flammable, so keep it away from naked flames, e.g. Bunsen burners.

Investigating Photosynthesis

The **Starch Test** Shows Whether **Photosynthesis** is **Taking Place**

If a plant can't photosynthesise, it can't make starch. You can use this principle to show that chlorophyll, light and CO_2 are needed for photosynthesis. Here's how...

Chlorophyll

You can show that chlorophyll is needed for photosynthesis using variegated (green and white) leaves. Only the green parts of the leaf contain chlorophyll.

1) Take a variegated leaf from a plant that's been exposed to light. Make sure you record which bits are green and which bits aren't.

2) Test the leaf for starch as on the previous page — only the bits that were green turn blue-black.

3) This suggests that only the parts of the leaf that contained chlorophyll are able to photosynthesise and produce starch.

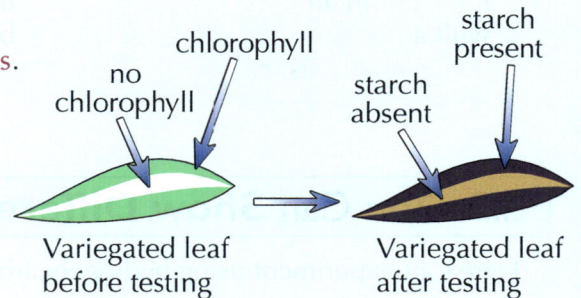

no chlorophyll · chlorophyll · starch absent · starch present

Variegated leaf before testing

Variegated leaf after testing

The white parts of the leaf go yellow/orange because the brown iodine solution stains them.

Light

1) To show that light is needed for photosynthesis you need a plant that's been grown without any light, e.g. in a cupboard for 48 hours. This will mean that it has used up its starch stores.

2) Cut a leaf from the plant and test it for starch — the leaf won't turn blue-black.

3) This shows that light is needed for photosynthesis, as no starch has been made.

Even though the plant is kept in the dark, you need to make sure it's warm enough to photosynthesise and that there's plenty of CO_2 — or it won't be a fair test.

CO_2

1) You can show that CO_2 is needed for photosynthesis with the apparatus shown on the right.

2) The soda lime will absorb CO_2 out of the air in the jar.

3) If you leave the plant in the jar for a while and then test a leaf for starch, it won't turn blue-black.

4) This shows that no starch has been made in the leaf, which means that CO_2 is needed for photosynthesis.

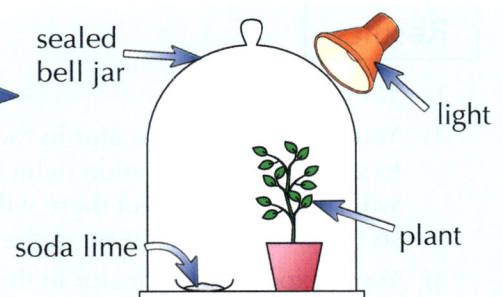

sealed bell jar · light · plant · soda lime

- For these experiments, it's important to use controls to make sure that only the factors being investigated (chlorophyll, light or CO_2) are affecting the results. This is why a variegated leaf is used in the first investigation — the green parts of the leaf are the control.

- For the other two investigations, the control should use identical plants that are kept in the same conditions, but they should also be provided with light and CO_2 respectively.

You might have to describe experiments like this in the exam

EXAM TIP If you're asked to describe an experiment, make sure you do it step-by-step, as if you're guiding someone who's never done it before through how to carry it out.

Investigating Gas Exchange in Plants

If you're not convinced about CO_2 being needed for photosynthesis, here's how you can see it for yourself...

Hydrogencarbonate Indicator Shows CO_2 Concentration...

A solution of hydrogencarbonate indicator in air with a normal CO_2 concentration is red.

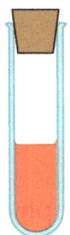

If the CO_2 concentration of the indicator increases, it becomes more yellow.

If the CO_2 concentration of the indicator decreases, it becomes purple.

...So You Can Show Differences in Net Gas Exchange in Plants

Here's an experiment using hydrogencarbonate indicator to show how light affects gas exchange:

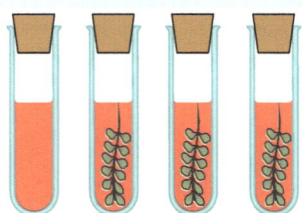

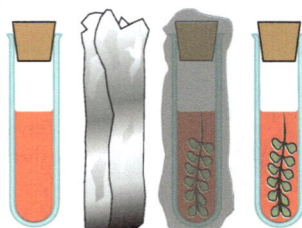

1) Add the same volume of hydrogencarbonate indicator to four boiling tubes.
2) Put similar-sized, healthy-looking pieces of Canadian pondweed into three of the tubes. Keep the fourth tube empty as a control. Seal the tubes with rubber bungs.
3) Completely wrap one tube in aluminium foil, and a second tube in gauze.
4) Place all the tubes in bright light. This will let plenty of light on to the uncovered pondweed, and a little light onto the pondweed covered in gauze. The pondweed covered in foil will get no light — assuming you've wrapped it up properly.
5) Leave the tubes for an hour, then check the colour of the indicator.

control   foil   gauze   uncovered

Results

1) There shouldn't be any change in the colour of the control tube.
2) You'd expect the indicator in the darkened tube (with the foil) to go yellow. Respiration (which produces CO_2 — see p.72) will still take place but there will be no photosynthesis, so the CO_2 concentration in the tube will increase.
3) You'd expect the indicator in the shaded tube (with the gauze) to stay a similar colour. With a little photosynthesis and some respiration taking place, roughly equal amounts of CO_2 will be taken up and produced by the pondweed, so the CO_2 concentration in the tube won't change very much.
4) You'd expect the indicator in the well-lit (uncovered) tube to go purple. There will be some respiration, but lots of photosynthesis, leading to net uptake of CO_2 by the pondweed. This will lower the CO_2 concentration in the tube.

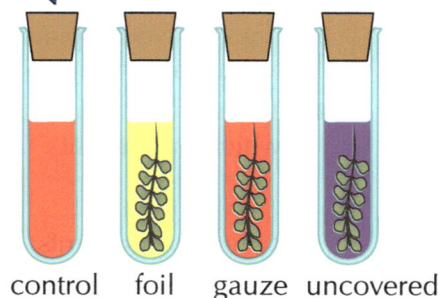

control   foil   gauze   uncovered

Make sure the colour change is really clear

PRACTICAL TIP

When checking for colour changes, it's a good idea to hold the boiling tube against a clear white background, such as a white tile. This helps make the colour change really clear and easy to spot.

Leaf Structure and Mineral Requirements

It's important that leaves are able to carry out photosynthesis and that plants get the minerals they need.

Leaves are Designed for Making Food by Photosynthesis

You need to know all the different parts of a typical leaf shown on the diagram:

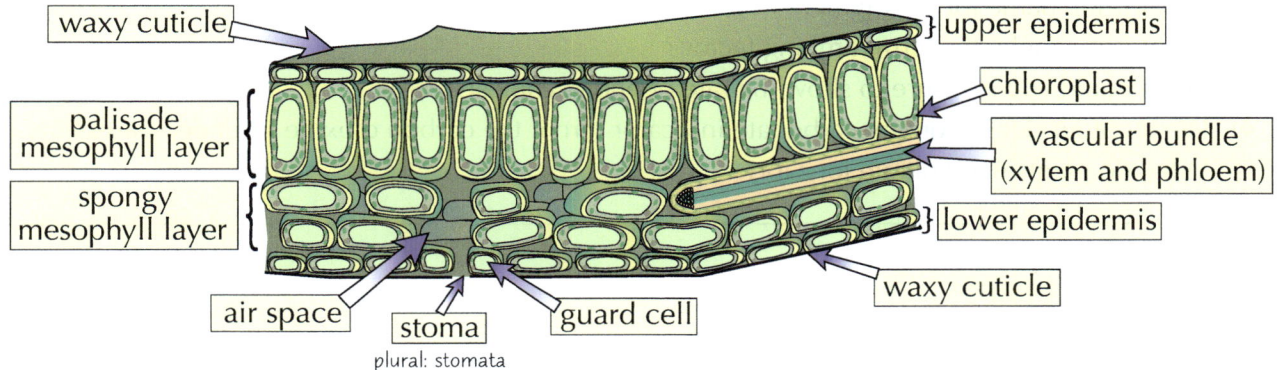

waxy cuticle — palisade mesophyll layer — spongy mesophyll layer — air space — stoma (plural: stomata) — guard cell — upper epidermis — chloroplast — vascular bundle (xylem and phloem) — lower epidermis — waxy cuticle

Leaves are Adapted for Efficient Photosynthesis

1) Leaves are usually broad, which gives them a large surface area. This maximises the leaf cells' exposure to light and speeds up gas exchange.

2) Leaves are thin, which also speeds up gas exchange as the distance for gases to diffuse is shorter.

3) Most of the chloroplasts are found in the palisade mesophyll layer. This is so that they're near the top of the leaf where they can get the most light.

4) The upper epidermis is transparent so that light can pass through it to the palisade mesophyll layer.

5) Leaves of dicotyledonous plants (see p.8) have a network of vascular bundles — these are the transport vessels xylem and phloem (p.48). They deliver water and other nutrients to the leaf and take away the glucose produced by photosynthesis. They also help to support the leaf structure.

6) The waxy cuticle on the top and bottom helps to reduce water loss by evaporation.

7) There are air spaces inside the leaf. These let gases like CO_2 and O_2 move easily between cells. They also increase the surface area for gas exchange and so make photosynthesis more efficient.

8) The lower surface is full of little holes called stomata. They're there to let CO_2 (necessary for photosynthesis — see p.34) and O_2 (produced by photosynthesis) diffuse in and out of the leaf. Water vapour is also lost through the stomata during transpiration (see p.50).

9) The size of the stomata is controlled by guard cells. These close the stomata if the plant is losing water faster than it is being replaced by the roots. Without guard cells, the plant would soon wilt.

Plants Need Mineral Ions For Growth

1) Plants need certain elements so they can produce important compounds.

2) They get these elements from mineral ions in the soil.

Nitrate Ions

Contain nitrogen for making amino acids and proteins, which are needed for cell growth.

Magnesium Ions

Magnesium ions are needed to make chlorophyll.

Warm-Up & Exam Questions

Before we move on to human nutrition, test that you've understood everything you need
to know about plant nutrition by answering the questions below and on the next page.

Warm-Up Questions

1) What is the name for the pigment inside chloroplasts that absorbs light?
2) What is meant by the term 'limiting factor'?
3) What could you measure to show the rate of photosynthesis?
4) What colour does hydrogencarbonate indicator turn if the carbon dioxide level decreases?
5) What do plants need nitrate ions for?

Exam Questions

1   Photosynthesis produces glucose using light.

(a)   Complete the word equation for photosynthesis.

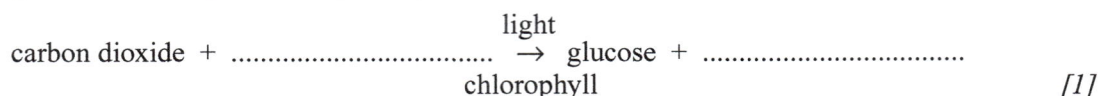

$$\text{carbon dioxide} + \text{.....................} \xrightarrow[\text{chlorophyll}]{\text{light}} \text{glucose} + \text{.....................}$$

[1]

(b)   Plants use some of the glucose they produce to make a substance which strengthens
their cell walls. Which of the following strengthens cells walls? Tick **one** box.

☐ **A** cellulose   ☐ **B** sucrose   ☐ **C** starch   ☐ **D** nectar

[1]

[Total 2 marks]

2   The diagram shows a cross-section through
a typical leaf. Some of the structures
in the leaf are labelled **A** to **E**.

The table below contains descriptions of how
the structures labelled in the diagram make the
leaf well-adapted for efficient photosynthesis.

Complete the table by matching the letters
in the diagram to the correct description.
The first one has been done for you.

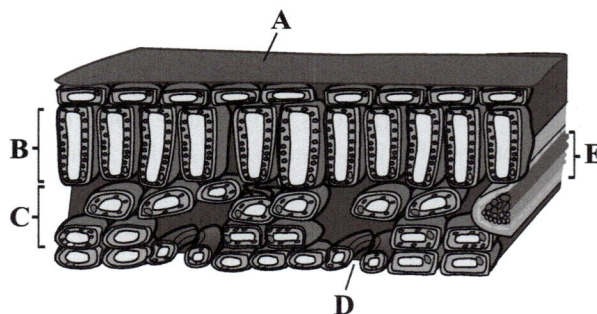

Description of structure	Letter
contains air spaces to aid gas exchange	C
delivers water and nutrients to the leaf	
helps to reduce water loss by evaporation	
where most of the chloroplasts in the leaf are located, to maximise the amount of light they receive	
allows carbon dioxide to diffuse directly into the leaf	

[Total 3 marks]

Exam Questions

3 The diagram below shows a variegated leaf. It is partly green and partly white. Chlorophyll is present in the green parts of the leaf but not the white parts.

A student did an experiment in which part of the leaf was covered with black paper, as shown in the diagram below. The leaf was then exposed to light for four hours and was then tested for starch.

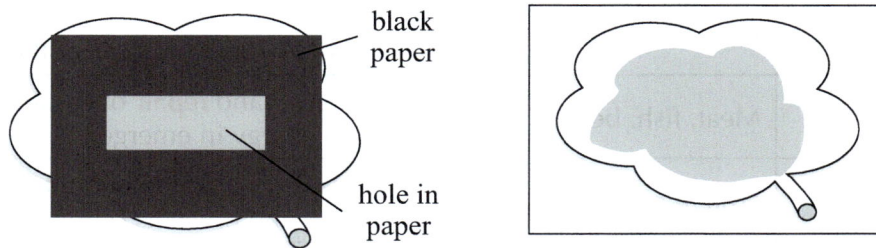

black paper

hole in paper

(a) Complete the diagram on the right by shading in the part(s) of the leaf that you would expect to contain **starch**.

[1]

(b) Explain your answer to **(a)**.

[2]

[Total 3 marks]

4 A student investigated the effect of limiting factors on the rate of photosynthesis of a plant.

The results are shown in the graph.

rate of photosynthesis

light intensity

- - - - 0.1% CO_2
——— 0.07% CO_2
——— 0.04% CO_2

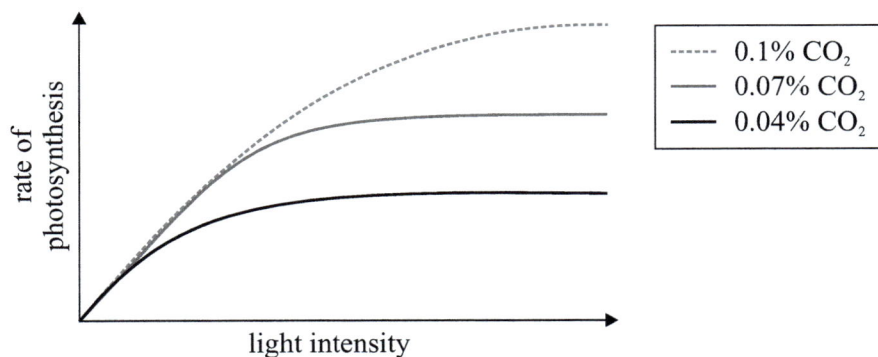

(a) Describe the effect that increasing the concentration of CO_2 has on the rate of photosynthesis as light intensity increases.

[2]

(b) Explain why all the lines on the graph level off eventually.

[1]

[Total 3 marks]

Supplement

Supplement

Human Diet

Your body needs the right fuel or it won't work properly — that means eating a balanced diet.

You Need to **Eat Different Foods** to Get **Different Nutrients**

Nutrient		Found in...	Function(s)
Carbohydrates		Pasta, rice, sugar	Provide energy.
Fats and oils		Butter, oily fish	Provide energy, act as an energy store, provide insulation and provide protection of the organs.
Proteins		Meat, fish, beans	Needed for growth and repair of tissue, and to provide energy in emergencies.
Vitamins	C	Fruit, e.g. oranges	Needed for tissue repair, is important for the immune system, and prevents scurvy (see below).
	D	Eggs, oily fish	Needed for calcium absorption. *Vitamin D is also made by your body when your skin is exposed to sunlight.*
Mineral ions	Calcium	Milk, cheese	Needed to make bones and teeth.
	Iron	Red meat, beans	Needed to make haemoglobin for healthy blood.
Water		Food and drink	Just about every bodily function relies on water — we need a constant supply to replace water lost through urinating, breathing and sweating.
Fibre (roughage)		Wholemeal bread, fruit	Aids the movement of food through the gut.

A **Balanced Diet** Supplies **All** Your **Essential Nutrients**

1) A balanced diet gives you all the essential nutrients you need — in the right proportions.
2) The six essential nutrients are carbohydrates, proteins, fats and oils, vitamins, mineral ions and water.
3) You also need fibre (or roughage) to keep the gut in good working order.

Not Getting Enough Nutrients can Cause **Problems**

A lack of certain nutrients in your diet can cause deficiency diseases. Here are two examples:

1) Scurvy — A lack of vitamin C can lead to a disease called scurvy. It causes bleeding gums, poor wound healing and pain, especially in the legs.
2) Rickets — A lack of vitamin D or calcium can cause rickets. It causes weak or brittle bones, bone deformation and bone pain in children. Adults can also experience brittle bones and bone pain as the result of vitamin D or calcium deficiency.

You need to eat the right nutrients in the right proportions...

...so that means having a diet which consists of the right amount of carbohydrates, proteins, fats and oils, vitamins, mineral ions and water. You also need fibre. Make sure that you can say what each of these nutrients is important for and can give some examples of foods they can be found in.

The Alimentary Canal

Digestion takes place in the alimentary canal — it's where the food you eat gets broken down into smaller molecules ready to be taken into your body cells (or passed out of the body as faeces).

Your Alimentary Canal Runs Through Your Body

The main organs of the alimentary canal are the mouth, oesophagus, stomach, small intestine and large intestine. The salivary glands, pancreas, liver and gall bladder are all associated organs.

The alimentary canal and its associated organs are known as the digestive system.

Mouth

1) Salivary glands in the mouth produce amylase enzyme (p.45) in the saliva.
2) Teeth (next page) break down food.

Oesophagus

The muscular tube that connects the mouth and stomach.

Liver

Where bile is produced (see page 46).

Gall bladder

Where bile is stored (see page 46).

Large intestine

1) Also called the colon.
2) Where excess water is absorbed from the food.

Rectum

1) The last part of the large intestine.
2) Where the faeces (made up mainly of indigestible food) are stored before they are passed out through the anus.

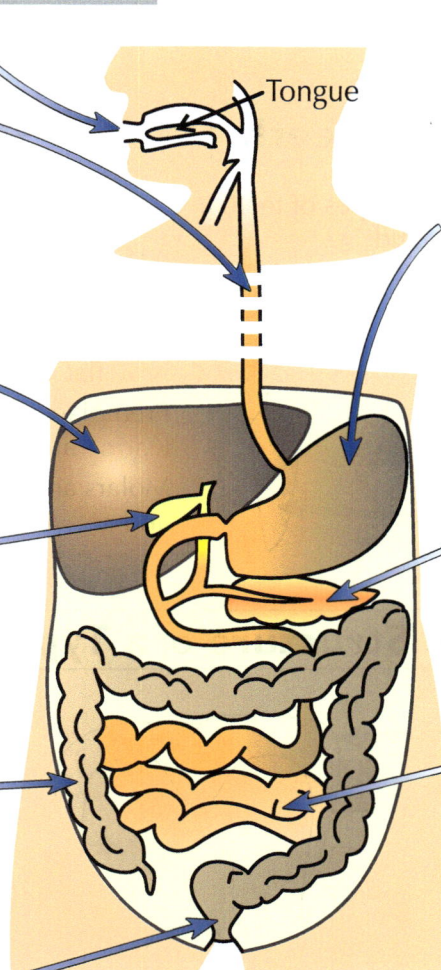

Tongue

Stomach

1) Churns the food up with its muscular walls. This is a type of physical digestion, see next page.
2) Produces a protease enzyme (pepsin) — this is involved in chemical digestion, see p.45.
3) Produces gastric juice (which contains hydrochloric acid) for two reasons:
   - To kill bacteria in food.
   - To provide the optimum acidic pH for the protease enzyme that works here.

Pancreas

Produces protease, amylase and lipase enzymes. Releases these into the small intestine.

Small intestine

1) Produces protease (trypsin), amylase and lipase enzymes to complete digestion.
2) Where nutrients are absorbed out of the alimentary canal into the body.
3) Where most of the water is absorbed into the body.
4) It has two parts — the duodenum and the ileum.

Look, cover, write, check...

REVISION TIP

Copy out the diagram and then try and label all the parts correctly without looking at the page.

Physical Digestion

The first step in digestion is physical — tearing, cutting and grinding down food into smaller pieces.

Ingestion Comes Before Physical Digestion

1) Ingestion is when substances such as food and drink are taken into the body. Food and drink are both ingested through the mouth.

2) After you've ingested food, teeth do the first part of physical digestion.

KEY TERM — Physical digestion is the breakdown of food into smaller pieces without the food molecules undergoing a chemical change.

3) By breaking down food into smaller pieces, physical digestion gives the enzymes involved in chemical digestion (see next page) a bigger surface area to work on.

There are Four Types of Teeth

You need to know what the different types of teeth are, what they do and where they're found:

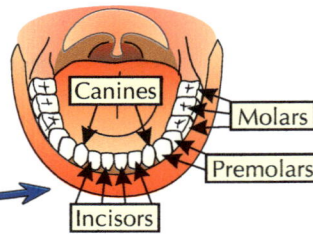

Canines
Molars
Premolars
Incisors

Incisors and canines have sharp biting surfaces.
Incisors are used for biting and cutting into food.
Canines are used for gripping and tearing food.

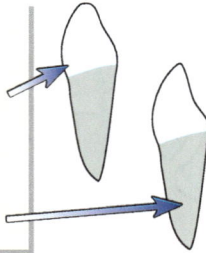

Premolars and molars have flat biting surfaces.
Premolars are used for tearing and crushing food.
Molars are used for crushing and grinding food.

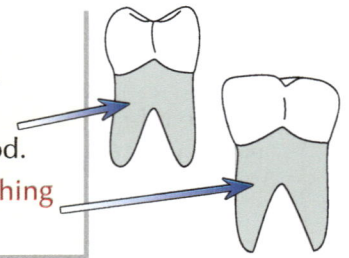

You Need to Know the Structure of a Typical Tooth

Enamel — a hard outer layer on the tooth.

Cement — bone-like tissue that surrounds the tooth and helps hold it in place.

Bone — where the tooth is embedded (held in position).

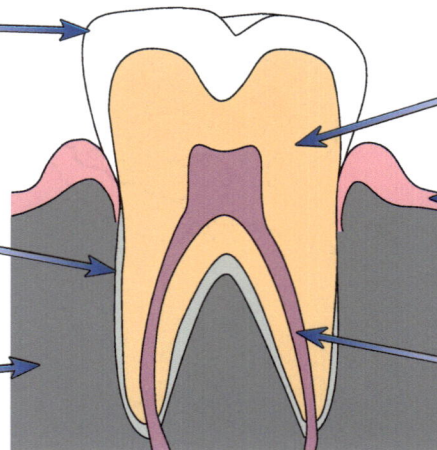

Dentine — a softer material that forms the bulk of the tooth.

Gum — soft tissue that surrounds and protects the tooth and bone.

Pulp — soft tissue that contains nerves and blood vessels.

Here's a page you can really get your teeth into

Remember, teeth aren't the only parts of the alimentary canal involved in physical digestion — the stomach also plays a role (it helps break down food by churning it up — see previous page). Unlike teeth, the stomach also has a role in chemical digestion, which comes up next...

Chemical Digestion

Chemical digestion involves the breakdown of food using enzymes.

Enzymes Break Down Food in Chemical Digestion

1) Starch, proteins and fats are BIG molecules. They're too big to pass through the walls of the alimentary canal. They're also insoluble.
2) Simple reducing sugars, amino acids, glycerol and fatty acids are much smaller molecules. They're soluble and can pass easily through the walls of the alimentary canal.

KEY TERM Chemical digestion is the breakdown of larger, insoluble molecules into smaller, soluble molecules.

3) The digestive enzymes break down the BIG molecules into the smaller ones.
4) You need to know about three digestive enzymes — where they're secreted from and what they do:

Amylase Breaks Down Starch into Simple Reducing Sugars

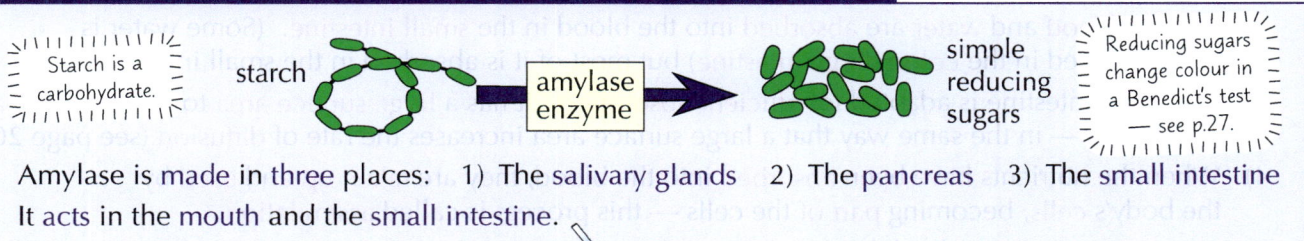

Starch is a carbohydrate.

starch → amylase enzyme → simple reducing sugars

Reducing sugars change colour in a Benedict's test — see p.27.

Amylase is made in three places: 1) The salivary glands 2) The pancreas 3) The small intestine
It acts in the mouth and the small intestine.

Amylase breaks down starch to a sugar called maltose. Maltose is broken down further by maltase to glucose. This happens on the membranes of the epithelium lining of the small intestine.

Proteases Break Down Proteins into Amino Acids

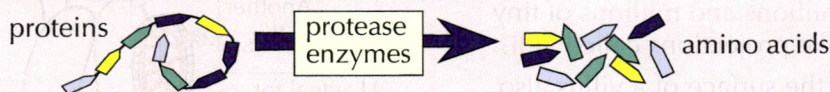

proteins → protease enzymes → amino acids

Proteases are made in three places: 1) The stomach 2) The pancreas 3) The small intestine
Proteases act in the stomach and small intestine.

The protease in the stomach is called pepsin. It works best in acidic conditions.
The one in the small intestine is called trypsin. It works best in alkaline conditions.

Lipases Break Down Fats and Oils into Glycerol and Fatty Acids

fats and oils → lipase enzymes → glycerol and fatty acids

Lipases are made in two places: 1) The pancreas 2) The small intestine
They act in the small intestine.

Make sure you really know this stuff before moving on

The next page is all about what happens to these smaller food molecules after chemical digestion has happened. So make sure you're confident with this page before moving on to the next one.

Chemical Digestion and Absorption

There's just a bit more on chemical digestion, then it's on to how these small food molecules are absorbed.

Supplement

Bile Neutralises the Stomach Acid and Emulsifies Fats and Oils

1) Bile is produced in the liver. It's stored in the gall bladder before it's released into the duodenum in the small intestine.

2) The hydrochloric acid in the stomach makes the pH too acidic for enzymes in the small intestine to work properly. Bile is a mixture of alkaline chemicals — it neutralises the acidic mixture of food and stomach acid, and makes conditions alkaline. The enzymes in the small intestine work best in these conditions.

3) Bile also emulsifies fats and oils (breaks them into tiny droplets). This gives a much bigger surface area of fat for the enzyme lipase to work on — which makes its digestion faster.

Most Absorption Happens in the Small Intestine

1) Absorption is the movement of nutrients through the wall of the intestines into the blood.

2) Digested food and water are absorbed into the blood in the small intestine. (Some water is also absorbed in the colon (large intestine) but most of it is absorbed in the small intestine.)

3) The small intestine is adapted for efficient absorption. It has a large surface area to increase the rate of absorption — in the same way that a large surface area increases the rate of diffusion (see page 20).

4) When the nutrients have been absorbed into the blood, they are taken up and used by the body's cells, becoming part of the cells — this process is called assimilation.

5) Egestion is when any food that hasn't been digested or absorbed is removed from the body as faeces.

Supplement

Villi Increase the Surface Area of the Small Intestine

1) The small intestine has a big surface area for absorption, because its walls are covered in millions and millions of tiny little finger-like projections called villi.

2) Each cell on the surface of a villus also has its own microvilli — little structures that increase the surface area even more.

3) These microvilli contain lots of mitochondria (p.11) which provide energy from respiration (p.72). This is used for active transport (p.24), to absorb molecules into the blood capillaries.

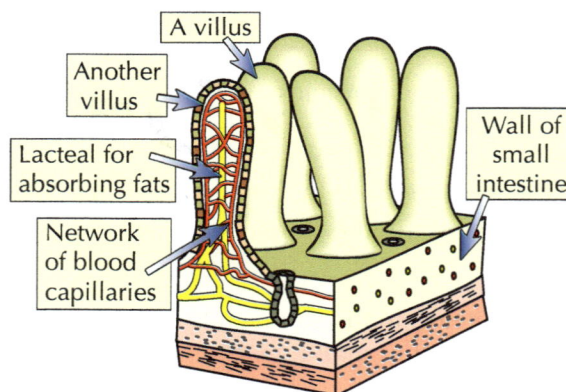

A villus

Another villus

Lacteal for absorbing fats

Network of blood capillaries

Wall of small intestine

4) The network of blood capillaries is needed so that the absorbed molecules can be transported round the body. A good blood supply allows for quick absorption.

5) Villi have a single permeable layer of surface cells which also allows for quick absorption. (The surface cells form a tissue called epithelium.)

6) The lacteals are tubes in the villi that absorb digested fats. Here's how they work:

- Fats move from the small intestine into the lacteals in the villi.
- Lacteals contain fluid called lymph that transports fats away from the small intestine.
- The lacteals merge to form larger vessels, before the lymph (and the fats it contains) empties into the blood.
- The fats can then be transported around the body in the blood.

Supplement

Warm-Up & Exam Questions

We've covered plant nutrition, now it's time for questions on human nutrition — then Section 5 is done.

Warm-Up Questions

1) Why are proteins needed for a balanced diet?
2) Name the **three** parts of the digestive system that produce protease enzymes.
3) What are canine teeth used for?
4) Which type of enzyme digests: (a) protein (b) fats?
5) What are the products of the digestion of: (a) starch (b) protein (c) fats?
6) What is egestion?
7) What are lacteals?

Exam Questions

1   The diagram shows part of the digestive system.

   (a)   Label the place where bile is produced.

   [1]

   (b)   Explain why bile needs to have an alkaline pH.

   [2]

   (c)   Outline how bile helps with the digestion of fats.

   [2]

   [Total 5 marks]

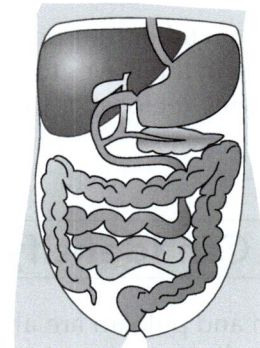

2   Starchy foods such as bread and pasta are used by the body as a source of energy.

   (a)   Name the enzyme used to digest starch.

   [1]

   (b)   Explain why starch must be digested before it can be absorbed into the blood.

   [3]

   [Total 4 marks]

3   Many years ago, sailors on long trips at sea would often suffer from scurvy.

   (a)   State the cause of scurvy.

   [1]

   (b)   Suggest why sailors who spent a long time at sea may have been likely to suffer from scurvy.

   [2]

   (c)   Scurvy can lead to gum disease. This can cause the gums to pull away from the teeth, leaving the bone and cement exposed. If left untreated, the bone and cement could become damaged, resulting in tooth loss. Suggest how gum disease could lead to tooth loss.

   [1]

   [Total 4 marks]

Transport in Plants

Water and food need to be transported throughout a plant. Flowering plants have two types of transport vessel — xylem and phloem. Both types of vessel go to every part of the plant, but they are totally separate.

Xylem Tubes Take Water UP

1) Xylem tubes carry water and mineral ions from the roots to the stem and leaves. They also provide support for the plant.

Supplement

2) They are made of dead cells joined end to end with no cross walls between them and a hole down the middle. The cells have no contents, so they form a continuous hollow tube. They have thick cell walls, which are strengthened with a material called lignin.

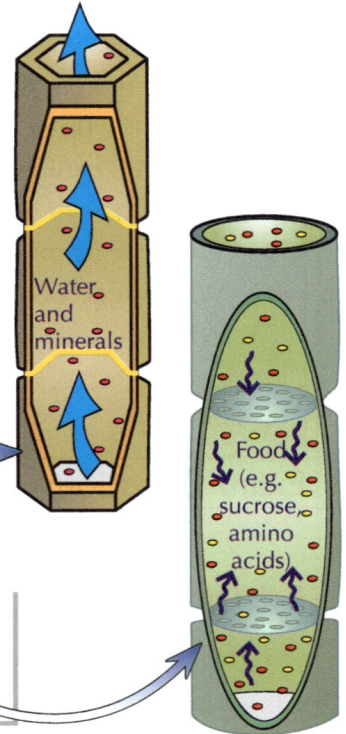

Water and minerals

Phloem Tubes Transport Food

Phloem tubes transport food substances (mainly sucrose and amino acids) made in the leaves to the rest of the plant for immediate use (e.g. in growing regions) or for storage. The transport goes in both directions.

Food (e.g. sucrose, amino acids)

You Can Identify Xylem and Phloem From Their Position

Xylem and phloem are always located in the same places in a stem, root or leaf, which allows you to identify them from cross-sections.

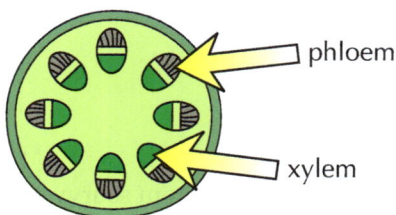

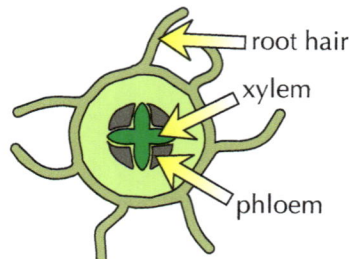

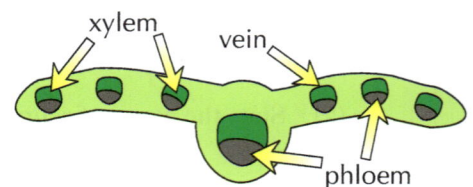

1) In a stem, the xylem and phloem are near the outside.
2) In a root, the xylem is in the centre surrounded by phloem to provide support.
3) In a leaf, xylem and phloem make up a network of veins.

The diagrams below all show the xylem and phloem in 'non-woody dicotyledonous plants' — basically just flowering plants (see p.8) without a woody stem.

Stem cross-section
phloem
xylem

Root cross-section
root hair
xylem
phloem

Leaf cross-section
xylem
vein
phloem

REVISION TIP

Xylem vessels carry water, phloem vessels carry sucrose

Make sure you don't get your phloem mixed up with your xylem. To help you to learn which is which, you could remember that phloem transports substances in both directions, but xylem only transports things upwards — xy to the sky. It might just get you a mark or two in the exam...

Water Uptake

Water from the soil enters the plant through the roots, then continues up through the plant. You can see the pathway that water takes in an experiment.

Root Hairs Take In Water and Mineral Ions

1) You might remember from page 12 that the cells on the surface of plant roots grow into "hairs", which stick out into the soil.
2) Each branch of a root will be covered in millions of these microscopic hairs.
3) The hairs give the plant roots a much larger surface area, which increases the rate of absorption of water by osmosis (see p.21) and mineral ions by active transport (see p.24).

Water Follows a Pathway Through The Plant

Water in the soil travels from the root hairs to the leaves through xylem vessels in the stem. The diagram below shows the pathway water takes:

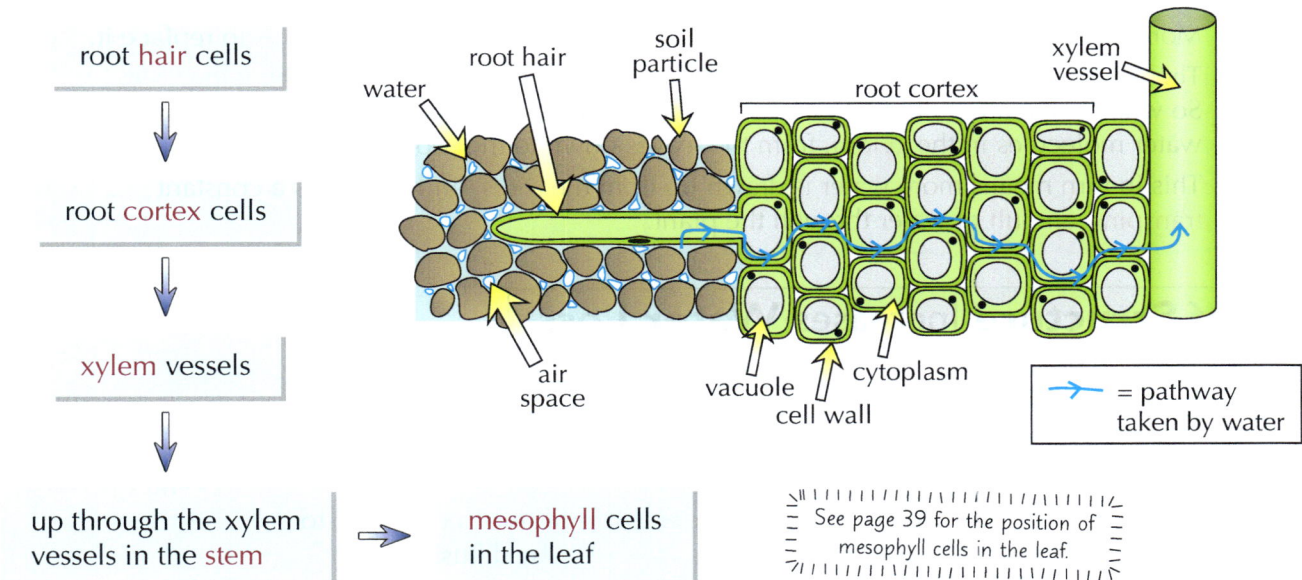

See page 39 for the position of mesophyll cells in the leaf.

You Can Investigate the Pathway of Water in a Plant

1) Place a plant stem (e.g. a celery stalk) into a beaker of water containing a stain, like coloured dye.
2) As water moves up the stem, you'll see the dye travel up the stem, staining the xylem.
3) If the plant stem has leaves, you'll see the dye reach the leaves too.

Plants take up water through root hair cells

EXAM TIP Make sure you know the pathway that water follows through the roots, stems and leaves of a plant, and that you are able to describe how to investigate the pathway of water through the above-ground parts of a plant (the stem and the leaves), in case it comes up in the exams.

Transpiration

If you don't water a house plant for a few days it starts to wilt (droop). Plants need water.

Plants Lose Water Through Transpiration

You need to know this definition of transpiration:

KEY TERM

Transpiration is the loss of water vapour from plant leaves.

Water evaporates from the surface of the mesophyll cells in the leaf, forming water vapour. This moves through the leaf's air spaces and then diffuses out of the leaf through the stomata (tiny holes in the leaf's surface).

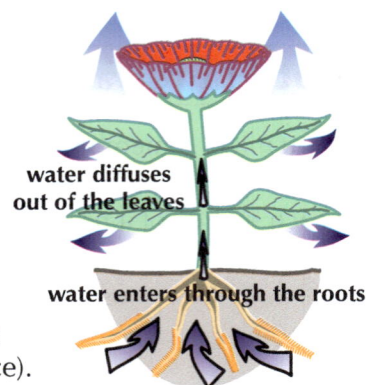

water diffuses out of the leaves

water enters through the roots

A Transpiration Pull Moves Water Up the Plant

1) Evaporation and diffusion of water from the leaves at the 'top' of the xylem creates a slight shortage of water in the leaf.

2) More water is drawn up from the rest of the plant through the xylem vessels to replace it.

3) There are forces of attraction between the water molecules, which hold them together. So when some are pulled into the leaf, others follow. This means the whole column of water molecules in the xylem, from the leaves down to the roots, moves upwards.

4) This in turn means more water is drawn up from the roots, and so there's a constant transpiration pull of water through the plant.

Leaf Structure Increases Water Loss

1) Transpiration is just a side-effect of the way leaves are adapted for photosynthesis (see p.39).

2) The interconnecting air spaces in the leaf give mesophyll cells a large surface area. This means that a lot of water can evaporate in a short period of time and diffuse through the leaf.

3) Guard cells are able to change the diameter (size) of stomata in order to control water loss. Reducing the size of the stomata reduces water loss by diffusion.

4) The number of stomata also affects water loss by diffusion — the greater the number of stomata, the more water can be lost.

Wilting Happens When There is a Lack of Water

1) Watering a plant increases the water potential (see p.21) of the soil around it. This means that all the plant cells draw in water by osmosis until they become turgid (plump and swollen). The contents of the cell push against the cell wall, creating a turgor pressure that helps to support the plant tissues (see p.23).

2) If there's no water in the soil, a plant starts to wilt (droop). This is because the cells become flaccid — they start to lose water. The plant doesn't totally lose its shape though, because the inelastic cell wall keeps things in position. It just droops a bit.

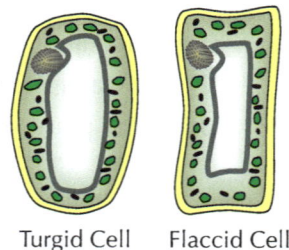

Turgid Cell   Flaccid Cell

Transpiration involves evaporation and diffusion

A big tree loses about a thousand litres of water from its leaves every single day. That's as much water as the average person drinks in a year, so the roots have to be very effective at drawing in water from the soil.

Supplement

The Rate of Transpiration

Here's another page on transpiration for you. But this time it's all about the rate of transpiration.

A **Potometer** can be Used to **Estimate Transpiration Rate**

1) You can estimate the rate of transpiration by measuring the uptake of water by a plant.
2) This is because you can assume that water uptake by the plant is directly related to water loss by the leaves (transpiration).
3) Set up the apparatus as in the diagram, and then record the starting position of the air bubble.
4) Start a stopwatch and record the distance moved by the bubble per unit time, e.g. per hour.
5) The set up below will be your control — you can vary an environmental condition, e.g. the temperature or wind speed, run the experiment again and compare the results to the control to see how the change affected the transpiration rate.

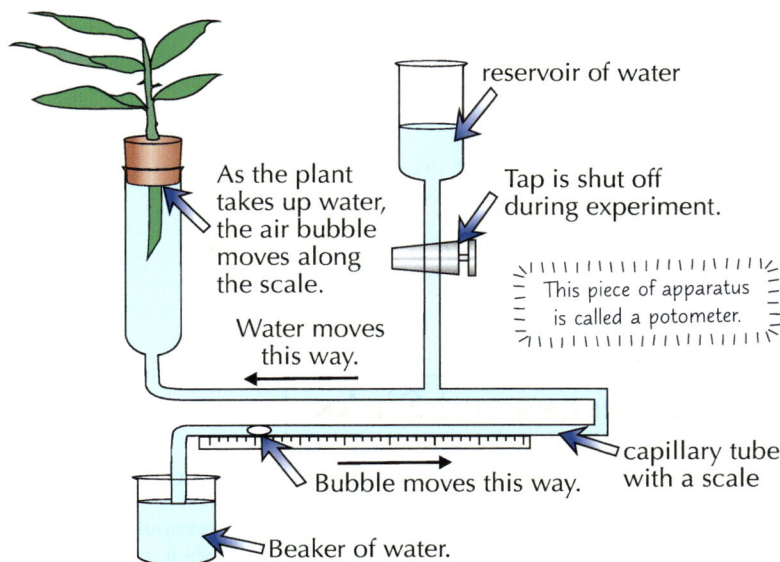

reservoir of water

As the plant takes up water, the air bubble moves along the scale.

Tap is shut off during experiment.

This piece of apparatus is called a potometer.

Water moves this way.

Bubble moves this way.

capillary tube with a scale

Beaker of water.

6) You can increase or decrease the temperature by putting the apparatus in a room that's warmer or colder than where you did the control experiment.
7) You can put the apparatus next to a fan to change the wind speed. You can increase or decrease the wind speed by changing the settings on the fan.

When plants lose water through transpiration, they also lose mass — so you can also estimate transpiration rate by measuring the rate at which a plant loses mass.

Transpiration Rate is Affected by Different Factors

Temperature

1) The warmer it is, the faster transpiration happens.
2) When it's warm the water particles have more kinetic energy to evaporate and diffuse out of the stomata.

s

Humidity

1) The more humid (full of water) the air around a leaf, the slower transpiration happens.
2) If the air is humid there's a lot of water in it already, so there's not much of a concentration gradient between the inside and the outside of the leaf.
3) Diffusion happens fastest if there's a really high concentration in one place, and a really low concentration in the other.

Supplement

Wind Speed

1) The higher the wind speed around a leaf, the greater the transpiration rate.
2) If it's windy, any water vapour surrounding the leaf is swept away, maintaining a low concentration of water in the air outside the leaf. This means diffusion happens faster.

Supplement

There's more on how temperature and concentration gradients affect the rate of diffusion on p.20.

Translocation

So now you know how plants transport water, it's time to learn how plants move the substances they make around. They do this by a process called translocation.

Translocation Happens in the Phloem

KEY TERM

Translocation is the movement of sucrose and amino acids through the phloem from a source to a sink.

1) Translocation moves solutes like sucrose and amino acids through the phloem to where they're needed in a plant.

2) Translocation always moves sucrose and amino acids from 'sources' to 'sinks'.

3) A source is any part of the plant that releases sucrose or amino acids.

4) A sink is any area where:

- sucrose or amino acids are stored.
- sucrose or amino acids are used up in respiration or growth.

5) The concentration of sucrose and amino acids is higher at a source than a sink.

Plant Organs Can Be Both Sources and Sinks

Some parts of a plant can act as sources or as sinks at different times during the life of the plant:

When plants are growing, the leaves are actively photosynthesising and producing lots of sucrose — they are sources.

Photosynthesis makes glucose, which is then converted to sucrose before it is transported around the plant.

Reproductive structures (e.g. flowers and fruits) and growing stems act as sinks when plants are growing, because they use the sucrose up. Places where sucrose is stored, like roots, tubers and bulbs also act as sinks.

During winter, when some plants lose their leaves, storage sites like roots, tubers and bulbs become the sources of sucrose.

Amino acids are made in the roots or the shoots (sources) then transported to developing roots, leaves, flowers and seeds (sinks).

The newly growing leaves act as sinks. Once they mature they will become sources once again.

Translocation moves substances from sources to sinks

Make sure you know the difference between a source and a sink. A source is the place where sucrose and amino acids are made and a sink is a part of a plant where sucrose and amino acids are used up or stored. Parts of a plant can act as both a source and a sink throughout a plant's life, as the plant grows and develops.

Supplement

Warm-Up & Exam Questions

That's the end of transport in plants. Before moving onto transport in animals, test that you've understood everything you need to know about plant transport by answering the questions below.

Warm-Up Questions

1) Outline the pathway taken by water through a plant.
2) What is transpiration?
3) Explain why wilting occurs.
4) What is the difference between a source and a sink?

Exam Questions

1   Aphids are insects. They feed on liquid which they extract from a plant's transport vessels, using their sharp mouthparts to pierce the stem. This liquid contains dissolved sucrose.

(a)   Name the process by which sucrose is transported around the plant.

[1]

(b)   Name the type of transport vessel that the aphids extract their liquid food from.

[1]

(c)   Which letter (**A** or **B**) points to the position of the transport vessel you named in (b) on the diagram on the right?

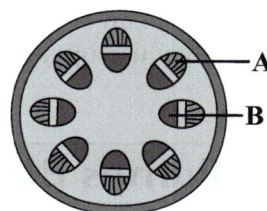

[1]

[3 marks]

2   A student investigated the effect of temperature on transpiration in basil plants.
She put groups of three plants in two different conditions. She weighed the plants before and after the experiment and calculated the % loss in mass for each plant.
Her results are shown in the table below.

plant	% loss in mass	
	Group A: 20 °C	Group B: 25 °C
1	5	10
2	5	11
3	4	9
mean	4.7	

(a)   Calculate the mean % loss in mass for the three plants in Group **B**.

[2]

(b)   Explain why the plants in Group **B** lost a greater percentage of their mass than the plants in Group **A**.

[3]

(c)   Explain how humidity can affect the rate of transpiration.

[2]

[7 marks]

Circulatory System — The Heart

The heart plays a major role in the circulatory system. It's needed to pump blood through the blood vessels.

The Circulatory System Moves Blood Through the Body

1) The circulatory system is a system of blood vessels with a pump (the heart) and valves to make sure that blood always flows in one direction.

Blood vessels are the tubes that blood flows through (p.57).

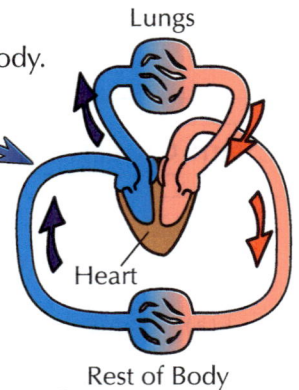

2) Fish have a single circulatory system — deoxygenated blood from the fish's body passes through the heart, which then pumps it right round the body again in a single circuit (via the gills where it picks up oxygen). Blood only goes through the heart once in each full circuit it makes of the body.

3) Mammals have a double circulatory system. This means that the heart pumps blood around the body in two circuits:

- In the first circuit, the heart pumps deoxygenated blood to the lungs to take in oxygen. Oxygenated blood then returns to the heart.

- In the second circuit, the heart pumps oxygenated blood around all the other organs of the body to deliver oxygen to the body cells. Deoxygenated blood then returns to the heart.

Lungs

Heart

Rest of Body

4) There are advantages of a double circulatory system over a single one:

- Returning blood to the heart after it has picked up oxygen at the lungs means it can be pumped out around the body at a much higher pressure.

- This means that blood can be pumped around the body much faster, so more oxygen can be delivered to the cells. This is important for mammals because they use up a lot of oxygen maintaining their body temperature.

The Heart Pumps Blood Through the Blood Vessels

In mammals, blood is pumped away from the heart into arteries and returns to the heart in veins.

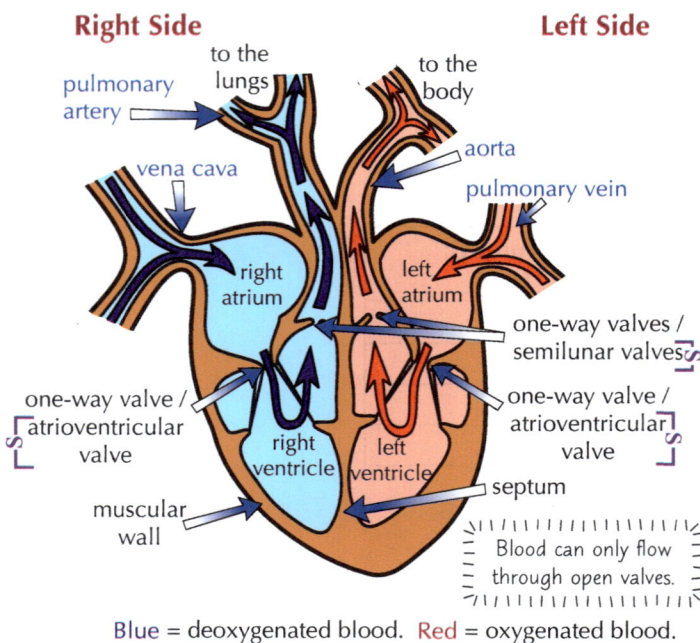

Right Side   **Left Side**

to the lungs   to the body

pulmonary artery

aorta

vena cava

pulmonary vein

right atrium

left atrium

one-way valves / semilunar valves

one-way valve / atrioventricular valve

one-way valve / atrioventricular valve

right ventricle   left ventricle

septum

muscular wall

Blood can only flow through open valves.

Blue = deoxygenated blood. Red = oxygenated blood.

1) The right atrium of the heart receives deoxygenated blood from the body through the vena cava (a large vein).

2) The left atrium receives oxygenated blood from the lungs via the pulmonary vein.

3) The atria pump blood into the ventricles.

4) The right ventricle pumps deoxygenated blood to the lungs via the pulmonary artery.

5) The left ventricle pumps oxygenated blood to the body via the aorta (an artery).

6) The muscular walls of the atria and ventricles contract to pump the blood.

7) Valves prevent the backflow of blood. E.g. when the ventricles contract, the atrioventricular valves shut to prevent blood flowing back into the atria.

8) The septum separates the left and right sides of the heart, so oxygenated and deoxygenated blood remain separate.

9) The left ventricle has a much thicker wall than the right ventricle. It needs more muscle because it has to pump blood around the whole body at high pressure, whereas the right ventricle only has to pump it to the lungs. The muscular walls of the atria are not as thick as those of the ventricles, as they only have to pump blood to the ventricles.

Circulatory System — The Heart

Different factors, like exercise, affect the heart rate. Changes in heart rate can be monitored.

There are **Different** Ways to **Monitor** the **Activity** of the **Heart**

1) By listening to it. The opening and closing of heart valves make a "lub dub" sound. A stethoscope can be used to listen to the heart sounds, to check that the heart is functioning normally.

2) By measuring the pulse rate (see below). This gives an idea of how quickly the heart is beating compared to what is expected.

3) By using an electrocardiogram (ECG). The heart's activity is controlled by electrical impulses. In an ECG, sensors are attached to a person's skin that detect these electrical impulses. These impulses are recorded by a machine, so that anything unusual can be detected.

You Can Investigate the **Effect** of **Physical Activity** on **Pulse Rate**

1) Each contraction of the ventricles creates a surge of blood in the arteries. This is your pulse.

2) To measure your pulse rate, put two fingers on the inside of your wrist or your neck and count the number of pulses in 1 minute.

3) You can investigate how physical activity affects your pulse rate. E.g. you could take your pulse after:

- sitting down for 5 minutes,
- then after 5 minutes of gentle walking,
- then again after 5 minutes of slow jogging,
- then again after running for 5 minutes.

Your pulse rate is equivalent to your heart rate.

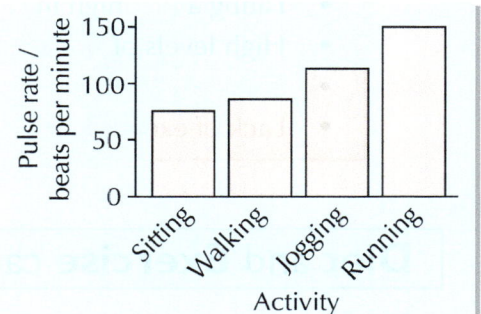

4) You could then plot your results in a bar chart.

5) Your pulse rate will increase the more intense the exercise is.

Physical Activity Increases **Heart Rate**

See pages 72-73 for more on respiration.

1) When you exercise, your muscles need more energy, so you respire more.

2) This means you need to get more oxygen into the cells and remove more carbon dioxide. For this to happen the blood has to flow faster, so your heart rate increases. Here's how:

- Exercise increases the amount of carbon dioxide (CO_2) in the blood.
- High levels of blood CO_2 are detected by receptors in two of the arteries.
- These receptors send impulses to the brain.
- The brain sends impulses to the heart, causing it to contract more frequently and with more force.

Physical activity causes the pulse rate to increase

EXAM TIP

Measuring pulse rate is one way that the activity of the heart can be monitored. Make sure you can describe how to do this, and know how physical activity affects pulse rate. If you're doing the Extended course, you'll need to explain the effect that physical activity has on heart rate too.

Coronary Heart Disease

Coronary heart disease (CHD) is a big problem. But there are things we can do to help prevent it.

CHD Happens When Coronary Arteries Get Blocked

1) The coronary arteries supply blood to the heart muscle.

2) Coronary heart disease is when the coronary arteries get blocked by layers of fatty material building up.

3) This causes the arteries to become narrow, so blood flow is restricted and there's a lack of oxygen to the heart muscle — this can lead to a heart attack.

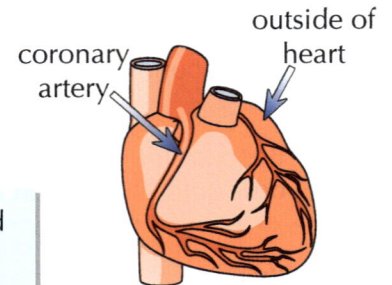

coronary artery

outside of heart

Several Factors can Lead to Coronary Heart Disease

1) Risk factors are things that are linked to an increase in the likelihood that a person will develop a certain disease during their lifetime.

2) There are many risk factors for coronary heart disease. They include:

- Eating a diet high in saturated fat and salt
- High levels of stress
- Smoking
- Lack of exercise
- The genes you inherit
- Getting older
- Being male rather than female

Both men and women can get coronary heart disease, but it's more likely if you're male.

Diet and Exercise can Help to Prevent Coronary Heart Disease

Diet

- High blood pressure and a high blood cholesterol level (specifically, a high level of LDL or 'bad' cholesterol in the blood) can cause fatty deposits to form in arteries.
- Reducing the amount of salt in your diet may help to reduce blood pressure.
  Reducing the amount of saturated fat in your diet will help to reduce the blood cholesterol level.
- So a diet low in salt and saturated fat is likely to reduce the risk of fatty deposits occurring and therefore help to prevent coronary heart disease.
- Eating plenty of fruits and vegetables is also thought to help protect the heart against CHD.

Exercise

Another risk factor for coronary heart disease is being inactive. Regular exercise can lower blood pressure and reduce the risk of coronary heart disease.

Coronary heart disease is associated with blood flow

Factors like age and family history can increase the risk of coronary heart disease but they can't be changed. It is possible to control and modify lifestyle-related risk factors, like diet, smoking and stress.

Circulatory System — Blood Vessels

Blood is carried round the body in a set of 'tubes' called blood vessels. Here's a page on the different types.

Arteries Carry Blood Under Pressure

1) Arteries carry blood from the heart to the rest of the body.
2) The walls are thick compared to the size of the hole down the middle (the "lumen"). They contain thick layers of muscle and elastic fibres.
3) The walls need to be thick to withstand the high pressure of blood in the arteries. They need to be elastic so they can stretch and recoil with each surge of blood as the heart beats.

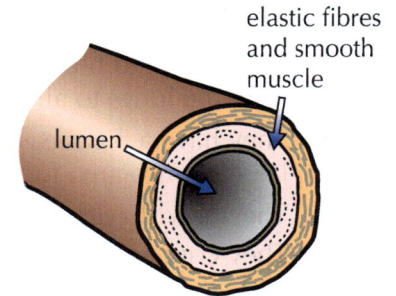

Supplement

elastic fibres and smooth muscle

lumen

Capillaries are Really Small

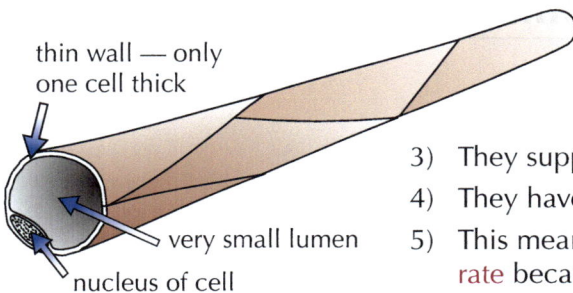

thin wall — only one cell thick

very small lumen

nucleus of cell

1) Capillaries are really tiny — too small to see.
2) They carry the blood really close to every cell in the body to exchange substances with them.
3) They supply glucose and oxygen, and take away wastes like CO_2.
4) They have permeable walls that are usually only one cell thick.
5) This means that substances can diffuse in and out at an increased rate because the distance over which diffusion happens is reduced.

Supplement

Veins Take Blood Back to the Heart

1) Their walls are not as thick as artery walls and they have a bigger lumen than arteries.
2) Veins also have one-way valves inside them.
3) The blood is at lower pressure in the veins so the walls don't need to be as thick.
4) They have a bigger lumen than arteries to help the blood flow despite the lower pressure.
5) The valves help keep the blood flowing in the right direction despite the lower pressure.

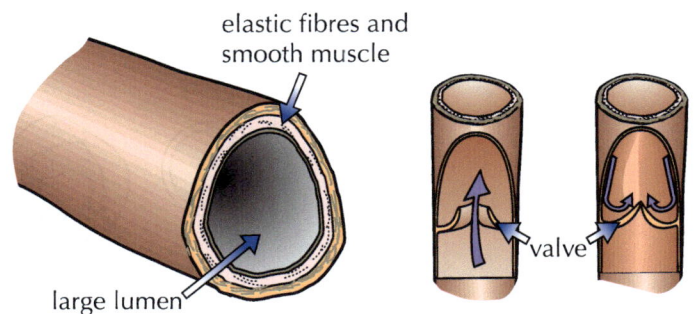

Supplement

elastic fibres and smooth muscle

large lumen

valve

Learn The Names of These Blood Vessels

You need to learn the names of the blood vessels going to and from the organs in this table.
You also need to be able to identify them in diagrams.

Organ	Main blood vessel(s) to...	Main blood vessel(s) from...
Heart	vena cava	aorta
Heart	pulmonary vein	pulmonary artery
Lungs	pulmonary artery	pulmonary vein
Kidney	renal artery	renal vein
Liver	hepatic artery	hepatic vein
Liver	hepatic portal vein	hepatic vein

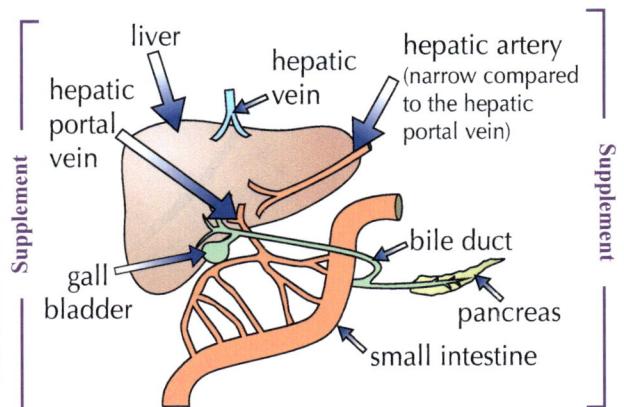

Supplement

liver

hepatic vein

hepatic artery (narrow compared to the hepatic portal vein)

hepatic portal vein

gall bladder

bile duct

pancreas

small intestine

There's more on the vena cava, aorta and pulmonary blood vessels on p.54. There's more on the renal artery and renal vein on p.77.

Section 6 — Transport in Plants and Animals

Circulatory System — Blood

Blood acts as a huge transport system — it is a tissue that contains different cells.

Red Blood Cells Carry Oxygen

1) The job of red blood cells is to carry oxygen from the lungs to all the cells in the body.

2) They have a biconcave disc shape to give a large surface area for absorbing oxygen.

3) They don't have a nucleus — this allows more room to carry oxygen.

4) They contain a red pigment called haemoglobin, which binds to oxygen in the lungs and releases it in body tissues, allowing it to be transported around the body to cells.

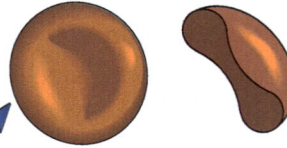

White Blood Cells Defend Against Infection

1) White blood cells are usually larger than red blood cells. Unlike red blood cells, white blood cells do have a nucleus.

2) White blood cells help to defend against infection by:

- Phagocytosis — engulfing and digesting disease-causing organisms.
- Producing antibodies — proteins that attach to disease-causing organisms and help to destroy them.

3) Phagocytes are white blood cells that carry out phagocytosis.

4) Lymphocytes are white blood cells that produce antibodies against microorganisms.

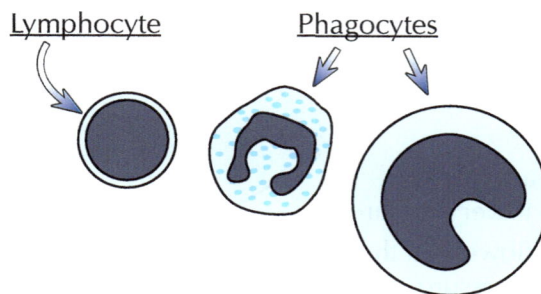

Lymphocyte   Phagocytes

There's more on white blood cells and how they work on page 64.

Make Sure You Can Identify Blood Cells in a Photomicrograph

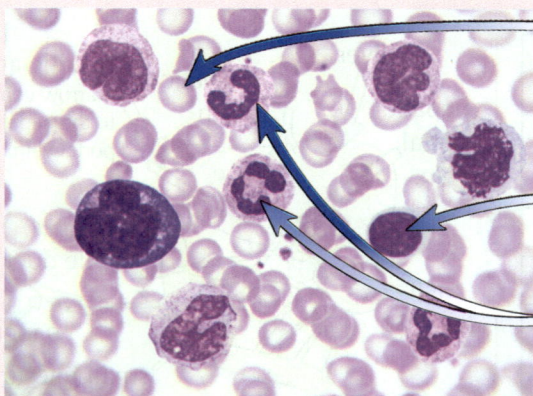

Most of the cells are red blood cells. They're easy to spot because they don't have a nucleus.

A photomicrograph is just a photo taken through a microscope.

The rest are white blood cells — they do have a nucleus.

This is a lymphocyte. The nucleus takes up most of the cell and there's very little cytoplasm to be seen.

These are different types of phagocytes. One has a 'multi-lobed' nucleus (a nucleus with several interconnected parts). The other has a c-shaped nucleus.

Circulatory System — Blood

Blood doesn't just contain red blood cells and white blood cells — it also contains platelets and plasma.

Platelets Help Blood Clot

1) These are small fragments of cells.
2) They have no nucleus.
3) When you damage a blood vessel, platelets clump together to 'plug' the damaged area. This is known as blood clotting.
4) Clotting stops you losing too much blood from a wound and stops pathogens (disease-causing organisms) from getting in.
5) Lack of platelets can cause excessive bleeding and bruising.

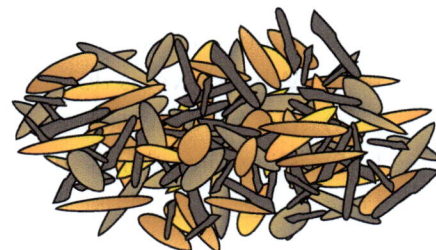

Blood Clotting Involves Proteins Too

1) Your blood contains a soluble protein called fibrinogen.
2) When you damage a blood vessel, it triggers a series of reactions that convert fibrinogen into another protein called fibrin.
3) Fibrin is made up of insoluble fibres. These tangle together and form a mesh in which platelets and red blood cells get trapped — this forms the blood clot.

Plasma is the Liquid That Carries Everything in Blood

This is a pale, straw-coloured liquid which carries just about everything, including:

1) Red and white blood cells and platelets.
2) Nutrients like glucose and amino acids. These are the soluble products of digestion which are absorbed from the gut and taken to the cells of the body.
3) Carbon dioxide from the organs to the lungs.
4) Ions.
5) Hormones.
6) Urea.

Blood — red blood cells, white blood cells, platelets and plasma

Sometimes, when you're ill, you might have a sample of your blood taken so that it can be analysed. Blood tests can be used to diagnose loads of things — not just disorders of the blood. This is because the blood transports so many chemicals produced by so many organs... and it's easy to take a sample of blood.

Warm-Up & Exam Questions

That's Section 6 finished. Have a go at these questions to see how much you know.

Warm-Up Questions

1) What is a circulatory system?
2) State three ways that the activity of the heart can be monitored.
3) What do veins do?
4) Describe the purpose of platelets in blood.
5) Give three things that are carried in blood plasma.

Exam Questions

1 Blood is a tissue that transports important substances around the body.
The cell shown below transports oxygen around the body.

View
from above

Cut through
view

(a) Name the type of cell shown.

[1]

(b) Describe and explain **one** way in which this cell is adapted for carrying oxygen.

[2]

(c) Name another type of blood cell, and state its function.

[2]

(d) Blood cells are carried in the bloodstream inside blood vessels.
Capillaries are one type of blood vessel.
State and explain **two** ways that the structure of a capillary enables it to carry out its function.

[4]
[Total 9 marks]

2 Doctors are assessing the heart of a patient with coronary heart disease.

(a) What is coronary heart disease?

[1]

(b) Explain why a high level of saturated fat in a person's diet might increase their risk of developing coronary heart disease.

[2]

(c) State **two** other possible risk factors for coronary heart disease.

[2]
[Total 5 marks]

Exam Questions

3   The diagram below shows the human heart, as seen from the front.
The left ventricle has been labelled.

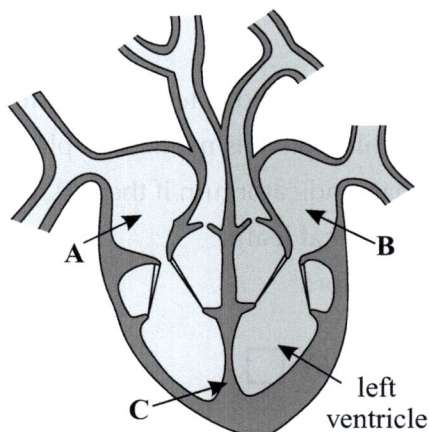

(a)   Name the parts labelled **A**, **B** and **C**.

[1]

(b)   Describe the passage of deoxygenated blood from the body
through the heart to reach the lungs.

[4]

Supplement

(c)   Explain why the wall of the left ventricle is thicker than the wall of the right ventricle.

[2]

(d)   Give the function of the valves in the heart.

[1]

(e)   The human heart is part of a double circulatory system. Give **one** advantage for
humans of having a double circulatory system instead of a single circulatory system.

[1]
[Total 9 marks]

Supplement

4   What is the name of the main blood vessel from the liver?

◻ **A**   hepatic vein   ◻ **B**   hepatic portal vein

◻ **C**   pulmonary vein   ◻ **D**   renal vein

[Total 1 mark]

5   Platelets help the blood to clot at a wound.

(a)   Give **two** reasons why it is important for blood to clot at a wound.

[2]

(b)   Describe the process of blood clotting.

[2]
[Total 4 marks]

Revision Summary for Sections 5 & 6

That's the end of Sections 5 and 6 — time to put yourself to the test and find out how much you really know.
- Try these questions and tick off each one when you get it right.
- When you've done all the questions for a topic and are completely happy with it, tick off the topic.

Photosynthesis and Gas Exchange in Leaves (p.34-39) ☐
1) What is photosynthesis?
s 2) Explain how a) light, b) CO_2 concentration and c) temperature limit the rate of photosynthesis.
3) Briefly describe a test to show that chlorophyll is needed for photosynthesis to take place.
4) What colour does hydrogencarbonate indicator turn if the CO_2 concentration increases?
5) Where are the stomata located in a typical leaf?
6) What do plants need magnesium ions for?

Diet, Digestion and Absorption (p.42-46) ☐
8) Why is having a balanced diet important?
9) Why does the stomach produce gastric juice?
10) What are incisor teeth used for?
11) What is the role of digestive enzymes in chemical digestion?
12) What is assimilation?
s 13) How do the villi in the small intestine help absorption?

Transport in Plants, Water Uptake, Transpiration and Translocation (p.48-52) ☐
15) What is the function of xylem?
16) Is the xylem or the phloem found in the centre of a root cross-section?
s 17) Explain how water moves upwards through a plant.
18) Describe how you'd use a potometer to estimate the rate of transpiration.
19) What is translocation?
s 20) Name a part of a plant that can be both a source and a sink.

The Circulatory System and The Heart (p.54-56) ☐
s 21) Do fish have a single or a double circulatory system?
22) Do arteries take blood to or from the heart?
s 23) Why do the ventricles have thicker muscular walls than the atria?
24) Describe how you can investigate the effect of physical activity on pulse rate.

Blood Vessels and Blood (p.57-59) ☐
s 25) How are arteries adapted to carry out their function?
26) Which blood vessels have valves?
27) What are the names of the two main blood vessels associated with the lungs?
28) Give one structural difference between red blood cells and white blood cells.
29) What is blood plasma?

Fighting Disease

Here's a page all about what causes disease and how disease can be spread — scary stuff.
Thankfully, you also need to know about the defences in the human body that help to protect us.

Some **Diseases** are **Caused** by **Pathogens**

KEY TERM — A pathogen is any organism that causes disease.

1) Pathogens can be bacteria, viruses, fungi or protoctists.
2) They cause transmissible (infectious) diseases in other organisms (called hosts).

KEY TERM — A transmissible disease is a disease where the pathogen can be passed from one host to another.

Pathogens are **Spread Through**...

...**Direct** Contact...

Pathogens spread through direct contact are spread directly from one organism to another.

For example, some pathogens are spread through contact with a host's blood or other body fluids, e.g. mucus or saliva.

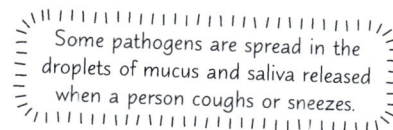

Some pathogens are spread in the droplets of mucus and saliva released when a person coughs or sneezes.

...And **Indirect** Contact

Pathogens spread through indirect contact are spread from one organism to another via an intermediate. For example:

- Some pathogens can be picked up by touching contaminated surfaces.
- Some pathogens are picked up by eating contaminated food.
- Some animals (insects in particular) carry pathogens from one organism to another.
- Some pathogens are breathed in as they are carried in the air.

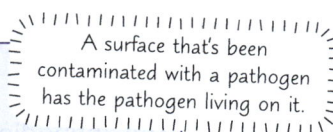

A surface that's been contaminated with a pathogen has the pathogen living on it.

The **Body** has its Own **Defences** to Stop **Pathogens** from Entering

The human body has many different defences against pathogen entry. You need to know these examples:

Defence	Function
Skin	Acts as a barrier to pathogens. If it gets damaged, blood clots quickly to seal cuts and keep microorganisms out.
Hairs in the nose	These trap particles from the air that could contain pathogens.
Mucus	Cells in your trachea and bronchi (airways in the lungs) produce mucus, which traps pathogens.
Stomach acid	The stomach produces acid, which kills most pathogens that are swallowed.

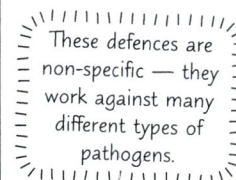

These defences are non-specific — they work against many different types of pathogens.

Fighting Disease — Immune System

Sometimes, pathogens do make it into your body — this page is all about what happens next.

Your **Immune System** Deals with **Pathogens**

1) Once pathogens have entered your body, they'll reproduce rapidly unless they're destroyed. That's the job of your immune system, and white blood cells (see p.58) are the most important part of it.

2) White blood cells have two different methods for defence that you need to know about: phagocytosis and antibody production.

Phagocytosis

1) Some white blood cells detect things that are 'foreign' to the body, e.g. pathogens. They then engulf (surround) the pathogens and digest them.

2) This process is called phagocytosis. The white blood cells are called phagocytes.

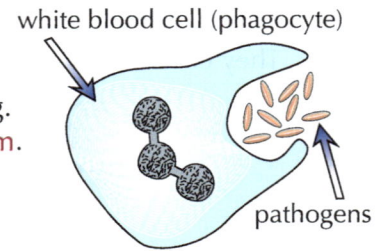

white blood cell (phagocyte)

pathogens

Production of **Antibodies**

Some white blood cells make proteins called antibodies. Antibodies are used to destroy pathogens. Here's how they work:

1) Every pathogen has unique molecules (called antigens) on its surface. These antigens have specific shapes.

2) When some types of white blood cell (called lymphocytes) come across a foreign antigen, they will start to produce antibodies. The antibodies have complementary shapes to fit the antigens.

3) The antibodies bind to the antigens on the invading pathogens, which either destroys the pathogens directly or marks them out for destruction by phagocytes.

4) The antibodies produced are specific to that antigen — they won't lock on to any others.

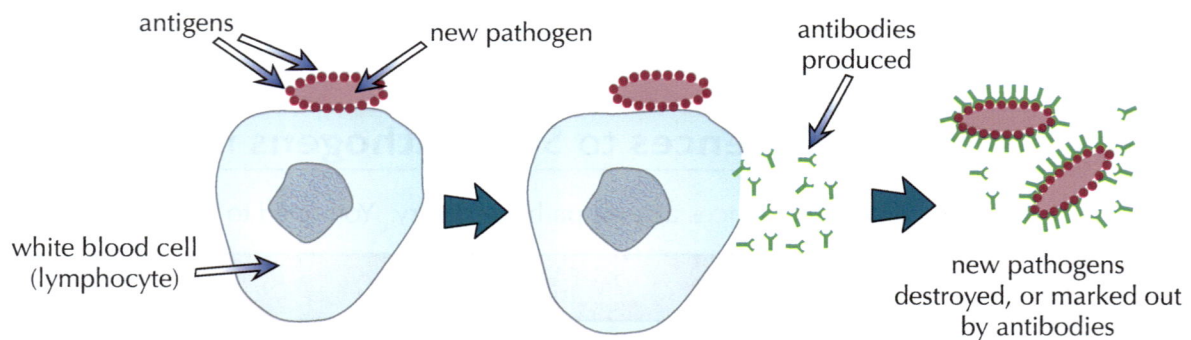

antigens   new pathogen   antibodies produced

white blood cell (lymphocyte)

new pathogens destroyed, or marked out by antibodies

5) Memory cells are also produced in response to the antigen. These are white blood cells that stay in the body and remember a specific antigen. They can produce antibodies very quickly if the same antigen enters the body again — so the pathogen can be destroyed before you get sick. This gives you long-term active immunity against the pathogen.

KEY TERM

Active immunity is the defence against a pathogen by the production of antibodies in the body.

Active immunity can be gained after infection by a pathogen or by vaccination (see p.65-66).

Supplement

Preventing the Spread of Disease

We don't always have to deal with the problem of disease once it's happened — we can prevent it happening in the first place. Here are a few ways to prevent the spread of disease.

The Spread of Disease Can Be Reduced

There are several measures that can be taken to control the spread of disease.

1) Hygienic food preparation — preparing food in hygienic (clean) conditions can reduce the spread of pathogens from work surfaces, chopping boards, etc. to food.

Certain foods also need thorough cooking to kill bacteria.

2) Good personal hygiene — simple hygiene measures, such as washing your hands after going to the toilet, can prevent the spread of disease.

3) Waste disposal — not letting rubbish build up, and having systems in place to safely dispose of things like soiled bandages and used needles, can prevent the spread of disease.

4) Clean water supply — having access to clean, fresh water for drinking and cooking reduces the spread of water-borne pathogens.

5) Sewage treatment — having a good system for the treatment of sewage (which prevents sewage from contaminating drinking water) will reduce the spread of water-borne pathogens.

Cholera is a Bacterial Disease that Causes Diarrhoea

Cholera is a disease caused by a bacterium that is transmitted through contaminated water. It causes diarrhoea, dehydration and loss of ions from the blood. Here's how cholera causes these effects:

1) The bacterium produces a toxin that causes the secretion of chloride ions into the small intestine. This decreases the water potential of the small intestine.

2) This decreased water potential causes water to move from the blood into the small intestine by osmosis (p.21), leading to diarrhoea and dehydration.

3) Chloride ions and other ions are then lost from the body due to the diarrhoea.

Vaccination Can be Used to Control the Spread of Disease

1) The body's defences can be enhanced through vaccination (see next page).

2) Individuals who have been vaccinated against a disease are immune — they won't develop the infection and pass it on to someone else.

3) When lots of people in a population have been vaccinated, it also helps to protect individuals that have not been vaccinated — they are less likely to catch the disease because there are fewer people to catch it from.

Supplement

Supplement

Preventing the Spread of Disease

Here's some more information about preventing the spread of disease.

Vaccination Can Enhance the Defences of the Body

Vaccination triggers the body to produce antibodies against a specific pathogen.

1) Vaccination usually involves injecting weakened pathogens or their antigens into the body. (Weakened pathogens are harmless, but they still carry antigens.)

2) The antigens in a vaccination stimulate an immune response by lymphocytes, which produce antibodies as normal.

3) The antigens also stimulate the production of memory cells. These give long-term active immunity against the pathogen.

Here's an example of a vaccination:

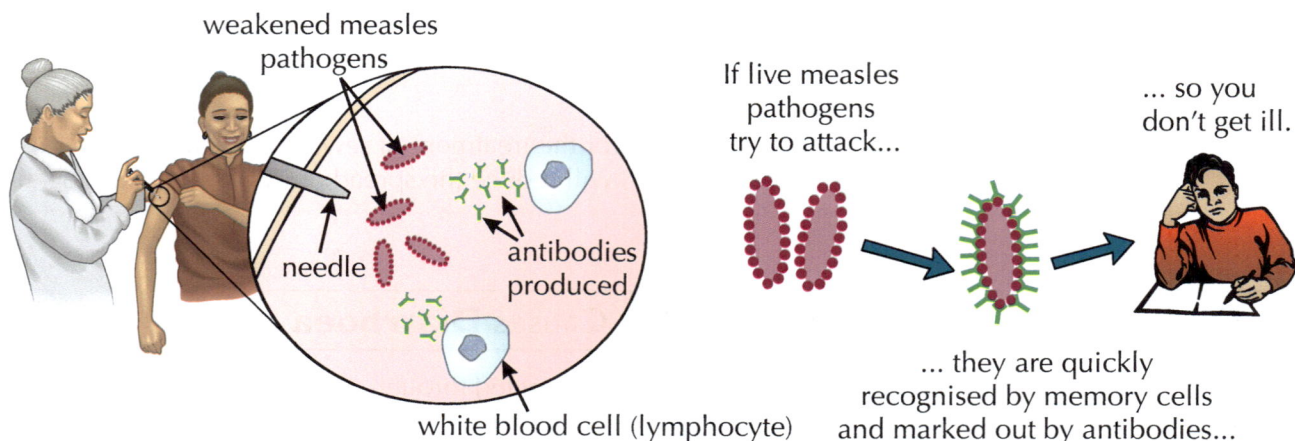

weakened measles pathogens

needle

antibodies produced

white blood cell (lymphocyte)

If live measles pathogens try to attack...

... they are quickly recognised by memory cells and marked out by antibodies...

... so you don't get ill.

Some Immunity Can be Passive

1) You can also become immune to a disease without producing your own antibodies. This is known as passive immunity.

KEY TERM

Passive immunity is the short-term defence against a pathogen by antibodies made by a different organism.

For example, a baby gets passive immunity from the antibodies it receives from its mother through the placenta and in breast milk. This is important because the immune systems of infants are not fully functional at birth, so they are at a greater risk of infection than older children and adults.

2) Passive immunity is short-term because the antibodies given do not remain in the blood long-term and memory cells are not produced. This means there is a risk of being infected by the same disease later on.

Memory cells speed up the next response to the pathogen

Vaccination has helped to save millions of lives — and it's all because of antibodies and memory cells.

Warm-Up & Exam Questions

It's easy to think you've learnt everything until you try some questions. Don't panic if there's a bit you've forgotten, just go back over that bit until it's firmly fixed in your brain.

Warm-Up Questions

1) What is meant by a transmissible disease?
2) How does the skin defend against the entry of pathogens?
3) What are the unique molecules found on the surface of pathogens called?
4) What is meant by passive immunity?

Exam Questions

1 There are many defences that help to prevent pathogens from entering the body.

(a) Describe the role of hairs in the nose.

[1]

(b) Describe a defence of the body against pathogens found in food.

[1]

[Total 2 marks]

2 The methods used to prevent the spread of a disease depend on how the disease is transmitted. It is important for chefs to wash their hands thoroughly before cooking. Suggest why.

[Total 1 mark]

3 The human immune system fights pathogens using a number of different mechanisms.

(a) Name and describe the mechanism for destroying pathogens which is shown in the diagram.

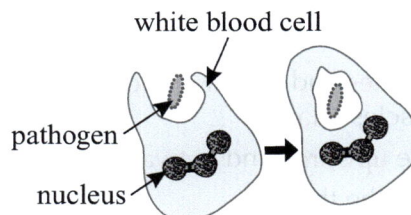

white blood cell

pathogen

nucleus

[2]

(b) Describe the role of antibodies in the immune response.

[3]

[Total 5 marks]

4 Child A and child B are born to different women on the same day.
Child A is vaccinated with the rubella vaccine, but child B is not.
Three years later the two children are exposed to the rubella virus.
Explain why child B becomes ill but child A does not.

[Total 5 marks]

Section 7 — Diseases and Immunity

The Breathing System

Your breathing system is found in your chest. It contains the lungs (the gas exchange organs).

The Breathing System has Lots of Parts

1) The lungs are protected by the ribs.

2) Intercostal muscles run between the ribs.

3) There are actually three layers of intercostal muscles. You need to know about two of them — the internal and external intercostal muscles.

4) The air you breathe in goes through the larynx and then the trachea.

5) The trachea is a hollow tube surrounded by C-shaped rings of cartilage. This makes it strong, but also allows it to move.

6) The trachea splits into two tubes called bronchi (each one is a bronchus), one going to each lung. The bronchi split into smaller tubes called bronchioles.

7) The bronchioles end at small sacs called alveoli where gas exchange takes place (see next page). The alveoli are surrounded by capillaries.

8) All of the structures mentioned above are separated from the lower part of the body by a muscle called the diaphragm.

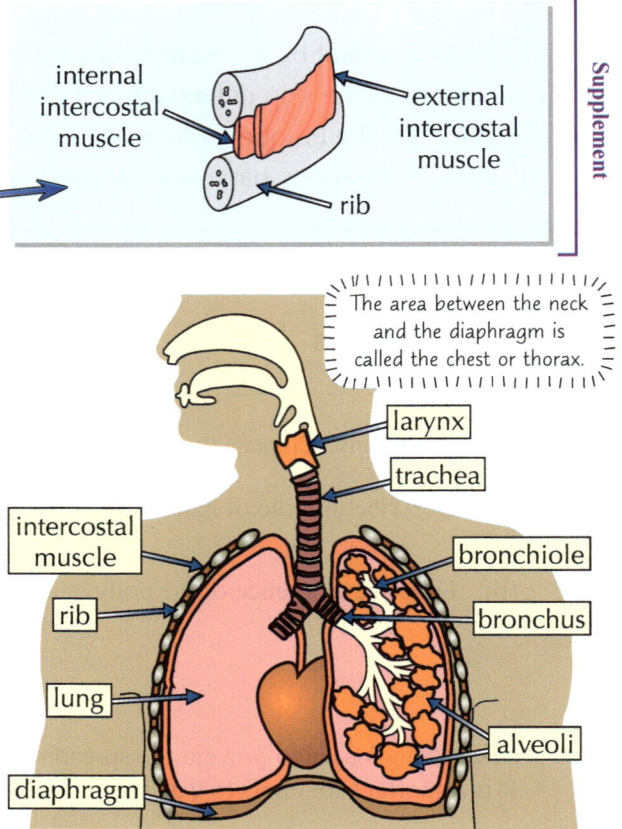

internal intercostal muscle

external intercostal muscle

rib

The area between the neck and the diaphragm is called the chest or thorax.

larynx

trachea

intercostal muscle

rib

lung

diaphragm

bronchiole

bronchus

alveoli

Ventilation is the Process of...

...Breathing In (Inspiration)...

1) The external intercostal muscles and diaphragm contract. The internal intercostal muscles relax.

2) This causes the ribs to move upwards and outwards.

3) This increases the volume of the thorax.

4) This decreases the pressure inside the thorax, drawing air in.

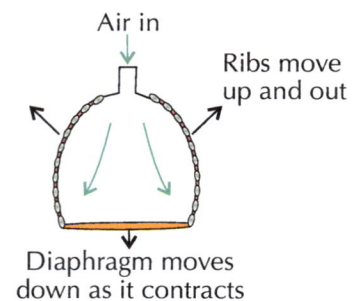

Air in

Ribs move up and out

Diaphragm moves down as it contracts

...and Breathing Out (Expiration)

1) The internal intercostal muscles contract. The external intercostal muscles and diaphragm relax.

2) This causes the ribs to move downwards and inwards.

3) This decreases the volume of the thorax.

4) This increases the pressure inside the thorax, so air is forced out.

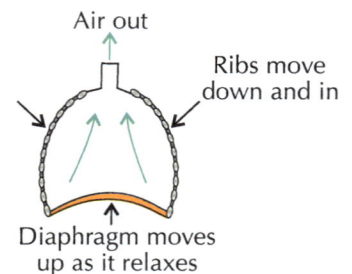

Air out

Ribs move down and in

Diaphragm moves up as it relaxes

Gas Exchange

Gas exchange isn't too tricky — it's just a simple trade of gases between the air and your blood.
You also need to know the differences between the air breathed in and air breathed out.

Gas Exchange Happens in the Lungs

1) The job of the lungs is to transfer oxygen to the blood and to remove waste carbon dioxide from it.

2) To do this the lungs contain millions of little air sacs called alveoli where gas exchange takes place.

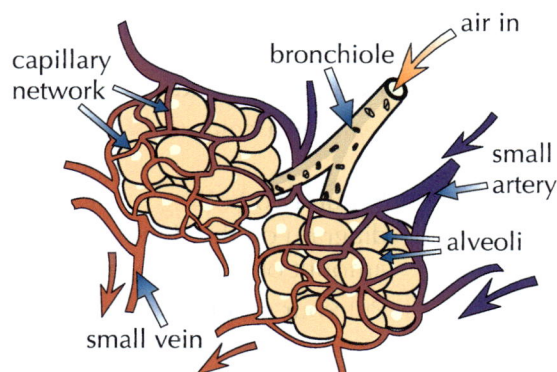

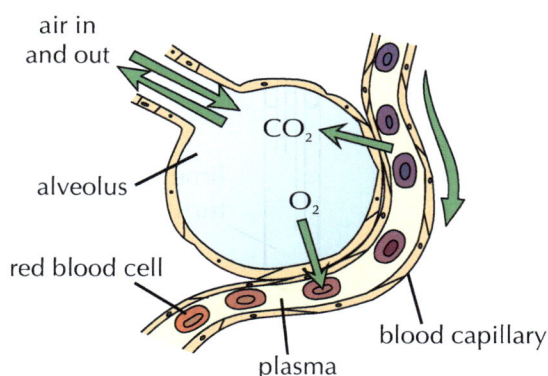

air in and out

CO_2

O_2

alveolus

red blood cell

plasma

blood capillary

Blue = blood with carbon dioxide.
Red = blood with oxygen.

capillary network

bronchiole

air in

small artery

alveoli

small vein

3) The alveoli form a specialised gas exchange surface. This means they have features to maximise the diffusion of oxygen and CO_2. They have:

- A large surface area (about 75 m^2 in humans).
- A very thin surface.
- A good blood supply.
- Good ventilation with air.

Gas exchange surfaces in other organisms tend to have similar features.

The Composition of Inspired and Expired Air is Different

The proportions of some gases in the air you breathe in are different from the proportions you breathe out.

	Oxygen / %	Carbon Dioxide / %	Water Vapour
Inspired Air	21	0.04	% Varies
Expired Air	16	4	Saturated (the air holds as much water as it can)

This is because aerobic respiration uses up oxygen and produces carbon dioxide — so there's less oxygen and more carbon dioxide in expired air than inspired air. The alveoli lining is kept moist to help gas exchange, so expired air becomes saturated with water as a result of body warmth causing it to evaporate.

There's more about respiration on page 72.

The Breathing System Has to be Protected

1) Your airways are lined with cells that have a protective role.

2) Goblet cells produce a sticky substance called mucus to coat the inner lining of the trachea and bronchi.

3) The mucus catches any pathogens and particles before they reach the lungs.

4) Ciliated cells are covered in tiny hair-like structures called cilia. These waft the mucus up to the back of the throat where it can be swallowed.

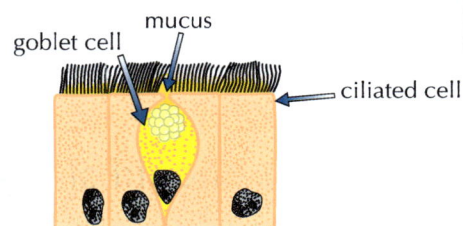

mucus

goblet cell

ciliated cell

Supplement

Investigating Breathing

Time for some investigating. On this page there's a test to show that the composition of inspired and expired air is different, and an investigation into how exercise affects your breathing rate.

You Can Show the **Release** of **Carbon Dioxide** in Your Breath

1) You can do an experiment with limewater to show that carbon dioxide (CO_2) is released when we breathe out.

2) Limewater is a colourless solution which turns cloudy in the presence of carbon dioxide.

- Set up two boiling tubes as in the diagram on the right. Put the same amount of limewater in each.
- Put your mouth around the mouthpiece and breathe in and out several times.
- As you breathe in, air from the room is drawn in through boiling tube A. This air contains very little carbon dioxide so the limewater in this boiling tube remains colourless.
- When you breathe out, the air you expire bubbles through the limewater in boiling tube B. This air contains CO_2 produced during respiration, so the limewater in this boiling tube turns cloudy.

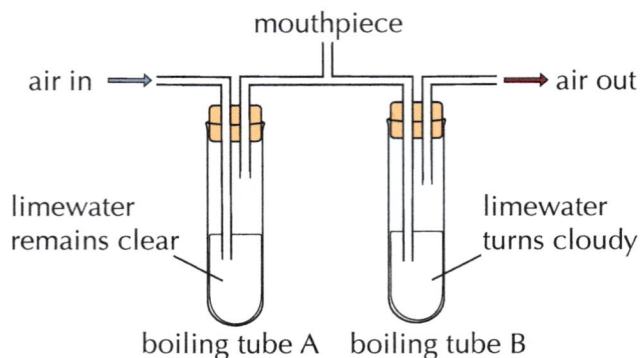

mouthpiece

air in ⇒   ⟶ air out

limewater remains clear

limewater turns cloudy

boiling tube A   boiling tube B

You Can Investigate the **Effect** of **Exercise** on **Breathing Rate**

1) When you exercise, your muscle cells need more oxygen (O_2) and produce more CO_2. So an increase in your breathing rate helps to deliver more O_2 to the cells and to remove the waste CO_2.

2) There's a simple experiment you can do to see what happens to breathing rate when you exercise:

- Firstly, sit still for five minutes. Then, for one minute, count the number of breaths you take.
- Now do four minutes of exercise (running, skipping...) and as soon as you stop count your breaths for a minute.
- Repeat the steps above, and work out your mean (average) results for resting and after exercise.
- You could also ask two other people to do the same so you get three sets of results to compare.

3) Your results should show that exercise increases breathing rate.

4) Exercise also increases the depth of breathing. When you breathe deeply, you inspire and expire a greater volume of air. This can be measured with a piece of equipment called a spirometer.

5) This all happens because the brain detects the increased concentration of CO_2 in the blood and increases the rate and depth of breathing so that more CO_2 is removed.

Supplement

You should always carry out repeats in an investigation

WORKING SCIENTIFICALLY

You should carry out repeats (at least three) and calculate a mean in order to see if your results are reliable. To calculate a mean, just add all your repeat results together (ignoring any anomalous results) and then divide the total by the number of repeats. Lovely.

Warm-Up & Exam Questions

The questions on this page are great practice for the exam. I'd give them a go if I were you...

Warm-Up Questions

1) True or False? Expired air has a greater proportion of oxygen than inspired air.
2) In the breathing system, what function do the ciliated cells have?
3) What solution can be used to test for the presence of carbon dioxide?
4) What effect does physical activity have on breathing rate?

Exam Questions

1   A diagram of the human breathing system is shown below.

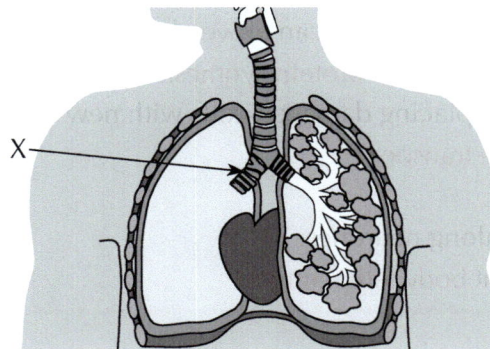

(a)   Label the diaphragm and a rib on the diagram.

[2]

(b)   A structure of the breathing system is labelled X on the diagram. Name structure X.

[1]

(c)   Name the structures in the breathing system where gas exchange takes place.

[1]

(d)   Give **two** ways in which these gas exchange structures are specialised for their function.

[2]

[Total 6 marks]

2   The statements below describe the events that take place when you breathe in.
Which of the options (**A-D**) shows the events in the correct order? Tick **one** box.

Event	Number
Pressure in thorax decreases	1
The external intercostal muscles and diaphragm contract, and the internal intercostal muscles relax	2
Air is drawn into the lungs	3
Thorax volume increases	4

☐ **A**   2, 1, 4, 3

☐ **B**   3, 4, 1, 2

☐ **C**   2, 4, 1, 3

☐ **D**   3, 2, 4, 1

[Total 1 mark]

Supplement

Respiration

You need energy to stay alive and to do all of the things that you love doing (like revising).
Energy comes from the food you eat, and it's transferred by respiration.

Respiration Involves Many Reactions

1) Respiration is the process of transferring energy from the breakdown of nutrient molecules, e.g. glucose (a sugar). It goes on in every cell in your body continuously.
2) Respiration transfers the energy that cells need to do just about everything.
3) There are two types of respiration, aerobic and anaerobic.

Respiration Transfers Energy for All Kinds of Things

Here are seven examples of how living organisms use the energy transferred by respiration:

1) To allow the muscles to contract (so they can move about).
2) To build proteins from amino acids in protein synthesis.
3) For cell division, e.g. when replacing damaged cells with new cells.
4) To move molecules by active transport.
5) So that they can grow.
6) For passing nerve impulses along neurones.
7) To maintain (keep) a constant body temperature.

Aerobic Respiration Needs Plenty of Oxygen

1) Aerobic just means "with oxygen" and it's the most efficient way to transfer energy from glucose.
2) Here's the definition you need to learn:

> **KEY TERM**
> Aerobic respiration is the series of chemical reactions in cells that uses oxygen to break down nutrient molecules (e.g. glucose) to release energy.

Aerobic respiration takes place in the mitochondria (see p.11).

3) This type of respiration goes on all the time in plants and animals. Here's the word equation:

$$\text{glucose} + \text{oxygen} \longrightarrow \text{carbon dioxide} + \text{water}$$

This is the reverse of the photosynthesis equation (see page 34).

Supplement

4) And here's the balanced chemical equation:

$$C_6H_{12}O_6 + 6O_2 \longrightarrow 6CO_2 + 6H_2O$$

Respiration releases energy

It's important to understand what respiration is and what it is used for. You're going to struggle to follow the next couple of pages if you don't. Read this page again if you need to, until you're sure you've got it.

Anaerobic Respiration

Now that you've learnt about aerobic respiration, it's time to learn about anaerobic respiration too.

Anaerobic Respiration is Used if There's Not Enough Oxygen

1) When you do vigorous (hard) exercise and your body can't supply enough oxygen to your muscles, they start doing anaerobic respiration as well as aerobic respiration. Here's the definition you need:

> **KEY TERM** Anaerobic respiration is the series of chemical reactions in cells that breaks down nutrient molecules to release energy without using oxygen.

2) Here's the word equation for anaerobic respiration in muscle cells:

glucose ⟶ lactic acid

3) Anaerobic respiration transfers much less energy per glucose molecule than aerobic respiration.

4) So, anaerobic respiration is only useful in emergencies, e.g. during exercise when it allows you to keep on using your muscles for a while longer.

Anaerobic Respiration Leads to an Oxygen Debt

1) Your muscles contract more frequently when you exercise, so you need more energy from respiration. This means you need to get more oxygen into your muscles for aerobic respiration.

2) Your breathing rate and breathing depth increase to get more oxygen into the blood, and your heart rate increases to get the blood (and the oxygen in it) around the body faster.

3) When you do really vigorous exercise your body can't supply oxygen to your muscles quickly enough for aerobic respiration alone, so they start respiring anaerobically as well. This causes lactic acid (see above) to build up in muscle cells and in the blood.

4) After respiring anaerobically, when you stop exercising you'll have an "oxygen debt".

5) An oxygen debt is the amount of extra oxygen your body needs to get rid of the lactic acid.

6) In other words you have to "repay" the oxygen that you didn't get to your muscles in time, because your lungs, heart and blood couldn't keep up with the demand earlier on:

- The blood that enters your muscles transports the lactic acid to the liver. The lactic acid is then broken down using oxygen, in aerobic respiration.
- Heart rate stays high after exercise to transport lactic acid in the blood from muscles to the liver. Breathing rate and depth stay high to supply oxygen for aerobic respiration of lactic acid.

Anaerobic Respiration in Yeast is Slightly Different

1) Yeast can respire without oxygen too, but they produce alcohol and carbon dioxide, not lactic acid.

2) Here's the word equation for anaerobic respiration in yeast:

Yeast are single-celled microorganisms.

glucose ⟶ alcohol + carbon dioxide

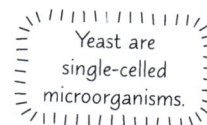

3) And here's the balanced chemical equation:

$$C_6H_{12}O_6 \longrightarrow 2C_2H_5OH + 2CO_2$$

EXAM TIP Aerobic and anaerobic respiration produce different products

Make sure you know the differences between aerobic and anaerobic respiration for your exam. Learn the products of each type, which transfers the most energy and which type requires oxygen.

Investigating Respiration

You can do experiments to investigate the rate of respiration in respiring organisms.

You Can Investigate the Rate of Respiration in Yeast

Respiring yeast produce carbon dioxide (CO_2) as a waste product, so you can use the volume of CO_2 produced in a given time to calculate their respiration rate. Here's an experiment you can do to investigate the effect of temperature on the rate of respiration in yeast:

1) Put a set volume and concentration of sucrose solution in a test tube.

2) Put the test tube in a water bath set to 15 °C.

3) Add a set mass of yeast to the test tube and stir for 2 minutes.

4) Attach the test tube to a gas syringe (as shown in the diagram) and leave the apparatus for a set amount of time (e.g. 10 minutes).

5) During this time, the yeast will respire and produce carbon dioxide. This is collected in the gas syringe, so the volume of CO_2 produced can be measured. If you divide the volume of CO_2 produced by the time taken to produce it, you can calculate the overall rate of respiration.

You could use the same mass of boiled yeast as a control (see p.162 for more on controls).

Diagram labels: bung, test tube, gas syringe, water bath, yeast and sucrose solution

6) Repeat steps 1-6 with the water bath set at different temperatures, e.g. 25 °C, 35 °C, 45 °C. This will allow you to see how changing the temperature affects the rate of respiration.

7) Respiration is controlled by enzymes — so as temperature increases, so should the rate of respiration, up until the optimum temperature (p.30). After the temperature increases past the optimum temperature, the rate of respiration decreases.

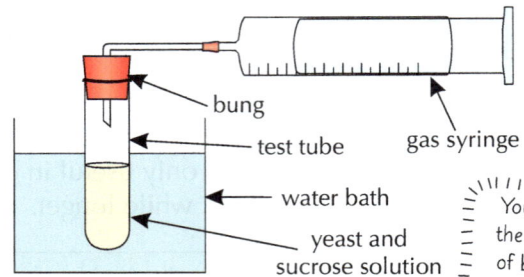

You Can Also Measure Oxygen Uptake by Respiring Organisms

You can use a piece of equipment called a respirometer to measure the uptake of oxygen by respiring organisms such as woodlice. You set it up as shown in the diagram.

1) The soda lime granules absorb the CO_2 produced by the respiring woodlice.

Safety goggles and gloves must be worn when handling soda lime.

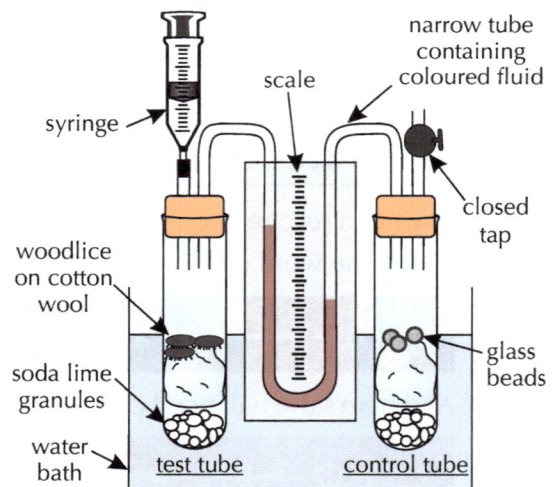

2) Glass beads (or another inert substance) with the same mass as the woodlice act as a control.

3) The syringe is used to set the fluid in the tube to a known level before the apparatus is left for a set time.

4) During this time, there'll be a decrease in the volume of air in the test tube containing the woodlice. This is because the woodlice use up oxygen in the tube as they respire. The decrease in volume reduces the pressure in the tube, causing the coloured fluid to move towards the test tube containing the woodlice. (The CO_2 they produce is absorbed by the soda lime so it doesn't affect the experiment.)

5) You can use the distance moved by the liquid to calculate the volume of oxygen taken in by the woodlice.

Diagram labels: syringe, scale, narrow tube containing coloured fluid, closed tap, woodlice on cotton wool, soda lime granules, water bath, test tube, control tube, glass beads

Learn how to investigate respiration in respiring organisms

PRACTICAL TIP

If you're given a method to follow in order to carry out an investigation, take your time and read each of the steps carefully before you begin — you might not get the right results if you don't.

Warm-Up & Exam Questions

You know the drill by now — work your way through the Warm-Up Questions, then the Exam Questions.

Warm-Up Questions

1) Give two examples of how organisms use the energy transferred by respiration.
2) What is produced by aerobic respiration in plants?
3) What is the balanced chemical equation for aerobic respiration?
4) State one way that the body clears the oxygen debt caused by vigorous exercise.
5) What is the balanced chemical equation for anaerobic respiration in yeast?

Exam Questions

1 Respiration is a process carried out by all living cells.
It can take place aerobically or anaerobically.

(a) State the purpose of respiration.

[1]

(b) Give **two** differences between aerobic and anaerobic respiration in animals.

[2]

(c) Write the word equation for aerobic respiration.

[2]
[Total 5 marks]

2 In the human body, respiration may be aerobic or anaerobic at different times.

(a) Write down the word equation for anaerobic respiration in humans.

[1]

(b) Glennon runs a 200 m race.
(i) State the type(s) of respiration Glennon will use when she is relaxing before the race.

[1]

(ii) State the type(s) of respiration Glennon will use towards the end of the race.

[1]
[Total 3 marks]

3 Outline an experiment that can be performed to measure the effect
of temperature on the rate of respiration in yeast.

[Total 4 marks]

4 A student investigated the effect of temperature
on the rate of respiration in yeast.
The results are shown in the graph on the right.

Describe how temperature affected the rate of respiration.

[Total 3 marks]

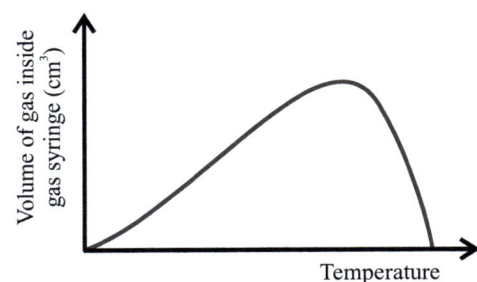

Revision Summary for Sections 7 & 8

That's the end of Sections 7 & 8 — time to see how much you can remember.
- Try these questions and tick off each one when you get it right.
- When you've done all the questions for a topic and are completely happy with it, tick off the topic.

Fighting Disease (p.63-64) ☐

1) What is a pathogen?
2) State two ways that pathogens can be spread.
3) How do cells in the lining of the trachea and bronchi defend against pathogens?
4) What is an antibody?

Preventing the Spread of Disease (p.65-66) ☐

5) State two ways that the spread of disease can be reduced.
6) State an example of a disease that can be transmitted through contaminated water.
7) How do vaccines prepare the immune system against infection by a particular pathogen?

The Breathing System (p.68-69) ☐

8) Name the key structures of the breathing system.
9) Name one of the functions of cartilage in the trachea.
10) What causes air to be forced out of the lungs when you breathe out normally?
11) Why do the alveoli have a very thin surface?
12) What is the percentage of carbon dioxide in: a) inspired air,   b) expired air?
13) Why is the composition of expired air different from the composition of inspired air?
14) What is the function of the goblet cells in the trachea?

Investigating Breathing (p.70) ☐

15) Describe an investigation that shows carbon dioxide is released on expiration.
16) What effect does physical activity have on depth of breathing?
17) Explain why physical activity affects breathing rate.

Respiration (p.72-73) ☐

18) Glucose is one reactant in aerobic respiration. What is the other?
19) What is produced by anaerobic respiration in muscle cells?
20) Which type of respiration releases the most energy per glucose molecule?
21) In what organ is lactic acid broken down using aerobic respiration?
22) What is produced by anaerobic respiration in yeast?

Investigating Respiration (p.74) ☐

23) What equipment can you use to change the temperature when investigating the effect of temperature on the rate of respiration in yeast?
24) When investigating the effect of temperature on the rate of respiration in yeast, what could you use as a control?

Excretion

Excretion means getting rid of waste products from metabolic reactions. Read on to find out more...

Excretion is an **Important Process**

1) Many metabolic reactions in the body produce unwanted substances as well as useful ones. For example, aerobic respiration produces carbon dioxide as a waste product.

2) The waste products of metabolic reactions need to be removed (excreted) from the body. For example, carbon dioxide is excreted through the lungs when you breathe out. Urea (another waste product) is excreted through the kidneys (see below).

3) Urea is produced in the liver from excess amino acids. The excretion of urea is important because its build-up is toxic and can harm body cells.

The **Kidneys** are **Excretory Organs**

1) The kidneys are part of the urinary system. The kidneys are involved in removing (excreting) these things from the body:

   - Urea
   - Excess ions
   - Excess water

2) Kidneys work by filtering stuff out of the blood under high pressure, and then reabsorbing the useful things. The end product is urine (wee), which leaves the body via the urethra.

3) Blood is carried to the kidneys by the renal arteries and removed by the renal veins.

4) The outer part of the kidney is called the cortex and the inner part is called the medulla.

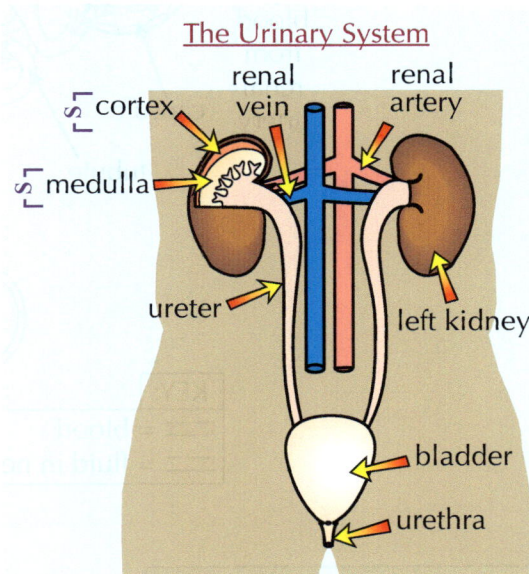

The Urinary System

renal cortex, renal vein, renal artery, medulla, ureter, left kidney, bladder, urethra

Urea is Produced as a Result of **Deamination**

1) We get amino acids from the breakdown of proteins during digestion.

2) These amino acids are then converted into new proteins. For example, the liver converts amino acids into proteins such as enzymes. The amino acids are said to have been 'assimilated' (see page 46) into our bodies.

3) As well as being involved in the assimilation of amino acids, the liver is also involved in the breakdown of excess amino acids (ones that aren't needed to make proteins) so they can be removed from the body. It does this through the process of deamination.

KEY TERM Deamination is the removal of the nitrogen-containing portion of amino acids to produce urea.

Excretion — The Kidneys

Blood is filtered in the kidneys in the kidney nephrons. These are positioned across the kidney cortex and medulla. Here's what happens as blood passes through the kidney nephrons...

1) Filtration:

1) Blood from the renal artery flows through the glomerulus — a bundle of capillaries at the start of the nephron (see diagram below).

2) A high pressure is built up which squeezes water, urea, ions and glucose out of the blood and into the capsule.

3) The membranes of the glomerulus act like filters, so big molecules like proteins and blood cells are not squeezed out. They stay in the blood. Due to the loss of water, the blood leaving the glomerulus is more concentrated than the blood entering it.

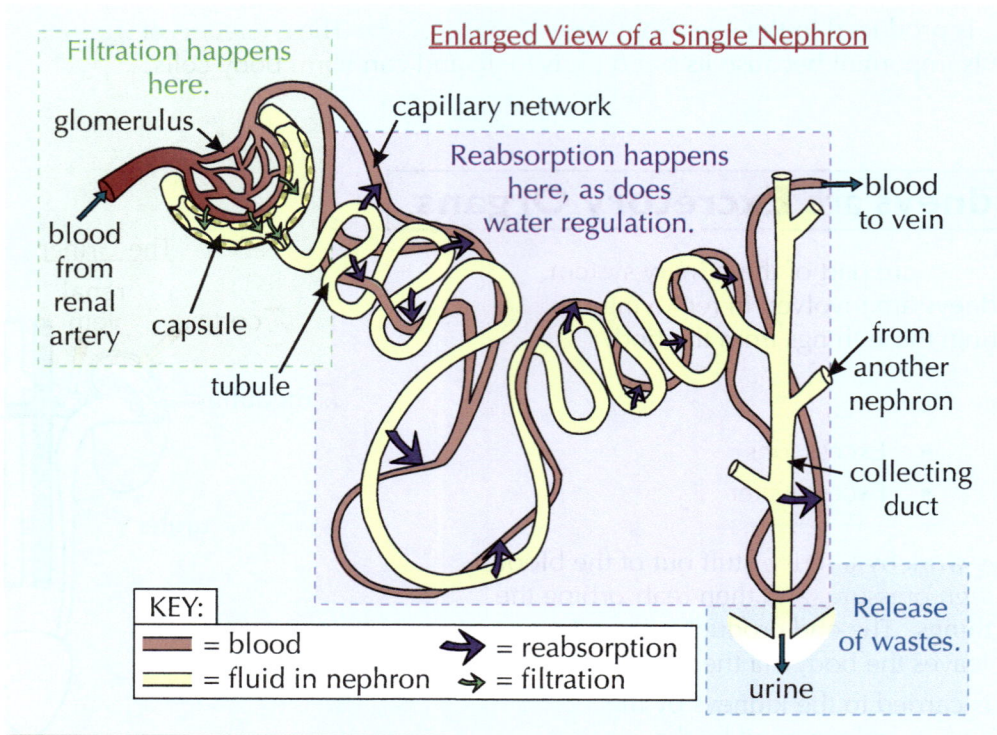

Filtration happens here.

glomerulus

blood from renal artery

capsule

tubule

Enlarged View of a Single Nephron

capillary network

Reabsorption happens here, as does water regulation.

blood to vein

from another nephron

collecting duct

Release of wastes.

urine

KEY:
- = blood
- = fluid in nephron
- = reabsorption
- = filtration

2) Reabsorption:

As the fluid flows along the nephron, useful substances are selectively reabsorbed back into the blood:

1) All the glucose is reabsorbed so that it can be used in respiration. The reabsorption of glucose involves the process of active transport (see p.24) against the concentration gradient.

2) Some ions are reabsorbed. Excess ions aren't.

3) Most water is reabsorbed. This happens by osmosis (see p.21) and leads to urea becoming more concentrated in the fluid.

It's called selective reabsorption because only some substances are reabsorbed.

3) Release of Wastes:

The remaining substances (including excess water, excess ions and urea) form urine. This continues out of the nephron, through the ureter and down to the bladder, where it is stored before being released via the urethra.

The kidneys remove urea and control ion and water levels

Remember the three subheadings on this page — they're key to understanding how the kidneys work.

Supplement

Warm-Up & Exam Questions

Think you know everything there is to know about excretion in humans? Time to put it to the test...

Warm-Up Questions

1) Through which organ is the waste product carbon dioxide excreted?
2) State three things that are excreted by the kidneys.
3) How are amino acids assimilated into the body?
4) What is the glomerulus?

Exam Questions

1 Part of the urinary system is shown in the diagram on the right.

   (a) Which of the labels identifies the bladder?

     ☐ **A**   ☐ **B**   ☐ **C**   ☐ **D**

[1]

   (b) Identify the part of the diagram labelled **Z**.

[1]

[Total 2 marks]

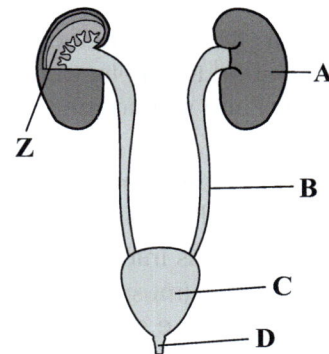

2 The substances below are all present in the blood before it passes through a glomerulus. Which of these substances are present in the fluid at the start of a kidney tubule?

    1. glucose
    2. ions
    3. proteins
    4. water

   ☐ **A** 1 and 2   ☐ **B** 1, 2 and 3

   ☐ **C** 1, 2 and 4   ☐ **D** 1, 2, 3 and 4

[Total 1 mark]

3 Urea is a waste product that is excreted from the body

   (a) Describe how urea is formed.

[3]

   (b) Outline how urea in the blood is excreted from the body.

[3]

   (c) Explain why it is important that urea is excreted.

[2]

[Total 8 marks]

Section 10 — Coordination and Response

The Nervous System

The nervous system allows humans (and other mammals) to react to their surroundings, coordinate their behaviour and regulate body functions. This page is all about how it works.

There are Two Parts to the Nervous System in Mammals

1) The nervous system contains neurones (nerve cells) which go to all parts of the body.

2) The nervous system is split into the central and peripheral nervous systems:

- The central nervous system (CNS) consists of the brain and the spinal cord.
- The peripheral nervous system (PNS) is made up of all the neurones outside of the CNS.

The CNS Coordinates a Response

1) The body has lots of sensory receptors — groups of cells that can detect a change in your environment (a stimulus).

2) When a stimulus is detected by receptors, the information is converted to an electrical impulse (also called a nervous impulse) and sent to the CNS along SENSORY NEURONES.

3) The CNS coordinates the response (in other words, it decides what to do about the stimulus and tells something to do it). Impulses travel through the CNS along RELAY (CONNECTOR) NEURONES.

4) The CNS sends information along a MOTOR (EFFECTOR) NEURONE to an effector (muscle or gland). The effector then responds accordingly — e.g. a muscle may contract or a gland may secrete a hormone (see p.85).

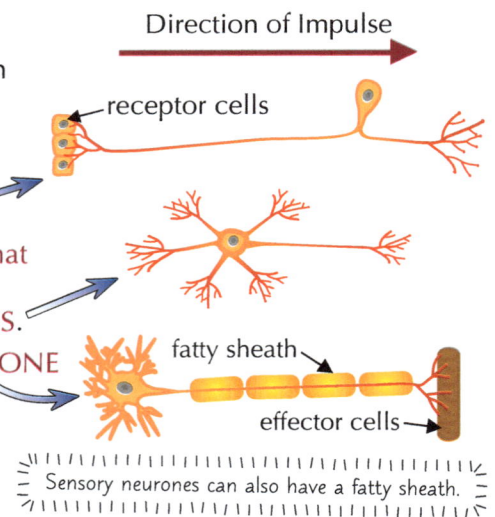

Direction of Impulse

receptor cells

fatty sheath

effector cells

Sensory neurones can also have a fatty sheath.

Neurones are Connected by Synapses

KEY TERM — A synapse is a junction between two neurones.

(see p.19)

1) A synapse consists of the ends of two neurones, separated by a synaptic gap.

2) The end of the neurone before the gap holds vesicles (membrane-bound sacs) filled with neurotransmitters (chemicals).

3) The end of the neurone after the gap has neurotransmitter receptor proteins in its membrane.

4) This is how a nerve impulse is passed across a synapse:

- The nerve impulse reaches the end of the neurone before the synaptic gap and triggers the release of neurotransmitter molecules from the vesicles into the synaptic gap.
- The neurotransmitters diffuse (see p.19) across the synaptic gap to bind with receptor proteins in the membrane on the next neurone.
- This stimulates an electrical impulse in the next neurone.

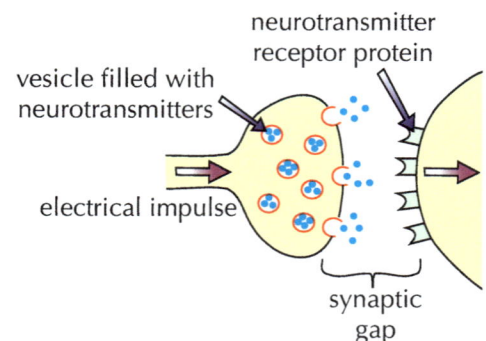

neurotransmitter receptor protein

vesicle filled with neurotransmitters

electrical impulse

synaptic gap

5) Because the receptors are only on one side of the synaptic gap, synapses make sure that impulses can only travel in one direction.

Reflex Actions

Neurones transmit information very quickly to and from the brain, and your brain quickly decides how to respond to a stimulus. But reflex actions are even quicker...

Reflex Actions Help Prevent Injury

1) Reflex actions are rapid, automatic responses to certain stimuli that don't involve the conscious part of the brain — it basically means your body reacts without you having to think about what to do.

2) The response of an effector is coordinated with a stimulus — this means that the response of an effector to a particular stimulus will always be the same.

> For example, if someone shines a bright light in your eyes, your pupils automatically get smaller so that less light gets into your eyes — this stops them from getting damaged (see p.83).

3) The passage of nerve impulses in a reflex action (from receptor to effector) is called a reflex arc.

The Reflex Arc Goes Through the Central Nervous System

1) The neurones in reflex arcs go through the spinal cord or through an unconscious part of the brain.

2) When a stimulus (e.g. a bee sting) is detected by receptors, impulses are sent along a sensory neurone to the CNS.

3) When the impulses reach a synapse between the sensory neurone and a relay neurone, the impulses cross the synapse and are sent along the relay neurone.

4) When the impulses reach a synapse between the relay neurone and a motor neurone, the same thing happens and the impulses are sent along the motor neurone.

4. Impulses are passed along a relay neurone, via a synapse.

3. Impulses travel along a sensory neurone.

5. Impulses travel along a motor neurone, via a synapse.

6. When impulses reach muscle, it contracts.

1. Bee stings finger.

2. Sting detected by pain receptors.

Relay neurones connect sensory neurones to motor neurones.

5) The impulses then travel along the motor neurone to the effector (in this example it's a muscle).

6) The muscle then contracts and moves your hand away from the bee.

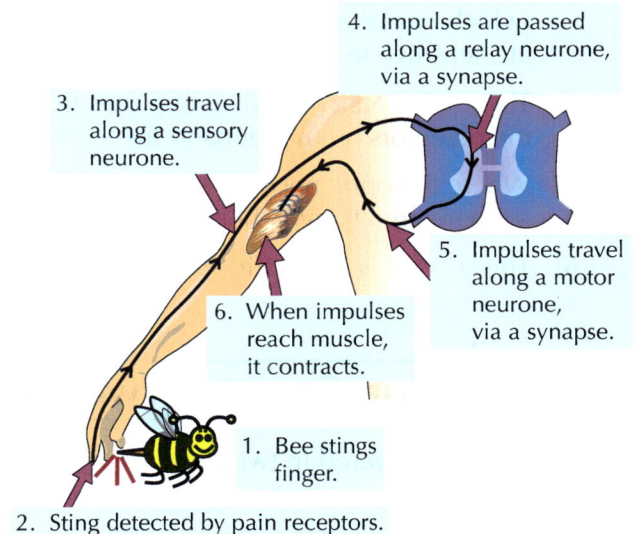

Don't get all twitchy — just learn it...

Reflex actions bypass your conscious brain completely when a quick response is essential — your body just gets on with things. If you had to stop and think first, you'd end up in a lot more pain (or worse).

The Eye

If you can read this, you're using your eyes. And that's great because you need to know all about them.

The Eye is a Sense Organ

KEY TERM: A sense organ is a group of receptor cells that respond to a specific type of stimulus (e.g. light, sound, touch, temperature or chemicals).

Different receptors in your body detect different stimuli. Receptors in your eyes detect light.

Learn the Eye with All Its Labels

1) The CORNEA is the transparent outer layer found at the front of the eye. It refracts (bends) light into the eye.

2) The IRIS contains muscles that allow it to control the diameter of the PUPIL (the hole in the middle) and therefore how much light enters the eye.

3) The LENS focuses the light onto the RETINA (which contains light receptors, some of which are sensitive to light of different colours).

4) The OPTIC NERVE carries impulses from the receptors on the retina to the brain.

5) Where the optic nerve leaves the eye is called the BLIND SPOT — there aren't any light receptors, so it's not sensitive to light.

6) The FOVEA is a specific area of the retina which contains cone cells (see below).

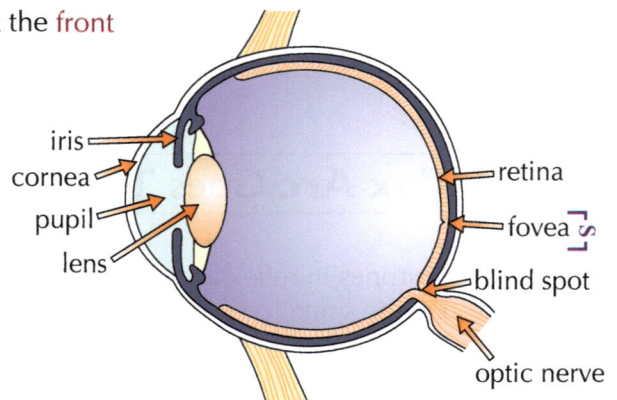

Diagram labels: iris, cornea, pupil, lens, retina, fovea, blind spot, optic nerve

The Retina Contains Two Types of Receptor

The retina is covered in two different types of receptor — rods and cones.

Rods

- Rods are mainly found in the peripheral parts (outside edges) of the retina.
- Rods are very sensitive to light, so work well in dim light (e.g. at night).
- There is one kind of rod, which gives information in black and white (not colour vision).

Cones

- Cones are mainly found packed together in the fovea.
- Cones are less sensitive to light than rods (they work best in bright light).
- There are three kinds of cones which give information in different colours for colour vision.

Supplement

Learn that diagram of the eye...

REVISION TIP: It'll help if you sketch the diagram out roughly, close this book and then try to label your sketch. If your artistic skills aren't great, you could even trace it, then label the traced version.

The Eye

This page is all about reflex actions in the eye. If you've forgotten anything about reflex actions, have a look back over page 81.

The **Pupil Reflex** — Adjusting for **Bright Light**

1) Very bright light can damage the retina — so you have a reflex action to protect it.
2) When light receptors in the eye detect a high light intensity (very bright light), a reflex action is triggered that reduces the diameter of the pupil (makes it smaller). This reduces the amount of light that can enter the eye.
3) The opposite process happens in a low light intensity (dim light) — the diameter of the pupil increases (it is made wider), which increases the amount of light that can enter the eye.

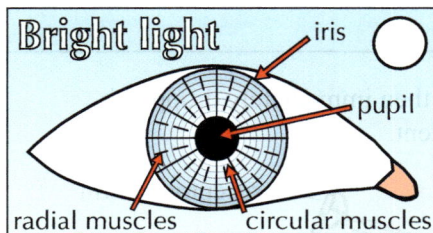

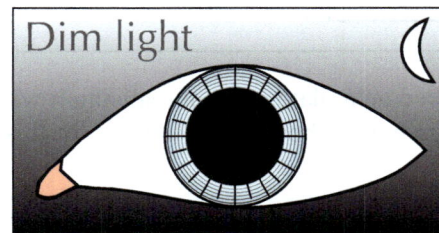

4) The iris contains two types of muscles to control pupil diameter — the radial and circular muscles.
5) These work by antagonistic action — when one muscle contracts, the other muscle relaxes.

- To make the pupil wider, the radial muscles in the iris contract and the circular muscles relax.
- To make the pupil smaller, the circular muscles in the iris contract and the radial muscles relax.

Focusing on Near and Distant Objects — Another **Reflex Action**

The eye focuses light on the retina by changing the shape of the lens — this is known as accommodation.

To Look at **Near Objects**:

1) The ciliary muscles contract, which slackens the suspensory ligaments.
2) The lens becomes fat (more curved).
3) This increases the amount by which it refracts (bends) light.

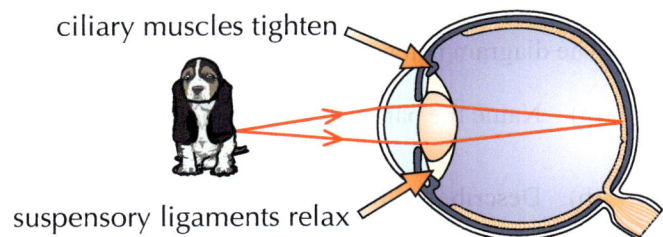

ciliary muscles tighten

suspensory ligaments relax

To Look at **Distant Objects**:

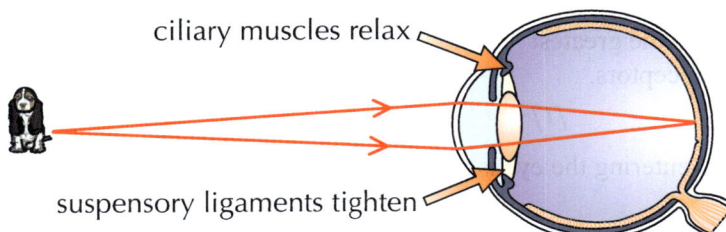

ciliary muscles relax

suspensory ligaments tighten

1) The ciliary muscles relax, which allows the suspensory ligaments to pull tight.
2) This makes the lens go thin (less curved).
3) So it refracts light by a smaller amount.

Section 10 — Coordination and Response

Warm-Up & Exam Questions

Welcome to the first set of questions in this section. Having a go at some questions is one of the best ways of figuring out just what you know. Time to get started...

Warm-Up Questions

1) Name the two parts of the body which make up the central nervous system.
2) In what form is information transmitted along neurones?
3) Give an example of a reflex action.

Exam Questions

1 A man picked up a plate without realising it was hot, then immediately dropped it. The diagram below shows the reflex arc for this incident.

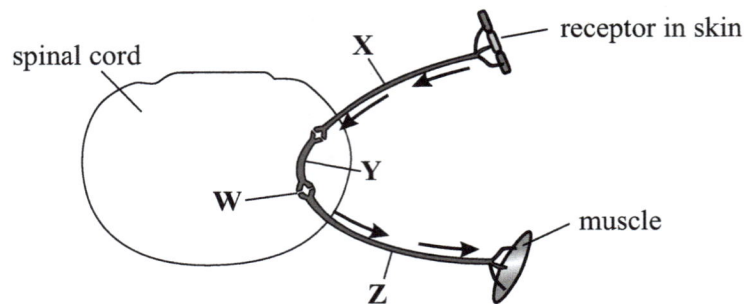

(a) Name the **three** types of neurone labelled **X**, **Y** and **Z**.

[3]

(b) Name the small gap between neurones, marked **W** on the diagram.

[1]

(c) State what the effector is in this reflex arc and describe its response.

[2]

[Total 6 marks]

2 The diagram below shows a cross section through the eye.

(a) Name the parts labelled **A** and **B**.

[2]

(b) Describe the function of the iris.

[1]

(c) (i) Name the **two** types of light receptor found on the retina.

[2]

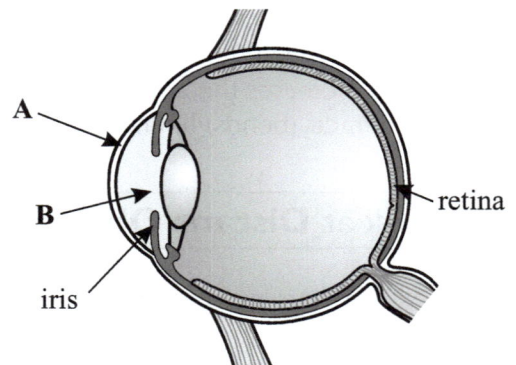

(ii) Name the part of the retina that has the greatest number of colour-sensitive light receptors.

[1]

(d) Describe how information about light entering the eye is passed to the brain.

[2]

[Total 8 marks]

Hormones

On page 80 you learnt how information is passed around the body via neurones.
The body also uses hormones as a way to communicate, which is what this page is all about.

Hormones Are Chemical Messengers Sent in the Blood

> **KEY TERM**
> Hormones are chemicals produced by glands and carried by the blood, which change the activity of a specific target organ or organs.

1) Hormones control things in organs and cells that need constant adjustment.
2) The glands that produce and secrete hormones are called endocrine glands. These glands make up your endocrine system.

Endocrine Glands Are Found in Different Places in the Body

You need to know about four endocrine glands, and which hormones they secrete:

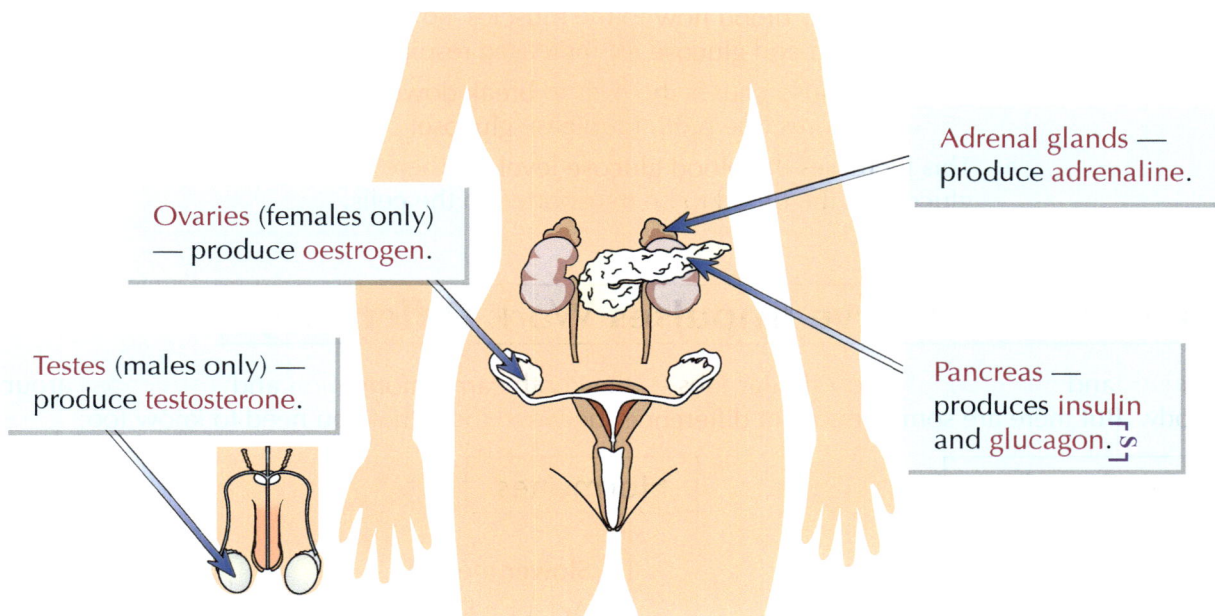

Ovaries (females only) — produce oestrogen.

Testes (males only) — produce testosterone.

Adrenal glands — produce adrenaline.

Pancreas — produces insulin and glucagon.

These Hormones Have Different Functions

1) Insulin acts to decrease the blood glucose level (see page 88) when it gets too high (e.g. after a meal containing carbohydrates is eaten).

The function of adrenaline is on the next page. The function of glucagon is on p.88.

2) Oestrogen is the main female sex hormone. It is involved in the menstrual cycle (see pages 105-106) and promotes the development of secondary sexual characteristics, e.g. breast development.

3) Testosterone is the main male sex hormone. It controls sperm production and promotes the development of secondary sexual characteristics, e.g. growth of hair on the chest.

Hormones

Adrenaline Prepares You for 'Fight or Flight'

1) Adrenaline is a hormone released by the adrenal glands (see previous page).

2) Adrenaline prepares the body for 'fight or flight' — in other words, standing your ground in the face of a threat (e.g. a predator) or running away.

3) When your brain detects a stressful, dangerous or exciting situation, it sends nerve impulses (see p.80) to the adrenal glands, which secrete adrenaline. This gets the body ready for action.

> Examples of situations when adrenaline is released include extreme sports (such as skydiving or bungee jumping), at the start of a race or test, or during an emergency.

4) Adrenaline causes an increase in breathing and heart rate. It also causes the pupils to widen (increase in diameter).

5) Increasing the breathing and heart rate increases the supply of oxygen and glucose to cells, which increases metabolic activity. Here's how:

- Adrenaline causes the heart muscle to contract more frequently and with more force, so heart rate increases.
- This increases blood flow to the muscles, so the cells receive more oxygen and glucose for increased respiration.
- Adrenaline also causes the liver to break down its glycogen stores (see p.88) to release glucose.
- This increases the blood glucose level, so there's more glucose in the blood to be transported to the cells.

Supplement

Hormones and Nerve Impulses Work Differently

Hormones and nerve impulses do similar jobs — they both carry information and instructions around the body. But there are some important differences between them that you need to know too:

Nerve Impulses

1) Very fast message.
2) Act for a very short time.

Hormones

1) Slower message.
2) Act for a long time.

If you're not sure whether a response is nervous or hormonal, have a think about the speed of the reaction and how long it lasts:

1) If the Response is Really Quick, It's Probably Nervous

1) Some information needs to be passed to effectors really quickly (e.g. pain signals, or the pupil reflex).
2) It's no good using hormones to carry the message — they're too slow.

2) But if a Response Lasts For a Long Time, It's Probably Hormonal

> For example, when you eat food, insulin is released in response to increased blood glucose levels (see page 88). This lasts until the blood glucose concentration has returned to normal.

Homeostasis

Homeostasis involves balancing body functions to keep everything at the level it is supposed to be at.

Homeostasis — it's all about Balance

1) Conditions in your body need to be kept steady so that cells can function properly. This involves balancing inputs (stuff going into your body) with outputs (stuff leaving). For example...

> Body temperature — you need to get rid of excess body heat when you're hot, but keep heat in when the environment is cold.

2) Homeostasis is what keeps conditions balanced. Here's the definition:

KEY TERM   Homeostasis is the maintenance of a constant internal environment.

3) Homeostasis controls the internal environment so conditions stay roughly constant. Each condition has a set point that is best for the body, e.g. the set point for body temperature is around 37 °C.

4) Conditions are kept steady using negative feedback systems. This means that when the body's receptors detect that a condition has gone above or below its normal level, they trigger a response to bring the level back to its set point again.

Internal Body Temperature Must Be Kept Constant

1) It's important for mammals to maintain the right core body temperature.

2) Mammals monitor their body temperature using blood temperature receptors and skin temperature receptors. The brain coordinates a response (see p.80) based on signals from these receptors and activates the necessary effectors to keep the body temperature just right.

3) There are different mechanisms that are used to change body temperature:

Mechanisms to REDUCE body temperature:	Mechanisms to INCREASE body temperature:

Hairs lie flat — a layer of hair provides insulation by trapping air. When it's hot, erector muscles relax so the hairs lie flat. Less air is trapped, so the skin is less insulated and heat can be lost more easily.

Hairs stand up — erector muscles contract when it's cold, which makes the hairs stand up. This traps an insulating layer of air near the surface of the skin and so prevents heat loss.

Sweating — more sweat is secreted from sweat glands when the body's too hot. The water in sweat evaporates from the surface of the skin and takes heat from the body. The skin is cooled.

Much less sweat — less sweat is secreted from sweat glands when it's cold, reducing the amount of heat loss.

Shivering — when it's cold, muscles contract in spasms. This makes the body shiver and more heat is produced from increased respiration.

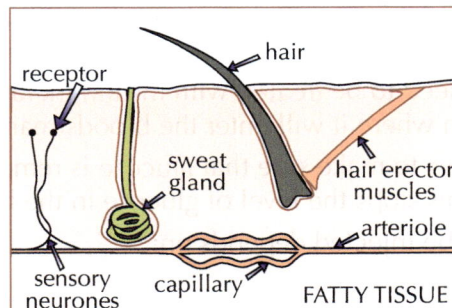

receptor — hair — sweat gland — hair erector muscles — arteriole — sensory neurones — capillary — FATTY TISSUE

Vasodilation — when it's hot, arterioles (small branches of arteries) near the surface of the skin dilate (this is called vasodilation). More blood flows through the capillaries (p.57) in the surface layers of the skin. This means more heat is lost from the skin and the temperature is lowered.

Vasoconstriction — when it's cold, arterioles near the surface of the skin constrict (this is called vasoconstriction) so less blood flows through the capillaries in the surface layers of the skin. This reduces heat loss.

Supplement

Controlling Blood Glucose

Insulin and glucagon are hormones that control how much glucose there is in your blood.

Insulin and Glucagon Control Blood Glucose Concentration

1) Eating foods containing carbohydrates puts glucose into the blood from the small intestine.
2) The normal metabolism of cells removes glucose from the blood.
3) Excess glucose can be stored as glycogen in the liver and in the muscles.
4) Changes in blood glucose concentration are monitored and controlled by the pancreas, using the hormones insulin and glucagon, as shown:

Blood glucose concentration too HIGH — INSULIN is secreted by the pancreas:

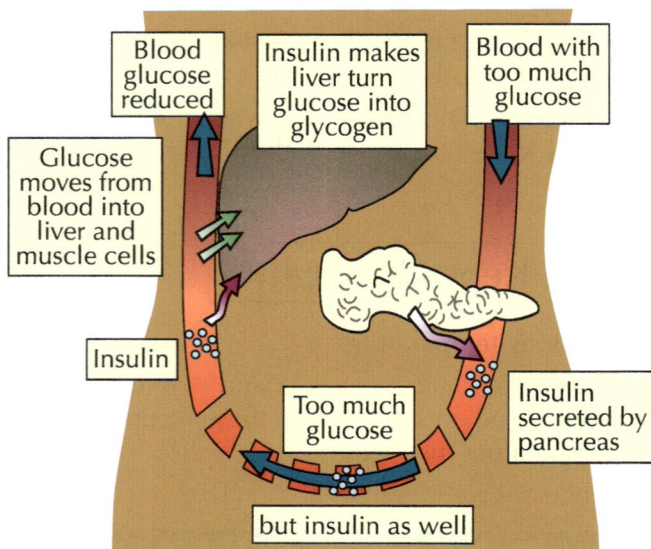

Blood glucose reduced

Insulin makes liver turn glucose into glycogen

Blood with too much glucose

Glucose moves from blood into liver and muscle cells

Insulin

Too much glucose

Insulin secreted by pancreas

but insulin as well

Blood glucose concentration too LOW — GLUCAGON is secreted by the pancreas:

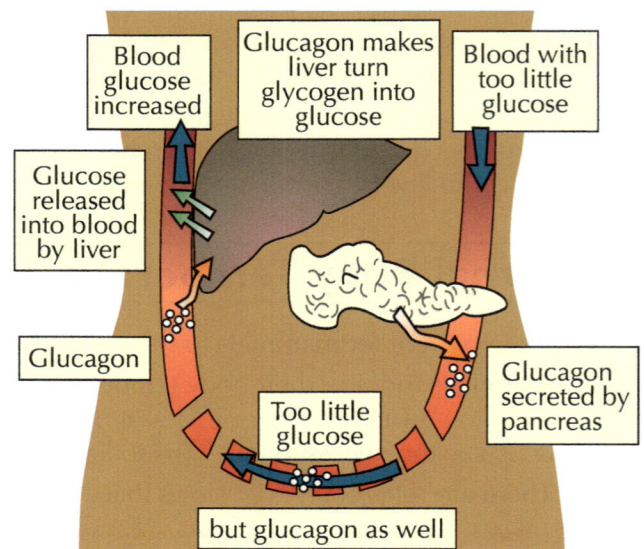

Blood glucose increased

Glucagon makes liver turn glycogen into glucose

Blood with too little glucose

Glucose released into blood by liver

Glucagon

Too little glucose

Glucagon secreted by pancreas

but glucagon as well

Type 1 Diabetes — Caused by a Lack of Insulin

1) Type 1 diabetes is a condition where the pancreas doesn't produce enough insulin. If untreated, a person's blood glucose can rise to a level that can kill them.
2) A person with Type 1 diabetes will need to be treated with insulin therapy — this usually involves injecting insulin under the skin, from where it will enter the bloodstream.
3) Injections are often done at mealtimes to make sure that glucose is removed from the blood quickly once the food has been digested. This stops the level of glucose in the blood from getting too high.
4) The amount of insulin that needs to be injected depends on:
   • the person's diet.
   • how active the person is.

Remember, insulin reduces blood glucose level.

REVISION TIP

And people used to think the pancreas was just a cushion...

This stuff can seem a bit confusing at first, but you could have a go at remembering it like this: if blood glucose is increasing, insulin's added. If blood glucose is almost gone, glucagon's added.

Supplement

Warm-Up & Exam Questions

Here are some more questions — they make for great practice.

Warm-Up Questions

1) What is a hormone?
2) State the sources of the following hormones: (a) oestrogen, (b) testosterone, (c) adrenaline.
3) What is homeostasis?

Exam Questions

1 Changes in the skin are an important part of temperature regulation. The diagram shows a cross-section through the skin of a person who is cold.

(a) Explain the response of the hairs when a person is cold.

[2]

(b) Explain the response of sweat glands when a person is cold.

[2]

[Total 4 marks]

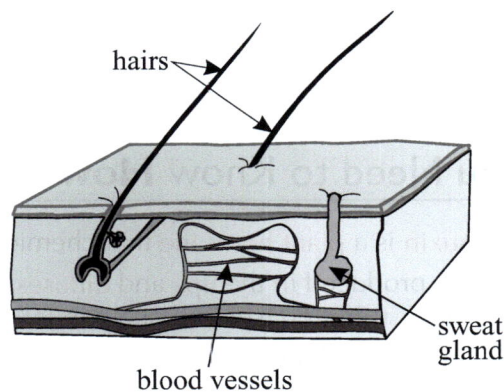

2 Responses to stimuli can be either nervous or hormonal. Describe the differences between responses brought about by hormones and those brought about by the nervous system.

[Total 2 marks]

3 The diagram shows how the blood glucose concentration is regulated in humans.

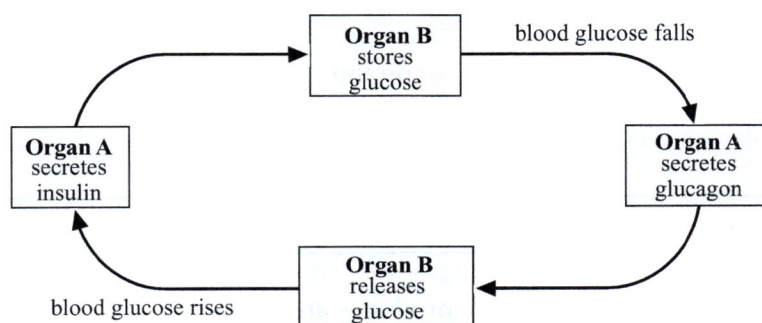

(a) Identify organs **A** and **B** in the diagram.

[2]

(b) With reference to the diagram, explain what goes wrong with the regulation of blood glucose level in people with Type 1 diabetes.

[3]

(c) Describe what the hormone glucagon does.

[1]

[Total 6 marks]

Section 10 — Coordination and Response

Tropic Responses

Plants don't just grow randomly. They grow in response to the things going on around them.

A Tropism is a Response to a Stimulus

There are two types of tropism that you need to know about:

KEY TERM — Phototropism is a response in which parts of a plant grow towards or away from a source of light.

KEY TERM — Gravitropism is a response in which parts of a plant grow towards or away from gravity.

> Shoots grow towards light and upwards against gravity, and roots grow away from light and downwards with gravity.

You Need to Know How This Works in Shoots

1) Auxin is a plant hormone that chemically controls growth near the tips of shoots.
2) It is produced in the tips and diffuses through the plant from there.
   The distribution (spread) of auxin is unequal, in response to light and gravity.
3) Auxin stimulates cell elongation in the cells just behind the tips.
4) If the shoot tip is removed, no auxin is available and the shoot may stop growing.
5) Phototropism and gravitropism are both examples of the chemical control of plant growth.

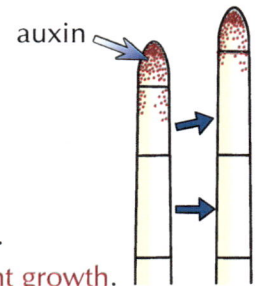

auxin

Shoots Grow Towards Light (Positive Phototropism)

1) When a shoot tip is exposed to light, more auxin accumulates (builds up) on the side that's in the shade than the side that's in the light.
2) This stimulates the cells to elongate faster on the shaded side, so the shoot bends towards the light.

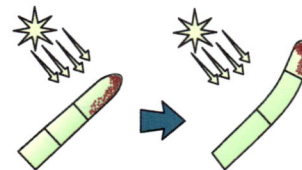

Shoots Grow Away From Gravity (Negative Gravitropism)

1) When a shoot grows sideways, gravity produces an unequal distribution of auxin, with more on the lower side of the tip.
2) This stimulates the cells of the lower side to elongate faster, bending the shoot upwards.

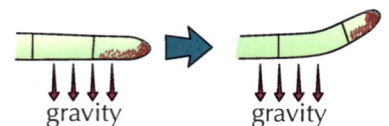

gravity   gravity

Supplement

Tropisms allow plants to react to their surroundings

By responding to stimuli in their environment, plants increase their chances of survival. For example, by growing towards the light, plants increase the amount of light they receive for photosynthesis.

Investigating Plant Growth Responses

Here are two investigations you need to know about that demonstrate plant growth responses.

You can **Investigate Plant Growth Responses**

You can investigate phototropism in the growth of shoots like this...

1) Put 10 seeds into three different Petri dishes, each lined with moist filter paper. (Remember to label your dishes, e.g. A, B, C.)

2) Put the dishes in a dark place and shine a lamp onto one of the dishes from above and two of the dishes from different directions.

> It needs to be dark to make sure that the light on each dish is only coming from one direction.

3) Leave your seeds alone for one week until you can observe their responses — you'll find the seedlings grow towards the light.

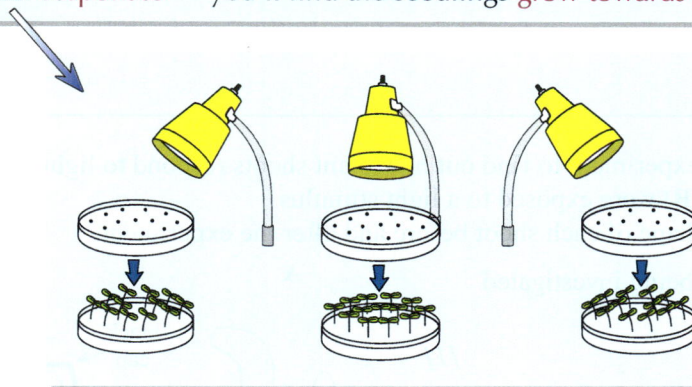

You can also investigate gravitropism in plant growth...

1) Place four seedlings on damp cotton wool in separate Petri dishes.

2) Store each Petri dish vertically in a dark place, each with their shoots and roots pointing in different directions.

3) Leave your seeds alone for one week and you should find that the shoots of each seedling grow upwards and that the roots of each seedling grow downwards.

Record your results using scientific drawings

PRACTICAL TIP

Labelled diagrams are a really good way to show the results of experiments like this. There's more about scientific drawings on page 168. Make sure your drawings are neat and useful — don't do any sketching or shading and label your drawing using straight, uncrossed lines.

Warm-Up & Exam Questions

You could skim through this page in a few minutes, but there's no point unless you check over any bits you don't know and make sure you understand everything. It's not quick, but it's the only way.

Warm-Up Questions

1) What is phototropism?
2) Name the plant hormone responsible for both phototropism and gravitropism.
3) Where is this plant hormone made?
4) By what process does this plant hormone spread through a plant?

Exam Questions

1   A student performed an experiment to find out how plant shoots respond to light.
Two plant shoots (**A** and **B**) were exposed to a light stimulus.
The diagram shows the shape of each shoot before and after the experiment.

(a)   Name the response being investigated
in this experiment.

[1]

(b)   Explain the results of shoot **B**.

[3]

[Total 4 marks]

A

B

black cap

Direction of light

Before   After   Before   After

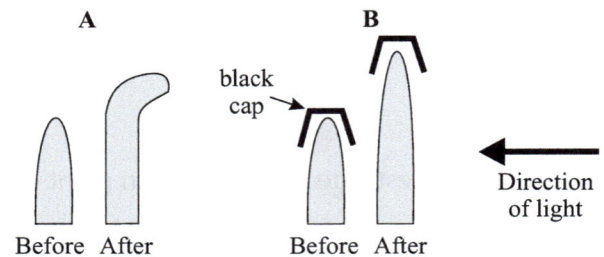

2   A student placed some germinating beans on the surface of some
damp soil and left them in the dark for five days. The appearance of
the beans before and after the five day period is shown in the diagram.

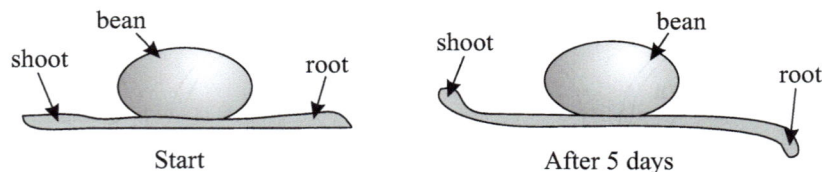

bean

shoot   root   shoot   bean   root

Start   After 5 days

Both the shoot and the root have undergone a gravitropic response after 5 days.

(a)   Describe the gravitropic response of the shoot.

[1]

(b)   Explain the mechanism behind this response.

[2]

(c)   The student wants to compare his findings with beans grown in the light.
He puts some new germinating beans on damp soil and shines a light on them.
Describe what the student would expect to see happen to the shoots.
Explain why this would happen.

[3]

[Total 6 marks]

Revision Summary for Sections 9 & 10

Nice work — you've finished Sections 9 & 10. Time to find out how much you know with some questions.
- Try these questions and tick off each one when you get it right.
- When you've done all the questions for a topic and are completely happy with it, tick off the topic.

Excretion in Humans (p.77-78)

1) Name a gas excreted by the lungs.
2) Name the waste product produced in the liver from excess amino acids.
3) Describe what is meant by amino acid assimilation.
4) What is reabsorbed by the nephron in the kidney?

The Nervous System, Reflex Actions and The Eye (p.80-83)

5) What is a nervous impulse?
6) How does an impulse travel across a synapse?
7) Explain how synapses ensure impulses travel in only one direction.
8) What is a reflex action?
9) Where do the electrical impulses in a reflex arc originate from?
10) What is a sense organ?
11) Describe the function of the cornea.
12) Describe the pupil reflex. Why is it needed?
13) How does accommodation of the eye work?

Hormones, Homeostasis and Controlling Blood Glucose (p.85-88)

14) Where is insulin made?
15) Name the main hormone produced by the testes.
16) What is the role of the hormone adrenaline? What effects does it have on the body?
17) Explain how negative feedback helps to maintain a stable internal environment.
18) Explain why we shiver when we get cold.
19) How is Type 1 diabetes treated?

Tropic Responses and Investigating Plant Growth (p.90-91)

20) What is gravitropism?
21) What is auxin?
22) Describe an experiment to investigate the effect of phototropism on some shoots.

Medicinal Drugs

Drugs can be used for lots of different reasons. Those that are used to help treat infections, cure diseases or reduce symptoms are known as medicinal drugs. These types of drugs are really important for health.

Drugs Have Effects **Inside the Body**

Before we get started, make sure you know the definition of a drug:

> **KEY TERM**
> A drug is any substance that when taken into the body will affect or change chemical reactions in the body.

Antibiotics are a Useful Type of **Medicinal Drug**

1) Antibiotics (e.g. penicillin) can be used to treat bacterial infections.
2) These drugs work by actually killing (or preventing the reproduction of) the bacteria causing the problem, without killing your own body cells.
3) Different antibiotics kill different types of bacteria, so it's important to be treated with the right one.
4) The use of antibiotics has greatly reduced the number of deaths from transmissible diseases (p.63) caused by bacteria.
5) But, antibiotics don't destroy viruses (e.g. flu or cold viruses) — they only target bacterial cells. So taking antibiotics will not help in treating a viral infection.

Bacteria Can Become **Resistant** to **Antibiotics**

1) Mutations (see page 122) can cause the genetic material in bacteria to change. Sometimes this change to bacteria's genetic material can make them resistant to (not killed by) an antibiotic.
2) So, if you have an infection, some of the bacteria might be resistant to antibiotics.
3) This means that when you treat the infection, only the non-resistant strains of bacteria will be killed.
4) The individual resistant bacteria will survive and reproduce, so the population of the resistant strain will increase.
5) This resistant strain could cause a serious infection that can't be treated by antibiotics.

- MRSA (methicillin-resistant *Staphylococcus aureus*) is a type of antibiotic-resistant bacteria. MRSA causes serious wound infections and is resistant to the powerful antibiotic methicillin.
- To slow down the rate of development of resistant strains such as MRSA, it's important for doctors to only provide antibiotics when they are really needed. So you won't get them for a sore throat, only for something more serious.
- It's also important that you finish the whole course of antibiotics and don't just stop once you feel better.

There's more on how bacteria become resistant to antibiotics on p.125.

Supplement

Antibiotic resistance is inevitable...

...but that doesn't mean we shouldn't try to do anything about it. We might not be able to stop it from ever happening, but we can limit how quickly it develops. So do your bit, and finish your courses of antibiotics.

Warm-Up & Exam Questions

That's the end of this (very short) section — try out these questions to make sure you've remembered it all.

Warm-Up Questions

1) Explain why strains of antibiotic-resistant bacteria can cause problems in humans.
2) Name a type of antibiotic-resistant bacteria.

Exam Questions

1   Which of the following statements best describes the term 'drug'?

☐ A   Any substance that treats bacterial or viral infections.

☐ B   Any substance that is taken into the body for medical purposes.

☐ C   Any substance that affects or changes chemical reactions in the body.

☐ D   Any illegal substance taken into the body for recreational use.

[Total 1 mark]

2   The table below shows the diagnoses of four different patients, **A-D**, and the causes and symptoms of these conditions.

Patient	Diagnosis	Cause	Symptoms
A	Cold sore	*Human alphaherpesvirus 1* virus	Small, painful blisters around the mouth
B	Pneumonia	*Streptococcus pneumoniae* bacterium	Cough, fever and difficulty breathing
C	Onychomycosis	*Trichophyton rubrum* fungus	Brittle, discoloured toenail
D	Molluscum contagiosum	*Molluscum contagiosum* virus	Sore, raised lesions on leg

One of the patients was prescribed antibiotics. Using the information in the table, state which patient, **A-D**, was prescribed antibiotics to treat their infection.

[Total 1 mark]

3   A doctor prescribed the correct antibiotics to treat a bacterial infection that a patient had.

(a)   Explain why the doctor shouldn't have prescribed antibiotics if the patient had a viral infection.

[1]

(b)   After taking all of the antibiotics, the patient still had the infection.
Suggest and explain why the patient still had the bacterial infection.

[3]

(c)   The doctor examines another patient with a mild bacterial ear infection.
Suggest why the doctor does not prescribe antibiotics for this patient.

[2]

[Total 6 marks]

Reproduction

Reproduction is important as it is how all organisms pass on their genes — there are two types to learn...

Asexual Reproduction

KEY TERM
Asexual reproduction is the process used to produce genetically identical offspring from one parent.

Asexual reproduction also occurs in some animals, e.g. certain types of lizard and starfish.

1) Bacteria and many plants reproduce this way, e.g. strawberry plants reproduce asexually using runners (stems that run along the ground). Tulips reproduce asexually using bulbs. Bacteria simply split in two.

2) You need to be able to describe some of the advantages and disadvantages of asexual reproduction:

Advantages

1) Lots of offspring can be produced very quickly. E.g. bacteria, such as *E. coli*, can divide every half an hour to colonise a new area very rapidly.

2) There's no need to attract a mate, so less energy is needed to reproduce asexually.

3) All offspring are genetically identical to their parents — so, for example, if a crop plant with beneficial features reproduces asexually, you can be certain that its offspring will inherit the same features. A crop with uniform features makes a consistent product.

4) Crop plants can be grown asexually from cuttings (off-cuts of the parent plant). Plants grown in this way reach maturity quicker, which means they can be harvested sooner.

Disadvantages

1) There's no genetic variation between offspring in the population. This means organisms are unlikely to be able to adapt to changes in the environment. If environmental conditions become unfavourable, the whole population may be affected. E.g. Black Sigatoka is a disease that affects banana plants, which reproduce asexually. An outbreak of the disease is likely to affect all plants in a population of the crop.

2) Overpopulation may occur if too many offspring are produced.

Supplement *Supplement*

Sexual Reproduction

Gametes are sex cells.

KEY TERM
Sexual reproduction is the process used to produce offspring that are genetically distinct from each other. It involves the fusion of the nuclei of two gametes (**fertilisation**) to form a zygote.

See p.111 for more on 'haploid' and 'diploid'.

1) The nuclei of gametes are haploid. When they fuse, they form a zygote with a diploid nucleus.

2) You need to be able to discuss some of the advantages and disadvantages of sexual reproduction:

Advantages

1) It produces genetic variation. If environmental conditions change, it's more likely that some individuals will have the characteristics to survive the change. E.g. if there is an outbreak of disease, it is unlikely that the disease will affect every individual.

2) Diversity can lead to natural selection (see p.124) and evolution as species become better adapted to their new environment.

3) Selective breeding (see p.126) can be used to improve crop production and quality.

Disadvantages

1) It takes more time and energy than asexual reproduction, so organisms produce fewer offspring in their lifetime. Organisms have to find and attract mates. E.g. male bowerbirds build twig structures and then dance to impress females.

2) Two parents are needed, which can be a problem if individuals are isolated. E.g. polar bears often live alone, so males may walk up to 100 miles to find a mate.

Supplement *Supplement*

Sexual Reproduction in Plants

You need to know all about sexual reproduction in plants. Here's how it works...

The Flower Contains Both Male and Female Gametes

Plants that reproduce sexually have both male and female gametes. Here's where they come from:

The Stamen

1) The stamen produces male gametes.
2) It consists of the anther and filament:

The anther contains pollen grains — these produce the male gametes.

Filament — holds up the anther.

In insect-pollinated flowers (see next page) the petals are often brightly coloured to attract insects needed for pollination.

The Carpel

1) The carpel produces female gametes.
2) It consists of the stigma, style and ovary:

The stigma is the end bit that the pollen grains attach to.

Style — supports the stigma and connects it to the ovary.

The ovary contains the female gametes (eggs) inside ovules. The ovules eventually develop into seeds after fertilisation.

The sepals are green and leaf-like. They protect the flower in the bud.

Sexual Reproduction in Plants Involves Pollination

1) In plants, for fertilisation to occur, a process called pollination has to take place.

KEY TERM Pollination is the transfer of pollen from an anther to a stigma.

2) There are different types of pollination, depending on where the pollen has come from:

KEY TERM Self-pollination is when pollen is transferred from an anther to a stigma on either the same flower or a different flower on the same plant.

KEY TERM Cross-pollination is when pollen is transferred from an anther to a stigma on a flower from a different plant of the same species.

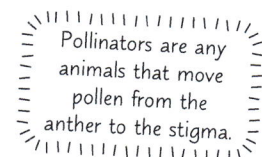

Pollinators are any animals that move pollen from the anther to the stigma.

3) Self-pollination and cross-pollination have different effects on a population of plants:

- Self-pollinating plants don't rely on pollinators. This means it is easier for the plant to spread to locations where there aren't pollinators available.
- Cross-pollinating plants rely on pollinators to transfer pollen grains elsewhere. If the pollinator population declines, it becomes harder for a plant to reproduce.
- Cross-pollination produces more variation, meaning cross-pollinating plants are more likely to be able to adapt and survive any changes in the environment.
- Self-pollination produces less variation because the gene pool (the mix of genes in a population) is smaller. This means that self-pollinating plants are less likely to be able to adapt to changes in the environment (see p.124).

Supplement

Plant Pollination

As you saw on the previous page, sexual reproduction in plants involves the transfer of pollen from an anther to a stigma. Plants sometimes need a bit of outside help to get it done.

Some Plants are Adapted for Insect Pollination

Here's how plants can be adapted for pollination by insects...

1) They have large brightly coloured petals to attract insects to the anthers and stigmas inside.

2) They also have scented flowers and nectaries (glands that secrete nectar) to attract insects.

3) The stigma is sticky so that any pollen picked up by insects on other plants will stick to the stigma.

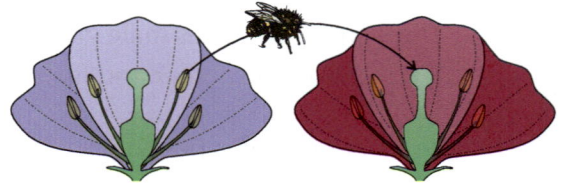

Insect-pollinated plants make big, sticky pollen grains — the grains stick to insects as they go from plant to plant.

Other Plants are Adapted for Wind Pollination

Features of plants that are adapted for pollination by wind include...

1) Small, dull petals (they don't need to attract insects).

2) No nectaries or strong scents (for the same reason).

3) Long filaments that hang the anthers outside the flower, so that a lot of the pollen gets blown away by the wind.

4) A large and feathery stigma to catch pollen as it's carried past by the wind. The stigma often hangs outside the flower too.

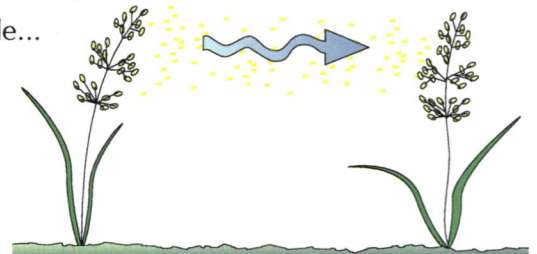

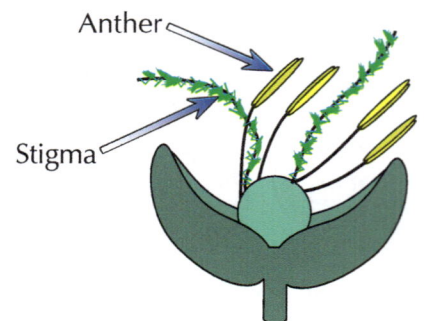

Anther

Stigma

Wind-pollinated plants have lots of small, light pollen grains — these grains can easily be carried to other plants by the wind.

EXAM TIP

Pollination is the transfer of pollen from an anther to a stigma

Flowers like roses (big, bright petals, a strong scent) are pollinated by insects. The feathery looking flowers you sometimes see in long grass, and fluffy willow catkins, are pollinated by the wind. If you're given a picture of a flower in the exam, you should be able to say whether it's most likely to be insect- or wind-pollinated and explain your answer. So get learning this page.

Fertilisation and Germination

On page 96, you saw that sexual reproduction can't occur without fertilisation. Here's more about fertilisation in plants, and what happens after that...

Fertilisation is the Fusion of Gametes

1) Plant fertilisation occurs when the nucleus from a pollen grain (the male gamete) fuses with the nucleus of the female gamete in an ovule.

2) Fertilisation doesn't happen when the pollen grain reaches the stigma — the pollen grain needs to get to the ovule:

- A pollen grain lands on the stigma of a flower, usually with help from insects or the wind (see previous page).

- A pollen tube grows out of the pollen grain and down through the style to the ovary and into the ovule.

- A nucleus from the male gamete moves down the tube to join with a female gamete in the ovule. Fertilisation is when the two nuclei fuse together to make a zygote. This divides by mitosis to form an embryo.

- Each ovule containing a fertilised female gamete forms a seed, which can then grow into a new plant.

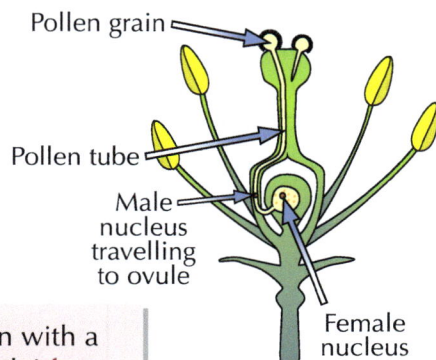

Pollen grain
Pollen tube
Male nucleus travelling to ovule
Female nucleus

Germination is when Seeds Start to Grow

1) Once a seed has formed following fertilisation, it will often lie dormant until the conditions around it are right for germination (growth into a plant).

2) Seeds need the right conditions to start germinating, and germination only starts when all of these conditions are suitable:

- Water — to activate the enzymes that break down the food reserves in the seed.
- Oxygen — for respiration (see page 72), which transfers the energy from food for growth.
- A suitable temperature — for the enzymes inside the seed to work. This depends on what type of seed it is.

Light isn't needed for germination because seeds contain enough food stores to support the plant during early development, so they don't need to photosynthesise.

You Can Examine the Inside of Seeds or Flowers using Dissection

If you want to examine the inside of a seed or flower, the easiest way is to just cut it open. Here's an experiment you can do to look at internal structures of a bean seed:

1) Choose the type of bean that you would like to examine. Try to pick a large bean as this will be easier to cut. Kidney beans are a good choice.

2) Soak your bean seed in water for at least 12 hours, so it becomes soft.

3) Pick up a soaked seed and rub it between your fingers. The seed coat should slide off the seed (if it doesn't you may need to soak the seed for longer).

4) Using a scalpel or sharp knife, make a cut lengthways along the middle of the seed.

5) Use a hand lens to magnify the inside of the seed so that you can observe it. You should be able to identify the embryo shoot and root, as well as the food store.

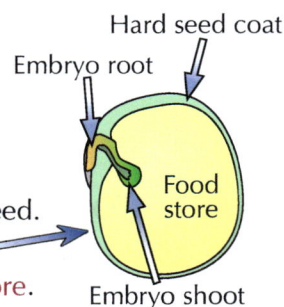

Hard seed coat
Embryo root
Food store
Embryo shoot

Section 12 — Reproduction

Investigating Seed Germination

If you've always wanted to investigate the different conditions needed for germination to take place, then today is your lucky day...

You Can Investigate the Conditions Needed for Germination

You saw on the previous page that seeds need water, oxygen and a suitable temperature for germination to happen. Here's an experiment you can do to investigate these conditions.

1) Take four boiling tubes and put some cotton wool at the bottom of each one.

2) Put 10 seeds on top of the cotton wool in each boiling tube.

3) Set up each boiling tube as follows:

Tube 1	water, oxygen, room temperature (the control).
Tube 2	no water, oxygen, room temperature.
Tube 3	water, oxygen, low temperature.
Tube 4	water, no oxygen, room temperature.

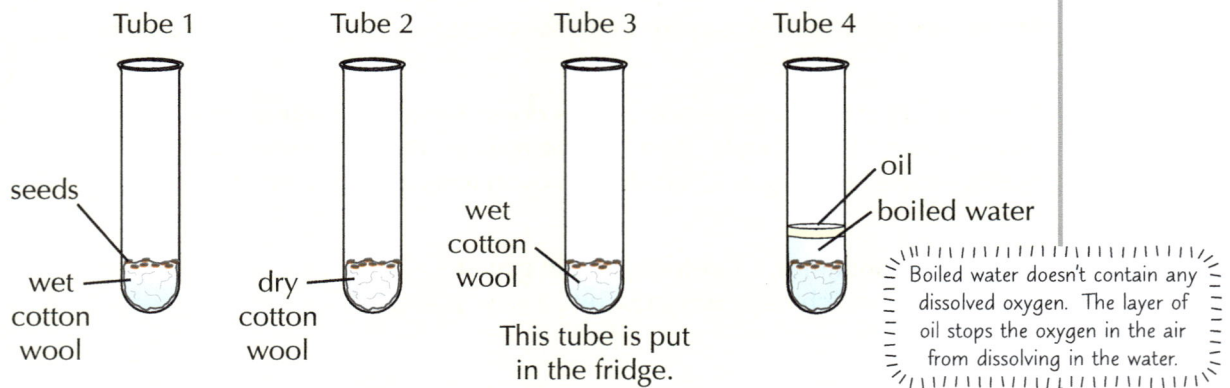

Tube 1 — seeds, wet cotton wool

Tube 2 — dry cotton wool

Tube 3 — wet cotton wool — This tube is put in the fridge.

Tube 4 — oil, boiled water — Boiled water doesn't contain any dissolved oxygen. The layer of oil stops the oxygen in the air from dissolving in the water.

4) Leave the tubes for a few days and then observe what has happened.

5) It's important to control all of the variables during the experiment. You should only be changing one condition at a time so you know that any effect on germination is due to the change in that one condition.

6) So, in Tube 2, the only change from the control (Tube 1) is a lack of water. In Tube 3, only the temperature has changed. In Tube 4, the only change is the lack of oxygen.

Interpreting Your Observations

1) You should only see germination happening in Tube 1.

2) This is because all of the conditions needed for germination are present.

3) The seeds in the other boiling tubes won't germinate — this shows that the seeds need water, oxygen and a suitable temperature to germinate.

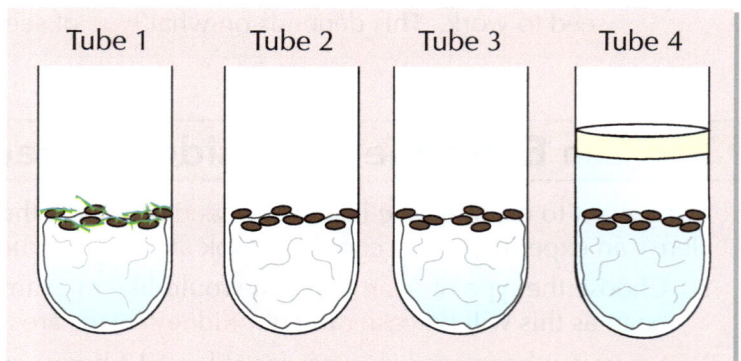

Tube 1   Tube 2   Tube 3   Tube 4

You need the right conditions for germination to happen

PRACTICAL TIP

It's really important that you label your four boiling tubes — if you don't, you'll end up with no idea about what conditions are set up in each tube, and your results won't mean anything.

Warm-Up & Exam Questions

It's that time again. Don't turn the page just yet — give these questions a go before you move on.
They're the only way of finding out if you really know your stuff.

Warm-Up Questions

1) What is sexual reproduction?
2) What is meant by the term 'fertilisation'?
3) What is meant by the term 'self-pollination'?

Exam Questions

1 The diagram below shows cross-sections through two flowers.

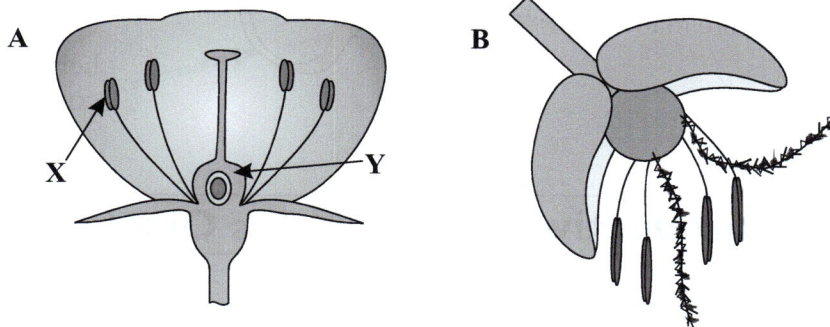

A   B

X   Y

(a) Look at flower **A**. State the name and function of the structures labelled **X** and **Y**.

[4]

(b) Identify which flower, **A** or **B**, is better adapted for wind pollination. Explain your answer.

[2]

(c) Describe and explain **two** ways in which flowers can be adapted for pollination by insects.

[2]

[Total 8 marks]

2 A student set up a controlled experiment to investigate the conditions needed for germination.

She placed moist cotton wool and soaked alfalfa seeds in two large sealed flasks.
Flask **A** contained sodium pyrogallate solution, which absorbs oxygen from the air.
Flask **B** contained sodium hydroxide solution, which absorbs carbon dioxide from the air.

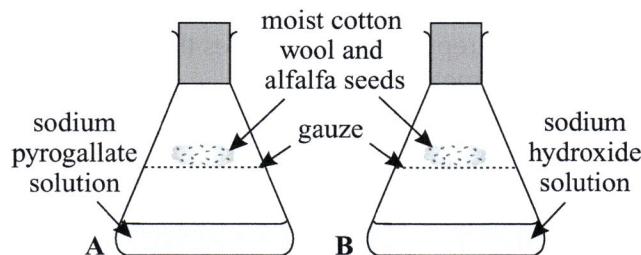

After 24 hours, the student found that the seeds had germinated in flask **B** only.

Explain why germination did not occur in flask **A**.

[Total 2 marks]

Sexual Reproduction in Humans

It's time to learn all about the male and female reproductive systems, and about fertilisation.

The Male Reproductive System Makes Sperm

to bladder

Urethra — a tube which carries sperm through the penis during ejaculation. Urine also passes through the urethra to exit the body.

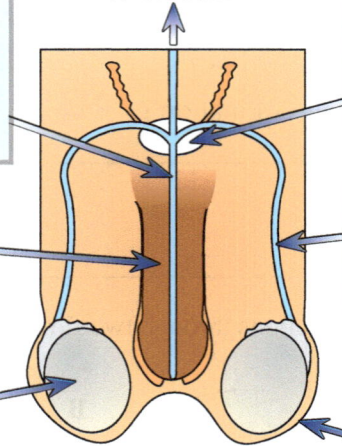

Prostate gland — produces the liquid that's added to sperm to make semen.

Penis — swells when filled with blood, for introducing sperm into the female.

Sperm duct — muscular tube that carries sperm from testis towards the urethra.

Testis — where sperm are made.

Scrotum — hangs behind the penis and contains the testes.

The plural is 'testes'.

The Female Reproductive System Makes Ova (Egg Cells)

Oviduct — a muscular tube that carries the ovum (egg) from the ovary to the uterus. Fertilisation happens in the oviduct.

Ovary — the organ that produces ova and sex hormones.

Cervix — the neck of the uterus.

Uterus — the organ where an embryo grows.

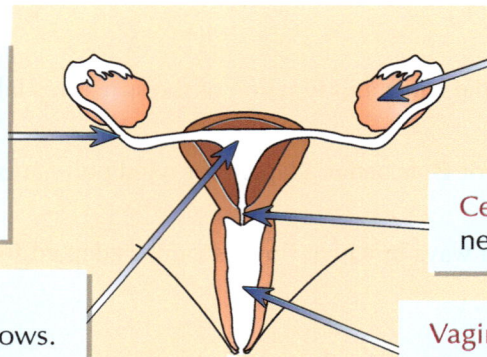

Vagina — where the sperm are deposited.

Fertilisation is the Fusion of the Nuclei of Sperm and Egg Cells

1) As you saw on page 96, sexual reproduction involves the fusion of the nuclei from a male gamete and a female gamete.

2) In humans, the male gametes are sperm and the female gametes are ova (egg cells).

3) During sexual reproduction, the nucleus of an egg cell fuses with the nucleus of a sperm to create a zygote, which then develops into an embryo (see p.104).

REVISION TIP

There's more to learn about sperm and egg cells coming up...

Try drawing out diagrams for both the male and the female reproductive system, with labels for all of the parts. Then make sure you know the function of each part too. Don't worry if your diagram isn't very artistic — it's the knowledge behind it that counts.

Sexual Reproduction in Humans

Fertilisation involves a sperm and an egg cell. The previous page told you where egg cells and sperm are made, but this page is all about how each type of cell is adapted for its function.

Egg Cells and Sperm Are Specialised for Reproduction

Egg Cells

The main functions of an egg cell are to carry the female DNA and to nourish the developing embryo in the early stages. Here are the adaptive features of an egg cell:

1) It contains energy stores in its cytoplasm. These provide nutrients for the zygote so that it can divide after fertilisation and form an embryo.

2) It has a jelly coating that changes at fertilisation. After fertilisation, the jelly coat changes structure to stop any more sperm getting in. This makes sure the offspring end up with the right amount of DNA.

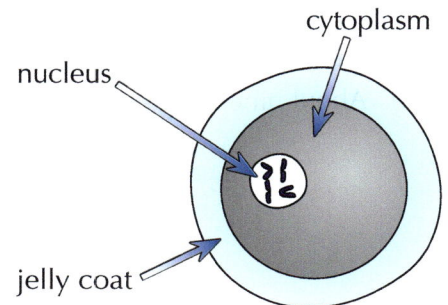

Sperm

The function of a sperm is to transport the male's DNA to the female's egg. Here are the adaptive features of a sperm:

1) It has a flagellum, which gives the sperm the ability to swim to the egg.

2) It has enzymes in a portion of its head called the acrosome. The enzymes are needed to digest a way through the jelly coat of the egg cell.

3) Sperm also contain lots of mitochondria. These provide energy for the flagellum to move.

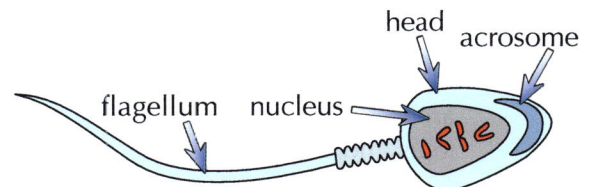

Egg Cells and Sperm are Quite Different

If you couldn't tell from the diagrams, there are some significant differences between female gametes (egg cells) and male gametes (sperm). Here's a table with a summary:

	Egg Cell	Sperm
Size	About 0.1 mm in diameter.	About 0.05 mm in length.
Structure	Spherical. Lots of cytoplasm surrounded by jelly coating.	Head and flagellum. Small amount of cytoplasm.
Motility (ability to move)	Do not move independently.	Able to move due to the presence of the flagellum.
Numbers	About 300 000 present at puberty. Released one at a time each month.	Millions produced every day. Millions released at a time.

Pregnancy

Pregnancy occurs if a sperm fertilises an egg cell and the fertilised egg implants into the uterus. You need to know about how that tiny fertilised egg grows and develops into a fetus.

The Embryo Develops During Pregnancy

1) Once an egg cell has been fertilised, it is called a zygote.
2) Within about four days, the zygote develops into an embryo by dividing several times. This is a ball of cells that implants into the lining of the uterus.
3) Once the embryo has implanted, the placenta develops.
4) The placenta is connected to the embryo by the umbilical cord.
5) The embryo is surrounded by the amniotic sac, which is filled with amniotic fluid.
6) About nine weeks after fertilisation, when it starts to look human, the embryo is called a fetus.

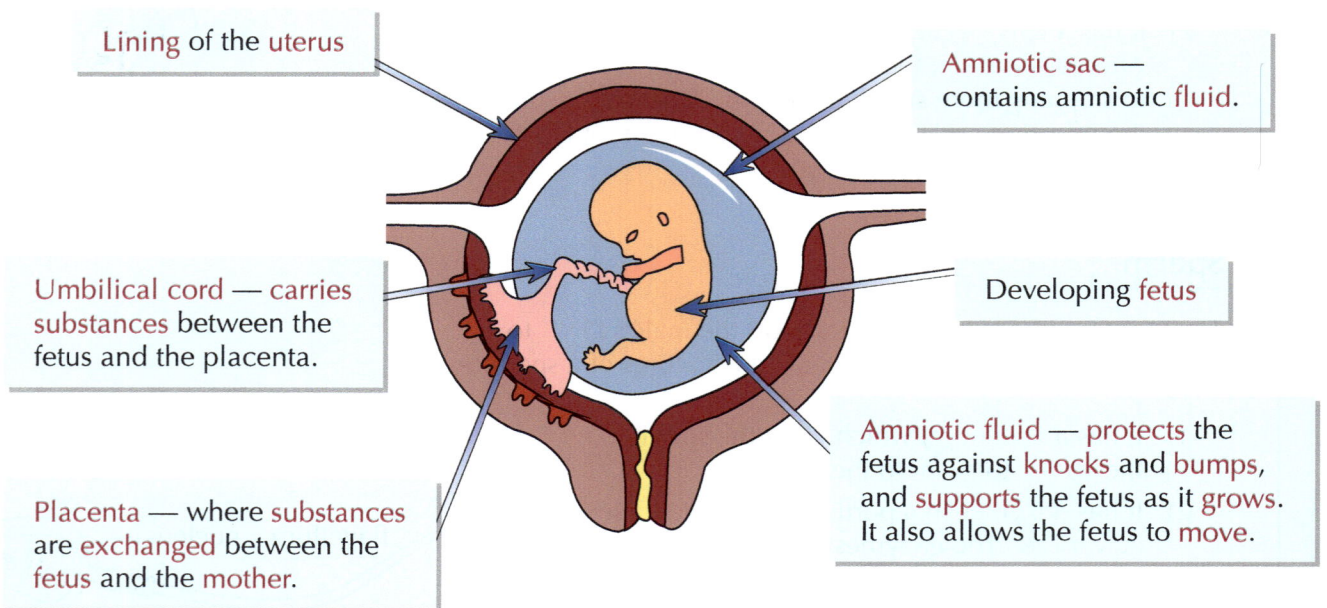

Lining of the uterus

Amniotic sac — contains amniotic fluid.

Umbilical cord — carries substances between the fetus and the placenta.

Developing fetus

Amniotic fluid — protects the fetus against knocks and bumps, and supports the fetus as it grows. It also allows the fetus to move.

Placenta — where substances are exchanged between the fetus and the mother.

The Placenta and Umbilical Cord Transfer Substances

1) The placenta allows the blood of the fetus to get very close to the blood of the mother.

2) This allows dissolved nutrients (e.g. glucose and amino acids) and dissolved oxygen to pass into the fetus's blood from the mother's blood. It also allows excretory products (wastes like urea and carbon dioxide) to diffuse in the opposite direction.

3) The placenta also provides a barrier to most toxins and pathogens, however some can still pass across the placenta and into the fetus.

Supplement

Supplement

The fetus is well protected during pregnancy

REVISION TIP

An embryo is formed from a zygote — it doesn't become a fetus until later in the pregnancy. You can remember that embryo comes before fetus by thinking that e comes before f in the alphabet.

Puberty and the Menstrual Cycle

You need to learn the science behind what happens at puberty. Read on, my friend...

Hormones Promote Sexual Characteristics at Puberty

At puberty, your body starts releasing sex hormones — testosterone in men and oestrogen in women. These trigger off the secondary sexual characteristics:

Testosterone in Men Causes...

1) Extra hair on face and body.
2) Muscles to develop.
3) Penis and testes to enlarge.
4) Sperm production.
5) Deepening of voice.

Oestrogen in Women Causes...

1) Extra hair on underarms and pubic area.
2) Hips to widen.
3) Development of breasts.
4) Egg release and start of periods.

See page 85 for more on hormones.

The Menstrual Cycle Has Four Stages

During the menstrual cycle, the uterus lining changes, and an egg develops and is released from an ovary.

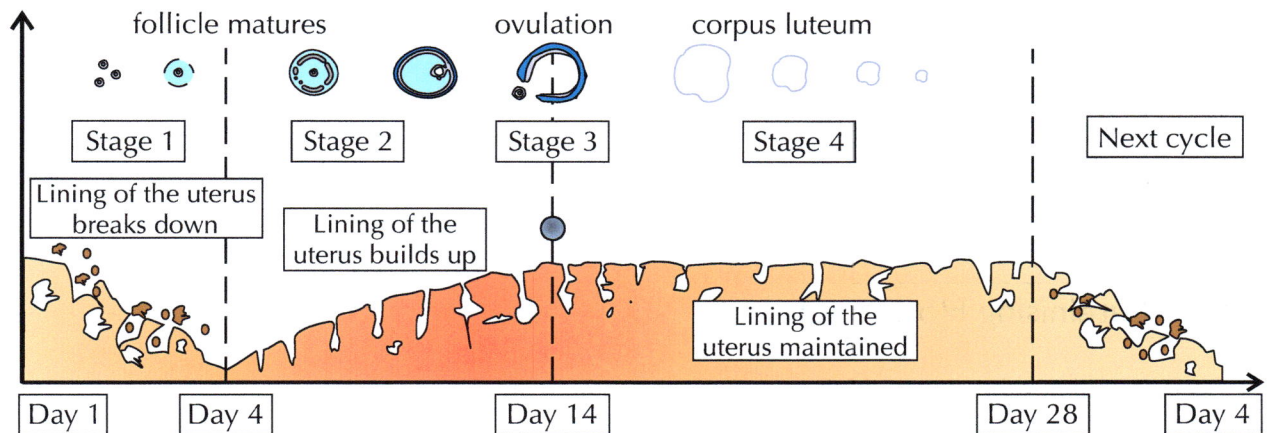

Stage 1: Day 1 — menstruation starts. The uterus lining breaks down for about four days.

Stage 2: The uterus lining builds up (day 4 to 14) into a thick spongy layer full of blood vessels, ready to receive a fertilised egg. A follicle (an egg and its surrounding cells) matures in one of the ovaries.

Stage 3: The egg is released from the follicle at around day 14 — this is called ovulation.

Stage 4: The remains of the follicle develop into a structure called a corpus luteum. The wall is then maintained for about 14 days until day 28. If no fertilised egg has implanted in the uterus wall by day 28, the spongy lining starts to break down and the whole cycle starts again.

Sperm can survive in the female reproductive system for up to five days. If sperm are deposited in the vagina in the five days before ovulation, up to the day after ovulation, there is a chance that the egg will be fertilised. On the rest of the days of the month, fertilisation will not take place.

The end of the cycle depends on whether the egg's fertilised...

REVISION TIP

You need to understand how the lining of the uterus changes throughout the menstrual cycle. Cover up the page and try drawing the graph from memory to see how much you know.

The Menstrual Cycle

If you're taking the Extended course, you need to understand the menstrual cycle in terms of hormones...

The **Menstrual Cycle** is **Controlled** by **Four Hormones**

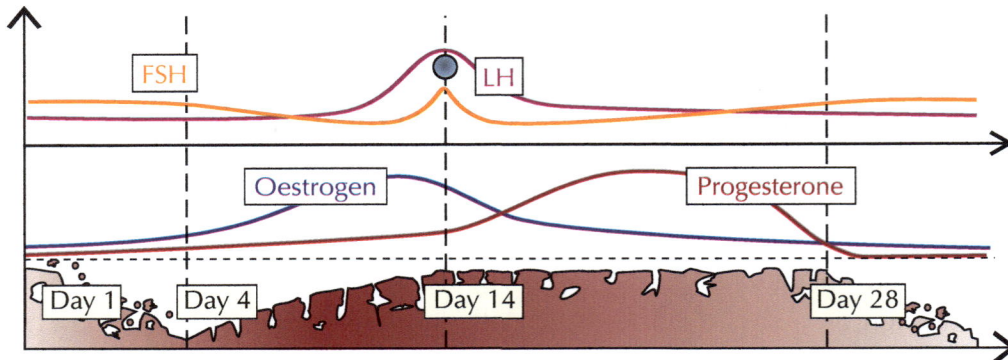

FSH (Follicle-Stimulating Hormone)

1) Causes a follicle to mature in one of the ovaries.
2) Stimulates the ovaries to produce oestrogen.

Oestrogen

1) Produced in the ovaries.
2) Causes the lining of the uterus to grow.
3) Stimulates the release of LH (causing the release of an egg) and inhibits the release of FSH.

LH (Luteinising Hormone)

1) Stimulates the release of the egg from the follicle at day 14 (ovulation).
2) Stimulates the remains of the follicle to develop into a corpus luteum, which secretes progesterone.

Progesterone

1) Produced in the ovaries by the corpus luteum after ovulation.
2) Prepares the uterus to receive a fertilised egg by maintaining the uterus lining during the second half of the cycle. When the level of progesterone falls, the lining breaks down.
3) Inhibits the release of LH and FSH.

The **Four Hormones** Have **Different Roles** During **Pregnancy**

1) During pregnancy, these hormones act in slightly different ways.
2) FSH and LH are inactive during pregnancy. The progesterone and oestrogen levels stay high to maintain the lining of the uterus, and stimulate breast growth and the development of milk ducts.
3) During pregnancy, progesterone is secreted mostly by the placenta and in smaller amounts by the ovaries. Oestrogen is also produced in the placenta.

Supplement

Sexually Transmitted Infections

Some transmissible diseases are transmitted sexually, but there are ways to prevent their spread.

STIs are Sexually Transmitted Infections

KEY TERM

A sexually transmitted infection (STI) is an infection that is transmitted through sexual contact.

You need to know about one example of a pathogen that causes an STI:

HIV is the Human Immunodeficiency Virus

1) HIV is a pathogen spread via infected bodily fluids (e.g. blood, semen, vaginal fluids) during sexual contact and non-sexually (e.g. through sharing needles). HIV can also spread from an infected mother to her baby during pregnancy, childbirth and breastfeeding.

HIV can't be spread through saliva, tears or sweat.

2) HIV infection may eventually lead to AIDS (Acquired Immune Deficiency Syndrome).

3) AIDS is when the infected person's immune system deteriorates and eventually fails — because of this, the person becomes very vulnerable to infections by other pathogens.

The Spread of STIs can be Controlled

Thankfully, it is possible to control the spread of STIs. Here are some methods:

1) It's important that people are educated and aware of STIs so that their spread can be reduced.
2) The best way to prevent the spread of STIs is abstinence — not having sexual intercourse.
3) Another way to prevent the spread of STIs is to use a condom when having sex.
4) Limiting the number of sexual partners also reduces the spread of infection.
5) Getting tested for infection after unprotected sex or after contact with several sexual partners will also help to control the spread of STIs.
6) Medication can reduce the risk of an infected individual passing some infections (e.g. HIV) on to others during sex or of a mother passing it to her baby during pregnancy.
7) Some vaccines protect against STIs caused by viruses.
8) Drug users should avoid sharing needles.

There isn't currently a vaccine against HIV but scientists are working on it.

HIV is an STI but isn't only transmitted sexually...

REVISION TIP

Draw a table with columns for 'how HIV is spread' and 'how to control spread of STIs', then fill it in with all the things you know. See how much you can write down without looking at this page.

Warm-Up & Exam Questions

Time for some Warm-Up Questions now, to see what you've remembered from the previous few pages.
Once you've finished those, move onto the Exam Questions.

Warm-Up Questions

1) What happens to the lining of the uterus at the start of the menstrual cycle?
2) Where is oestrogen produced during the menstrual cycle?

Exam Questions

1 The diagram on the right shows the male reproductive system.

(a) Name the structures labelled **X** and **Y**.

[2]

(b) The structure labelled **Z** is a gland. State its function.

[1]

(c) Add an arrow to the diagram to show where
sperm are produced.

[1]
[Total 4 marks]

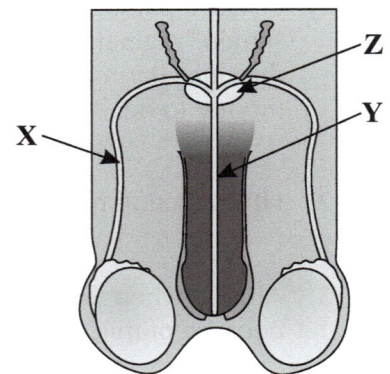

2 The diagram on the right shows the uterus during pregnancy.
State the role of the following features shown in the diagram:

(a) the placenta

[1]

(b) the amniotic fluid

[1]
[Total 2 marks]

placenta   amniotic
fluid

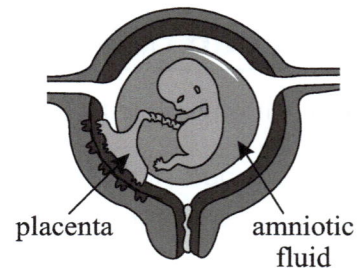

3 The release of sex hormones begins at puberty.

(a) Name the male sex hormone.

[1]

(b) Give **two** secondary sexual characteristics caused by the male sex hormone.

[2]

(c) Give **one** secondary sexual characteristic that is caused by the female sex hormone, oestrogen.

[1]
[Total 4 marks]

Exam Questions

4 HIV is a sexually transmitted infection that eventually leads to AIDS in the people it infects.

(a) State what is meant by the term 'sexually transmitted infection'.

[1]

(b) Drug users are advised not to share needles in order to protect themselves from HIV. Suggest why.

[2]

(c) Describe **one** other way of controlling the spread of HIV.

[1]
[Total 4 marks]

5 Sperm cells are specialised to help them achieve their function.
The digram below shows the structure of a sperm cell.

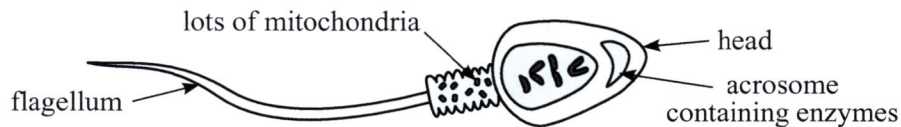

(a) State the function of a sperm cell.

[1]

(b) Explain how the structure of a sperm cell helps it to carry out its function. Use the diagram to help you.

[3]
[Total 4 marks]

6 The menstrual cycle is controlled by several different hormones.

(a) Describe the effect of progesterone on the release of FSH.

[1]

(b) State the day of a 28 day menstrual cycle on which the egg is usually released.

[1]

Towards the end of the menstrual cycle, the oestrogen level is low and the progesterone level begins to fall.

(c) Describe the effect that this will have on the uterus lining.

[1]

(d) When a fertilised egg implants in the uterus, the level of progesterone remains high. State **one** reason why this happens.

[1]

(e) State the main site of production of progesterone during pregnancy.

[1]
[Total 5 marks]

Supplement

Revision Summary for Sections 11 & 12

Well, that's Sections 11 and 12 finished. Now it's time to test how much you've taken in...
- Try these questions and tick off each one when you get it right.
- When you've done all the questions for a topic and are completely happy with it, tick off the topic.

Drugs (p.94) ☐
1) What is the definition of a drug?
2) What type of infections are antibiotics used to treat?

Reproduction (p.96) ☐
3) What is asexual reproduction?
4) Give two advantages of asexual reproduction compared to sexual reproduction.
5) Give one difference between the nucleus of a gamete and the nucleus of a zygote.
6) Give one advantage of sexual reproduction compared to asexual reproduction.

Sexual Reproduction in Plants (p.97-100) ☐
7) On a plant, what is the function of: a) the petals, b) the sepals?
8) What is pollination?
9) What is cross-pollination?
10) Describe the pollen grains of a wind-pollinated plant.
11) What happens during plant fertilisation?
12) How does pollen get from the stigma to the ovule?
13) Give three conditions that are needed for germination to happen.

Sexual Reproduction in Humans (p.102-104) ☐
14) Give the name and function of three structures in the female reproductive system.
15) State and explain two features of an egg cell that make it adapted for its function.
16) Compare egg cells and sperm in terms of their size and numbers.
17) Describe how a fertilised egg becomes a fetus.
18) What is the name of the structure that amniotic fluid is contained in?
19) State one substance that passes between the umbilical cord and placenta.

Puberty and the Menstrual Cycle (p.105-106) ☐
20) Name the main female sex hormone.
21) Describe the changes that take place in the ovary during the menstrual cycle.
22) Describe two effects of FSH on the ovaries.
23) Where is progesterone released from during the menstrual cycle?

Sexually Transmitted Infections (p.107) ☐
24) What does HIV stand for?
25) HIV can be spread via blood through sexual contact.
    State two other bodily fluids in which HIV can be spread.

Chromosomes and Sex Inheritance

A molecule called DNA carries your genetic code — here's how it is stored and how it determines your sex.

DNA is Stored as Chromosomes and Contains Genes

1) Chromosomes are found in the nucleus of eukaryotic cells.

> **KEY TERM** — A chromosome is a long length of DNA, which carries genetic information in the form of genes.

> **KEY TERM** — A gene is a section of DNA that codes for a protein.

2) By controlling the production of proteins, genes also control our characteristics.

3) There can be different versions of the same gene, which give different versions of a characteristic — like blue or brown eyes.

> **KEY TERM** — An allele is an alternative version of a gene.

For example, you might have the alleles for blue eyes and your friend might have the alleles for brown eyes.

Two Chromosomes Determine Sex in Humans

1) In humans, there are two chromosomes responsible for sex determination (whether you turn out male or female). These are the sex chromosomes and can be labelled as either X or Y.

2) Males have an X and a Y chromosome (XY). The Y chromosome causes male characteristics.

3) Females have two X chromosomes (XX). The XX combination allows female characteristics to develop.

4) All eggs have one X chromosome, but a sperm can have either an X chromosome or a Y chromosome. So sex determination in humans depends on whether the sperm that fertilises an egg (see p.102) carries an X or a Y.

5) There's a 50:50 chance that a sperm contains an X or Y chromosome, so there's a 50:50 chance of a child having XX (and being a girl) or XY (and being a boy).

Chromosomes Can Come in Pairs

1) Human body cells are diploid — there are two copies of each chromosome, arranged in pairs.

> **KEY TERM** — A diploid nucleus is a nucleus that contains two sets of chromosomes.

2) There are 23 pairs of chromosomes in human diploid cells, so there are 46 chromosomes in total.

3) Gametes (sex cells) are haploid — they have half the number of chromosomes in a normal cell.

> **KEY TERM** — A haploid nucleus is a nucleus that contains a single set of chromosomes.

4) Human gametes each contain 23 chromosomes.

Supplement

Protein Synthesis

This page is all about how your body uses the genes in DNA to make the proteins it needs.

Proteins are Made by Reading the Code in DNA

1) DNA strands contain bases (see page 26) which make up genes (see previous page).

2) The order of bases in a gene is the genetic code that determines the order (sequence) of amino acids in a protein.

3) Each amino acid is coded for by a sequence of three bases in the gene.

4) Amino acids are joined together to make specific proteins, depending on the order of the gene's bases.

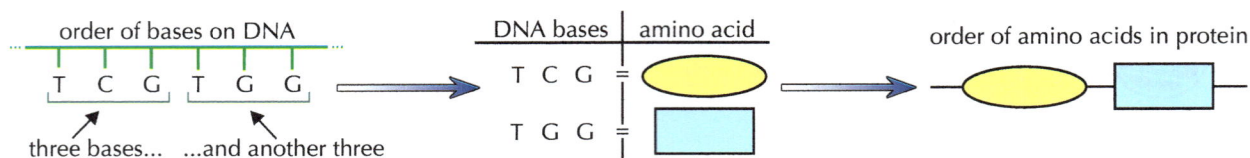

order of bases on DNA

T C G T G G

three bases... ...and another three

DNA bases	amino acid
T C G =	
T G G =	

order of amino acids in protein

5) When a chain of amino acids has been assembled, it folds into a unique shape which allows the protein to perform the task it's meant to do. Different sequences of amino acids result in proteins with different shapes.

- A cell's function is controlled by DNA, because DNA controls the production of proteins, including enzymes (p.29), membrane carriers (proteins in the membrane that move substances across the membrane) and neurotransmitter receptors (p.80).
- Most body cells in an organism have the same genes, but cells don't express (make proteins from) all of their genes. Cells only express those genes that lead to the production of the specific proteins they need to carry out their function.

Proteins are Made in the Cytoplasm

1) DNA is found in the cell nucleus. It can't move out of the nucleus because it's really big. The cell needs to get the information from the DNA into the cytoplasm.
2) This is done using a molecule called messenger RNA (mRNA).
3) Like DNA, mRNA is made up of bases. Each mRNA molecule is a copy of a gene.
4) mRNA is made in the nucleus and then moves to the cytoplasm.
4) Once in the cytoplasm, the mRNA passes through a ribosome (see page 11).
5) The ribosome assembles amino acids into protein molecules.
6) The sequence of bases in the mRNA determines the specific order of amino acids in the protein.

DNA and mRNA decide the order of amino acids in the protein

It's important that you know why the order of bases in a section of DNA (and the mRNA copy) affects which protein is made. If you're unsure, it's all covered on this page — go back and take another look.

Mitosis and Meiosis

In order to survive and grow, our cells have got to be able to divide. This involves nuclear division (division of the nucleus). There are two types of nuclear division that you need to know about.

Mitosis Makes New Cells for Growth, Development and Repair

1) Body cells divide to produce new cells during mitosis.

KEY TERM Mitosis is a nuclear division that results in two genetically identical cells.

2) Mitosis is used in growth, cell replacement, and in the repair of damaged tissues.
3) It is also used in asexual reproduction (see page 96).
4) Before mitosis can happen, the cell's chromosomes are replicated (copied) exactly — so you end up with twice the normal diploid number of chromosomes (see p.111).
5) During mitosis, the chromosome copies separate and the nucleus divides — one copy of each chromosome ends up in each daughter (new) cell. This means that each daughter cell is diploid and the original chromosome number is maintained.

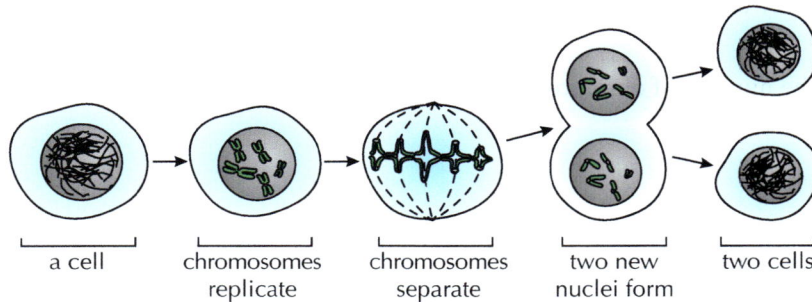

a cell — chromosomes replicate — chromosomes separate — two new nuclei form — two cells

Mitosis is Important in Stem Cells

1) Stem cells are unspecialised cells.
2) Depending on what instructions they're given, stem cells divide by mitosis to produce identical daughter cells that can then become specialised for specific functions.
3) Stem cells in embryos allow an organism to grow and develop. Stem cells in adults are used to replace damaged cells.

Meiosis is Another Type of Division

Meiosis is used to produce haploid gametes for use in sexual reproduction (see p.96).

KEY TERM Meiosis is a reduction division, which halves the chromosome number from diploid to haploid, resulting in four genetically different cells.

Meiosis is different from mitosis

Don't get meiosis mixed up with mitosis. Try remembering m**it**osis has "IT" in it and "IT" stands for **I**dentical **T**wins, because the two cells produced are genetically identical to the original cell. Meiosis doesn't have "IT" and produces four daughter cells which are genetically different.

Warm-Up & Exam Questions

Take a deep breath and go through these Warm-Up and Exam Questions one by one.
Don't panic if you get something wrong — go back to the relevant page and have another look.

Warm-Up Questions

1) What combination of sex chromosomes do human males have?
[S] 2) Does mitosis or meiosis produce genetically identical cells?

Exam Questions

1 DNA in plants and animals is found in the form of chromosomes.

(a) Describe what is meant by the term chromosome.

[1]

[S] (b) (i) Each body cell in most mammals has a **diploid** nucleus. Explain what this means.

[1]

(ii) State the number of chromosomes in a human **haploid** cell.

[1]

[Total 3 marks]

2 To make a protein, mRNA carries a copy of the gene from the DNA in the nucleus to the cytoplasm.

(a) Name the part of the cell that assembles amino acids into protein molecules.

[1]

(b) State what determines the order of amino acids in a protein.

[1]

(c) Briefly explain how genes affect cell function.

[2]

[Total 4 marks]

3 Mosquitoes have three pairs of chromosomes in their body cells.
The diagram below shows a mosquito cell which is about to divide by meiosis.

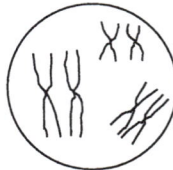

How many chromosomes will be present in each new cell produced?

☐ **A** 2   ☐ **B** 3

☐ **C** 6   ☐ **D** 12

[Total 1 mark]

Supplement

Supplement

Section 13 — Inheritance

Monohybrid Inheritance

Chromosomes contain the same genes in the same places. The genes have different alleles (versions, see p.111), so the characteristics you have depends on which alleles you inherited from your parents.

Here are Some **Definitions** to Learn...

KEY TERMS

Term	Definition
Inheritance	The transmission of genetic information (DNA) between generations.
Genotype	The alleles an organism has (its genetic make-up).
Phenotype	The observable features of an organism.
Homozygous	Having two identical alleles for a particular gene.
Heterozygous	Having two different alleles for a particular gene.
Dominant allele	An allele that is always expressed if it is present.
Recessive allele	An allele that is only expressed when the dominant version of the allele is not present in the organism's genotype.

Monohybrid inheritance is the inheritance of a single characteristic.

Genes are **Inherited** From Your **Parents**

1) You have two alleles of every gene in your body — one from each parent.

> The combination of alleles that you inherit is your genotype.

> Your genotype determines what features you have (your phenotype).

> So different combinations of alleles give rise to different phenotypes.

2) Different genotypes arise from different combinations of alleles.

> If an organism has two of the same alleles for a particular gene, then it's homozygous for that trait. Two identical homozygous individuals that breed together will be pure-breeding (they can only pass on one allele, and therefore only one phenotype).

> If an organism has two alleles for a particular gene that are different, then it's heterozygous. A heterozygous organism will not be pure-breeding, as it can pass on two different alleles.

3) Alleles that are dominant (shown with capital letters, e.g. 'C') overrule alleles that are recessive (shown with small letters, e.g. 'c'). If an organism has one dominant and one recessive allele for a gene (e.g. 'Cc'), then the dominant allele will determine the characteristic present.

4) To display a dominant characteristic, an organism can have either two dominant alleles (CC) for a particular gene, or one dominant and one recessive allele (Cc) for that gene.

5) For an organism to display a recessive characteristic, both its alleles must be recessive (cc).

Genetic Diagrams

You can work out the probability of offspring having certain characteristics by using a genetic diagram.

Genetic Diagrams Show the Possible Alleles of Offspring

The allele which causes cats to have short hair is dominant ('H'), whilst long hair is due to a recessive allele ('h'). A cat with long hair must have the genotype hh. But a cat with short hair could be HH or Hh.

1) Here's what happens if you cross a pure-breeding (homozygous) short-haired cat (HH) with a pure-breeding (homozygous) long-haired cat (hh):

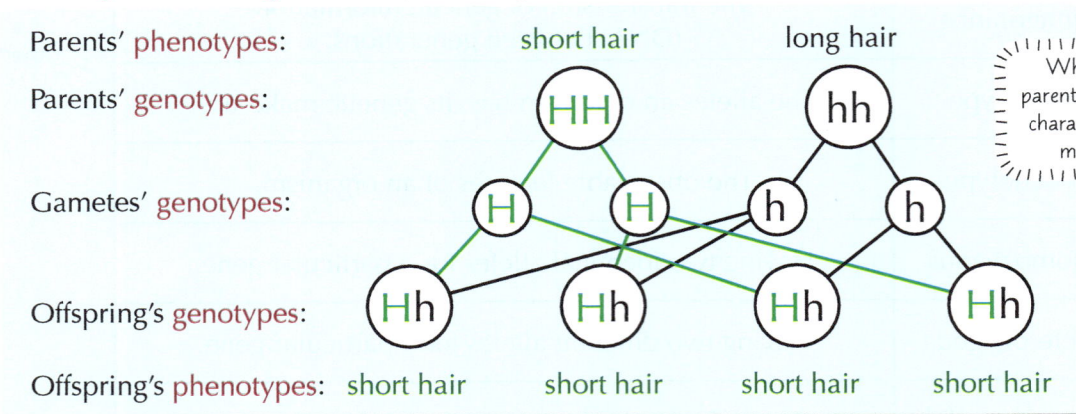

Parents' phenotypes: short hair   long hair

Parents' genotypes: HH   hh

Gametes' genotypes: H H   h h

Offspring's genotypes: Hh   Hh   Hh   Hh

Offspring's phenotypes: short hair   short hair   short hair   short hair

When you cross two parents to look at just one characteristic, it's called a monohybrid cross.

2) All the offspring are heterozygous for short hair.

3) Now, here's what happens if you breed two of these heterozygous individuals together. This time, the genetic cross is shown in a Punnett square:

4) This cross produces a 3 : 1 ratio of short-haired to long-haired offspring in this generation (a 1 in 4 or 25% probability of long hair).

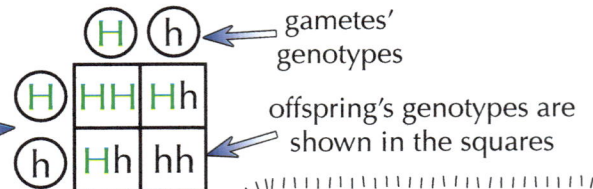

gametes' genotypes ← H h

H | HH | Hh
h | Hh | hh

offspring's genotypes are shown in the squares

The first set of offspring here is called the F_1 generation. The second set of offspring is called the F_2 generation.

There Can Be a 1 : 1 Ratio in the Offspring

1) A cat with short hair (Hh) was bred with another cat with long hair (hh).

2) The cats had 8 kittens — 4 with short hair and 4 with long hair.

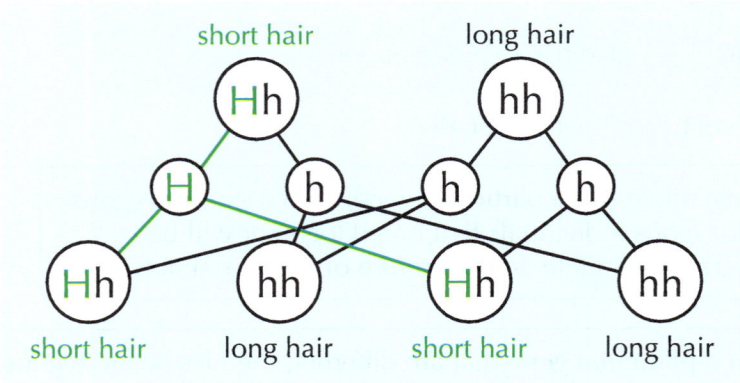

short hair   long hair

Hh   hh

H h   h h

Hh   hh   Hh   hh

short hair   long hair   short hair   long hair

Remember — genetic diagrams only tell you probabilities. They don't say definitely what will happen.

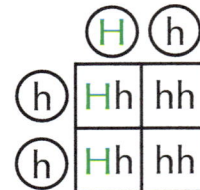

H h
h | Hh | hh
h | Hh | hh

3) This is a 1 : 1 ratio — it's what you'd expect when a parent with only one dominant allele (heterozygous — Hh) is crossed with a parent with two recessive alleles (homozygous — hh).

EXAM TIP

Genetic diagrams aren't that scary

You should know how to produce and interpret both of these types of genetic diagram before exam day. Try drawing a Punnett square from a genetic cross diagram like the ones above, and then try the same but the other way round. Always remember the genotypes and the phenotypes.

Genetic Diagrams

Coming up on this page — another type of genetic diagram you need to know about...

Pedigree Diagrams Can Show How Characteristics Are Inherited

1) Knowing how inheritance works can help you to interpret a pedigree diagram
   — this is one for a genetic (inherited) disorder called cystic fibrosis.

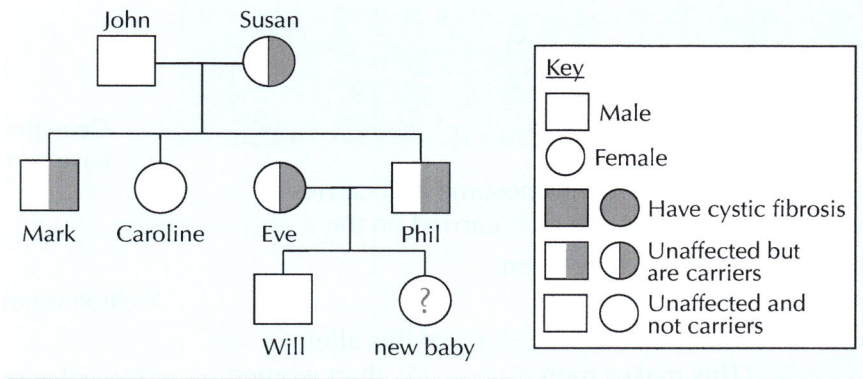

Key

- ☐ Male
- ○ Female
- ◼ ● Have cystic fibrosis
- ◼ ◐ Unaffected but are carriers
- ☐ ○ Unaffected and not carriers

A carrier is someone who doesn't have the disorder, but can pass it on.

(Pedigree diagram showing: John & Susan parents; children Mark, Caroline, Eve & Phil; Eve & Phil have children Will and new baby with "?")

2) From the pedigree diagram, you can tell that the allele for cystic fibrosis isn't dominant because plenty of the family carry the allele but don't have the disorder. The allele must be recessive (f).

3) Both of the baby's parents are unaffected but are carriers, meaning they both have the genotype Ff.

4) As both parents are Ff, there is a 25% chance that the new baby will be unaffected and not a carrier (FF), a 50% chance that it will be unaffected but a carrier (Ff), and a 25% chance that the new baby will have the disorder (ff).

This is the same as the 3 : 1 ratio shown on page 116.

Test Crosses Can Be Used to Identify Unknown Genotypes

1) A test cross can be used to determine the unknown genotype of an organism, by analysing the ratio of phenotypes in the offspring.

2) You can use genetic diagrams when carrying out test crosses.

3) Let's say you're breeding cats again (see p.116). You breed a long-haired cat with a short-haired cat.

A test cross has to involve a homozygous recessive individual — in this case the long-haired cat with the genotype hh.

4) The long-haired cat must have the genotype hh, because long hair is due to a recessive allele.

5) The genotype of the short-haired cat is unknown — it could be homozygous dominant (HH) or heterozygous dominant (Hh). Here's how you can work out which it is:

When the two cats breed, the ratio of the phenotypes in the offspring will be the same as the ratio of the genotypes of the short-haired cat's gametes.

1) If the short-haired parent cat is homozygous (HH), it will produce only one gamete genotype (H). Therefore, when it is bred with the long-haired cat (hh) only one type of offspring phenotype will be produced (Hh — short hair). If all of the offspring produced in a test cross have short hair, the short-haired parent cat must be homozygous (HH).

	h	h
H	Hh	Hh
H	Hh	Hh

2) A heterozygous short-haired cat (Hh) bred with the long-haired cat (hh) will produce two gamete genotypes (H and h) in the ratio 1 : 1, and therefore two offspring phenotypes (Hh — short hair, hh — long hair) in the same ratio. If short-haired and long-haired offspring are produced in a test cross, the short-haired cat must be heterozygous (Hh).

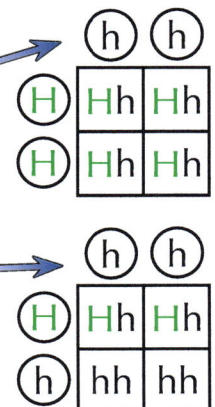

	h	h
H	Hh	Hh
h	hh	hh

This is the same as the 1 : 1 ratio shown on page 116.

Supplement

Sex-Linked Genetic Disorders

There are some disorders that you're more likely to end up with if you're a certain sex. This is because these disorders are linked to the sex chromosomes, which are different in males and females (see p.111).

Some Genetic Characteristics Are Sex-Linked

1) A characteristic is sex-linked if the gene that codes for it is located on a sex chromosome (X or Y).

> **KEY TERM**
> A sex-linked characteristic is a feature that is coded for by a gene located on a sex chromosome, making it more common in one sex than in the other.

X chromosome

Gene that men have two alleles for.

Y chromosome

Gene that men have only one allele for.

2) The Y chromosome is smaller than the X chromosome and carries fewer genes. So most genes on the sex chromosomes are only carried on the X chromosome.

3) As men only have one X chromosome they often only have one allele for sex-linked genes.

4) Because men only have one allele, the characteristic of this allele is shown even if it is recessive. This makes men more likely than women to show recessive characteristics for genes that are sex-linked.

5) Disorders caused by faulty alleles located on sex chromosomes are called sex-linked genetic disorders.

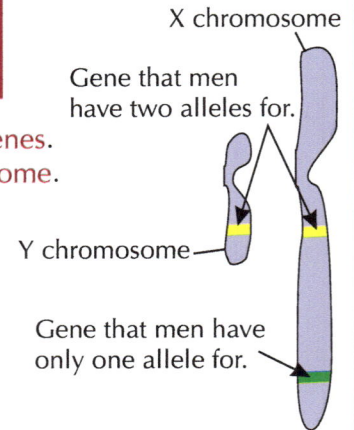

Red-Green Colour Blindness is a Sex-Linked Disorder

1) Red-green colour blindness is caused by a faulty allele carried on the X chromosome.

2) As it's sex-linked, both the chromosome and the allele are written in the genetic diagram, e.g. X^n, where X represents the X chromosome and n the faulty allele for colour vision. The Y chromosome doesn't have an allele for colour vision so is just represented by Y.

3) Women need two copies of the recessive allele to be colour blind, while men only need one copy. This means colour blindness is much rarer in women than men.

4) A woman with only one copy of the recessive allele is a carrier of colour blindness. This means that she isn't colour blind herself, but she can pass the allele on to her offspring.

5) Here's a genetic diagram showing a carrier female and an unaffected (non-colour blind) male:

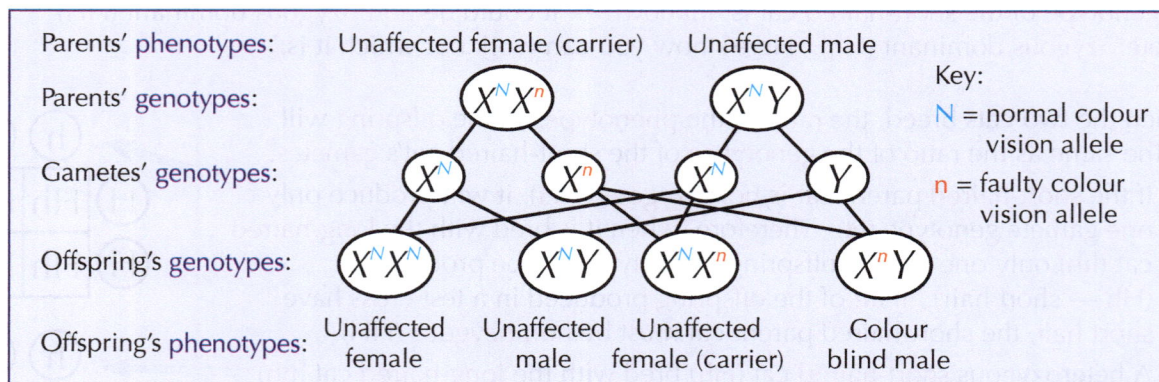

Parents' phenotypes:	Unaffected female (carrier) Unaffected male	Key:
Parents' genotypes:	$X^N X^n$ $X^N Y$	N = normal colour vision allele
Gametes' genotypes:	X^N X^n X^N Y	n = faulty colour vision allele
Offspring's genotypes:	$X^N X^N$ $X^N Y$ $X^N X^n$ $X^n Y$	
Offspring's phenotypes:	Unaffected female Unaffected male Unaffected female (carrier) Colour blind male	

6) In the example above, the ratio of unaffected : colour blind offspring is 3 : 1. Be careful with this one, it could also be called a 2 : 1 : 1 ratio (unaffected : carrier : colour blind), but it means the same thing.

7) In other words, there's a 1 in 4 (25%) chance of a child being colour blind. This rises to 1 in 2 (50%) if you know that the child will be a boy.

Supplement

Supplement

Inheritance of Blood Groups

This is a bit more complicated than the previous examples, but don't worry, just go through it slowly.

There Are **Multiple Alleles** That Determine **Blood Group**

1) So far you've probably only come across cases where there are two possible alleles for a gene — one that's recessive and one that's dominant.

2) Well, sometimes you'll get more than two (multiple) alleles for a single gene. This makes studying the inheritance of characteristics controlled by these genes a little more complicated.

3) For example, humans have four potential blood types — A, B, AB and O. These are the phenotypes. The gene for blood type in humans has three different alleles — I^A, I^B and I^o.

4) I^A and I^B are codominant with each other. That means that when an individual has both of these alleles (genotype $I^A I^B$), then they'll have the blood type AB — one allele isn't dominant over the other one. Here's the definition of codominance:

> **KEY TERM**
> Codominance is when both of the alleles in a heterozygous organism are expressed and so both determine the organism's phenotype.

5) When it comes to blood groups, I^o is recessive. So when you get I^o with I^A (genotype $I^A I^o$) you only see the effect of I^A — giving blood type A. In the same way, I^o with I^B (genotype $I^B I^o$) only gives the effect of I^B, making you blood type B.

6) You only get blood type O when you have two of the recessive alleles ($I^o I^o$).

You Can Predict **Blood Groups** Using **Genetic Diagrams**

1) You can draw genetic diagrams for codominant alleles in the same way that you would for alleles that are recessive and dominant.

2) The tricky bit is predicting the potential phenotypes in the offspring once you've worked out what the potential genotypes are. You need to remember how the different alleles interact with each other to produce a phenotype.

3) Here's an example showing how you can use genetic diagrams to predict the blood type inherited by the offspring:

1) A man and a woman are both blood group AB with the genotype $I^A I^B$. The diagram shows the alleles that they can produce.

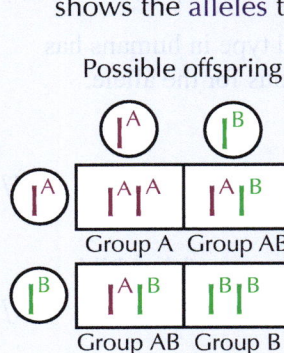

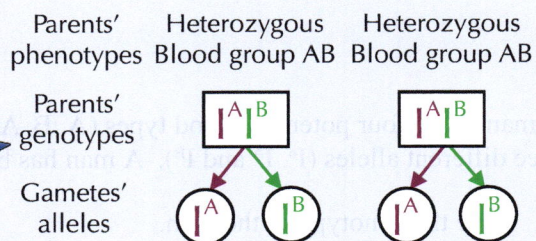

2) The man and the woman have a child. The possible genotypes and phenotypes are shown in the Punnett square on the left.

3) As you can see from the diagram, there is a 1 : 2 : 1 ratio in the offspring of blood group A : blood group AB : blood group B (or 1 homozygous for one allele : 2 heterozygous : 1 homozygous for the other allele).

Codominance — both alleles are visible in the phenotype

You need to be able to use genetic diagrams to predict results for codominant genotypes. If you're still confused by the diagrams, read over the last few pages again — it will really help for this example.

Warm-Up & Exam Questions

You need to test your knowledge with a few Warm-Up Questions, followed by some Exam Questions.

Warm-Up Questions

1) Define inheritance.
2) What is genotype? What is phenotype?
s 3) Where is a gene that codes for a sex-linked characteristic located?

Exam Questions

1 Polydactyly is a genetic disorder transmitted by the dominant allele **D**. The corresponding recessive allele is **d**. The pedigree diagram of a family with a history of polydactyly is shown.

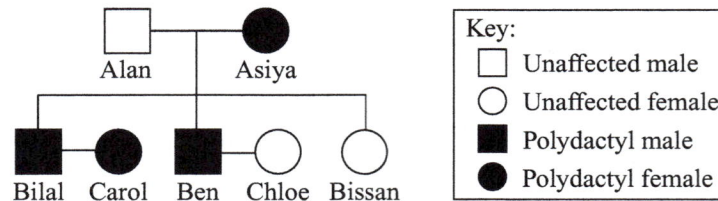

Alan — Asiya

Bilal Carol Ben Chloe Bissan

Key:
☐ Unaffected male
○ Unaffected female
■ Polydactyl male
● Polydactyl female

Using the information given above, state what Asiya's genotype must be.
Explain your answer.

[Total 2 marks]

2 Fruit flies usually have red eyes. However, there are a small number of white-eyed fruit flies. Having white eyes is a recessive characteristic. Two fruit flies with red eyes have the heterozygous genotype for this characteristic. They are crossed to produce offspring.

(a) Draw a genetic diagram to show the possible genotypes and phenotypes of the offspring. Use **R** to represent the dominant allele and **r** to represent the recessive allele.

[3]

(b) State the probability that one of the fruit flies' offspring will have white eyes.

[1]

[Total 4 marks]

3 Humans have four potential blood types (A, B, AB and O). The gene for blood type in humans has three different alleles (I^o, I^A and I^B). A man has blood type **A** and is heterozygous for the allele.

(a) Give the genotype of the man.

[1]

(b) The man has a child with a homozygous woman who has blood group **B**.
    (i) Draw a Punnett square to show the possible genotypes for the blood group of the child.

[2]

    (ii) State the probability that the child will have blood type **B**.

[1]

    (iii) State and explain the phenotype of a child who inherits an I^A allele and an I^B allele.

[2]

[Total 6 marks]

Supplement

Variation

You have probably noticed that not all people are identical. There are reasons for this.

Organisms of the Same Species Have Differences

1) Different species look different — my dog definitely doesn't look like a daisy.

2) But even organisms of the same species usually look at least slightly different — e.g. in a room full of people you'll see different eye colour, individually shaped noses, a variety of heights, etc. This is known as variation.

3) Here's the definition you need to know:

KEY TERM — Variation is the differences between individuals of the same species.

4) Variation can be caused by genes (genetic variation), the environment, or a combination of the two.

Variation can be Continuous or Discontinuous

1) Continuous variation is when the individuals in a population have a range of phenotypes which vary between two extremes — there are no distinct categories. E.g. an organism can have any body length within a range, not just long or short.

2) Other examples include body mass, and the number of leaves on a tree.

3) Continuous variation is caused by both genes and the environment.

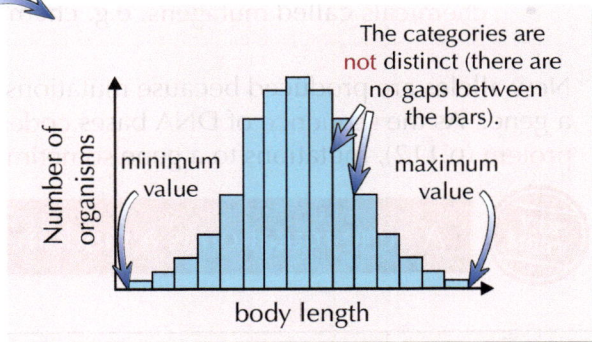

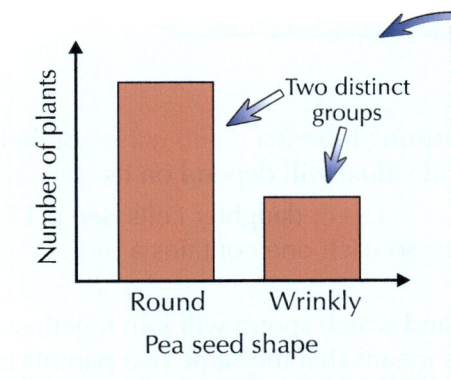

The categories are not distinct (there are no gaps between the bars).

Number of organisms — minimum value — maximum value — body length

4) Discontinuous variation is when there are two or more distinct categories. Each individual falls into only one of these categories, so there is a limited number of phenotypes with no intermediates (nothing in between) — e.g. pea seeds can be either round or wrinkly in shape, and green or yellow in colour.

5) Discontinuous variation is usually caused by genes alone. Blood groups in humans are an example of this. Humans can only be blood group A, B, AB or O (see p.119). This is determined by genes and is not affected by environmental factors.

Number of plants — Two distinct groups — Round — Wrinkly — Pea seed shape

Variation is caused by differences in genotype and phenotype

Make sure you properly understand all of the new terms you've come across on this page. It's pretty important stuff, so if you forget what they mean you can always come back to refresh your memory.

Variation

There's more you need to learn about variation I'm afraid — including a practical...

You can **Investigate Variation** in Organisms

An example of a way you can investigate continuous variation is by collecting data on the height of everyone in a group, such as your class. To do this, follow this method:

1) Ask each person to remove their shoes.
2) Use a measuring tape to measure from the top of a person's head to the ground.
3) Record the height of the person using a suitable table (see page 169).
4) Plot your height data against the number of people, and compare the shape of your plot to the graph on the previous page.

You could investigate discontinuous variation too, e.g. by recording the eye colour of everyone in the group.

Genetic Variation Can Arise Due to **Mutations**

KEY TERM Mutation is genetic change.

1) When mutations occur within a gene they result in a different version of the gene called an allele.
2) Having different alleles increases genetic variation.
3) Mutations can happen spontaneously, but the rate of mutation is increased by exposing yourself to:

- ionising radiation, e.g. X-rays, gamma rays or ultraviolet rays,
- chemicals called mutagens, e.g. chemicals in tobacco.

4) New alleles are produced because mutations change the sequence of the DNA bases (p.26) in a gene. As the sequence of DNA bases codes for the sequence of amino acids that make up a protein (p.112), mutations to a gene sometimes lead to changes in the protein that it codes for.

KEY TERM A gene mutation is a random change in the base sequence of DNA.

There are **Other Sources** of **Genetic Variation** too

The following are all additional sources of genetic variation:

1) Random mating — when two organisms mate, their offspring inherit a combination of their genes. So the combination of alleles inherited by an individual will depend on its parents.
2) Meiosis — this type of cell division produces genetically different daughter cells (see p.113). Gametes (sperm and egg cells) are produced by meiosis, so each one contains a different combination of alleles.
3) Random fertilisation — it's random chance which egg and which sperm will join together at fertilisation to produce an embryo (see page 102). This means that the same two parents can produce multiple offspring with a different combination of alleles to each other and themselves.

Mutations are very common, but are rarely noticeable

Mutations sound pretty scary (especially if you're thinking about all those mutant creatures in sci-fi movies). But in reality, mutations occur all the time and hardly ever affect the structure or function of a protein.

Adaptive Features

It's variation that has allowed life to adapt to so many different environments.

Adaptive Features Allow Organisms to Survive

1) Different organisms are adapted to live in different environmental conditions.
2) The features or characteristics that allow them to do this are called adaptive features.

KEY TERM — Adaptive features are characteristics that an organism inherits which help it to survive and reproduce in its environment.

3) Here are some examples of adaptive features:

Arctic animals like the Arctic fox have white fur so they're camouflaged against the snow. This helps them to avoid predators and to catch prey.

Animals that live in cold places (like whales) have a thick layer of blubber (fat) and a small surface area for their size to help them retain heat.

Animals that live in hot places (like camels) have a thin layer of fat to help them lose heat.

Some Plants are Adapted to Live in Extreme Environments

Xerophytes

- Xerophytes are plants like marram grass (which grows on sand dunes). They're adapted to live in dry climates.
- Marram grass has stomata that are sunk in pits and surrounded by hairs. These slow transpiration (p.50) down because they both trap a layer of humid air close to the leaf's surface.
- Marram grass plants have rolled leaves to trap humid air.
- Marram grass has a thick, waxy layer on the epidermis to reduce water loss by evaporation.

Look at page 39 again if you need a reminder of a typical leaf structure.

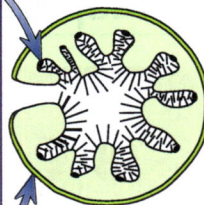

Hydrophytes

- Hydrophytes are plants like water lilies, which are adapted to live in water.
- The leaves contain air spaces, so they can float on the surface of the water and be exposed to the most light.
- Stomata are usually only present on the upper surface of floating leaves. This helps to maximise gas exchange.
- The stems are flexible to help prevent damage from currents.

Supplement

Organisms can adapt to life in a variety of environments

EXAM TIP — You might be given a picture of an organism in the exam, and asked to suggest what its adaptive features are. Think about things like the type of environment that it lives in (e.g. hot or cold, in water or on land) and its interactions with other organisms (e.g. whether it needs to catch prey or run away from predators).

Natural Selection

Natural selection is all about the organisms with the best characteristics surviving to pass on their alleles.

Natural Selection Means there is a Struggle for Survival

Natural selection results in those organisms that are better adapted to their environment being more likely to survive and reproduce. Here's how it happens:

1) Individuals in a population show genetic variation (see page 121) because of differences in their alleles.

2) Some organisms produce many offspring. This means that there aren't enough resources (e.g. food, water, mates, etc.) to support all of the offspring and so there is competition between them.

3) Competition for resources and things like predation and disease affect an organism's chance of surviving and reproducing. There is a 'struggle for survival'.

4) Those individuals with characteristics that make them better adapted to their environment have a better chance of survival and so are more likely to reproduce successfully.

5) This means the alleles that are responsible for beneficial characteristics are more likely to be passed on to the next generation and become more common in the population.

Natural Selection Results in Adaptation

KEY TERM Adaptation is the process by which populations become more suited to their environment over several generations. It happens as a result of natural selection.

EXAMPLE: Imagine that all rabbits used to have short ears and managed OK. Then one day a rabbit was born with big ears who could hear better and so was always the first to hide from predators. Soon the big-eared rabbit had produced a whole family of rabbits with big ears — they all hid from predators before the other rabbits. After more time there were only big-eared rabbits left. The short-eared rabbits couldn't hear the predators coming quick enough.

Organisms that are better adapted to their environment survive

Natural selection needs variation in a population and something that causes a struggle for survival, such as competition for resources. Don't forget that successful reproduction is needed to complete the process.

Antibiotic Resistance

We can observe the process of natural selection happening in real time in bacteria.

Natural Selection May Result in New Strains of Bacteria

1) Like all organisms, bacteria sometimes develop random mutations in their DNA. These can create new alleles, which can change the bacteria's characteristics — e.g. a bacterium could become less affected by a particular antibiotic (a drug designed to kill bacteria or prevent them from reproducing — p.94).

'Bacterium' is singular and 'bacteria' is plural. So you can talk about a bacterium or multiple bacteria.

2) For the bacterium, the ability to resist this antibiotic is a big advantage in the 'struggle for survival'. In a person who's being treated to get rid of the infection, a resistant bacterium is better able to survive than a non-resistant bacterium — and so it lives for longer and reproduces many more times.

3) This leads to the allele for antibiotic resistance being passed on to lots of offspring — it's just natural selection. This is how it spreads and becomes more common in a population of bacteria over time. Eventually a new antibiotic-resistant strain of bacteria is created.

Variation in the population

Bacterium with antibiotic resistance allele

Bacterium without resistance allele

Bacteria exposed to antibiotic

Survival

Resistant bacteria are more likely to survive

Non-resistant bacteria die

Resistant bacteria reproduce and pass on resistance allele

Reproduction

Resistance allele becomes more common in the population

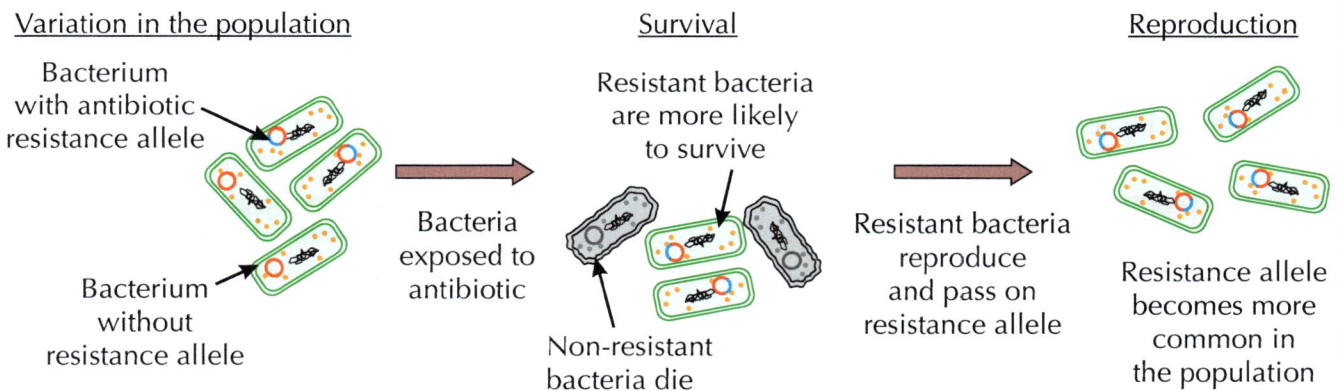

4) Antibiotic resistance shows adaptation taking place — over several generations, the bacterial population becomes better suited to an environment in which antibiotics are present.

See p.94 for more on antibiotic resistance.

Don't become resistant to revision...

REVISION TIP

A good way of testing whether you really know something is to try and teach it to someone else. Cover up this page and explain to a friend how natural selection produces strains of antibiotic-resistant bacteria. You'll soon find out whether you need to do some more revision.

Selective Breeding

'Selective breeding' sounds like it has the potential to be a tricky topic, but it's actually quite simple. You take the best plants or animals and breed them together to get the best possible offspring. That's it.

Selective Breeding is Very Simple

Selective breeding is when humans artificially select the plants or animals that are going to breed so that the frequency of the alleles for desired characteristics increases in a population. Organisms are selectively bred to develop features that are useful or attractive, for example:

- Animals that produce more meat or milk.
- Crops with disease resistance.
- Dogs that are well-behaved and gentle.
- Decorative plants with big or unusual flowers.

This is the basic process involved in selective breeding:

1) Select the plants or animals which have desirable features.
2) Cross them with each other to produce the next generation.
3) Select the offspring showing the desirable features, and cross them together.
4) Continue this process over several generations, and the desirable features become more and more common. Eventually, all the offspring will have those features.

> Selective breeding is also known as 'artificial selection'.

In agriculture (farming), selective breeding can be used to improve crop plants and farm animals. E.g. to increase the amount of meat produced, a farmer could breed together the cows and bulls with the best characteristics for producing meat, e.g. large size. By repeating this over generations the farmer would get cows that produce lots of meat.

Natural and Artificial Selection are Different

You might be able to think of some obvious differences between natural and artificial selection from what you've already read. But here are some differences that you need to know:

Artificial Selection

- The individuals that reproduce have characteristics that humans think are desirable.
- It's a faster process than natural selection.
- It only happens to the organisms humans choose.
- Artificial selection involves breeding from closely related organisms, which causes inbreeding — this is where variation in a population is reduced and individuals may be more likely to have genetic disorders.
- If a new disease appears, or the environment changes, the chances that the population will survive are lower for the offspring of artificially selected organisms because there's not much variation in the population.

Natural Selection

- The individuals that survive and reproduce have characteristics that suit their environment.
- It's a long and slow process.
- It happens to all wild organisms.
- Individuals are 'healthier' because they are less likely to be inbred.
- The chances of survival are increased for the population of offspring because there's more variation in the population.

Supplement

Selective breeding is just breeding the best to get the best...

Different breeds of dog came from selective breeding. For example, somebody thought 'I really like this small, yappy wolf — I'll breed it with this other one'. After thousands of generations, we got poodles.

Warm-Up & Exam Questions

That's the end of this section — have a go at these questions to see how much you know.

Warm-Up Questions

1) What is variation?
2) Give an example of a characteristic that shows discontinuous variation.
3) State how new alleles arise in a population.
4) What sort of conditions are xerophytes adapted to?

Exam Questions

1   The penguin shown on the right lives in Antarctica, where the temperature is very cold. It moves between the land and the sea.

Give **one** adaptive feature of the penguin and briefly suggest how it allows it to survive and reproduce in its environment.

[Total 2 marks]

2   The characteristics of two varieties of wheat plants are shown in the table below.

Variety	Grain yield	Resistance to bad weather
Tall stems	High	Low
Dwarf stems	Low	High

Selective breeding is used to create a wheat plant with a high grain yield and high resistance to bad weather. Choose words from the list to complete the sentences about this process. Each word may be used once, more than once or not at all.

increases   tall   lowest   stronger   highest   dwarf   weaker   decreases

A tall stem plant and a .... stem plant could be bred together. The offspring with the

.... grain yield and .... resistance to bad weather could then be bred together.

Repeating this over several generations means the frequency of the desirable features ....

[Total 4 marks]

3   Explain **two** ways in which hydrophytes are adapted to their environment.

[Total 4 marks]

4   The image on the right shows a type of stingray. The stingray's appearance mimics a flat rock. It spends most of its time on a rocky seabed.

Explain how natural selection might have caused the stingray to look like this.

[Total 6 marks]

Revision Summary for Sections 13 & 14

So you've finished Sections 13 and 14 — time to do some questions to test your knowledge.
- Try these questions and tick off each one when you get it right.
- When you've done all the questions for a topic and are completely happy with it, tick off the topic.

Chromosomes and Sex Inheritance (p.111) ☐

1) What is a gene?

2) What is an allele?

3) A couple have a child.
   What's the probability that the child will have the XX combination of sex chromosomes?

4) How many pairs of chromosomes are there in a human diploid cell?

Protein Synthesis, Mitosis and Meiosis (p.112-113) ☐

5) What happens at the ribosomes during protein synthesis?

6) a) Name the type of cell division used in asexual reproduction.
   b) Apart from asexual reproduction, what else is this type of cell division used for?

7) What happens to the chromosomes in a cell before mitosis takes place?

8) State the type of cell division used to make gametes in humans.

Inheritance and Genetic Diagrams (p.115-119) ☑

9) What does it mean if an organism is: a) homozygous for a gene? b) heterozygous for a gene?

10) True or False? A heterozygous individual will be pure-breeding.

11) Explain how a test cross can be used to identify an unknown genotype.

12) Why are men more likely to show recessive characteristics that are sex-linked?

13) What is codominance?

14) What blood group does an individual have if they have the genotype $I^B I^O$?

Variation (p.121-122) ☐

15) What type of variation results in a range of phenotypes between two extremes?

16) Is body mass usually controlled by genes, the environment or both?

17) How can the rate of mutation be increased?

18) Apart from mutations, list three sources of genetic variation.

Adaptive Features, Natural Selection and Selective Breeding (p.123-126) ☐

19) What is an adaptive feature?

20) Describe the process of natural selection.

21) What is the process of adaptation?

22) Describe how bacteria can become resistant to antibiotics.

23) What is selective breeding?

24) How might farmers use selective breeding?

25) State two differences between natural and artificial selection.

Food Chains and Food Webs

Food chains and food webs are a way of representing feeding relationships between organisms.

Food Chains Show the Transfer of Energy Between Organisms

1) Food chains always start with a producer, e.g. a plant. Producers make (produce) their own organic nutrients (food), usually using energy from the Sun during photosynthesis.
2) Energy is then transferred through the ecosystem when organisms are eaten (ingested).
3) Consumers are organisms that get energy by feeding on other organisms. Producers are eaten by primary consumers. Primary consumers are then eaten by secondary consumers and secondary consumers are eaten by tertiary consumers. Tertiary consumers are eaten by quaternary consumers.
4) All these organisms eventually die and get ingested by decomposers, e.g. bacteria. Decomposers get energy by breaking down (decomposing) dead material and waste.

Here's an example of a food chain:

The arrows show the direction of energy flow.

Producers	Primary consumers	Secondary consumer
5000 dandelions...	feed... 100 rabbits...	which feed... 1 fox.

5) In the food chain above, the rabbits are herbivores — this means they get their energy by eating plants. Carnivores, e.g. foxes, are animals that get their energy by eating other animals.
6) The position an organism occupies in a food chain, food web or ecological pyramid (see next page) is called a trophic level.
7) You may be asked to construct a simple food chain in your exam or to interpret a food chain or food web (see below).

A Food Web is a Network of Interconnected Food Chains

1) There are many different species within an environment — which means lots of different possible food chains that are all interconnected. You can draw a food web to show this. For example:

PART OF A FOOD WEB FROM A STREAM

Pike, Frog, Stickleback, Diving beetle, Waterboatman, Water spider, Stonefly larvae, Blackfly larvae, Mayfly larvae, Algae

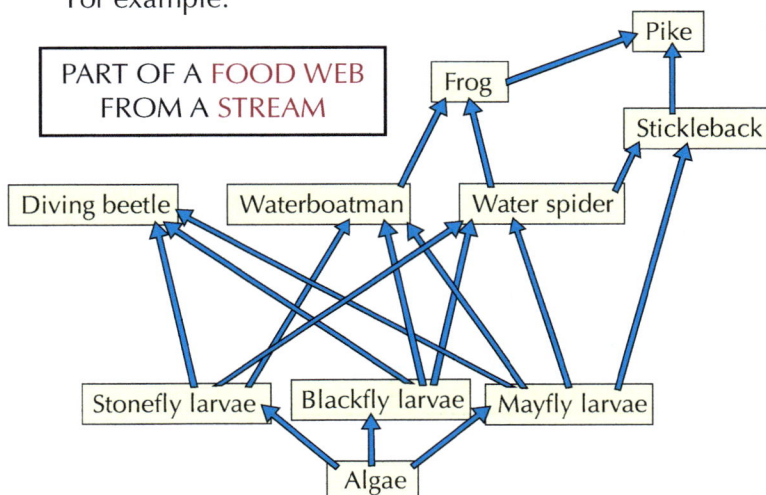

The algae are the producers in this food web. Stonefly, blackfly and mayfly larvae are all primary consumers, frogs and sticklebacks are tertiary consumers, etc.

2) If one species changes in a food web, it affects all the others. In this food web, if lots of water spiders died, then:

- There would be less food for the frogs, so their numbers might decrease.
- The number of mayfly larvae might increase since the water spiders wouldn't be eating them.
- The diving beetles wouldn't be competing with the water spiders for food, so their numbers might increase.

3) Organisms in a food web can feed at more than one trophic level (e.g. they might be both a secondary and a tertiary consumer).

Ecological Pyramids

Food chains can be represented visually with ecological pyramids.

You Need to Understand Pyramids of Numbers

Here's a pyramid of numbers for the dandelions, rabbits and fox food chain on the previous page.

A pyramid of numbers is one type of ecological pyramid. A pyramid of biomass (see below) is another.

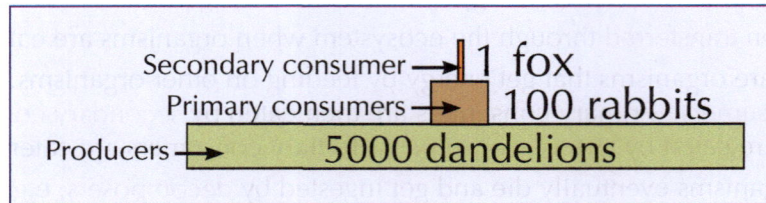

Secondary consumer → 1 fox
Primary consumers → 100 rabbits
Producers → 5000 dandelions

1) Each bar on a pyramid of numbers shows the number of organisms at a particular trophic level in the food chain.

2) So the 'dandelions' bar on this pyramid would need to be longer than the 'rabbits' bar, which in turn should be longer than the 'fox' bar.

3) Dandelions go at the bottom because they're at the bottom of the food chain.

4) This is a typical pyramid of numbers, where every time you go up a level, the number of organisms goes down. This is because it takes a lot of food from the level below to keep one animal alive.

Pyramids of Biomass Show the Relative Masses of Trophic Levels

1) Sometimes pyramids of numbers are not shaped like true pyramids (the bars don't always get progressively smaller from the bottom to the top).

2) This happens when an organism in a food chain is much bigger than the organism that eats it. For example, in the food chain above, there could be 500 fleas feeding on the one fox — the number of organisms would therefore increase when you moved up to the next trophic level.

3) This means that a pyramid of numbers doesn't always represent what's happening in a food chain very well. Often a better way to look at the food chain is to think about biomass instead.

4) Biomass is the mass of living material in a food chain — it's a store of energy.

5) Pyramids of biomass are almost always pyramid-shaped:

- Each bar on a pyramid of biomass shows the relative mass of living material at a trophic level — basically how much all the organisms at each level would "weigh" if you put them all together.

- So the one fox above would have a big biomass and the hundreds of fleas would have a very small biomass. The pyramid of biomass would look like this:

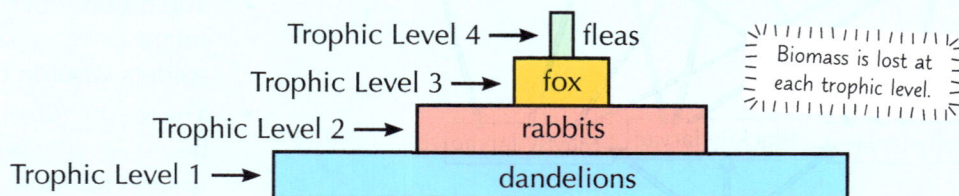

Trophic Level 4 → fleas
Trophic Level 3 → fox
Trophic Level 2 → rabbits
Trophic Level 1 → dandelions

Biomass is lost at each trophic level.

- The big bar along the bottom of the pyramid shows trophic level 1. It always represents the producer (e.g. plants or algae).

- The next bar will be the primary consumer (trophic level 2), then the secondary consumer (trophic level 3) and so on up the food chain.

More on Ecological Pyramids

We've not finished with ecological pyramids just yet, so keep reading...

Pyramids of Energy Model Energy Transfer in a Food Chain

1) There are actually a couple of exceptions where pyramids of biomass aren't quite pyramid-shaped, or where the pyramid is upside down.

2) This can happen when the producer has a very short life but reproduces a lot — for example, plankton at certain times of year.

There's more on energy transfer in a food chain on the next page.

3) At any one point in time, the tiny plankton have a small biomass (store of energy). However, because they reproduce very quickly, they can transfer energy to the next trophic level at a very high rate.

4) This can be shown using a pyramid of energy — these usually show the rate of energy transfer between trophic levels, rather than the amount of energy stored at each trophic level.

5) Pyramids of energy therefore allow the efficiency with which different food chains transfer energy to be directly compared. Using a pyramid of biomass to do this might be misleading.

6) Pyramids of energy show that the majority of energy present at one trophic level will not be available to the next (see next page). They are always shaped like a true pyramid and the pyramid is always the right way up.

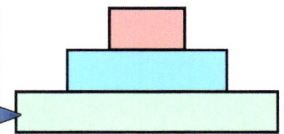

Make Sure You Can Draw Ecological Pyramids

1) If you're given numbers, or figures for biomass or energy transfer, you can use them to draw bars of the correct scale.

If you're studying the Core course, you only need to be able to draw pyramids of numbers and biomass.

2) Don't forget that the order of organisms in the pyramid must follow the order of the food chain (starting with the producer).

3) Each bar must also be labelled. If you've been given units for biomass or the rate of energy transfer, you should include them.

EXAM TIP

Use a sharp pencil and a ruler to draw pyramids

If you need to draw an ecological pyramid to scale in the exam, you may be given a grid or graph paper to draw it on. You'll need to work out a sensible scale to use — think about how easy your diagram will be to draw and interpret (something like '5 small squares on the grid = 1 kg of biomass' might work) and make sure that your pyramid takes up at least half the space available.

Supplement

Energy Flow

Some organisms get their energy from the Sun and some get it from other organisms.

Energy is Transferred Along a Food Chain

1) The Sun is the source of energy for nearly all life on Earth.

2) Plants use light energy from the Sun to make glucose during photosynthesis. They then use some of this glucose to make biomass — a store of chemical energy. This chemical energy gets transferred to other organisms in the food chain when animals eat the plants and each other.

Animals also use some of their food to produce biomass.

3) Biomass and energy are lost at each trophic level in the food chain.

4) Some parts of food, e.g. roots or bones, aren't eaten by organisms so the energy isn't taken in. Some parts of food are indigestible (e.g. fibre) so pass through organisms and come out as waste, e.g. faeces.

5) A lot of the energy that does get taken in is used for staying alive, i.e. in respiration (see page 72), which powers all life processes.

ENERGY LOST AS HEAT

MATERIALS LOST IN ANIMALS' WASTE

6) Most of this energy is eventually transferred to the environment as heat.

7) Only around 10% of the total energy available to a trophic level becomes biomass, i.e. it's stored or used for growth. The other 90% is lost in the ways described above, making the transfer of energy between trophic levels very inefficient.

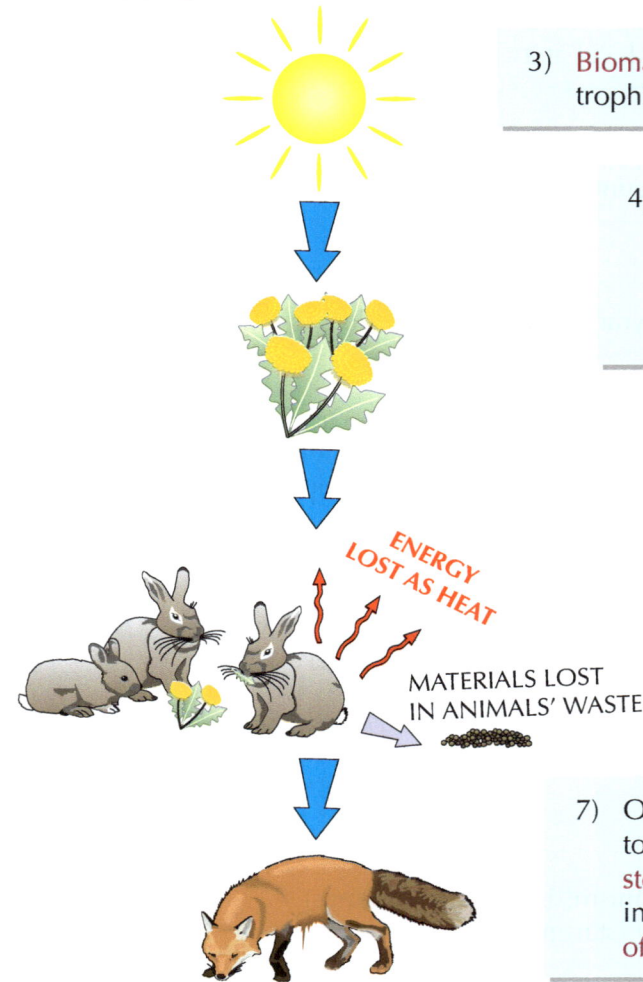

Supplement

8) This explains why you hardly ever get food chains with more than about five trophic levels. So much energy is lost at each stage that there's not enough left to support more organisms after four or five stages. You also tend to get fewer organisms at each trophic level (although this isn't always the case).

Supplement

The organisms at the top of a food chain with five trophic levels are called quaternary consumers.

Food chains rely on the Sun for energy

Most of the energy from the producers doesn't make it up to the top of the food chain. If you're doing the Extended course, you need to make sure you know the different reasons why energy is lost.

Humans and Food Webs

Looking at food chains and food webs can help us to understand how human activities affect habitats.

Humans Impact Food Webs Through Overharvesting

1) Overharvesting is when people take so much of an organism that its population is unable to reproduce quickly enough to keep up, and the population size falls. Eventually, this can lead to extinction.

2) When one species is overharvested, the other species connected to it in the food web are all affected.

> Overfishing is a type of overharvesting. For example, there used to be a lot of cod in the Grand Banks area of the Atlantic Ocean, but their numbers had dropped significantly by the 1990s due to overfishing. Cod are consumers in several different food chains, so the disappearance of so many led to a huge increase in the populations of species that the cod used to feed on, such as shrimp and crab.

Introducing Foreign Species to a Habitat Affects Food Webs

1) A foreign species is one that doesn't naturally occur in an area. They can be introduced intentionally (e.g. for food or hunting) or unintentionally (e.g. accidentally on a ship).

2) Introducing a foreign species to a food web may affect the populations already in the habitat. E.g.:

Cane toads were introduced to Australia in the 1930s, to eat beetles that were damaging crops. ⟹ Water monitors (a type of lizard in Australia) ate the cane toads. They were poisoned by chemicals in the toads and died. ⟹ The water monitor population fell, which led to an increase in the crimson finch population, as fewer of them were eaten by water monitors.

Plants are a More Efficient Source of Human Food than Animals

1) Because energy is lost at each trophic level in a food chain (see previous page), it is more efficient for humans to eat plants than to eat animals.

2) For example, if you were to eat meat from a pig that had been fed on vegetables, you would be higher up the food chain than if you were eating the vegetables themselves. This means that less of the energy originally in the vegetable plants would reach you, because there would be an extra trophic level between you and the plants (in which energy is lost):

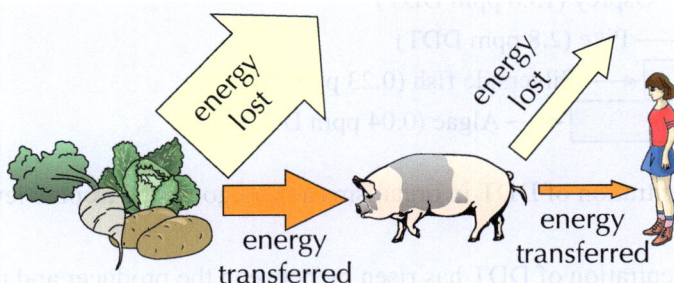

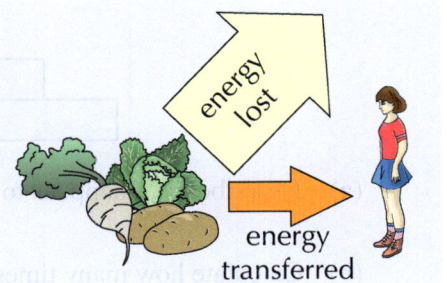

3) So, farming crops to directly feed humans is a lot more efficient than farming crops to feed livestock (farm animals) that are then used to feed humans.

Supplement

The whole food web can be affected when a species is added or lost

As well as being at the top of many food chains, humans have disturbed natural food webs in a number of ways — e.g. through farming, fishing, and introducing species to areas where they didn't previously exist.

Warm-Up & Exam Questions

Right, now you've got to grips with how energy is transferred through a food chain, have a go at these practice questions. If there's anything you're struggling with, go back and read that bit again.

Warm-Up Questions

1) What is the word for an organism that makes its own organic nutrients?
2) What is meant by the term herbivore? What is a carnivore?
3) What is a trophic level?
4) Why do you hardly ever get food chains with more than five trophic levels?

Exam Questions

1 The diagram shows part of a food web from Nebraska, USA. The flowerhead weevil is not native to this area. It was introduced by farmers to eat the musk thistle, which is a weed.

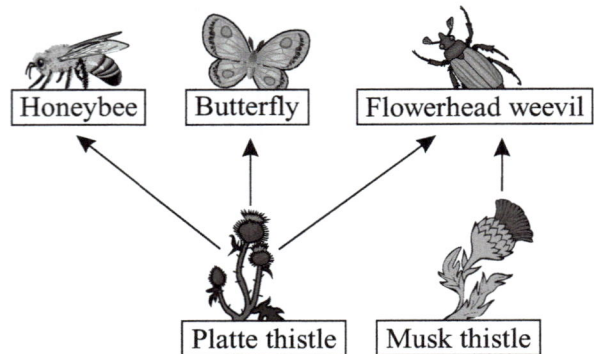

(a) Explain how the introduction of the flowerhead weevil could affect the amount of wild honey produced in the area.

[2]

(b) When the organisms in the food web above die, they are broken down by microorganisms. What name is given to the organisms that break down dead material?

[1]

[Total 3 marks]

2 In the 1950s a chemical called DDT was used to control insect pests. DDT was later discovered to be toxic to other animals and was detected at very high levels in the tissues of organisms across food chains. The pyramid of biomass below shows the concentration of DDT in the tissues of organisms at each trophic level in parts per million (ppm).

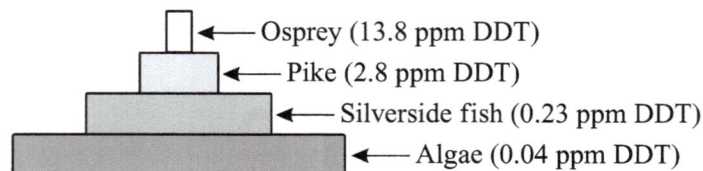

(a) Describe what happens to the concentration of DDT in organisms as you go up the trophic levels.

[1]

(b) Calculate how many times the concentration of DDT has risen by between the producer and the tertiary consumer. Show your working.

[2]

(c) Suggest why a pyramid of biomass is a suitable diagram for displaying the problem with DDT.

[1]

[Total 4 marks]

The Carbon Cycle

All the nutrients in our environment are constantly being recycled — it's all about balance.

Materials are Constantly Recycled in an Ecosystem

1) Living things are made of materials they take from the world around them. E.g. plants turn elements like carbon, oxygen, hydrogen and nitrogen from the soil and the air into the complex compounds (carbohydrates, proteins and fats) that make up living organisms. These get passed up the food chain.
2) These materials are returned to the environment in waste products, or when the organisms die.
3) Dead or waste organic material is broken down (decomposed) — usually by microorganisms.
4) Decomposition puts the stuff that plants need to grow (e.g. mineral ions) back into the soil.

The Constant Cycling of Carbon is called the Carbon Cycle

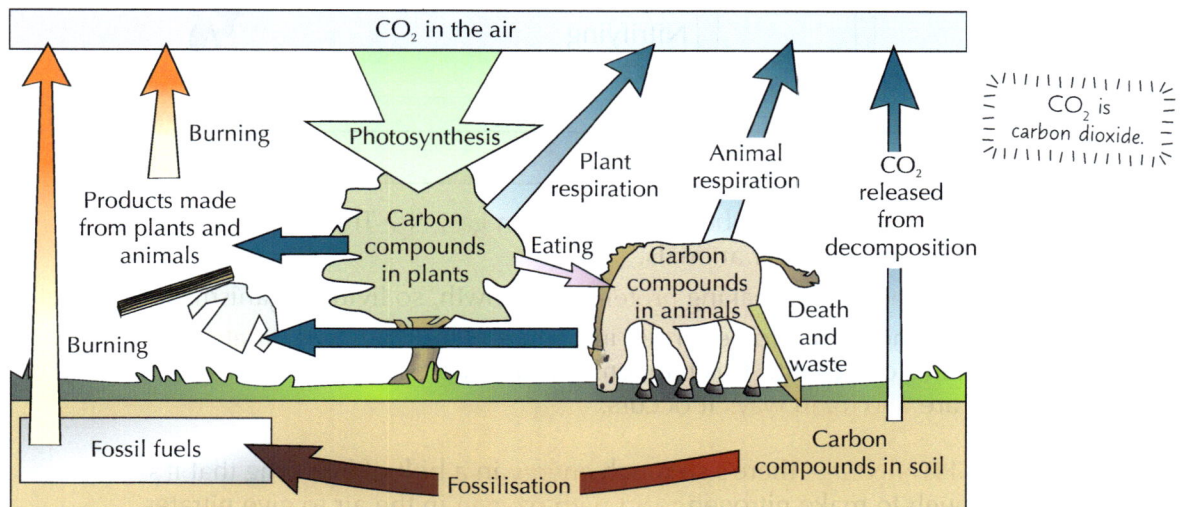

That can look a bit complicated at first, but it's actually pretty simple:

1) CO_2 is removed from the atmosphere by green plants and algae during photosynthesis. The carbon is used to make glucose, which can be turned into carbohydrates, fats and proteins that make up the bodies of the plants and algae.
2) When the plants and algae respire, some carbon is returned to the atmosphere as CO_2.
3) When the plants and algae are eaten by animals, some carbon becomes part of the fats and proteins in their bodies. The carbon then moves through the food chain.
4) When the animals respire, some carbon is returned to the atmosphere as CO_2.
5) When plants, algae and animals die, decomposers feed on their remains. Decomposers can be types of animal (detritus feeders) or microorganisms. When these organisms respire, CO_2 is returned to the atmosphere.
6) Animals also produce waste that is broken down by decomposers.
7) Not all dead organic material decomposes — some dead organisms have been compressed over millions of years, forming fossil fuels (coal, oil and natural gas).
8) The combustion (burning) of wood and fossil fuels also releases CO_2 back into the air.
9) So the carbon (and energy) is constantly being cycled — from the air, through food chains (via plants, algae and animals, and decomposers) and eventually back out into the air again.

The Nitrogen Cycle

Nitrogen, just like carbon, is constantly being recycled. So the nitrogen in your proteins might once have been in the air. And before that it might have been in a plant. Or even in some horse urine. Nice.

Nitrogen is Recycled in the Nitrogen Cycle

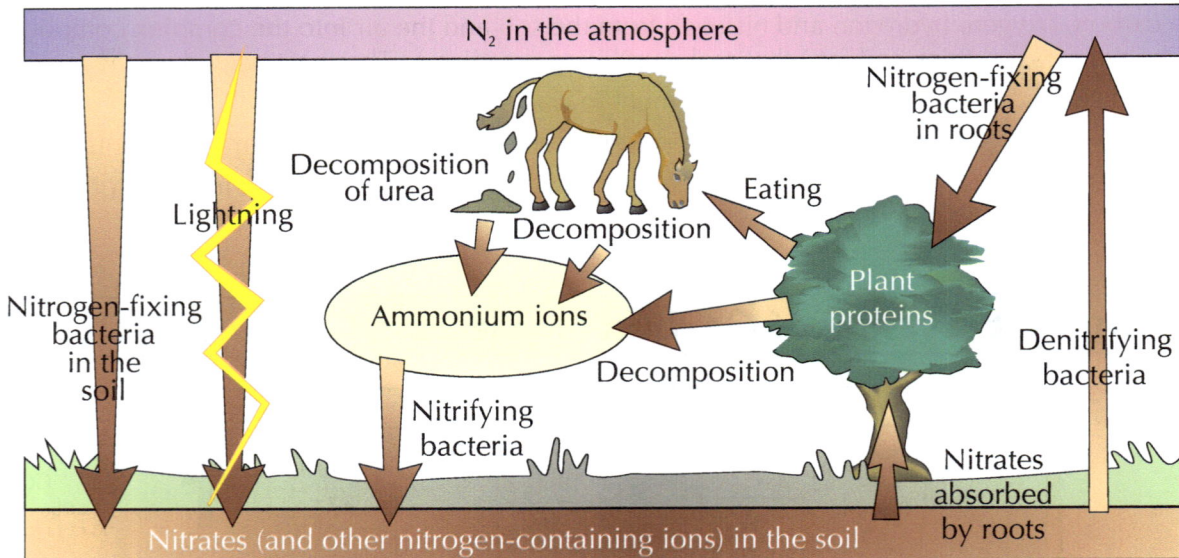

N_2 in the atmosphere

Nitrogen-fixing bacteria in roots

Decomposition of urea

Lightning

Decomposition

Eating

Plant proteins

Nitrogen-fixing bacteria in the soil

Ammonium ions

Denitrifying bacteria

Decomposition

Nitrifying bacteria

Nitrates absorbed by roots

Nitrates (and other nitrogen-containing ions) in the soil

1) The atmosphere contains about 78% nitrogen gas, N_2. This is very unreactive and so it can't be used directly by plants or animals.

2) Nitrogen is needed for making proteins for growth, so living organisms have to get it somehow.

3) Nitrogen in the air has to be turned into mineral ions, such as nitrate ions (NO_3^-), in the soil before plants can use it. This happens through a process called nitrogen fixation — there are two main ways it occurs:

   a) LIGHTNING — there's so much energy in a bolt of lightning that it's enough to make nitrogen react with oxygen in the air to give nitrates.

   b) NITROGEN-FIXING BACTERIA in soil and the roots of some plants (see below).

   Compounds containing nitrate ions are called nitrates.

4) Plants absorb these ions from the soil and use the nitrogen in them to produce amino acids, which join together to make proteins.

5) Nitrogen is then passed along food chains in the form of proteins, as animals eat plants (and each other). When the proteins are digested, they are converted back into amino acids (see p.45).

6) In animals, excess amino acids are broken down in the liver in a process called deamination. Ammonia (a nitrogen compound, NH_3) is a waste product from this process, which gets converted to urea and excreted. The urea is then decomposed and nitrogen ions are eventually returned to the soil.

7) There are four different types of microorganisms involved in the nitrogen cycle:

   a) DECOMPOSERS — break down proteins (in rotting plants and animals) and urea (in animal waste) and turn them into ammonia. This forms ammonium ions (NH_4^+) in the soil.

   b) NITRIFYING BACTERIA — turn ammonium ions in decaying matter into nitrite ions (NO_2^-) and then nitrates. This process is called nitrification.

   c) NITROGEN-FIXING BACTERIA — turn atmospheric N_2 into nitrogen compounds that plants can use (e.g. ammonia).

   When ammonia is dissolved in water, ammonium ions are formed.

   d) DENITRIFYING BACTERIA — turn nitrates back into N_2 gas (denitrification). This is of no benefit to living organisms (other than the denitrifying bacteria themselves).

Most of these bacteria live in the soil. Some nitrogen-fixing bacteria live in nodules (swellings) on plant roots.

Population Sizes

Over time, the sizes of populations might increase, decrease, or remain stable.

Here are Some Terms You Need to Know

KEY TERM

Term	Definition
Population	A group of organisms of one species living in the same place at the same time.
Community	All the populations of different species living in an ecosystem.
Ecosystem	A unit containing a community and its environment, interacting together.

Population Growth Rate is Affected by Several Factors

The rate at which population size increases or decreases depends on various factors, including:

Food supply

1) If more food is available, a population is likely to grow.
2) E.g. during a year when plants produce an unusually high number of berries, the population of blackbirds might increase because there'll be enough food for all of them, so they're more likely to survive and reproduce.

Disease

1) The presence of pathogens (disease-causing organisms — see p.63) in the environment affects a population's growth rate.
2) E.g. if a new pathogen is introduced then a population may decrease in size due to illness.

Predation

1) Consumers that hunt and kill other animals are called predators. Their prey are what they eat.
2) If the population of prey increases, then it's likely that the population of predators will too. For example, if the number of gazelles (prey) increases then the number of lions (predators) is also likely to increase because there are more gazelles available to be eaten by the lions.
3) As the predator population increases, it's likely that the number of prey will decrease. E.g. its likely that more lions will eat more gazelles, causing the gazelle population to decrease.
4) It takes time for one population to respond to changes in the other population, so predator-prey cycles are always out of phase with each other.

A peak in prey numbers is followed by a peak in predator numbers.

Population / Prey / Predator / Time

5) Population sizes often start to increase slowly. The rate of increase then gets faster as the number of organisms reproducing increases.
6) If the predator population was removed, the population size of the prey would increase until the number of prey reached the maximum the environment could support. The prey population would then level off or start to decrease.

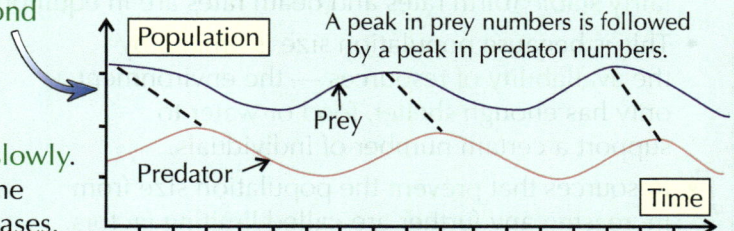

The population size may temporarily overshoot the maxiumum the environment can support, then decrease as food starts to run out.

Competition

1) Organisms compete for the resources they need to survive and reproduce. Plants compete for light, space, water and mineral ions. Animals compete for space, food, water and mates.
2) The presence of competitors affects population size. E.g. if a new species is introduced to an area it may out-compete existing populations, reducing their population size.

Section 15 — Organisms and Their Environment

Population Growth

Populations don't just grow at the same rate over time — their growth tends to follow a standard pattern.

Learn the **Phases** of the **Sigmoid Curve of Population Growth**

1) If a population were to have an unlimited supply of the resources it needs (e.g. water, nutrients) then it would grow exponentially (more and more rapidly).

2) However, populations usually exist in an environment with limited resources, where population growth tends to take the shape of a sigmoid curve ('sigmoid' means 's'-shaped).

3) There are four phases to the curve:

Lag phase

- The population size is increasing slowly.
- At the beginning, there are just a few individuals, so the rate of reproduction is low.

Exponential (log) phase

- There are an increasing number of individuals reproducing, so the population size increases more and more quickly.
- There are plenty of resources available for the number of individuals. The population is able to rapidly reproduce, as the environment has enough resources to support more individuals.

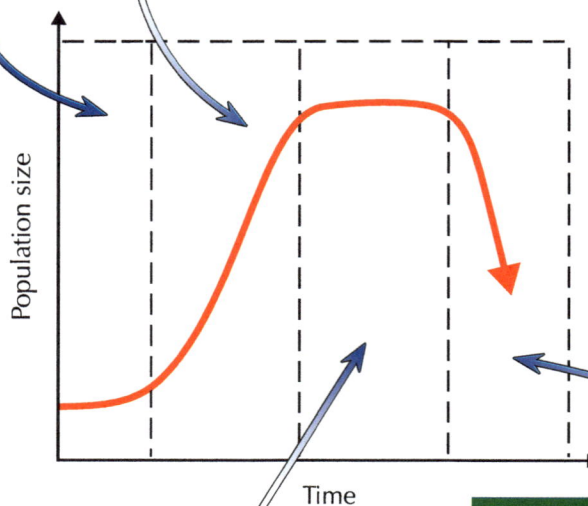

Stationary phase

- Eventually, the population size levels off and stays fairly stable (birth rates and death rates are in equilibrium).
- This is because population size is limited by the availability of resources — the environment only has enough shelter, food or water to support a certain number of individuals.
- Resources that prevent the population size from increasing any further are called limiting factors.
- During the stationary phase, the population reaches the carrying capacity (the maximum population size that the environment can support).

Death phase

- Some populations have a phase where the rate at which individuals are dying is faster than the reproductive rate, and the population size drops.
- This might happen because the population has used up so many of the resources that the environment can no longer support it. Waste products can also build up to toxic levels, e.g. in populations of microorganisms.

EXAM TIP

The population growth curve levels off due to limited resouces

Don't get put off if you get a population graph in the exam and it doesn't match this exactly. The stationary phase is usually actually quite a wobbly line, as the population rises slightly above and below a certain level — just look for part of the graph where there's no overall growth or decline.

Warm-Up & Exam Questions

You can't just stare at these pages and expect it all to go in. Have a go at these questions to see how well you really know the two nutrient cycles, and the factors affecting population growth.

Warm-Up Questions

1) Describe the role of lightning in the nitrogen cycle.
2) Describe the effect of decomposers on proteins in dead plant and animal matter.
3) What is a population?
4) What is an ecosystem?

Exam Questions

1   Carbon is constantly being recycled. The diagram below shows some of the processes occurring in the carbon cycle.

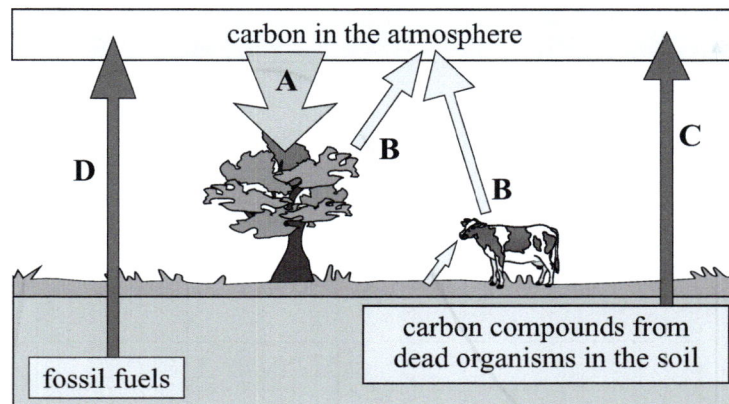

(a)   (i)   Name the process, labelled **A**, that removes carbon from the atmosphere.

[1]

(ii) Name the gas in which carbon is removed from the atmosphere by process **A**.

[1]

(b)   Name the process, labelled **B**, by which all living organisms return carbon to the atmosphere.

[1]

(c)   Explain how carbon is released from dead organisms in the soil (process **C**).

[2]

(d)   (i)   Explain why fossil fuels contain carbon.

[1]

(ii) Describe how the carbon from fossil fuels is released back into the atmosphere (process **D**).

[1]

[Total 7 marks]

2   Several different types of bacteria are involved in the nitrogen cycle. Which bacteria convert nitrogen in the atmosphere into nitrogen compounds that plants can use?

☐ **A** nitrifying   ☐ **B** denitrifying   ☐ **C** nitrogen-fixing   ☐ **D** decomposers

[Total 1 mark]

Exam Questions

3   Walruses are a predator of clams. Which **one** of the following statements describes how the population sizes of walruses and clams are likely to be related to one another?

☐   **A**   If the walrus population increases, the clam population will then increase.

☐   **B**   If the walrus population decreases, the clam population will then decrease.

☐   **C**   If the clam population increases, the walrus population will then increase.

☐   **D**   If the clam population decreases, the walrus population will then increase.

[Total 1 mark]

4   A population of microorganisms was grown in a liquid culture medium under constant conditions. The graph below shows how the size of the population changed over time.

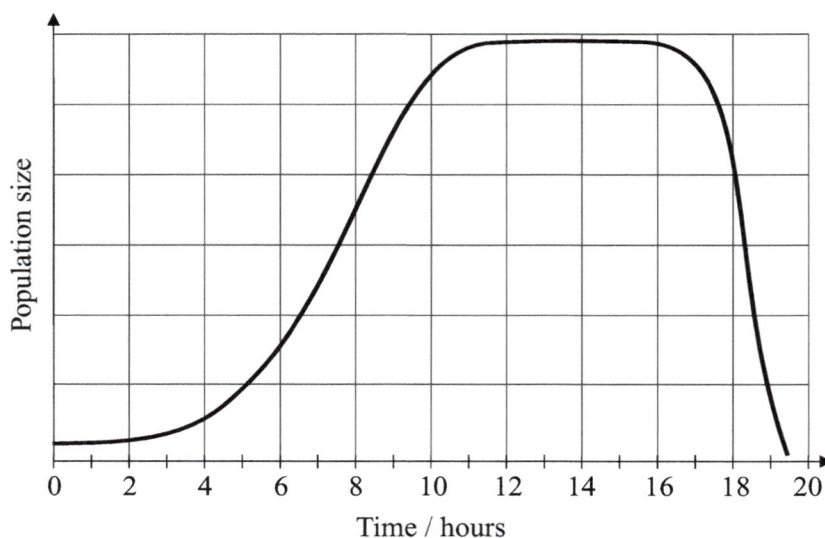

(a)   State which phase of the sigmoid curve the population was in at:

(i)   2 hours.

[1]

(ii) 7 hours.

[1]

(iii) 12 hours.

[1]

(b)   Suggest why the rate of population change at 12 hours was different to that at 7 hours.

[2]

(c)   Explain one reason for the change in population size between 16 and 19.5 hours.

[2]

[Total 7 marks]

Revision Summary for Section 15

Sections 15 is now complete. Now would be a great time to figure out what you do and don't know.
- Try these questions and tick off each one when you get it right.
- When you've done all the questions for a topic and are completely happy with it, tick off the topic.

Food Chains, Food Webs and Ecological Pyramids (p.129-131) ☐
1) What is a food chain? ☐
2) How is energy transferred between organisms in a food chain? ☐
3) What is a food web? ☐
4) What does a pyramid of numbers show? ☐
5) Why might it be better to draw a pyramid of biomass to represent a food chain instead of a pyramid of numbers? ☐
6) Why might it be better to draw a pyramid of energy to represent a food chain instead of a pyramid of biomass? ☐

Energy Flow, Humans and Food Webs (p.132-133) ☐
7) Give one way in which energy is lost from a food chain. ☐
8) How can overharvesting affect food webs? ☐
9) How can introducing a foreign species to an area negatively affect food webs? ☐
10) Why are plants a more efficient source of human food than animals? ☐

Nutrient Cycles (p.135-136) ☐
11) Name three processes that return carbon to the atmosphere. ☐
12) What are fossil fuels? ☐
13) What role do nitrifying bacteria play in the nitrogen cycle? ☐
14) Name two types of nitrogen-containing ion in the nitrogen cycle. ☐

Ecosystems and Populations (p.137-138) ☐
15) What name is given to all the organisms of different species living in an ecosystem? ☐
16) How does competition affect the growth of a population? ☐
17) Give three other factors that affect the growth of a population. ☐
18) What's happening in the lag phase of a sigmoid curve of population growth? ☐

Food Production

Maintaining our food supply is important — there are more than 7 billion people on our planet to feed.

Humans have Increased Food Production

Farms and gardens supply a lot of the food that we eat. Humans have increased the amount of food that can be produced. For example:

Agricultural Machinery

1) Agricultural machinery includes tractors and combine harvesters.
2) This machinery can be used instead of manual labour (people) and working animals.
3) Using machinery is quicker and more efficient than manual labour and means that crops can be grown and harvested over larger areas of land.

Chemical Fertilisers

1) Plants need certain mineral ions (see page 39).
2) If they don't get enough mineral ions, their growth can be affected.
3) Sometimes these ions are missing from the soil because they've been used up by a previous crop planted in the same soil.
4) Farmers use chemical fertilisers to replace these missing ions or to provide more of them. This helps to improve crop yields by boosting plant growth.

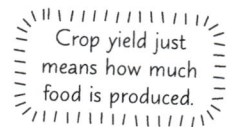

Crop yield just means how much food is produced.

Insecticides

1) Insects that eat or damage crops can be killed using insecticides.
2) These are chemicals that are sprayed onto crops by farmers.
3) They kill the insects without killing the actual crop.
4) This means that fewer plants are damaged or destroyed by insects, which increases crop quality and yield.

Herbicides

1) Herbicides are chemicals that can be sprayed around crops to kill weeds.
2) This means that crop plants face less competition from weeds for nutrients, water and light.
3) This increases the quality and yield of crop plants.

Selective Breeding

1) Humans use selective breeding (p.126) to improve crops and livestock.
2) This includes cattle (cows), fish and poultry that are larger and produce more meat, and crop plants that grow faster and are disease-resistant.

Food Production

Modern farming methods have both advantages and disadvantages.

Monoculture Means Growing a Single Crop Species

A monoculture is where a single crop species is grown at one time on a large area of land.
It has advantages and disadvantages over more traditional farming methods,
in which a variety of crops are grown side by side.

Advantages

1) It's more efficient — all the plants are planted, taken care of and harvested in the same way, using the same chemicals and machinery. This makes it easier to manage the crops and is more cost-effective too.

2) All of this results in higher yields from the same area of land, which means more food and a greater profit for farmers.

3) It also means that the food produced is cheaper for the people buying it (consumers).

Disadvantages

1) Genetic variation amongst the crop is low, so if there's a pest or disease that affects the species, it could kill all of the crop being grown.

2) Farmers use a lot of pesticides (chemicals that kill pests) to stop this from happening. Excess pesticides can be washed into water and pollute the freshwater environment. They can also kill beneficial insects, and build up in food chains.

3) Monocultures can also reduce biodiversity (p.144) because they contain fewer plant species than a natural ecosystem. Having fewer plant species means they don't provide habitats (see next page) for as many organisms.

Intensive Livestock Production Aims to Maximise Meat Yield

Intensive livestock production involves limiting the movement of animals (e.g. pigs and chickens) and keeping them in a temperature-controlled environment. This has advantages and disadvantages over 'free-range' farming methods, which allow animals to roam more widely and forage for food.

Advantages

1) The animals use less energy moving around and controlling their own body temperature, so they have more energy available for growth, and so more meat can be produced.

2) Keeping the animals in a confined space makes it easier for the farmer to monitor the animals and protect them from predators.

3) Again, all of this means a greater profit for the farmer and cheaper food for the consumer.

Disadvantages

1) Waste from the livestock can build up, meaning that diseases can spread easily between animals. The waste can run into water sources and pollute them (see p.146).

2) The chemicals used to treat diseases, like antibiotics, can also pollute the environment.

3) Producing feed for animals raised in this way is inefficient. It is more efficient to farm crops that are used to feed humans directly (see page 133).

4) Some people have ethical objections to this farming method, as they think that making animals live in unnatural and uncomfortable conditions is cruel.

Intensive livestock production is sometimes called 'factory farming'.

There are pros and cons to all farming methods...

Monoculture and intensive livestock farming allow more (and cheaper) food to be produced from the same area of land. But they can both have serious negative consequences for the environment.

Habitat Destruction

Human activities destroy many different kinds of habitats and have many undesirable effects.

Habitats are Destroyed for Different Reasons

1) A habitat is a place where an organism lives.
2) Human activities can have a negative impact on habitats by affecting food webs and chains. E.g. if a predator is removed, its prey may increase in numbers and destroy the habitat by consuming more vegetation (trees or plants).
3) Habitat destruction can also negatively affect food webs. E.g. if habitat destruction causes the numbers of a prey species to decrease, predator numbers may decrease too.
4) Many human activities destroy habitats. For example:

- As the human population increases, more habitats are being destroyed to increase the area of land available for crop plant growth, livestock production and housing.
- Habitats are often destroyed during the extraction of natural resources. For example, the extraction of fossil fuels often requires road and pipeline construction which breaks up and destroys habitats. Extracting wood involves cutting down trees (see below).
- Cities and factories create waste that is often dumped in rivers and ends up in the sea. This causes both freshwater and marine pollution that can harm aquatic environments.

Deforestation is an Example of Habitat Destruction

1) Deforestation is the clearing of forests.
2) The effects of deforestation can have a big impact on the environment:

Effect	Explanation
Loss of biodiversity	Biodiversity is the number of different species that live in an area. Forest habitats can contain a wide variety of different plant and animal species, so they often have a high biodiversity. When these habitats are destroyed, the species that live in them will die or move away, reducing biodiversity in the area.
Extinction	There is a danger that some species could die out completely if they can't find, or are unable to move to, other suitable habitats. This is known as extinction (see p.151).
Loss of soil	When trees are removed, there are no roots to stabilise the soil during heavy rain. Soil is easily washed away and nutrients are lost. This makes it harder for new trees to grow later.
Flooding	Trees slow down rain as it falls because the rain hits leaves first. The water is then more gradually absorbed by the soil then the roots. Without trees, flooding is more likely. Flooding can destroy habitats and kill wildlife.
Increase of carbon dioxide in the atmosphere	Photosynthesis removes CO_2 from the atmosphere and stores it as carbon in trees. CO_2 is then released when trees are burnt to clear land (see p.147). Increased concentrations of CO_2 contributes to global warming.

Human activities can have a negative impact on habitats

The huge increases in human population mean that more land is required to provide food and shelter for everyone. However, clearing land has negative impacts on many organisms. It can even lead to extinction.

Warm-Up & Exam Questions

Time to see how much you've learnt over the previous few pages. Have a go at these questions.

Warm-Up Questions

1) State three ways that humans have increased food production.
2) How does intensive livestock farming increase food production compared to free-range methods?
3) Give one ethical objection to intensive livestock farming.
4) What is biodiversity?

Exam Questions

1   Methods of food production often have advantages and disadvantages.

   (a)   (i)   Describe **two** advantages to the farmer of using monocultures to grow crops, rather than more traditional farming methods.

[2]

   (ii)   Describe **one** benefit to the consumer of crops being grown via monoculture.

[1]

   (b)   Describe **two** ways that monocultures can negatively impact ecosystems.

[2]

[Total 5 marks]

2   The photo below shows a type of habitat destruction taking place.

   (a)   Give **two** reasons why the trees might be being removed.

[2]

   (b)   Loss of biodiversity and extinction can be undesirable effects of the above type of habitat destruction. State **two** other undesirable effects of the above type of habitat destruction.

[2]

   (c)   Explain how the two effects you gave in **(b)** impact the environment.

[2]

[Total 6 marks]

Water Pollution

Here's another environmental problem for you to learn about — pollution of water.

Sewage and Fertilisers can Run into Water

1) Nitrates and other ions are put onto fields as mineral fertilisers.

2) If too much fertiliser is applied and it rains afterwards, nitrates are easily leached (washed through the soil) into rivers and lakes.

3) Nitrates can also find their way into rivers and lakes from untreated sewage.

4) The result is eutrophication, which can cause serious damage to river and lake ecosystems and eventually lead to the death of aquatic organisms.

If untreated sewage contaminates drinking water, the pathogens in it can also cause problems for humans, e.g. diarrhoea.

Here's How Eutrophication Happens

1) Fertiliser (or untreated sewage) enters the water, adding extra nutrients (nitrates and other ions).

2) The extra nutrients cause producers like algae to grow faster and block out the light.

3) Plants can't photosynthesise due to lack of light and start to die.

4) With more food available, microorganisms that feed on dead plants (decomposers) increase in number. They respire aerobically (see p.72) so the amount of dissolved oxygen in the water is reduced as decomposition increases.

5) Organisms that need the oxygen dissolved in water (e.g. fish) die.

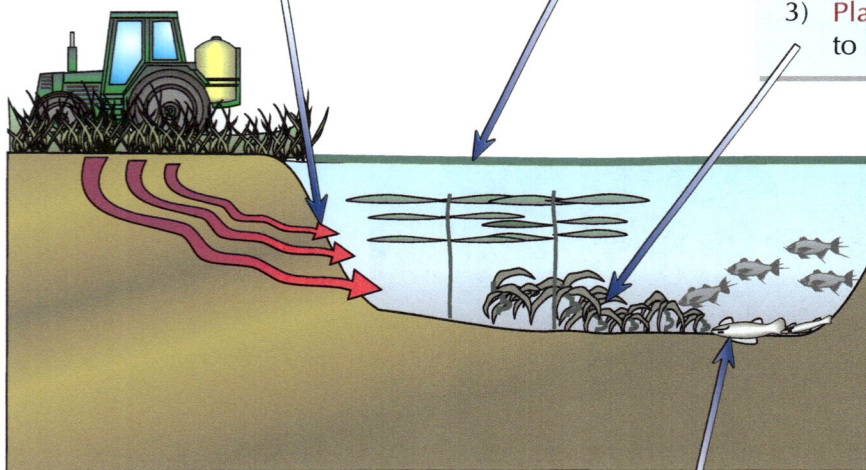

Pollution has negative impacts on water

Pollution often remains in the environment for a long time and can have devastating effects on organisms and their habitats. Make sure you have learnt everything you need to on this page before moving on.

Air Pollution

Human activities can cause air pollution by increasing the quantities of certain gases in the atmosphere.

Burning Fossil Fuels Releases Carbon Dioxide

1) Fossil fuels are fuels that have formed over millions of years from the remains of dead organisms. Coal, oil and natural gas are all types of fossil fuel.

2) When fossil fuels are burnt, they release lots of carbon dioxide. During the last century, humans have been releasing increasing levels of carbon dioxide through the burning of fossil fuels, e.g.:

- Fossil fuels are burnt in power stations — they are the major source of electricity for most of the world.
- We also rely on them for transport — most cars, lorries, ships and planes run on fossil fuels.

3) Deforestation (see page 144) is also increasing the level of carbon dioxide in the atmosphere. This is because:

- Cutting down trees reduces the amount of carbon dioxide removed from the atmosphere during photosynthesis.
- Carbon dioxide is released when trees are burnt to clear land or when dead wood is left to decompose (see page 135).

Certain Types of Farming Release Methane

1) Methane gas is produced naturally from various sources, e.g. rotting plants in marshland.

2) However, two 'man-made' sources of methane are on the increase: growing rice and raising cattle.

Carbon Dioxide and Methane are Greenhouse Gases

1) Gases in the atmosphere absorb most of the heat that would normally be radiated out into space, and re-radiate it in all directions (including back towards the Earth). This is the greenhouse effect.

2) If this didn't happen, then at night there'd be nothing to keep any energy in, and it would be very cold.

3) There are several different gases in the atmosphere that help keep the energy in. They are called "greenhouse gases" and include carbon dioxide and methane.

4) Increasing levels of these greenhouse gases are enhancing (increasing) the greenhouse effect.

5) This enhanced greenhouse effect is causing the Earth to heat up — this is global warming. Global warming is a type of climate change and causes other types of climate change, e.g. changing rainfall patterns.

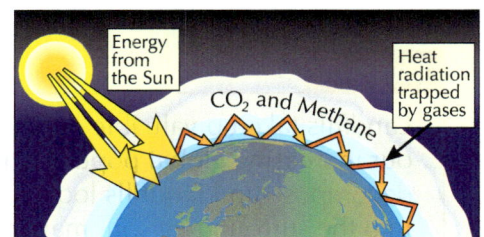

We need the greenhouse effect, but it's starting to go too far
The greenhouse effect is linked to climate change. We don't know yet what the long-term effects will be.

Non-Biodegradable Plastics

It's easy to throw away old plastic bottles and plastic packaging without giving it much thought — but doing this can have negative impacts on both aquatic (water) and terrestrial (land) ecosystems.

Non-Biodegradable Plastics Cannot be Broken Down

1) Decomposing microorganisms have not evolved to break down the chemicals found in most plastics.
2) So non-biodegradable plastics cannot be broken down through biological decomposition.
3) This means that they will remain in the environment for a very long time.
4) Common causes of plastic pollution are plastic bags and plastic bottles.
5) They often build up in landfills (sites where waste is disposed of by burying it), litter public spaces and can wash into aquatic ecosystems.

Non-Biodegradable Plastics Affect Aquatic Ecosystems

Food Chain Contamination

Eating plastic items after mistaking them for food can cause intestinal blockages in organisms or poisoning from chemicals that slowly leak from the plastics. It also means that plastic enters the food chain — e.g. consumers eat plastic by eating organisms with plastic inside them.

Entrapment of Organisms

Large quantities of plastic, along with other kinds of rubbish, can build up in the ocean. Rotating ocean currents can form the build up into an 'island'. Organisms can get entangled, trapped or strangled by plastic islands or even just by individual plastic items.

Non-Biodegradable Plastics Affect Terrestrial Ecosystems

Food Chain Contamination

Over time, plastics can give out poisonous toxins and chemicals that cause land pollution. Once they enter the food chain they can kill many organisms.

Air Pollution

If not carefully controlled, toxic gases can be released into the atmosphere when plastics are disposed of by burning. Carbon dioxide is also produced, which contributes to global warming (see p.147).

Landfill

Landfills take up valuable space that could be used to feed and house our increasing global population. Plastic in landfills takes a long time to decompose and landfills look unsightly. The buried waste also releases toxins into the surrounding soil, making it unsuitable for crops or grazing animals.

REVISION TIP

Non-biodegradable plastics remain in the environment

Non-biodegradable plastics can create serious problems in the environment. Cover up this page and write a list of effects that plastics can have in aquatic and terrestrial ecosystems. It's a good way of testing what you've learnt — you may be asked to discuss these effects in the exam.

Warm-Up & Exam Questions

Pollution isn't the most exciting topic, but it's important for you to learn about.
Have a go at these questions to see what you can remember from the last few pages.

Warm-Up Questions

1) State two gases that cause air pollution.
2) What does non-biodegradable mean?

Exam Questions

1 Non-biodegradable plastics can have negative effects on ecosystems.

(a) Give **two** ways that non-biodegradable plastics can affect aquatic ecosystems.

[2]

(b) Give **two** ways that non-biodegradable plastics can affect terrestrial ecosystems.

[2]

[Total 4 marks]

2 Increasing levels of greenhouse gases in the atmosphere are contributing to the enhanced greenhouse effect.

a) Methane is a greenhouse gas.
State **one** human activity that is increasing the level of methane in the atmosphere.

[1]

b) Explain how deforestation is contributing to increasing greenhouse gas levels.

[2]

[Total 3 marks]

3 Human activities can pollute rivers, lakes and the sea.

(a) Describe **one** way in which agriculture can pollute water.

[2]

(b) An investigation was carried out into the number of decomposer microorganisms along a stream. A sewage pipe was located midway along the study site. The results are shown below.

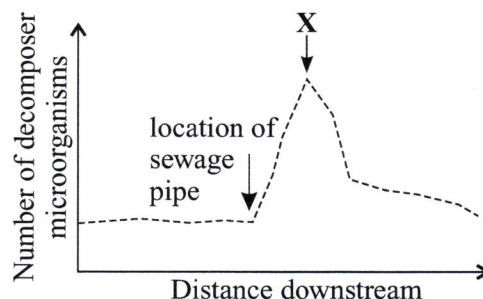

Describe and explain the change in number of decomposer microorganisms between the sewage pipe and point **X**.

[4]

[Total 6 marks]

Sustainable Resources

Some resources will run out, but others are sustainable if we maintain them.

Resources can be Renewable or Non-Renewable

1) Non-renewable resources include energy resources such as fossil fuels (coal, oil and gas).

2) Fossil fuels are typically burnt to release energy or used to make products (such as making plastics from oils).

3) They take a very long time to form, so we can't replace them. If no new resources are found, some fossil fuel stocks may run out within a hundred years. This means that it's important to conserve them.

4) Some resources are renewable, which means they are sustainable.

KEY TERM — A sustainable resource is one which does not run out because it is made as rapidly as it is removed from the environment.

Fish Stocks and Forests are Sustainable Resources

Fish Stocks

Fish stocks are particular populations of fish in the sea. Many of them are getting smaller because we're fishing so much. We can maintain (conserve) fish stocks by keeping them at a level where fish are able to breed at a fast enough rate to replace the fish taken.

Fish stocks can be conserved using these methods:

1) Legal quotas — there are limits on the number and size of fish that can be caught in certain areas. This helps to prevent certain species from being overfished.

2) Closed seasons — there are rules about the time of year you can catch fish in certain areas. This bans fishing during the breeding season, allowing fish stocks to replenish.

3) Protected areas — certain types of fishing are restricted or banned in these areas.

4) Controlled net types and mesh sizes — there are different limits to the mesh size of the fishing net, depending on what's being fished. This is to reduce the number of 'unwanted' and discarded fish — the ones that are accidentally caught, e.g. shrimp caught along with cod. Using a bigger mesh size will let the 'unwanted' species escape. It also means that younger fish will slip through the net, allowing them to reach breeding age.

5) Monitoring — surveys and sampling techniques are used to keep an eye on the size of fish stocks, as well as things like the size, age and movement of the fish. This helps to inform other policies.

6) Education — knowing about the importance of conserving fish stocks means that people shopping for fish can make better choices.

Supplement

Forests

Deforestation removes trees in an area (see p.144). We can plant trees to replace the ones that are removed (reforestation). This means that the number of trees can be maintained, so we can continue to use them to make, e.g. paper.

As well as replanting trees, forests can be conserved using these methods:

1) Legal quotas — limits can be applied to the number of trees that can be cut down in forests.

2) Protected areas — deforestation is banned in these areas by law.

3) Education — if people understand the value of the biodiversity in forests, more people will want to protect them from deforestation.

Supplement

Endangered Organisms

When the population size of a species drops, the species can become endangered.

Several Factors Cause Organisms to Become Endangered

Extinction is when no individuals of a species remain. An endangered species is one that is considered to be at a high risk of extinction. The reasons for organisms becoming endangered or extinct include:

Climate Change

- Global warming is a type of climate change (p.147) that is causing the Earth to heat up.
- All organisms have an ideal temperature range. If they can't adapt to changing temperatures or other environmental conditions quickly enough, they are at risk of becoming extinct.
- For example, whales need specific ocean temperatures for feeding and reproduction. Rising sea temperatures mean the whales might not be able to survive.

Habitat Destruction

- As a species' habitat is destroyed, fewer of the organisms can be supported. As their numbers start to decrease, the species can become endangered.
- For example, great apes live in forests in Southeast Asia. They risk extinction because large areas are being deforested.

> Competition from humans for resources can decrease the population size of an endangered species.

Hunting

- Many species are hunted for, e.g. food, fur or medicines. If endangered species are hunted, they can quickly become extinct.
- For example, the great auk and the passenger pigeon were both hunted to extinction.
- Endangered animals may also be killed by accident if hunters mistake an endangered species for a non-endangered species.

Pollution

- A species can also be affected by pollution in its environment.
- For example, the oceans are heavily polluted with plastics (p.148). Sea turtles can mistake plastic bags for jellyfish and eat them. This often causes their death.

Introduced Species

- Introduced species often thrive in their new environment and become invasive. Native species often can't defend themselves against, or compete with, the invaders.
- For example, a species of lake newt went extinct in China because it couldn't compete with introduced fish and frog species in its environment.

> An invasive species is a species that threatens local biodiversity.

Overharvesting

If people take so much of an organism that its population is unable to reproduce quickly enough to keep up, the population size falls. This is overharvesting — see p.133 for more.

Supplement

Endangered species have a reduced population size and reduced genetic variation (see p.121).

Variation is not restored if the population size simply increases again — mutations also need to happen over many generations. This means that even if a population recovers its size, it can still face extinction if it has low variation and can't adapt to changing environmental conditions.

Conserving Endangered Species

We can try to conserve endangered species before they become extinct.

There are **Several** Ways to **Conserve Endangered Species**

There are several different ways to try and stop the population sizes of endangered species decreasing. These include:

Monitoring and Protecting Species and Habitats

1) Monitoring species' numbers helps scientists to identify the species that are most under threat.

2) Protected areas can be set up to protect organisms and habitats that are under threat, e.g. from hunting.

3) Protected areas include places like national parks and nature reserves, where development of the land is restricted — including the building of houses and using the land for farming.

Education

Teaching people about the natural world helps them to understand the importance of conservation and what they can do to help.

Seed Banks

1) The seeds of endangered plant species can be kept in a seed bank.

2) This is a place with the conditions necessary to keep the seeds alive for a long time.

3) This protects and saves plant genetic diversity.

Captive Breeding Programmes

1) Captive breeding programmes are where animals are bred in captivity (e.g. zoos). Many have been set up to help prevent endangered species from becoming extinct.

2) This is because it's easier for animals to increase their numbers in captivity — there is less infant mortality (death), so more offspring survive to reproduce.

3) Some of these individuals may then be released into the wild to boost or re-establish a population. This can help make sure the species survives if it dies out in the wild.

4) Captive breeding programmes can involve artificial insemination (AI) or *in vitro* fertilisation (IVF).

- AI involves artificially inserting sperm collected from the male into the female's cervix to allow fertilisation to take place. This helps individuals who are unable to breed together naturally (e.g. because of reproductive difficulties, or because they are being kept very far apart) to reproduce. This helps to increase genetic variation.

- IVF is where an egg is removed from a female's ovaries and fertilised using sperm in the laboratory. The resulting embryo is then implanted into the female. Again, this can help individuals to reproduce when they are unable to breed together naturally.

Supplement

There are **Different Reasons** for **Conservation Programmes**

1) Conserving one species may stop others from becoming extinct. If one species becomes extinct it will affect all the organisms that feed on and are eaten by that species, so the whole food web (see p.129) is affected.

2) Conserving species means that ecosystem functions like nutrient cycling (p.135-136) can be maintained.

3) It also helps to maintain or even increase biodiversity (see p.144).

4) Protecting vulnerable environments means organisms can continue to live in their natural habitat. For example, controlling water levels will help to conserve wetlands and trimming trees will help to conserve woodlands. This also helps to maintain biodiversity.

5) Humans rely on many resources from the environment, such as animals for food, plants for drugs, wood for fuel and genes from organisms. Conservation programmes mean that resource provision from the environment can continue.

Supplement

Warm-Up & Exam Questions

That's the end of this section. Have a go at these questions to see how much you know.
If there's anything you've forgotten, have a look back over the previous few pages to remind yourself.

Warm-Up Questions

1) Define the term 'sustainable resource'.
2) What is a seed bank?
3) What is the purpose of a seed bank?

Exam Questions

1   The Siberian tiger is an endangered species. Explain how captive breeding
     programmes could help to increase the number of Siberian tigers in the wild.

[Total 2 marks]

2   Give **three** reasons why organisms become endangered or extinct.

[Total 3 marks]

3   Which **one** of the following statements describes what can happen
     if the population size of a species drops?

     ☐ **A**   The species will lose genetic variation, but it will regain variation quickly
                 if its population size recovers.

     ☐ **B**   The species will lose genetic variation, and it may still face extinction even
                 if its population size recovers.

     ☐ **C**   The species will lose genetic variation, but it won't risk extinction if its
                 population size recovers.

     ☐ **D**   The population will gain genetic variation, so it won't risk extinction if its
                 population size recovers.

[Total 1 mark]

4   A fish stock is a particular population of fish in the sea.

     (a)   Suggest **one** reason why it might be important to conserve fish stocks.

[1]

     (b)   Give **three** ways that fish stocks can be conserved.

[3]

[Total 4 marks]

Genetic Modification

Genetic modification is a relatively new area of science (well, it began in the 1970s). We've already put the technology to good use and it has many more exciting possibilities too...

Genetic Modification is Used to Transfer Genes

KEY TERM

Genetic modification is the alteration of an organism's genetic material by removing, changing or inserting individual genes.

Genetic modification allows us to transfer a gene responsible for a desirable characteristic from one organism into another organism, so that it also has the desirable characteristic.

Bacteria can be Modified to Produce Human Proteins

Human genes can be inserted into bacteria. The bacteria are then able to produce human proteins. For example, insulin can be made by inserting the gene for human insulin into bacteria. You need to learn the process used to modify bacteria:

1) The DNA making up the human gene is isolated using a restriction enzyme. Restriction enzymes recognise specific sequences of DNA and cut the DNA at these points. The cut leaves the DNA strands with unpaired bases — these are called 'sticky ends'.

2) A plasmid (a loop of DNA) is removed from a bacterium. The plasmid is cut open using the same restriction enzyme that was used to isolate the human gene — leaving complementary (matching) sticky ends.

3) The human gene is inserted into the bacterial plasmid DNA by mixing them together with DNA ligase (an enzyme). This joins the sticky ends together to produce a recombinant plasmid (a plasmid made of two different bits of DNA stuck together).

4) The recombinant plasmid is inserted into a bacterium.

5) The modified bacterium multiplies, leading to millions of bacteria that express the human gene and so produce the human protein.

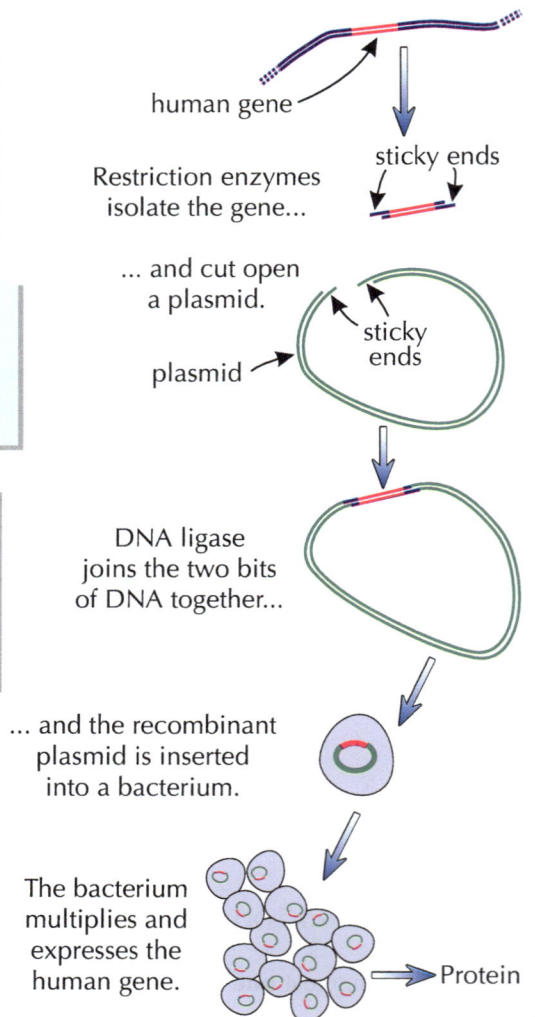

human gene

Restriction enzymes isolate the gene...

sticky ends

... and cut open a plasmid.

plasmid

sticky ends

DNA ligase joins the two bits of DNA together...

... and the recombinant plasmid is inserted into a bacterium.

The bacterium multiplies and expresses the human gene.

Protein

Supplement

It looks hard, but it's just like a fancy cut and paste...

Bacteria aren't the only organisms that can be genetically modified for human benefit (there are more examples coming up on the next page) but the process can be a bit more complicated in larger organisms.

Genetic Modification

You need to know about some more examples of genetic modification.

Bacteria are Really Useful for Genetic Modification

Bacteria are useful for genetic modification and biotechnology (see pages 156-158) for several reasons:

1) They reproduce very quickly in the right conditions.
2) They are able to produce complex molecules.
3) There aren't many ethical concerns over the modification and growth of bacteria.
   (Some people don't agree with the modification of animals and plants.)
4) Bacteria have plasmids — small rings of DNA that are easy to modify and transfer between cells.

Supplement

Crops can be Genetically Modified Too

1) Crops can be made herbicide-resistant by inserting herbicide resistance genes. This means farmers can spray areas where crops are grown to kill weeds, without affecting the crop itself.

> One type of soya has been genetically modified to be resistant to a herbicide called glyphosate.

2) Crops can be made insect-resistant by inserting insect resistance genes. This improves crop yield, because less of the crop is eaten by insects.

> Insect resistance also means farmers don't have to spray as many insecticides (see page 142) — so wildlife that doesn't eat the crop isn't harmed.

> One type of maize has been genetically modified to be resistant to the larvae of certain moths, which normally eat the crop.

3) Crops can be genetically modified by inserting genes to improve their nutritional quality.

> 'Golden Rice' has been made to produce a chemical that's converted in the body to vitamin A.

Genetic Modification of Crops has Advantages and Disadvantages

Supplement

Crops such as soya, maize and rice can all be genetically modified to produce crops that have different characteristics. There are advantages and disadvantages to this:

- Herbicide- and insect-resistant crops have improved yields. Crops can also be modified to grow in poor conditions, which also improves yield.
- Crops with additional nutritional value could be valuable in places where there isn't enough food to eat or where the diet is not sufficiently varied.

- There is a concern that transplanted genes may be passed on to other organisms, e.g. weeds may become herbicide-resistant.
- Changing an organism's genes could also create unforeseen problems that get passed on to the organisms' offspring.
- Some people are worried that genetically modified crops might affect food chains and human health.
- Crops could become more expensive.

WORKING SCIENTIFICALLY

Genetic modification has huge potential benefits...

Scientists have used genetic modification to produce organisms that benefit humans in all sorts of ways — but, as with any new technology, we need to be aware of the risks that it carries too.

Biotechnology

Biotechnology is where living things and biological processes are manipulated to produce a useful product. Using yeast to make bread is an example of biotechnology, so put your apron on and read on.

We Use Yeast for Making Bread

1) Yeast is a fungus that respires both aerobically and anaerobically (see p.72-73) to produce CO_2.
2) It's used in baking, where it's mixed into dough to create bubbles of CO_2 that make the dough rise:

1) A bread dough is made by mixing yeast (e.g. *S. cerevisiae*) with flour and water.

2) The dough is then left in a warm place to rise — this happens with the help of the yeast.

3) Enzymes break down the carbohydrates in the flour into sugars.

4) The yeast then uses these sugars in aerobic respiration, producing carbon dioxide.

5) When the oxygen runs out, the yeast switches to anaerobic respiration. This is also known as fermentation, and it produces carbon dioxide and alcohol (ethanol).

6) The carbon dioxide produced is trapped in bubbles in the dough.

7) These pockets of gas expand, and the dough begins to rise.

8) The dough is then baked in an oven, where the yeast continues to ferment until the temperature of the dough rises enough to kill the yeast. Any alcohol produced during anaerobic respiration is boiled away.

9) As the yeast dies, the bread stops rising, but pockets are left in the bread where the carbon dioxide was trapped.

We Also Use Yeast to Make Biofuels

1) Biofuels are fuels made from living material (biomass). Bioethanol is one of the most common biofuels.
2) The biomass is processed (e.g. using enzymes) to break down large carbohydrates into sugars.
3) Yeast then breaks down these sugars to produce ethanol during anaerobic respiration.
4) This is carried out on a large scale in vessels called fermenters (see p.158). The ethanol produced can be collected, purified and used as a biofuel.

Respiration in yeast produces carbon dioxide, making bread rise

You might not have thought there was much of an overlap between baking and biology, but you thought wrong. Understanding how yeast works has allowed humans to make bread for thousands of years.

Uses of Biotechnology

As you saw on p.29, enzymes are important molecules in living organisms. Here are some more of their uses.

Pectinase is Used in Fruit Juice Production

1) Pectin is a carbohydrate found in plant cell walls.

2) Pectinase is an enzyme that breaks down pectin. It is produced by bacteria and fungi to speed up fruit and vegetable decomposition.

3) Fruit juice manufacturers use pectinase help break down the cell walls in fruit so that the juice can be extracted more easily.

Biological Washing Powders Contain Enzymes

1) Biological washing powders contain enzymes to break down and remove stains from clothes.

2) A few different enzymes are used. For example, lipases digest fat stains, amylases digest carbohydrate-based stains and proteases digest protein-based stains.

There's more about these enzymes on page 45.

3) Because they contain enzymes, biological washing powders are more effective at low temperatures (e.g. 30 °C) than other types of washing powders.

4) You can investigate the effectiveness of biological versus non-biological washing powders at 30 °C:

- Prepare stained samples of fabric with, for example, ketchup, juice or gravy.
- Prepare dilute solutions of biological and non-biological washing powders in separate beakers.
- Add a fabric sample to each beaker and place them in a water bath at 30 °C for an hour.
- Remove and rinse the fabric samples, and leave them to dry. Assess the stain removal.

5) The fabric sample that was in the solution of biological washing powder is likely to look cleaner than the sample in the solution of non-biological washing powder. You could carry out the same experiment at different temperatures to investigate the effect of temperature on enzyme activity.

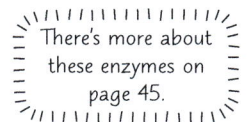

Lactase is Used in the Production of Lactose-Free Milk

1) Lactose is a sugar that is found in milk. Some people are lactose intolerant — they cannot digest lactose because they don't produce the enzyme lactase.

2) Lactase breaks lactose down into glucose and galactose. It can be used to make lactose-free milk.

3) To make the milk, the lactase is first immobilised (trapped) — usually by encasing it in alginate beads. Milk is then passed over the beads and the lactose in it is broken down.

Supplement

More Uses of Biotechnology

In industry, if you want to grow lots of microorganisms, it's best to use a big vessel called a fermenter.

Fermenters Can Be Used to Manufacture Useful Products

1) Microorganisms, such as fungi and bacteria, can be grown on a huge scale inside an industrial fermenter. The products they make can be collected and processed for a variety of applications.
2) For example, the fungus *Fusarium* can be used to grow the meat-substitute mycoprotein.
3) Another fungus, *Penicillium*, can be used to produce the antibiotic penicillin.
4) Genetically modified bacteria can also be grown to produce insulin, which is used to treat diabetes.

The Conditions in Fermenters are Carefully Controlled

1) The fermenters used to grow microorganisms are full of a liquid 'culture medium' in which they can grow and reproduce.
2) The conditions inside the fermenters are kept at the optimum (best) levels for growth — this means the yield of the product is as big as possible. Here's how:

Nutrients needed for growth are provided in the liquid culture medium.

Vessels are sterilised between uses with superheated steam that kills unwanted microbes. This increases the product yield because there is less competition with other organisms. It also means that the product doesn't get contaminated.

Carbon dioxide and other waste gases are removed via the exhaust. This helps to stop levels of waste gases becoming too high and maintains optimum conditions for growth.

The pH is monitored and kept at the optimum level by adding acid or alkali. This allows the microorganism's enzymes to work more efficiently (see p.30). This keeps the rate of reaction and therefore the product yield as high as possible.

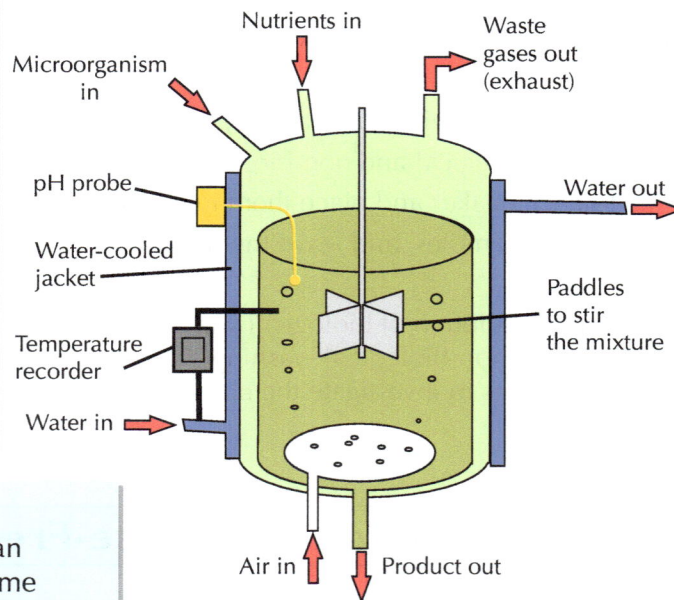

The temperature is monitored and kept at an optimum level for enzyme action. Heat is released as the microorganisms respire, causing the temperature inside the fermenter to increase. A water-cooled jacket makes sure it doesn't get so hot that the enzymes denature.

Oxygen is needed for respiration, so it's added by pumping in sterile air. This increases the product yield because there is always oxygen available for respiration to provide the energy for growth.

The microorganisms are kept in contact with fresh medium by paddles that circulate (or agitate) the medium around the vessel. This increases the product yield because the microorganisms can always access the nutrients needed for growth. It also helps to keep an even temperature and pH throughout the mixture.

Microorganism in
Nutrients in
Waste gases out (exhaust)
pH probe
Water-cooled jacket
Water out
Paddles to stir the mixture
Temperature recorder
Water in
Air in
Product out

Supplement

Optimum conditions for the microorganism = high yield of product

You can control all the conditions inside a fermenter so microorganisms will happily grow even when it's cold outside. The more microorganisms that grow, the more product you can make.

Warm-Up & Exam Questions

Now's your chance to practise some incredibly life-like Exam Questions, but do the Warm-Up first — you don't want to end up straining something.

Warm-Up Questions

1) Name a type of organism that has been genetically modified to produce a human protein.
2) How are plasmids involved in genetic modification?
3) Apart from restriction enzymes, name another type of enzyme needed for the process of genetic modification.
4) State two enzymes that might be found in biological washing powders.
5) State two conditions that are controlled in fermenters.

Exam Questions

1   Genetic modification is being investigated for use in a wide variety of applications.

   (a)   What is genetic modification?

[1]

The process of genetic modification has several steps.

   (b)   The useful gene is first isolated from an organism's DNA.
          Explain how this is done.

[2]

   (c)   The gene is then inserted into the target organism's DNA. Explain how this is achieved
          in bacteria, resulting in a large number of bacteria with the desired characteristics.

[4]

[Total 7 marks]

2   Biotechnology is the use of living organisms and processes to produce useful products.

   (a)   Describe **two** benefits of using bacteria in biotechnology.

[2]

Yeast have a variety of applications in biotechnology.

   (b)   Describe how yeast are used to make biofuels.

[2]

Lactose-free milk is produced using the enzyme lactase, which breaks lactose down.
Lactase can be produced industrially by a fungus called *Aspergillus niger*.

   (c)   When producing lactose-free milk using lactase from *A. niger*, it is important
          that the temperature is carefully controlled. Explain why.

[2]

[Total 6 marks]

Exam Questions

3 Genetically modified maize plants can be produced.

(a) (i) State **one** characteristic which a maize crop might be genetically modified to have.

[1]

(ii) Suggest **one** way in which genetically modifying maize plants to have this characteristic could help to feed people in areas with a growing population.

[1]

(b) Give **two** reasons why some people may have concerns about the use of genetically modified crops in agriculture.

[2]

[Total 4 marks]

4 The diagram below shows a fermenter that could be used to produce penicillin.

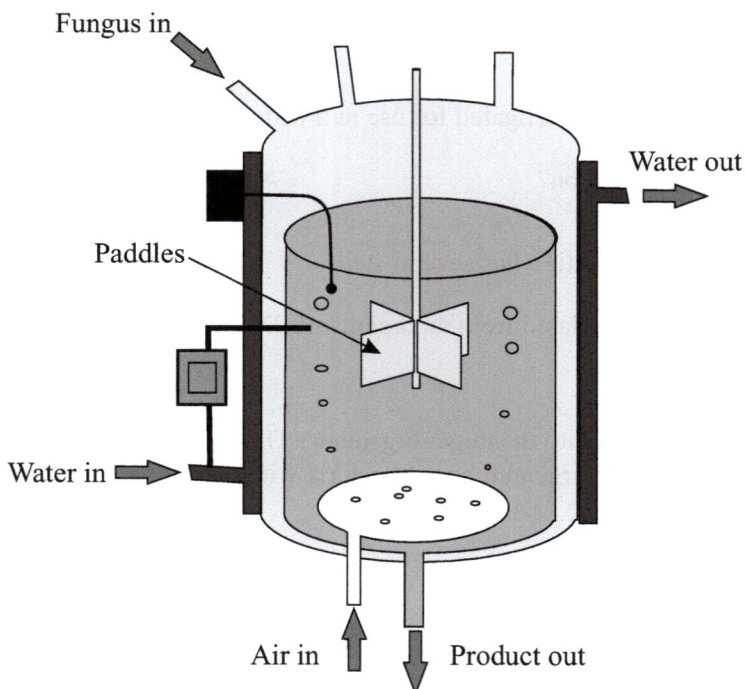

(a) Suggest another product that could be produced by fungi in a fermenter.

[1]

(b) Explain the purpose of the air supply in the fermenter.

[2]

(c) Suggest and explain why paddles are used in the fermenter.

[2]

(d) Give **one** substance not labelled in the diagram that would also need to be added to the fermenter in order to produce penicillin.

[1]

[Total 6 marks]

Revision Summary for Sections 16 & 17

So you've finished Sections 16 & 17 and you're nearly at the end of the book.
Here are some questions to see what you've learnt in these sections.
- Try these questions and tick off each one when you get it right.
- When you've done all the questions for a topic and are completely happy with it, tick off the topic.

Food Production and Habitat Destruction (p.142-144) ☐

1) How does using agricultural machinery help to increase food production? ☐
2) How do herbicides increase food production? ☐
3) How does selective breeding increase food production? ☐
4) What is a monoculture? ☐
5) What is intensive livestock production? ☐
6) What is deforestation? ☐

Pollution and Non-Biodegradable Plastics (p.146-148) ☐

7) What is the name of the process that occurs when fertilisers run into bodies of water and cause rapid growth of producers? ☐
8) Explain the effects of this process on aquatic organisms. ☐
9) Name a greenhouse gas released through the growing of rice. ☐
10) State two human activities which are increasing levels of greenhouse gases in the atmosphere. ☐
11) What are non-biodegradable plastics? ☐
12) True or false? Non-biodegradable plastics only pollute aquatic ecosystems. ☐

Sustainable Resources and Conservation (p.150-152) ☐

13) Describe three methods of conserving forests. ☐
14) Explain why climate change can cause a species to become extinct. ☐
15) Explain why introduced species can cause native species to become extinct. ☐
16) Describe how monitoring and protecting species and habitats can conserve endangered species. ☐
17) Describe how education can be used to help conserve endangered species. ☐
18) Describe how artificial insemination can be used in captive breeding programmes. ☐

Genetic Modification (p.154-155) ☐

19) What is meant by the term 'sticky ends'? ☐
20) Describe the function of DNA ligase. ☐
21) What is a recombinant plasmid? ☐
22) Give one reason why bacteria are useful for genetic modification. ☐

Biotechnology (p.156-158) ☐

23) Describe how yeast is used to make bread rise. ☐
24) Explain why pectinase is used in fruit juice production. ☐
25) Name three things that could be produced in a fermenter. ☐

Designing Investigations

Before you start carrying out an investigation, it's important to spend some time designing it.

Evidence Can Support or Disprove a Hypothesis

1) Scientists observe things and come up with hypotheses to test them.
   A hypothesis is just a possible explanation for what they've observed. For example:

   > Observation: People with big feet have spots. Hypothesis: Having big feet causes spots.

2) To determine whether or not a hypothesis is right, you need to do an investigation to gather
   evidence. To do this, you need to use your hypothesis to make a prediction — something you
   think will happen that you can test. E.g. people who have bigger feet will have more spots.

3) Investigations are used to see if there are patterns or relationships between two variables, e.g. to
   see if there's a pattern or relationship between the variables 'number of spots' and 'size of feet'.

Results Need to be Reliable and Valid

1) RELIABLE results come from experiments that give the same data each time the experiment is
   repeated (by you) and each time the experiment is reproduced (copied) by other scientists.

2) VALID results are both reliable and come from experiments that were designed to be a fair test.

Make an Investigation a Fair Test By Controlling the Variables

1) In a lab experiment you usually change one variable and measure how it affects another variable.

2) To make it a fair test, everything else that could affect the results should stay the same
   — otherwise you can't tell if the thing you're changing is causing the results or not.

3) The variable you CHANGE is called the INDEPENDENT variable.

4) The variable you MEASURE when you change the independent variable is the DEPENDENT variable.

5) The variables that you KEEP THE SAME are called CONTROL variables.

   > You could find how temperature affects reaction rate. The independent variable is temperature.
   > The dependent variable is rate. Control variables include concentration of reactants, pH, etc.

6) Because you can't always control all the variables, you often need to use a control experiment. This is
   an experiment that's kept under the same conditions as the rest of the investigation, but doesn't have
   anything done to it. This is so that you can see what happens when you don't change anything at all.

Results Also Need to be Accurate

1) Accurate results are those that are close to the true answer.

2) The accuracy of your results usually depends on your method. To make sure your results are as
   accurate as possible, you need to make sure you're measuring the right thing and that you don't
   miss anything or include anything that you shouldn't include.

   > E.g. if you wanted to measure the amount of gas released from an enzyme-controlled reaction you
   > could estimate how much gas is produced by counting the number of bubbles that are released. But
   > the bubbles could be different sizes, and if they're produced really quickly you might miss some when
   > counting. It would be more accurate to collect the gas (e.g. in a gas syringe) and measure its volume.

Designing Investigations

You Need to Look out for **Errors** and **Anomalous Results**

1) The results of your experiment will always vary a bit because of random errors — unpredictable differences caused by things like human errors in measuring. E.g. the errors you make when reading from a measuring cylinder are random. You have to estimate or round the distance when it's between two marks (see page 166) — so sometimes your figure will be a bit above the real one, and sometimes it will be a bit below.

2) You can reduce the effect of random errors by taking repeat readings and finding the mean (a type of average — see page 169). This will make your results more reliable.

3) If a measurement is wrong by the same amount every time, it's called a systematic error. For example, if you measured from the very end of your ruler instead of from the 0 cm mark every time, all your measurements would be a bit small. Repeating the experiment in the exact same way and calculating a mean won't correct a systematic error.

If there's no systematic error, then doing repeats and calculating a mean could make your results more accurate.

4) Just to make things more complicated, if a systematic error is caused by using equipment that isn't zeroed properly, it's called a zero error. For example, if a mass balance always reads 1 gram before you put anything on it, all your measurements will be 1 gram too heavy.

5) You can make up for some systematic errors if you know about them, e.g. if a mass balance always reads 1 gram before you put anything on it, you can subtract 1 gram from all your results.

Sometimes you get a result that doesn't fit in with the rest at all. This is an anomalous result. You should investigate it and try to work out what happened. If you can work out what happened (e.g. you measured something wrong) you can ignore it when processing your results.

Make Sure You're **Working Safely** in the **Lab**

1) Before you start any experiment, make sure you know about any safety precautions to do with your method or the chemicals you're using. You need to follow any instructions that your teacher gives you carefully. The chemicals you're using may be hazardous — for example, they might be flammable (catch fire easily), or they might irritate or burn your skin if it comes into contact with them.

2) Make sure that you're wearing sensible clothing when you're in the lab (e.g. open shoes won't protect your feet from spillages). When you're doing an experiment, you should wear a lab coat to protect your skin and clothing. Depending on the experiment, you may need to also wear safety goggles and gloves.

3) You also need to be aware of general safety in the lab, e.g. keep anything flammable away from lit Bunsen burners, don't directly touch any hot equipment, handle glassware (including microscope slides) carefully to avoid breakages, etc.

Designing an investigation is an involved process...

WORKING SCIENTIFICALLY

Collecting data is what investigations are all about. Designing a good investigation is really important to make sure that any data collected is reliable, valid, accurate and done in a safe way.

Planning Experiments

In the exam, you could be asked to plan or describe how you'd carry out an experiment. It might be one you've already come across or you might be asked to come up with an experiment of your own.

You Need to Be Able to Plan a **Good Experiment**

Here are some general tips on what to include when planning an experiment:

1) Say what you're measuring (i.e. the dependent variable).

2) Say what you're changing (i.e. the independent variable) and describe how you're going to change it.

3) Describe the method and the apparatus you'd use (i.e. to measure the variables).

4) Describe what variables you're keeping constant — and how you're going to do it.

5) Say that you need to repeat the experiment at least three times, to make the results more reliable.

6) Say whether you're using a control or not.

Here's an idea of a type of question you might be asked in the exam and what you might write as an answer...

Exam-style Question:

1   Describe an investigation to find out what effect temperature has on the rate of photosynthesis in Canadian pondweed.   *[6]*

Example Answer:

Set up a test tube containing a measured amount of Canadian pondweed, water and sodium hydrogencarbonate. Connect the test tube up to a capillary tube containing water and a syringe, then place it in a water bath in front of a source of white light.

Leave the pondweed to photosynthesise for a set amount of time. As it photosynthesises, the oxygen released will collect in the capillary tube. At the end of the experiment, use the syringe to draw the gas bubble in the tube up alongside a ruler and measure the length of the gas bubble. This is proportional to the volume of O_2 produced.

Repeat the experiment with the water bath set to different temperatures (e.g. 10 °C, 20 °C, 30 °C and 40 °C).

The pondweed should be left to photosynthesise for the same amount of time at each temperature (monitored using a stopwatch). The test tubes should also be set up the same distance away from the light source (measured using a ruler) and the same mass of pondweed should be used in each test tube (measured using a balance).

A control should also be set up at each temperature. This should be a test tube containing water and boiled pondweed (so that it can't photosynthesise).

Repeat the experiment three times at each temperature. Use the results to find a mean rate of photosynthesis at each temperature. This will make the results more reliable.

You Can Make **Reasoned Predictions** Based on Your **Knowledge**

1) You can use your hypothesis (p.162) and the stuff you know to make sensible predictions about what the results of an experiment might be.

2) For example, you can use your knowledge of the effects of temperature on the rate of photosynthesis to predict the results of the experiment above. You might predict that as the temperature increases, the rate of photosynthesis increases up to a point.

3) The results of your experiment would then tell you if your prediction was correct. This will help you to determine if your hypothesis is likely to be correct, or whether it needs to change.

Taking Measurements

There are lots of pieces of equipment you can use to take measurements. You need to know how to use each one correctly and when you need to use them. Luckily, that's what these next two pages are all about.

The **Right Apparatus** Depends on **What** You're **Measuring**

1. **Length**

1) Length can be measured in different units (e.g. mm, cm, m). Smaller units have a higher degree of accuracy. You'll need to decide on the appropriate level of accuracy for your experiment. For example, the length of a leaf would be better measured in mm, but the length of a field would be better measured in m.

2) It is also important to choose the right equipment — a ruler would probably be best for measuring short lengths, but a metre rule or tape measure would be better for larger distances.

2. **Mass**

1) To weigh a solid, put the container you are weighing your substance into on a balance.

2) Set the balance to exactly zero and then weigh out the correct amount of your substance.

3. **Temperature**

1) You can use a thermometer to measure the temperature of a solution.

2) Make sure that the bulb of the thermometer is completely submerged in the solution and that you wait for the temperature to stabilise before you take your initial reading.

3) Read off the scale on the thermometer at eye level to make sure it's correct.

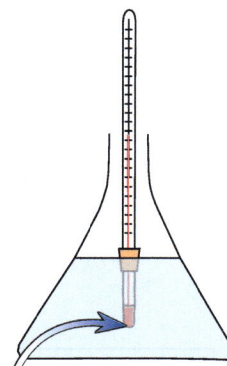

thermometer bulb

4. **Volume** of a **Liquid**

There's more than one way to measure the volume of a liquid. Whichever method you use, always read the volume from the bottom of the meniscus (the curved upper surface of the liquid) when it's at eye level.

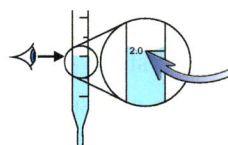

Read volume from here — the bottom of the meniscus.

Using a pipette

- Pipettes are used to suck up and transfer volumes of liquid between containers.
- Dropping pipettes are used to transfer drops of liquid.
- Graduated pipettes are used to transfer accurate volumes.
- A pipette filler is attached to the end of a graduated pipette, to control the amount of liquid being drawn up.

Syringes can also be used to measure small volumes of liquids.

Using a measuring cylinder

Measuring cylinders come in many different sizes (ranging from about 10 cm³ to several dm³). Make sure you choose one that's the right size for the measurement you want to make (see next page for more).

Taking Measurements

5. Volume of a Gas

1) To accurately measure the volume of gas, you should use a gas syringe.

2) Alternatively, you can use an upturned measuring cylinder filled with water. The gas will push the water out so you can read the volume of gas off the scale.

3) Other methods to measure the amount of gas include:
   * counting the bubbles produced,
   * measuring the length of a gas bubble drawn along a tube (see page 36).

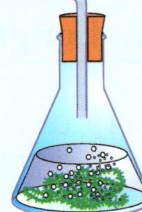

   These methods are less accurate, but will give you relative amounts of gas to compare results.

4) When you're measuring a gas, you need to make sure that the equipment is set up so that none of the gas can escape, otherwise your results won't be accurate.

6. pH

The method you should use to measure pH depends on what your experiment is.

1) Indicators are dyes that change colour depending on whether they're in an acid or an alkali. You use them by adding a couple of drops of the indicator to the solution you're interested in. Universal indicator is a mixture of indicators that changes colour gradually as pH changes. It's useful for estimating the pH of a solution based on its colour.

2) Indicator paper is useful if you don't want to colour the entire solution that you're testing. It changes colour depending on the pH of the solution it touches. You can also hold a piece of damp indicator paper in a gas sample to test its pH.

> Blue litmus paper turns red in acidic conditions and red litmus paper turns blue in alkaline conditions.

3) pH meters have a digital display that gives an accurate value for the pH of a solution.

Your Equipment has to be Right for the Job

1) The measuring equipment you use has to be sensitive enough to measure the changes you're looking for. For example, if you need to measure changes of 1 cm³ you need to use a measuring cylinder that can measure in 1 cm³ steps — it'd be no good trying with one that only measures 10 cm³ steps.

2) The smallest change a measuring instrument can detect is called its resolution. E.g. some mass balances have a resolution of 1 g, some have a resolution of 0.1 g, and some are even more sensitive.

3) The more sensitive your equipment is, the more precise your measurements will be. E.g. a measurement of 10.1 g is more precise than a measurement of 10 g. You should make sure you record your measurements with the same precision (number of digits) as your measuring instrument.

4) Unfortunately, your readings may not always perfectly match the scale on the instrument. When this happens, you need to interpolate (estimate) where your reading lies between two marks on the scale.

5) Also, equipment needs to be calibrated by measuring a known value. If there's a difference between the measured and known value, you can use this to correct the inaccuracy of the equipment.

PRACTICAL TIP

Read off the scale carefully when taking readings

Whether you're reading off a thermometer, a pipette, syringe or a measuring cylinder, take all readings at eye level. And, if it's volume you're measuring, read from the bottom of the meniscus.

Sampling

You need to be able to carry out sampling that'll give you non-biased results. First up why, then how...

Sampling Should be Random

1) When you're investigating a population, it's generally not possible to study every single organism in the population. This means that you need to take samples of the population you're interested in.

2) The sample data will be used to draw conclusions about the whole population, so it's important that it accurately represents the whole population.

3) If a sample doesn't represent the population as a whole, it's said to be biased.

4) To avoid bias, a sample should be random.

Organisms Should Be Sampled At Random Sites in an Area

For example, if you're looking at plant species in a field...

1) Divide the field into a grid.

2) Label the grid along the bottom and up the side with numbers.

3) Use a random number generator (on a computer or calculator) to select coordinates, e.g. (2,6).

4) Take your samples at these coordinates.

Non-random sampling
Only looks at a small part of the field.

Random sampling
Randomly selects squares from all over the field.

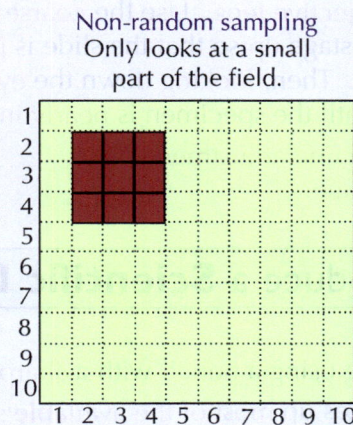

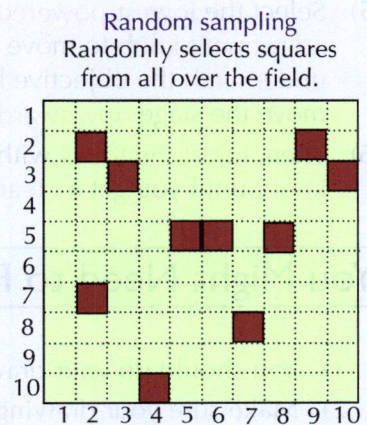

5) If you are estimating the population size of the plant species, you can count the number of plants at each sample site, and then use the mean number of plants at each site to estimate the population size of the plant species in the whole field.

Health Data Should be Taken from Randomly Selected People

For example, a health professional is investigating how many people diagnosed with Type 1 diabetes in a particular country also have coeliac disease:

1) All the people who have been diagnosed with Type 1 diabetes in the country of interest are identified by hospital records. In total, there are 270 196 people.

2) These people are assigned a number between 1 and 270 196.

3) A random number generator is used to choose the sample group (e.g. it selects the individuals #72 063, #11 822, #193 123, etc.)

4) The proportion of people in the sample that have coeliac disease can be used to estimate the total number of people with Type 1 diabetes that also have coeliac disease.

The Bigger the Sample Size the Better

1) Data based on small samples isn't as good as data based on large samples. A sample should represent the whole population (i.e. it should share as many of the characteristics in the population as possible) — a small sample can't do that as well. It's also harder to spot anomalies (see p.163) if your sample size is too small.

2) The bigger the sample size the better, but scientists have to be realistic when choosing how big. E.g. if you were studying how lifestyle affects people's weight it'd be great to study a million people, but it'd take ages and cost a lot. It's more realistic to study 1000 people, with a mixture of ages, sex and race.

Observing and Drawing Biological Specimens

You need to be able to observe, record and measure biological specimens, e.g. cells in a microscope image.

This is How to View a Specimen Using a Light Microscope:

1) Take a thin slice of your specimen, e.g. a layer of onion cells.

2) Next, take a clean slide and use a pipette to put one drop of water in the middle of it — this will hold the specimen in place. Use tweezers to place your specimen on the slide.

3) Add a drop of stain if your specimen is transparent or colourless — this makes the specimen easier to see.

4) Place a cover slip over the specimen. Press it down gently so that no air bubbles are trapped under it. Then clip the slide onto the stage.

5) Select the lowest-powered objective lens. Use the coarse adjustment knob to move the stage up so that the slide is just underneath the objective lens. Then, looking down the eyepiece, move the stage downwards until the specimen is nearly in focus.

6) Then adjust the focus with the fine adjustment knob, until you get a clear image.

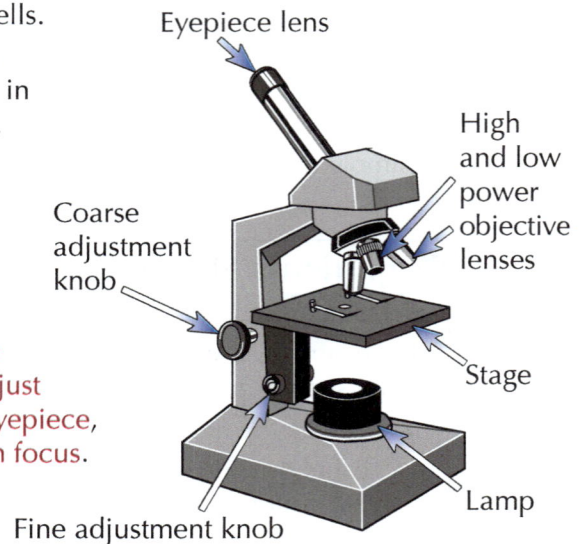

Eyepiece lens

High and low power objective lenses

Coarse adjustment knob

Stage

Lamp

Fine adjustment knob

You Might Need to Produce a Scientific Drawing of a Specimen

1) You should do your drawing using a pencil with a sharp point.

2) Make sure your drawing takes up most of the available space and that it is drawn with clear, unbroken lines.

3) Your drawing should not include any colouring or shading.

4) If you are drawing cells, the structures inside them should be drawn in proportion.

5) Remember to include a title of what you were observing and write down the magnification that it was observed under.

6) You should also label the important features of your drawing (e.g. nucleus, chloroplasts), using straight lines drawn with a ruler. Make sure that none of these lines cross each other because this can make them hard to read. Make sure your lines actually touch the features that you are labelling too.

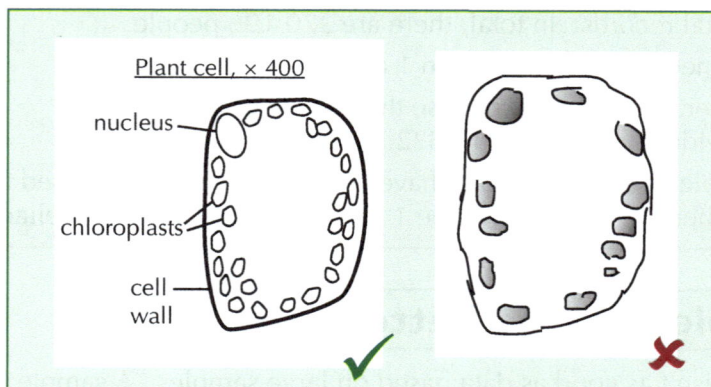

Plant cell, × 400

nucleus

chloroplasts

cell wall

✔

✗

If you know the power of the microscope lenses used to view an image, you can work out the magnification of the image using the formula:
total magnification = eyepiece lens magnification × objective lens magnification.
Otherwise, you can use the magnification formula on page 16.

Take your time when you're doing scientific drawings

PRACTICAL TIP

When you look at a real specimen under a microscope, it might not look exactly like the diagrams you see in books. But don't be put off — just draw what you can see.

Processing Data

Once you've had fun collecting all your data, a few calculations might be needed to work out what your data actually shows. Some simple calculations include the mean, range, median and mode.

Data Needs to be Organised

1) Tables are useful for organising data. E.g. to record the volumes of gas collected in two test tubes, you might draw a table like the one on the right.

Test tube	Volume / cm³		
	Repeat 1	Repeat 2	Repeat 3
A	28	37	32
B	47	51	16

2) When you draw a table, use a ruler to make sure your rows and columns are straight.

3) Make sure each result column has a heading that includes a physical quantity, e.g. volume, and units.

4) You should draw a table for your results before you begin an experiment. It allows you to record your results in a neat and organised way.

5) Recording your results in a table can also help you spot any results that might be anomalous (p.163) more easily, so you can try to figure out what's gone wrong or correct them early in your investigation.

You Might Have to Process Your Data

1) When you've done repeats of an experiment you should always calculate the mean (average). To do this add together all the data values and divide by the total number of values in the sample.

2) You might also need to calculate the range (how spread out the data is). To do this find the largest number and subtract the smallest number from it.

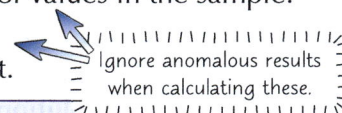

Ignore anomalous results when calculating these.

Example: The results of an experiment to find the volume of gas produced in an enzyme-controlled reaction are shown below. Calculate the mean volume and the range.

Volume / cm³				
Repeat 1	Repeat 2	Repeat 3	Mean	Range
28	37	32	(28 + 37 + 32) ÷ 3 = 32	37 − 28 = 9

3) You might also need to calculate the median or mode (two more types of average). To calculate the median, put all your data in numerical order — the median is the middle value. The number that appears most often in a data set is the mode.

If you have an even number of values, the median is halfway between the middle two values.

Example: If you have the data set: 1 2 1 1 3 4 2
The median is: 1 1 1 2 2 3 4. The mode is 1 because 1 appears most often.

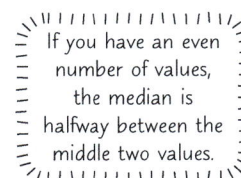

Round to the Lowest Number of Significant Figures

The first significant figure of a number is the first digit that's not zero. The second and third significant figures come straight after (even if they're zeros). You should be aware of significant figures in calculations.

1) In any calculation where you need to round, you should round the answer to the lowest number of significant figures (s.f.) given.

2) Remember to write down how many significant figures you've rounded to after your answer.

3) If your calculation has multiple steps, only round the final answer, or it won't be as accurate.

EXAMPLE: **A plant produces 10.2 cm³ of oxygen in 6.5 minutes whilst photosynthesising. Calculate the rate of photosynthesis.**

rate = 10.2 cm³ ÷ 6.5 min = 1.5692... = 1.6 cm³/min (2 s.f.)

3 s.f.   2 s.f.   Final answer should be rounded to 2 s.f.

More on Processing Data

Another way to process data is to calculate percentage change.

Percentage Change Allows you to Compare Results

1) When investigating the change in a variable, you may want to compare results that didn't have the same initial value.

> For example, you may want to compare the change in mass of potato cylinders left in different concentrations of sugar solution that had different initial masses (see page 22).

2) One way to do this is to calculate the percentage change. You work it out like this:

$$\text{percentage (\%) change} = \frac{\text{final value} - \text{original value}}{\text{original value}} \times 100$$

3) Below is an example that shows how percentage change can be calculated:

EXAMPLE: A student is investigating the effect of the concentration of sugar solution on potato cells. She records the mass of potato cylinders before and after placing them in sugar solutions of different concentrations. The table below shows some of her results. Which potato cylinder had the largest percentage change?

Potato cylinder	Concentration / M	Mass at start / g	Mass at end / g
1	0.0	7.5	8.7
2	1.0	8.0	6.8

1) Put each set of results into the equation:

$$\frac{\%}{\text{change}} = \frac{\text{final value} - \text{original value}}{\text{original value}} \times 100$$

1. $\frac{8.7 - 7.5}{7.5} \times 100 = 16\%$

The mass at the start is the original value and the mass at the end is the final value.

2. $\frac{6.8 - 8.0}{8.0} \times 100 = -15\%$

Here, the mass has decreased so the percentage change is negative.

2) Compare the results.

16% is greater than 15%, so the potato cylinder in the 0.0 M sugar solution had the largest percentage change.

Don't forget your calculator...

EXAM TIP It's not only important that you're able to collect and record the data, but that you can then do something with it once you've got it. In the exam you could be given some data and be expected to process it in some way. Even if it looks easy enough to do in your head, it's always worth checking on a calculator just to be sure. You don't want to lose marks by making a silly error.

Presenting Data

Once you've processed your data, e.g. by calculating the mean, you can present your results in a nice chart or graph. This will help you to spot any patterns in your data.

Bar Charts can be Used to Show Categoric Data

1) Bar charts are used to display categoric data — data that comes in distinct categories, e.g. flower colour, blood group, that is not numerical.

2) There are some golden rules you need to follow for drawing bar charts:

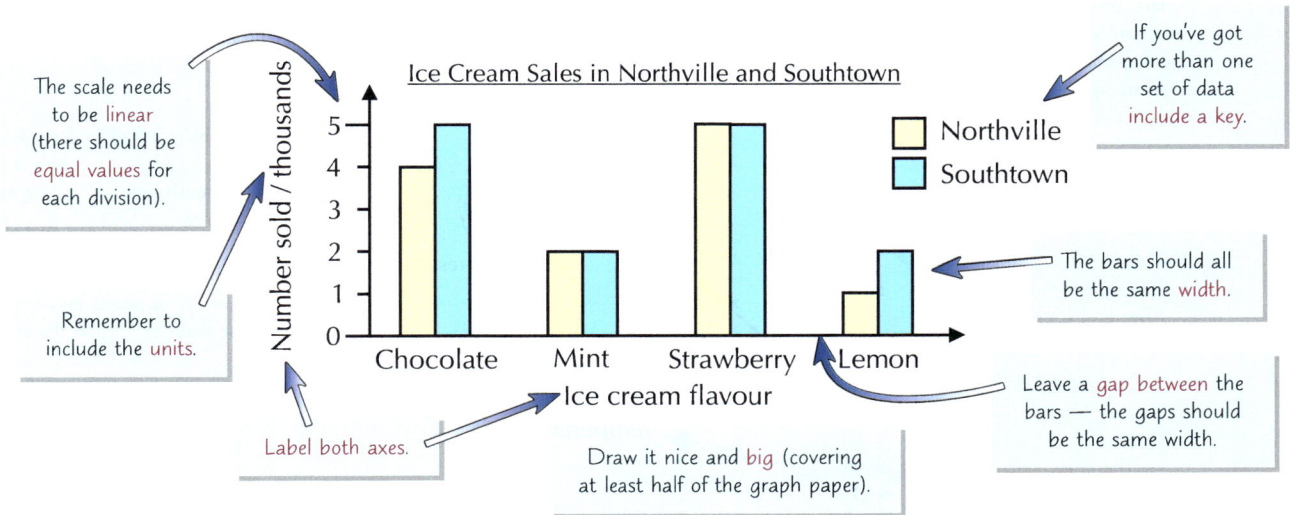

The scale needs to be linear (there should be equal values for each division).

Remember to include the units.

Label both axes.

If you've got more than one set of data include a key.

Ice Cream Sales in Northville and Southtown

Number sold / thousands

Northville
Southtown

Chocolate Mint Strawberry Lemon

Ice cream flavour

The bars should all be the same width.

Leave a gap between the bars — the gaps should be the same width.

Draw it nice and big (covering at least half of the graph paper).

With Histograms it's the Area NOT the Height that Matters

1) Histograms are a way to show frequency data (data on the number of times something occurs) when the independent variable is continuous. Continuous data is numerical data that can have any value in a range, e.g. length, volume, temperature.

2) Histograms may look like bar charts, but it's the area of the bars that represents the frequency rather than the height.

3) The continuous data is divided into groups called classes. For example, if the data relates to body temperature, you might have the classes: $35.5\ °C \leq x < 36.5\ °C$, $36.5\ °C \leq x < 37.5\ °C$, $37.5\ °C \leq x < 38.5\ °C$, etc. The width of each bar on a histogram is the class width.

4) When all the classes (bars) are the same width, you can just plot the frequency on the y-axis.

5) Here's what a histogram with equal class widths might look like:

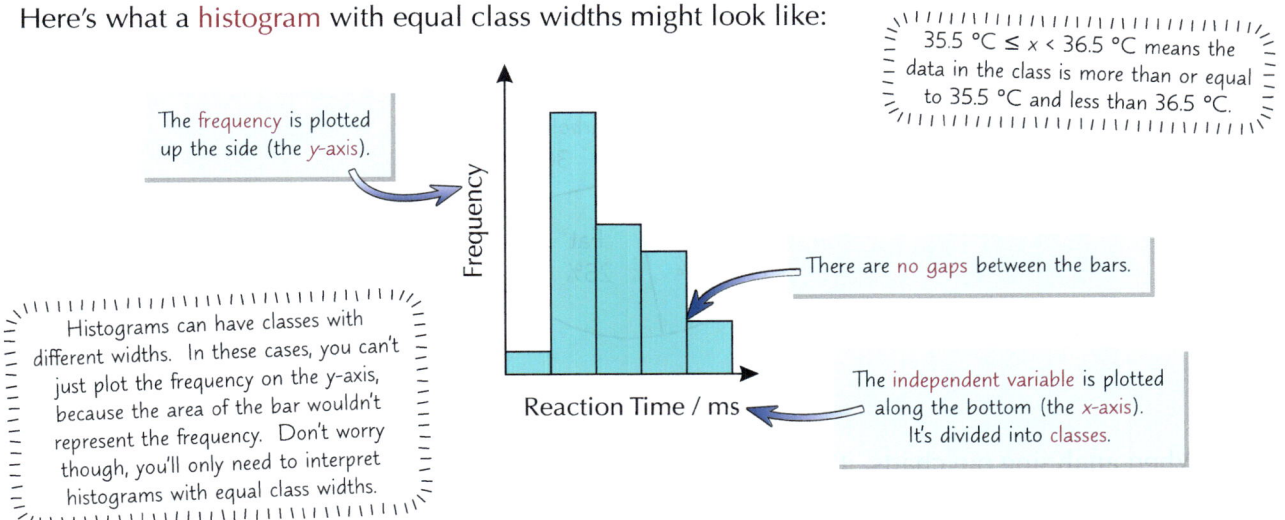

The frequency is plotted up the side (the y-axis).

$35.5\ °C \leq x < 36.5\ °C$ means the data in the class is more than or equal to $35.5\ °C$ and less than $36.5\ °C$.

Frequency

Reaction Time / ms

There are no gaps between the bars.

The independent variable is plotted along the bottom (the x-axis). It's divided into classes.

Histograms can have classes with different widths. In these cases, you can't just plot the frequency on the y-axis, because the area of the bar wouldn't represent the frequency. Don't worry though, you'll only need to interpret histograms with equal class widths.

Presenting Data

Graphs can be Used to Plot Continuous Data

1) If both variables are continuous you should use a graph to display the data.

2) Here are the rules for plotting points on a graph:

Use the biggest data values you've got to draw a sensible scale on your axes. Here, the highest rate of reaction is 22 cm³/s, so it makes sense to label the y-axis up to 25 cm³/s.

To plot points, use a sharp pencil and make neat little crosses (don't do blobs).

nice clear mark

smudged unclear marks

Graph to Show Rate of Enzyme-controlled Reaction Against Temperature

Rate of reaction / cm³/s

Temperature / °C

anomalous result

If you're asked to draw a line (or curve) of best fit, draw a single, smooth line through or as near to as many points as possible, ignoring any anomalous results. There should be a roughly even number of points on either side of the line. Don't join the crosses up.

The dependent variable goes on the y-axis (the vertical one).

The independent variable goes on the x-axis (the horizontal one).

Remember to include the units.

Draw it nice and big (covering at least half of the graph paper).

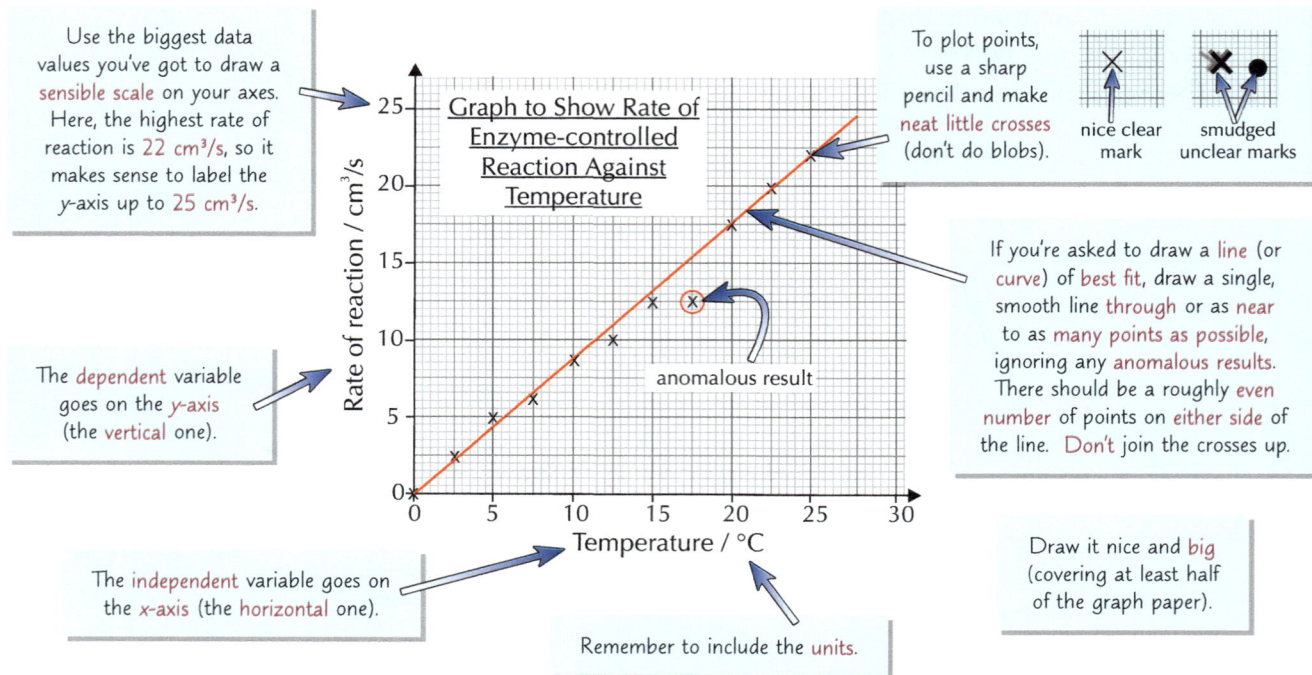

3) If you have a graph of the amount of product formed (or reactant used up) against time, then the gradient (slope) of the graph will be equal to the rate of the reaction — the steeper the slope, the faster the rate.

4) The gradient of a straight line is given by the equation:

$$\text{gradient} = \text{change in y} \div \text{change in x}$$

Pie Charts Show Proportions

1) Pie charts are a good way to compare different categories in data.

2) The amount of the whole chart a section takes up tells you the proportion (e.g. a percentage) of results in that category — the whole chart represents the entire data set.

3) When drawing pie charts there are a few rules you need to follow:

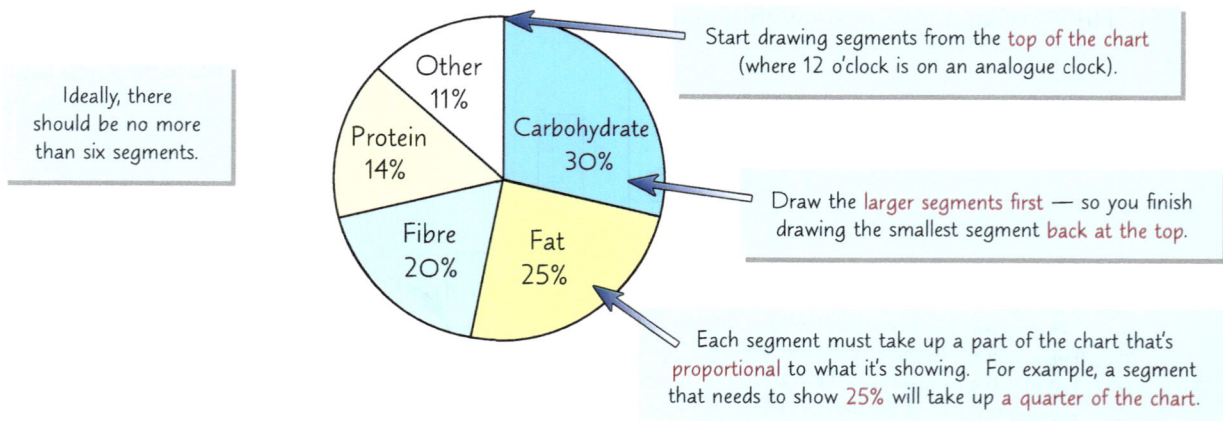

Ideally, there should be no more than six segments.

Other 11%

Protein 14%

Carbohydrate 30%

Fibre 20%

Fat 25%

Start drawing segments from the top of the chart (where 12 o'clock is on an analogue clock).

Draw the larger segments first — so you finish drawing the smallest segment back at the top.

Each segment must take up a part of the chart that's proportional to what it's showing. For example, a segment that needs to show 25% will take up a quarter of the chart.

4) When analysing pie charts, it's important to remember that they show proportions, not the actual number in each category.

Interpreting Data

Graphs aren't just fun to plot, they're also really useful for showing trends in your data.

You Need to be Able to **Interpret** Graphs

1) A graph is used to show the relationship between two variables — you need to be able to look at a graph and describe this relationship.

> *A relationship is directly proportional if one variable increases at the same rate as the other variable. E.g. if one variable doubles, the other also doubles. This is only true if the line is straight and goes through the origin (O,O).*

Example: The graph on the previous page shows that as temperature increases, so does rate of reaction.

2) You also need to be able to read information off a graph. In the example on the previous page, to find what the rate of reaction was at 11 °C, you'd draw a vertical line up to the graph line from the *x*-axis at 11 °C and a horizontal line across to the *y*-axis. This would tell you that the rate of reaction at 11 °C was around 9.7 cm^3/s.

Graphs Show the **Correlation** Between Two Variables

1) You can get three types of correlation (relationship) between variables:

2) Just because there's correlation, it doesn't mean the change in one variable is causing the change in the other — there might be other factors involved.

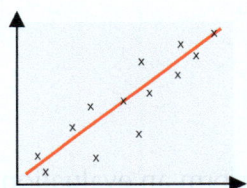

POSITIVE correlation:
as one variable increases
the other increases.

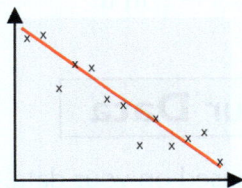

INVERSE (negative) correlation:
as one variable increases
the other decreases.

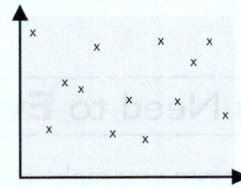

NO correlation:
no relationship between
the two variables.

3) There are three possible reasons for a correlation:

- CHANCE: It might seem strange, but two things can show a correlation purely due to chance.

- LINKED BY A 3RD VARIABLE: A lot of the time it may look as if a change in one variable is causing a change in the other, but it isn't — a third variable links the two things.

- CAUSE: Sometimes a change in one variable does cause a change in the other. You can only conclude that a correlation is due to cause when you've controlled all the variables that could, just could, be affecting the result.

A correlation is a relationship between two variables

WORKING SCIENTIFICALLY

Don't assume that two things changing together means that one is causing the other to change — it could be due to chance or to a third variable. Stop and think about what your results are really showing before drawing any sort of conclusion.

Conclusions and Evaluations

Hurrah! The end of another investigation. Well, now you have to worry about conclusions and evaluations.

You Can **Only Conclude** What the Data Shows and **NO MORE**

1) Drawing conclusions might seem pretty straightforward — you just look at your data and say what pattern or relationship you see between the dependent and independent variables.

> The table on the right shows the heights of pea plant seedlings grown for three weeks with different fertilisers.
>
> CONCLUSION: Fertiliser B makes pea plant seedlings grow taller over a three week period than fertiliser A.

Fertiliser	Mean growth / mm
A	13.5
B	19.5
No fertiliser	5.5

2) But you've got to be really careful that your conclusion matches the data you've got and doesn't go any further.

> You can't conclude that fertiliser B makes any other type of plant grow taller than fertiliser A — the results could be totally different.

3) You also need to be able to use your results to justify your conclusion (i.e. back up your conclusion with some specific data).

> Over the three week period, fertiliser B made the pea plants grow 6 mm more on average than fertiliser A.

4) When writing a conclusion you need to refer back to the original hypothesis and say whether the data supports it or not. If data backs up a prediction, it increases confidence in the hypothesis (although it doesn't prove the hypothesis is correct). If the data doesn't support the prediction, it can decrease confidence in it.

> The hypothesis for this experiment might have been that adding fertiliser would increase the growth of plants because it would provide plants with nutrients. The prediction may have been that fertiliser B contained more nutrients and so would increase growth more than fertiliser A. If so, the data increases confidence in the hypothesis.

You Need to **Evaluate** Your **Data**

1) Before you make any conclusions based on your data, you need to perform an evaluation. An evaluation is a critical analysis of the whole investigation, including the data you obtained.

2) You should comment on the method — was it valid? Did you control all the other variables to make it a fair test?

3) Comment on the quality of the results — were the results reliable and accurate? Were there sources of random or systematic error?

4) Were there any anomalous results? If there were none then say so. If there were any, try to explain them — were they caused by errors in measurement? Were there any other variables that could have affected the results?

5) All this analysis will allow you to say how confident you are that your conclusion is right.

6) Then you can suggest any changes to the method that would improve the quality of the results, so that you could have more confidence in your conclusion. For example, you might suggest changing the way you controlled a variable, carrying out further repeats or increasing the number of measurements you took. Taking more measurements at narrower intervals could give you a more accurate result.

> When suggesting improvements to the investigation, always make sure that you say why you think this would make the results better.

7) You could also make more predictions based on your conclusion, then further experiments could be carried out to test them.

Always look for ways to improve your investigations

EXAM TIP

There are 40 marks available in the practical assessment part of your exam (Paper 5 or 6). So you need to be able to describe experiments, process data, draw conclusions, etc. all in an appropriate way. Make sure you're happy with everything in this section. Best of luck.

Practice Papers

Once you've been through all the questions in this book, you should feel pretty confident about the exams. As final preparation, here is a set of <u>practice exam papers</u> to really get you ready for the real thing.

CGP Practice Exam Paper
Cambridge International
GCSE Biology

Cambridge International GCSE Biology

Paper 1 Multiple Choice (Core)

In addition to this paper you should have:
- A soft pencil.
- A calculator.
- An eraser.

Centre name					
Centre number					
Candidate number					

Time allowed:
- 45 minutes

Candidate name
Candidate signature

Instructions to candidates
- Write your name and other details in the spaces provided above.
- Use pencil to record your answers.
- For each question, clearly shade the oval next to your chosen answer. For example: ●
  If you wish to change your answer, use an eraser to remove your original answer.
- Do all rough work on the paper.

Information for candidates
- There are 40 marks available for this paper.
- Each question is worth one mark.

Turn over ▶

1   Where is DNA found in plant and animal cells?

    A cytoplasm

    B cell membrane

    C nucleus

    D vacuoles

2   A bean plant produces carbohydrate during photosynthesis.
    Which structure allows the cells of a bean plant to photosynthesise?

    A cell wall

    B chloroplast

    C cytoplasm

    D vacuole

3   The diagram shows a root hair cell viewed under a microscope at × 100 magnification.

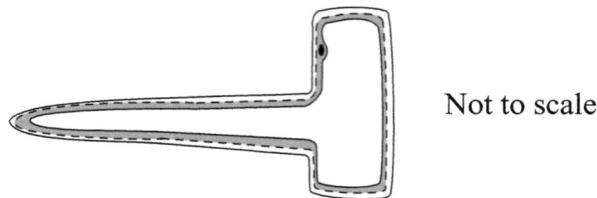

Not to scale

The actual length of the root hair cell is 0.08 mm.
What is the length of the root hair cell in the microscope image?

    A 0.0008 mm

    B 0.8 mm

    C 8 mm

    D 8 cm

4   The diagram shows a cell and the surrounding tissue fluid.
    Oxygen moves between the cell and the tissue fluid by diffusion.

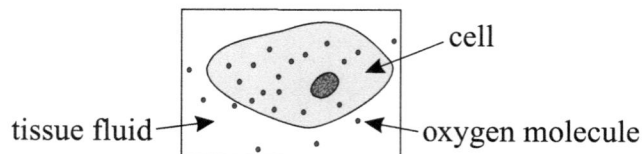

Which row describes how most of the oxygen molecules in the diagram will move?

	Direction of movement	Description of movement
A ◯	cell → tissue fluid	against concentration gradient
B ◯	cell → tissue fluid	down concentration gradient
C ◯	tissue fluid → cell	against concentration gradient
D ◯	tissue fluid → cell	down concentration gradient

5   In which of these examples is osmosis occurring?

    A A plant is absorbing water from the soil.

    B Sugar is being taken up into the blood from the gut.

    C Water is evaporating from a leaf.

    D Oxygen is entering the blood from the lungs.

6   Which statement about active transport is correct?

    A It is the way in which oxygen enters the blood from the lungs.

    B It can only occur down a concentration gradient.

    C It needs energy from respiration.

    D Particles move from a region of higher concentration to a region of lower concentration.

7   The biuret test is used on a sample of an unknown substance in solution. The solution turns purple.
    What is the unknown substance in the solution?

    A carbohydrate

    B fat

    C protein

    D water

8   A student investigates how temperature affects the rate at which starch is broken down
    by the enzyme amylase. Which graph correctly shows how the rate of the reaction is
    affected by temperature?

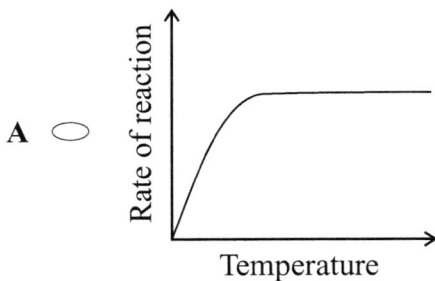

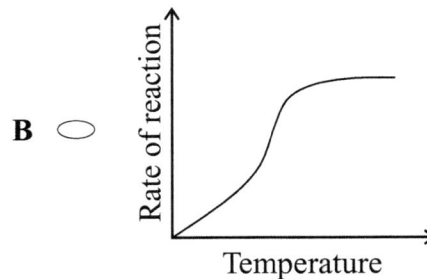

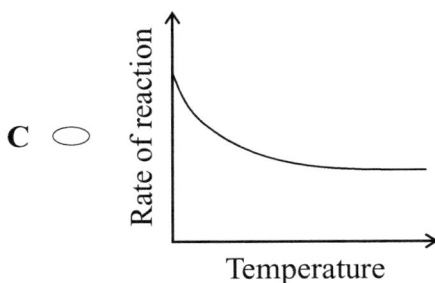

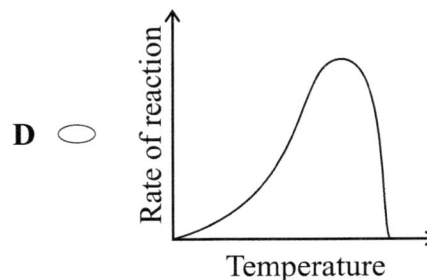

178

9   Which of these is **not** part of the overall equation for photosynthesis?

    A carbon dioxide

    B nitrates

    C light

    D chlorophyll

10 The apparatus below is used to investigate the effect of different factors on the rate of photosynthesis.

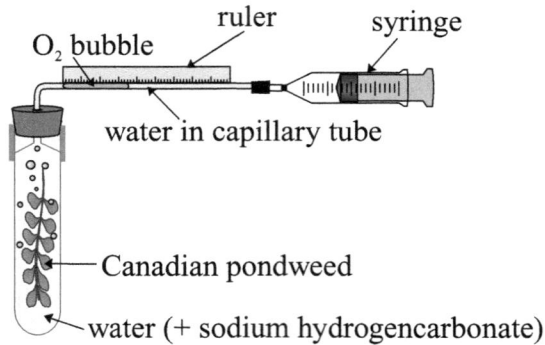

The apparatus is left in the following places for one hour.
In which place will the longest oxygen bubble be produced?

    A a dark fridge

    B a dark room

    C a fridge with the light switched on

    D a room with the light switched on

11 Which row shows a correct source of the nutrients needed for the body to carry out each function?

	Function			
	Making bones and teeth	Calcium absorption	Making haemoglobin	Maintaining the immune system
A	milk	citrus fruits	red meat	eggs
B	milk	eggs	red meat	citrus fruits
C	red meat	eggs	milk	citrus fruits
D	red meat	citrus fruits	milk	eggs

12 What is 'assimilation'?

A The uptake of nutrients into the cells of the body
where they are used, becoming part of the cells. ◯▶

B The taking of substances into the body through the mouth. ◯

C The passing out of food that has not been digested or absorbed, through the anus. ◯

D The movement of small food molecules and ions through the intestine wall into the blood. ◯

13 What molecule is digested by amylase and where in the alimentary canal is amylase produced?

		molecule digested	where produced
A	◯	starch	salivary glands
B	◯	protein	salivary glands
C	◯	starch	stomach
D	◯	protein	stomach

14 The diagram shows a section through a leaf.

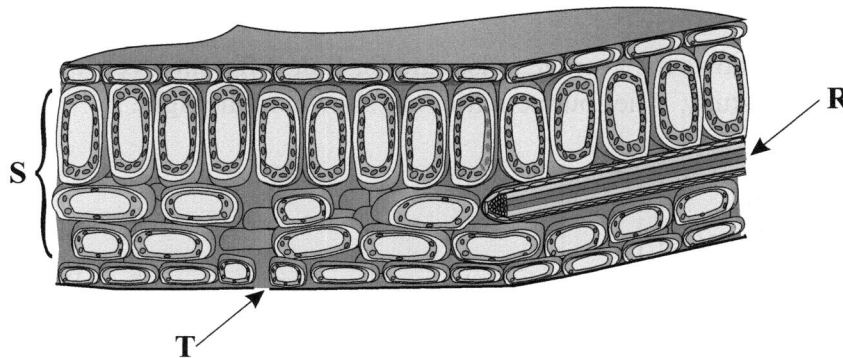

Which statement correctly describes how water is lost from the leaf via transpiration?

A Water evaporates from **R**, then diffuses through **T**. ◯

B Water diffuses through **R**, then evaporates at **T**. ◯

C Water evaporates from cells in **S**, then diffuses through **T**. ◯

D Water evaporates from cells in **S**, then diffuses through **R**. ◯

15 The diagram shows the equipment used to investigate transpiration rate.

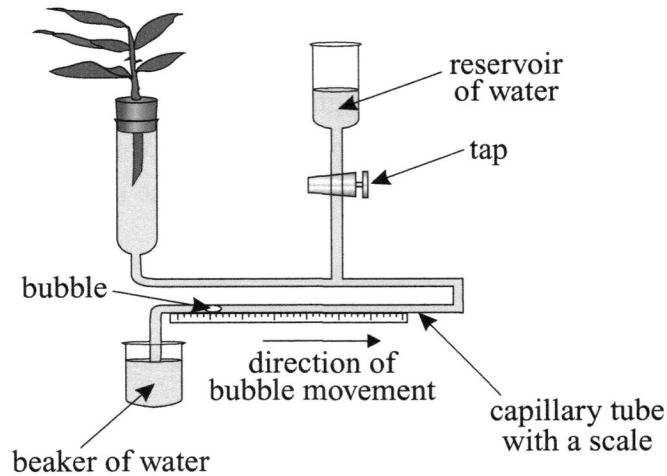

The experiment is carried out once as a control, and the distance moved by the bubble in 30 minutes is recorded. The experiment is then repeated in different environmental conditions. In which conditions will the bubble travel furthest?

A   warm, slow moving air

B   warm, fast moving air

C   cool, slow moving air

D   cool, fast moving air

16 The bar chart below shows the average pulse rate for four different levels of physical activity in a study. The four activities are shown on the right.

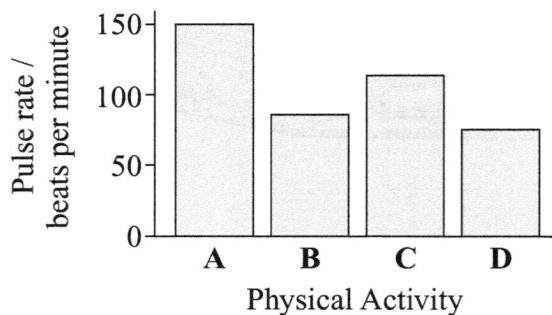

1.   Sitting

2.   Walking

3.   Jogging

4.   Running

Which physical activity on the graph is likely to be jogging?

A

B

C

D

17 Blood is carried around the body in blood vessels.
Three types of blood vessel are shown below.

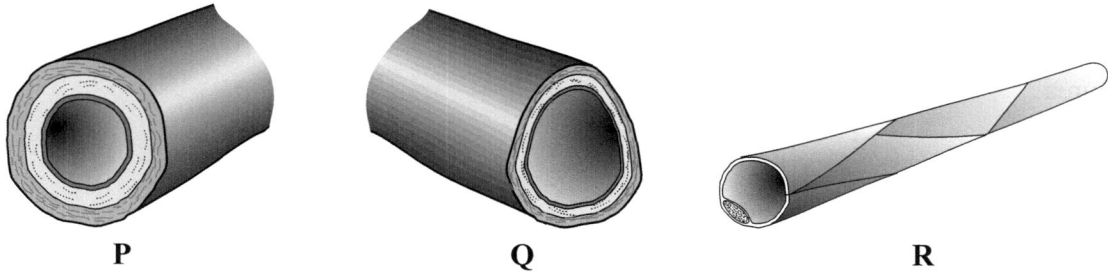

P   Q   R

Which statement is correct?

  A Vessels **Q** and **R** have one-way valves. ◯

  B Vessel **P** carries blood to the heart from the rest of the body. ◯

  C Vessel **R** carries blood really close to every cell in the body. ◯

  D Vessel **Q** carries blood from the heart to the rest of the body. ◯

18 Which of these is an example of a direct contact route by which a disease could be spread?

  A An insect transfers a pathogen from an infected person to an uninfected person. ◯

  B A person drinks some water that has been contaminated with a pathogen. ◯

  C A person breathes in a pathogen which is being carried in the air. ◯

  D An uninfected person kisses an infected person. ◯

19 What reacts with glucose in aerobic respiration?

  A water ◯

  B carbon dioxide ◯

  C lactic acid ◯

  D oxygen ◯

20 Which of these is **not** a possible product of anaerobic respiration?

  A water ◯

  B carbon dioxide ◯

  C lactic acid ◯

  D alcohol ◯

21   What substance is filtered out of the blood in the kidneys for removal in the urine?

    A proteins

    B carbon dioxide

    C oxygen

    D urea

22   Which row is correct for a reflex action?

	speed of action	decision
A ⬭	slow	under conscious control
B ⬭	slow	automatic
C ⬭	rapid	under conscious control
D ⬭	rapid	automatic

23   The diagram shows a section through the human eye.

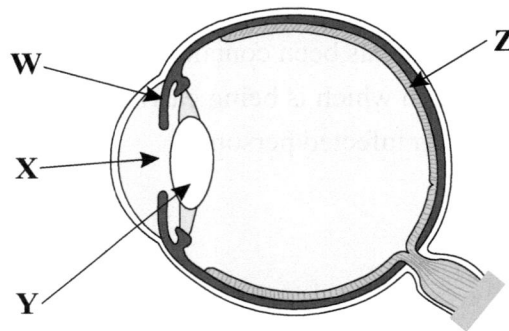

Which statement about the diagram is **false**?

    A **W** controls how much light enters **X**.

    B **Y** focuses light onto **Z**.

    C The diameter of **X** increases in bright light.

    D **Z** contains light receptors.

24   The optic nerve carries impulses.
Where do the impulses go once they have left the retina?

    A cornea

    B brain

    C blind spot

    D lens

25 Parts of the endocrine system are shown below.

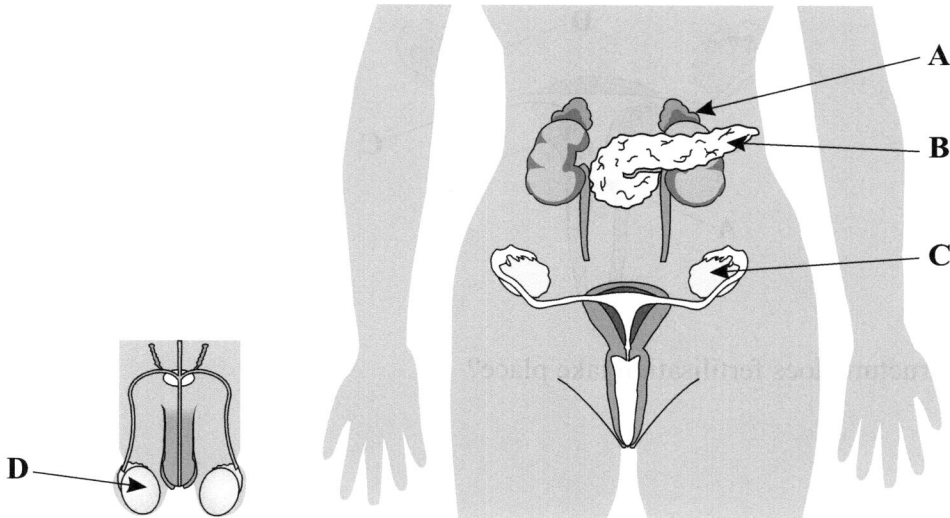

A hormone causes increased breathing and heart rate in 'fight or flight' situations. Which labelled gland is this hormone secreted from?

A ◯
B ◯
C ◯
D ◯

26 Which type of pathogen is targeted by antibiotics?

A viruses ◯
B bacteria ◯
C fungi ◯
D protoctists ◯

27 Part of a flower is shown below.

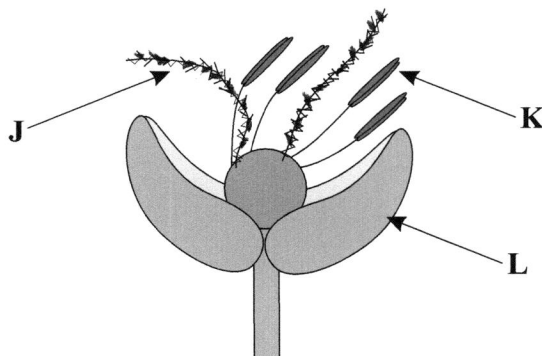

Which statement about the diagram is correct?

A Structure **K** catches pollen from other plants. ◯
B Structure **L** is likely to be brightly coloured. ◯
C Structure **J** produces big, sticky pollen grains. ◯
D Structure **K** releases many small, light pollen grains. ◯

28 The female reproductive system is shown below.

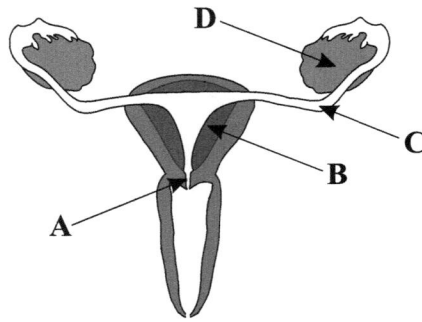

In which labelled structure does fertilisation take place?

A ⬭

B ⬭

C ⬭

D ⬭

29 The male reproductive system is shown below.

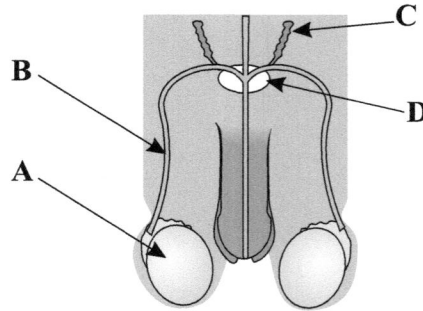

In which labelled structure is sperm produced?

A ⬭

B ⬭

C ⬭

D ⬭

30 A woman has the human immunodeficiency virus (HIV).
In which of these activities would she **not** be risking the transmission of HIV?

   A Having unprotected sex.   ○

   B Breastfeeding her baby.   ○

   C Coughing and sneezing on a crowded train.   ○

   D Sharing a needle with a drug user after using it to inject herself.   ○

31 Biological sex in humans is determined by sex chromosomes.
Which statement is **true**?

   A The presence of a Y chromosome results in male features.   ○

   B The presence of two X chromosomes results in male features.   ○

   C The presence of an X and a Y chromosome results in female features.   ○

   D The presence of two Y chromosomes results in female features.   ○

32 What term is used to describe the observable features of an organism?

   A genotype   ○

   B homozygous   ○

   C phenotype   ○

   D heterozygous   ○

33 Fruit flies can either have normal wings or small, deformed wings. The gene for normal wings is dominant (N). In an experiment, a scientist wanted to produce a population of fruit flies made up of 75% flies with normal wings and 25% flies with small, deformed wings.

Which cross would have the best chance of producing this population?

   A NN × Nn   ○

   B NN × nn   ○

   C nn × Nn   ○

   D Nn × Nn   ○

34 Which row gives correct causes and examples of continuous and discontinuous variation?

	Continuous variation		Discontinuous variation	
	Usual cause	Example	Usual cause	Example
A ⬭	Both genes and environment	ABO blood groups	Both genes and environment	Body mass
B ⬭	Both genes and environment	Body mass	Genes only	ABO blood groups
C ⬭	Genes only	Body mass	Environment only	ABO blood groups
D ⬭	Environment only	ABO blood groups	Genes only	Body mass

35 Which description would **not** be used when describing selective breeding?

A Competition for resources and struggle for survival. ⬭

B Selection by humans of individuals with desirable features. ⬭

C Selection of offspring showing desirable features. ⬭

D Crossing individuals with desirable features to produce a new generation. ⬭

36 The statements below describe how different organisms obtain energy or nutrients.

   1. By eating plants.

   2. By eating other animals.

   3. By breaking down dead material and waste.

   4. From the soil.

How do carnivores get their energy?

A 1, 2, 3 and 4 ⬭

B 1, 2 and 3 only ⬭

C 1 only ⬭

D 2 only ⬭

37 The diagram shows some of the feeding relationships in a rocky shore environment.

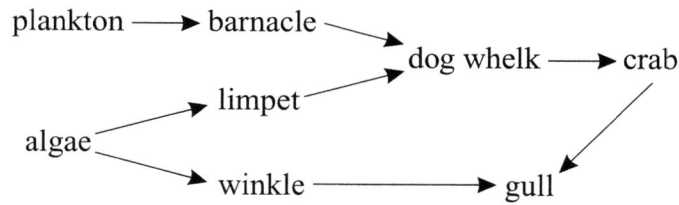

plankton ⟶ barnacle
algae ⟶ limpet
algae ⟶ winkle
barnacle ⟶ dog whelk
limpet ⟶ dog whelk
dog whelk ⟶ crab
winkle ⟶ gull
crab ⟶ gull

Which of the following organisms is **not** a secondary or a tertiary consumer?

A crab

B limpet

C gull

D dog whelk

38 A student wrote some sentences about how intensive livestock production is different from 'free-range' farming. He wrote:

'In intensive livestock production, animals use ......1...... energy for moving around.

This means ......2...... meat can be produced.

Diseases are more likely to spread in ......3.......·

Which row contains the words that correctly complete gaps 1, 2 and 3?

	1	2	3
A ○	less	less	'free-range' farming
B ○	more	less	'free-range' farming
C ○	more	more	intensive livestock production
D ○	less	more	intensive livestock production

39 Which of the following is **not** an effect of deforestation?

A increased risk of flooding

B increase in biodiversity

C increase of carbon dioxide in the atmosphere

D extinction

40 Which of these is an example of genetic modification?

A The production of ethanol for biofuels using yeast.

B The production of a bacterium that can produce human insulin.

C The production of fruit juice using the enzyme pectinase.

D The use of enzymes in biological washing powders.

END OF QUESTIONS

CGP — Practice Exam Paper
Cambridge International
GCSE Biology

Cambridge International GCSE Biology

Paper 2 Multiple Choice (Extended)

In addition to this paper you should have:
- A soft pencil.
- A calculator.
- An eraser.

Centre name					
Centre number					
Candidate number					

Time allowed:
- 45 minutes

Candidate name	
Candidate signature	

Instructions to candidates

- Write your name and other details in the spaces provided above.
- Use pencil to record your answers.
- For each question, clearly shade the oval next to your chosen answer. For example: ●
  If you wish to change your answer, use an eraser to remove your original answer.
- Do all rough work on the paper.

Information for candidates

- There are 40 marks available for this paper.
- Each question is worth one mark.

1   Which of the following organisms is a myriapod?

    A ◯   B ◯   C ◯   D ◯

2   Which row correctly shows two features of fungi?

		Feature 1	Feature 2
A	◯	Can store carbohydrate	Has cell walls containing cellulose
B	◯	Reproduce using spores	Has cell walls containing chitin
C	◯	Can photosynthesise	Reproduce using spores
D	◯	Has cell walls containing chitin	Can photosynthesise

3   The diagram shows a cell.

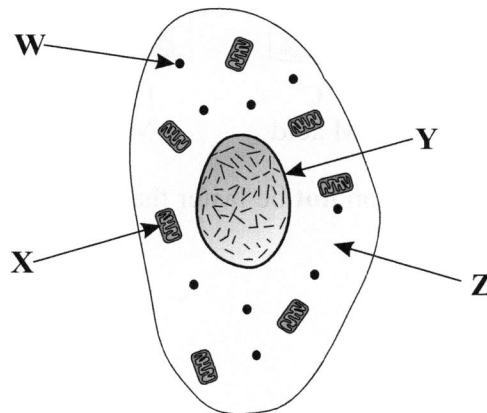

Which of these statements is **false**?

A   Z is where most chemical reactions in the cell take place.   ◯

B   This cell can photosynthesise.   ◯

C   Prokaryotes do not have structures **X** or **Y**.   ◯

D   Structure **W** is where proteins are made in the cell.   ◯

4 The diagram shows a blood cell viewed under a microscope.
   The real width of the blood cell is 12 μm.

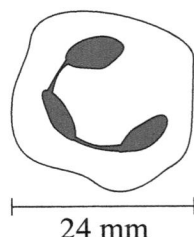

24 mm

What is the magnification of the cell?

A × 500   ◯
B × 1000   ◯
C × 2000   ◯
D × 4000   ◯

5 The diagram shows the set-up for an investigation into the rate of diffusion.
   The faster the rate of diffusion, the quicker the agar cubes turn colourless.

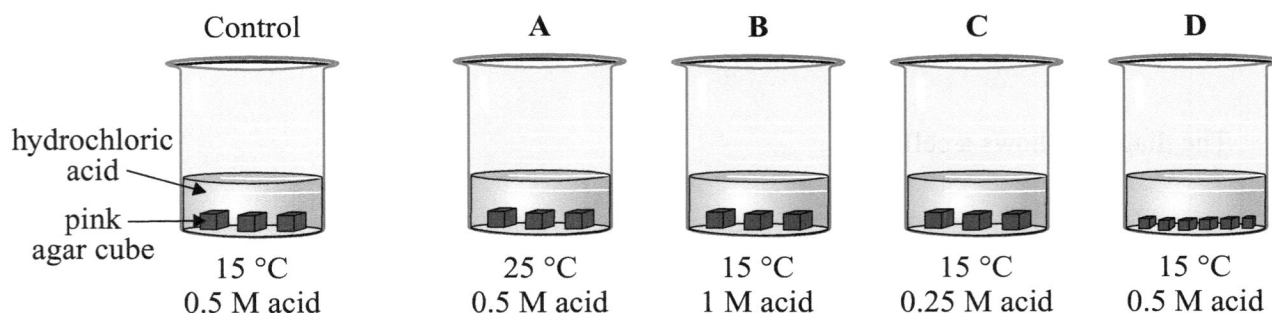

| Control | A | B | C | D |

hydrochloric acid

pink agar cube

| 15 °C | 25 °C | 15 °C | 15 °C | 15 °C |
| 0.5 M acid | 0.5 M acid | 1 M acid | 0.25 M acid | 0.5 M acid |

In which beaker will the rate of diffusion **not** be faster than in the control?

A ◯
B ◯
C ◯
D ◯

6 A plant tissue is placed in a solution with a higher water potential than itself.

Which statement correctly describes the effect on the plant tissue?

A The cells will become turgid.   ◯
B There will be no turgor pressure in the cells.   ◯
C The cells will become flaccid.   ◯
D Plasmolysis of the cells will occur.   ◯

7 In which scenario does active transport occur?

    A Movement of ions into root hair cells from the soil. ◯

    B Movement of water into the tissue fluid from the capillaries. ◯

    C Movement of oxygen into the blood from the alveoli. ◯

    D Movement of water into root hair cells from the soil. ◯

8 Which of the following can be used to test for vitamin C in a food sample?

    A Benedict's solution ◯

    B DCPIP solution ◯

    C ethanol ◯

    D biuret solution ◯

9 The graph below shows how the rate of an enzyme-controlled reaction is affected by pH.

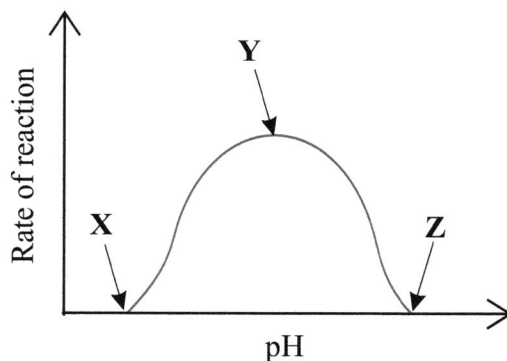

Which row provides correct labels relating to the enzyme for the points **X**, **Y** and **Z** on the graph?

	X	**Y**	**Z**
A ◯	at optimum pH	denatured	at optimum pH
B ◯	denatured	at optimum pH	at optimum pH
C ◯	at optimum pH	denatured	denatured
D ◯	denatured	at optimum pH	denatured

10 Which row shows the correct use of the ion in plants?

	Ion	Use
A ⬭	Nitrate	Making chlorophyll
B ⬭	Magnesium	Making amino acids and proteins
C ⬭	Nitrate	Making cell membranes
D ⬭	Magnesium	Making chlorophyll

11 The graph below shows the results of an investigation into the effect of different limiting factors on photosynthesis.

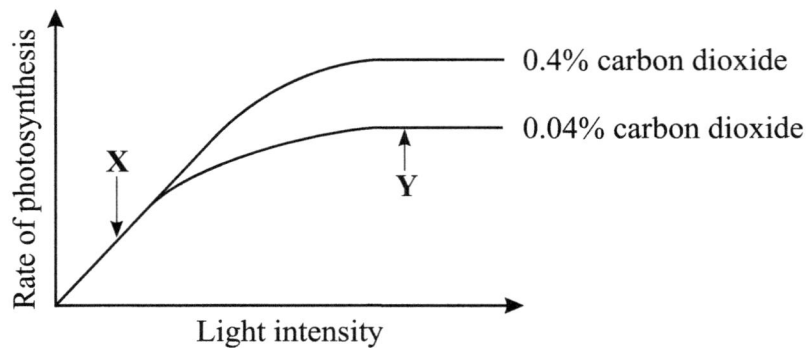

What are the limiting factors at points **X** and **Y**?

	Limiting Factor at **X**	Limiting Factor at **Y**
A ⬭	carbon dioxide concentration	temperature
B ⬭	carbon dioxide concentration	light intensity
C ⬭	light intensity	carbon dioxide concentration
D ⬭	temperature	carbon dioxide concentration

12 A certain organ in the digestive system has the following characteristics:

1. Produces a protease enzyme

2. Has a muscular wall

3. Produces hydrochloric acid

Which organ has **all** of these characteristics?

A pancreas

B liver

C stomach

D oesophagus

13 Which row shows two correct functions for the chemical involved in digestion?

	Chemical	Function 1	Function 2
A ○	hydrochloric acid	Giving the optimum pH for pepsin activity	Killing harmful microorganisms in food
B ○	bile	Neutralising the acidic mixture of food and stomach acid entering the duodenum	Giving the optimum pH for pepsin activity
C ○	hydrochloric acid	Emulsifying fats and oils to increase the surface area for digestion	Killing harmful microorganisms in food
D ○	bile	Giving the optimum pH for pepsin activity	Emulsifying fats and oils to increase the surface area for digestion

14 The diagram shows the structure of a villus in the small intestine.

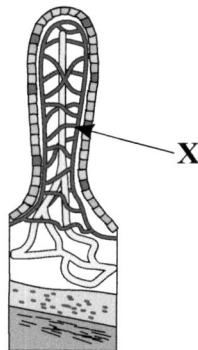

What is the role of structure **X**?

A To provide a good blood supply. ○

B To absorb digested fats. ○

C To provide energy from respiration. ○

D To increase the surface area of the small intestine. ○

15 How do nutrients move through a plant in translocation?

A In the xylem, from the source to the sink. ○

B In the phloem, from the source to the sink. ○

C In the xylem, from the sink to the source. ○

D In the phloem, from the sink to the source. ○

16 Which of the following statements describes capillaries?

    A They have a wide lumen.

    B They have permeable walls that are usually one cell thick.

    C Their walls have thick layers of muscle and elastic fibres.

    D They have valves.

17 The diagram below shows some blood cells under a microscope.

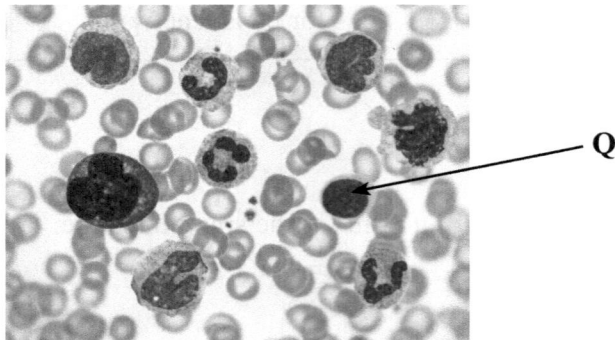

    What is the function of the cell marked **Q**?

    A producing antibodies

    B clotting

    C phagocytosis

    D transporting oxygen

18 Which statement would **not** be used when describing vaccination?

    A Antigens trigger an immune response by lymphocytes.

    B A weakened pathogen with antigens is given.

    C Memory cells are produced to give short-term, passive immunity.

    D Lymphocytes produce antibodies against the antigens.

19   The diagram shows cells in the airways.

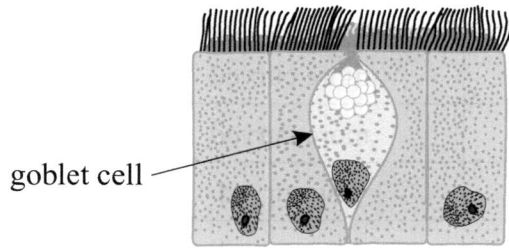

goblet cell

What is the purpose of the goblet cell?

A   wafting mucus back up to the top of the throat   ⃝
B   producing antibodies   ⃝
C   transporting carbon dioxide   ⃝
D   producing mucus   ⃝

20   Which statement about the removal of an oxygen debt is correct?

A   Oxygen is needed for the aerobic respiration of lactic acid.   ⃝
B   Anaerobic respiration is used to break down lactic acid.   ⃝
C   Lactic acid is transported from the liver to the muscles.   ⃝
D   All lactic acid is broken down in the muscles.   ⃝

21   The diagram shows the structure of the urinary system.

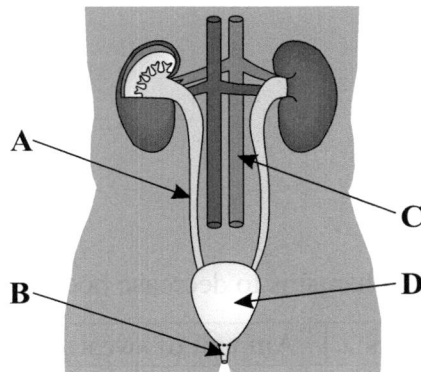

Which labelled structure is the urethra?

A   ⃝
B   ⃝
C   ⃝
D   ⃝

22 Which row correctly describes accommodation in the eye to look at distant objects?

	The ciliary muscles...	The lens becomes...	The amount of refraction...
A ○	contract	more curved	decreases
B ○	relax	more curved	increases
C ○	contract	less curved	increases
D ○	relax	less curved	decreases

23 Parts of the endocrine system are shown below.

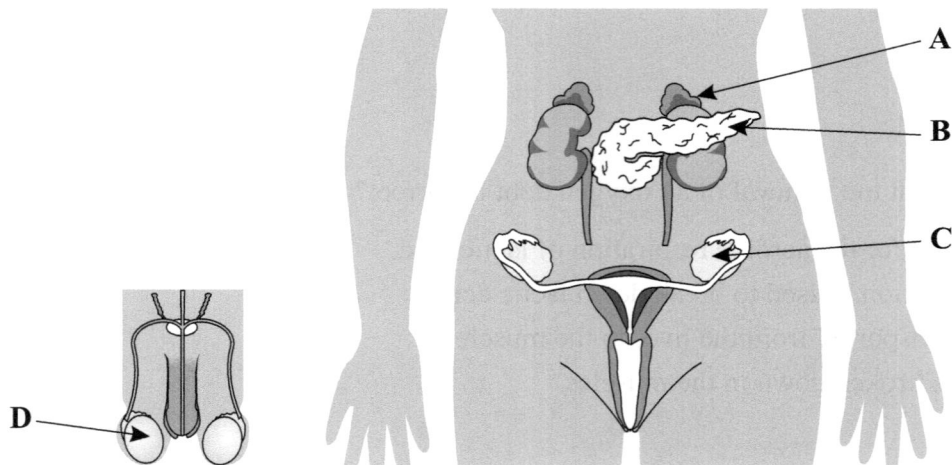

Which gland in the human body secretes insulin?

A ○

B ○

C ○

D ○

24 Which row correctly describes mechanisms to decrease body temperature?

	Erector muscles in hairs...	Amount of sweat...	Arterioles near the skin surface...
A ○	contract	decreases	dilate
B ○	relax	increases	constrict
C ○	contract	increases	constrict
D ○	relax	increases	dilate

25 The diagram shows an investigation into phototropism in cress seedlings.
    The arrow shows the direction from which the light is coming.

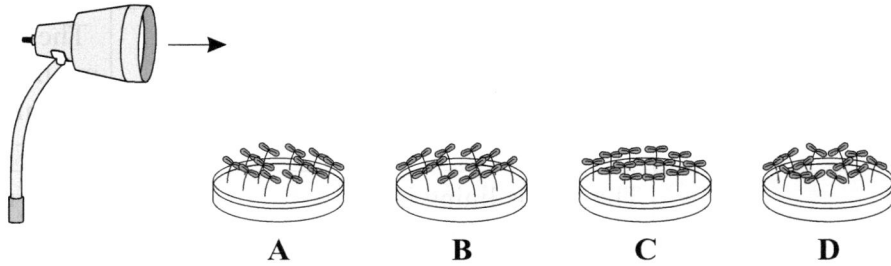

    Which Petri dish shows the direction of seedling growth after two days?

    A   ◯
    B   ◯
    C   ◯
    D   ◯

26 Which of the following statements best describes the term antibiotic?

    A A drug used to kill all pathogens, including bacteria and viruses.   ◯
    B A drug used to treat viral infections.   ◯
    C A drug used to kill every type of bacteria.   ◯
    D A drug used to treat a bacterial infection.   ◯

27 Which row is correct?

	Produces genetic variation	Requires two parents	Produces offspring more quickly
A ◯	sexual reproduction	asexual reproduction	sexual reproduction
B ◯	asexual reproduction	sexual reproduction	sexual reproduction
C ◯	sexual reproduction	sexual reproduction	asexual reproduction
D ◯	asexual reproduction	asexual reproduction	asexual reproduction

28 The stages of development of a baby are shown.

    1. fetus

    2. zygote

    3. embryo

    What is the correct sequence of the stages?

    A $2 \rightarrow 1 \rightarrow 3$ ◯
    B $1 \rightarrow 3 \rightarrow 2$ ◯
    C $2 \rightarrow 3 \rightarrow 1$ ◯
    D $3 \rightarrow 2 \rightarrow 1$ ◯

Turn over ▶

29 Which row correctly describes what happens at each stage of the menstrual cycle?

	Stage 1	Stage 2	Stage 3	Stage 4
A ○	The uterus lining builds up.	The uterus lining breaks down, and a follicle matures in an ovary.	The egg is released from the follicle.	The uterus lining is maintained, ready for the implantation of a fertilised egg.
B ○	The egg is released from the follicle.	The uterus lining is maintained, ready for the implantation of a fertilised egg.	The uterus lining breaks down.	The uterus lining builds up, and a follicle matures in an ovary.
C ○	A follicle matures in an ovary.	The uterus lining breaks down.	The uterus lining is maintained, ready for the implantation of a fertilised egg.	The uterus lining builds up, and the egg is released from the follicle.
D ○	The uterus lining breaks down.	The uterus lining builds up, and a follicle matures in an ovary.	The egg is released from the follicle.	The uterus lining is maintained, ready for the implantation of a fertilised egg.

30 The steps in protein synthesis are shown.

1. The gene coding for the protein remains in the **X**.

2. An mRNA molecule is a copy of the gene, which moves to the **Y**.

3. The mRNA passes through a **Z**.

4. The **Z** assembles amino acids into protein molecules.

What are the correct names for structures **X**, **Y** and **Z**?

	X	Y	Z
A ○	nucleus	cytoplasm	ribosome
B ○	cytoplasm	nucleus	ribosome
C ○	nucleus	cytoplasm	mitochondrion
D ○	cytoplasm	nucleus	mitochondrion

31 A diploid armadillo zygote contains 64 chromosomes.

How many chromosomes are in an armadillo gamete?

A 23

B 32

C 64

D 128

32 The graph shows the percentage of UK blood donors with different blood groups.

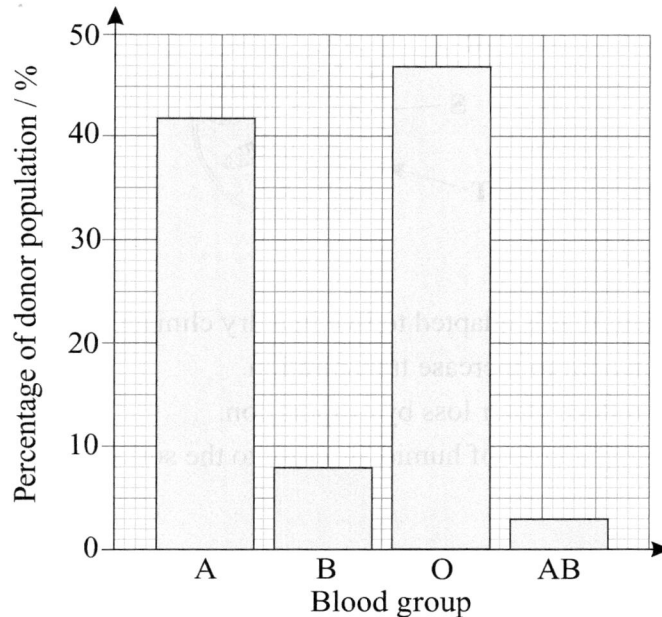

What percentage of donors have the I^B allele?

A 3%

B 8%

C 11%

D 55%

33 Red-green colour blindness is caused by a recessive allele (n) on the X chromosome. A man with red-green colour blindness has a child with a woman who is a carrier for the condition. The genetic diagram is shown.

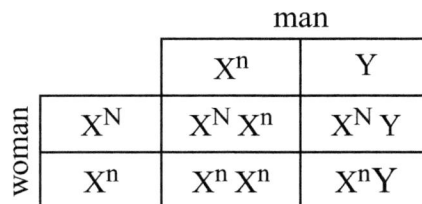

		man	
		X^n	Y
woman	X^N	$X^N X^n$	$X^N Y$
	X^n	$X^n X^n$	$X^n Y$

What is the probability that the couple will have a child with red-green colour blindness?

A 0%

B 25%

C 50%

D 75%

34 Which of the following is **not** a source of genetic variation in a population?

    A random fertilisation

    B mutation

    C random mating

    D mitosis

35 The diagram below shows a cross-section of a plant leaf.

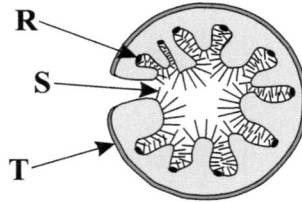

Which statement is **false**?

    A The leaf is from a plant that is adapted to live in a dry climate.

    B Structure **R** is sunk in a pit to increase transpiration.

    C Structure **T** helps to reduce water loss by evaporation.

    D Structure **S** helps to trap a layer of humid air close to the surface.

36 The diagram shows a pyramid of biomass.

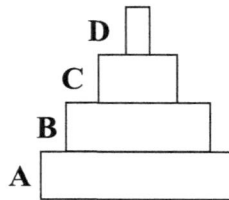

Which bar represents a primary consumer?

    A

    B

    C

    D

37 What is 'denitrification'?

    A Turning NO_3^- in the soil into N_2 in the air.

    B Turning NH_4^+ into NO_2^- and then NO_3^-.

    C Turning N_2 in the air into nitrogen compounds.

    D Turning proteins and urea into NH_4^+.

38 What is a 'community'?

A   All of the populations of different species in an ecosystem.

B   A group of organisms of one species, living in the same place at the same time.

C   A unit containing organisms and their environment interacting together.

D   A group of organisms that can reproduce to produce fertile offspring.

39 The steps in eutrophication are shown.

1.   The amount of dissolved oxygen in the water decreases.

2.   The amount of decomposition increases, so aerobic respiration of decomposers increases.

3.   Growth of producers such as algae increases, which blocks out the light, leading to the death of producers.

4.   Organisms in the water that need dissolved oxygen die.

5.   Fertilisers enter the water, providing extra nitrates and other ions.

What is the correct sequence of the steps?

A $5 \rightarrow 3 \rightarrow 1 \rightarrow 2 \rightarrow 4$

B $5 \rightarrow 3 \rightarrow 2 \rightarrow 1 \rightarrow 4$

C $5 \rightarrow 2 \rightarrow 3 \rightarrow 1 \rightarrow 4$

D $5 \rightarrow 1 \rightarrow 2 \rightarrow 3 \rightarrow 4$

40 The diagram shows the genetic modification of a bacterial plasmid.

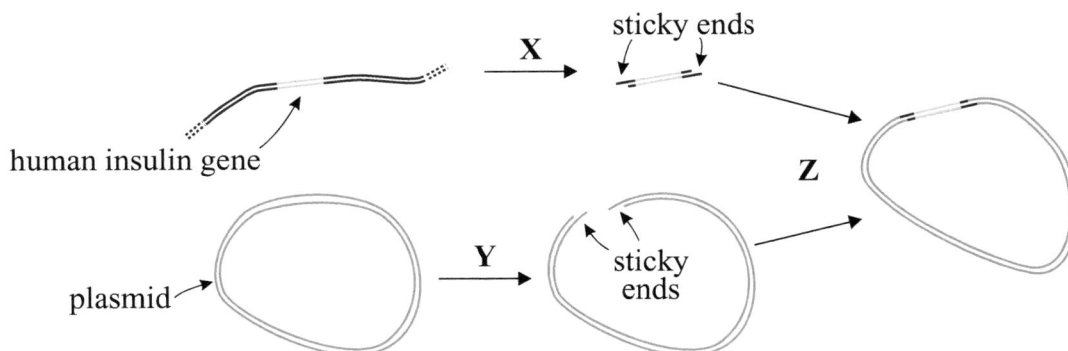

Which row of the table shows the correct enzymes for processes **X**, **Y** and **Z**?

	X	Y	Z
A	restriction enzymes	DNA ligase	restriction enzymes
B	DNA ligase	restriction enzymes	restriction enzymes
C	restriction enzymes	restriction enzymes	DNA ligase
D	DNA ligase	DNA ligase	restriction enzymes

END OF QUESTIONS

CGP Practice Exam Paper Cambridge International GCSE Biology

Cambridge International GCSE Biology

Paper 3 Theory (Core)

In addition to this paper you should have:
- A pen and pencil.
- A ruler.
- A calculator.

Centre name					
Centre number					
Candidate number					

Candidate name	
Candidate signature	

Time allowed:
- 1 hour 15 minutes

Instructions to candidates
- Write your name and other details in the spaces provided above.
- Use blue or black ink to write your answers.
- Answer all questions in the spaces provided.
- Do all rough work on the paper.
- Cross out any work you do not want to be marked.
- In calculations, show clearly how you worked out your answers.

Information for candidates
- The marks available are given in brackets at the end of each question part.
- There are 80 marks available for this paper.

1   **Figure 1** shows a plant cell.

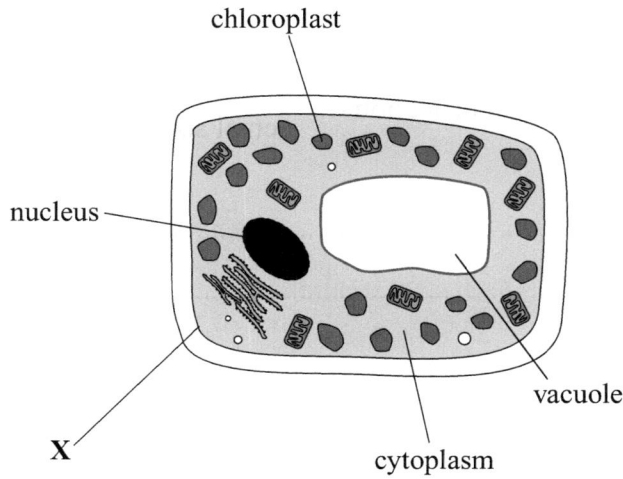

Figure 1

(a) (i)   State the name of part **X**.

....
                                                                                                    [1]

   (ii)   State the function of part **X**.

....
                                                                                                    [1]

(b) Name the part of the cell containing genetic material that controls the activities of the cell.

....
                                                                                                    [1]

(c) Explain how this cell gets its food.

....

....

....
                                                                                                    [2]

(d) (i)   Give **two** differences between this cell and an animal cell.

   1. ....

   2. ....
                                                                                                    [2]

   (ii)   Give **one** similarity between this cell and an animal cell.

....
                                                                                                    [1]

(e) A scientist viewed an individual plant cell under a microscope with × 150 magnification.
He calculated the actual length of the plant cell to be 0.054 mm.
Calculate the length of the image of the plant cell. Use the formula:

$$\text{magnification} = \frac{\text{image size}}{\text{actual size}}$$

....

....

.... mm

[2]

[Total 10 marks]

2 Enzymes are important in all living organisms.

(a) Define enzyme.

....

....

[1]

Biotechnology is where living organisms and biological processes are manipulated to produce a useful product. One use of biotechnology is in fruit juice production.

(b) (i) Name an enzyme commonly used in fruit juice production.

....

[1]

(ii) Explain why the enzyme you named in **(b) (i)** is used.

....

....

....

[2]

The anaerobic respiration of yeast is also exploited in biotechnology.

(c) (i) Complete the word equation for the anaerobic respiration of yeast.

.... $\rightarrow$ .... + carbon dioxide

[1]

(ii) State **two** uses of the anaerobic respiration of yeast in biotechnology.

1. ....

2. ....

[2]

[Total 7 marks]

3   The lung is a specialised gas exchange organ.

(a) Describe what is meant by the term organ.

....

....

[1]

The lung contains millions of air sacs called alveoli.
Figure 2 shows an alveolus and a blood capillary.

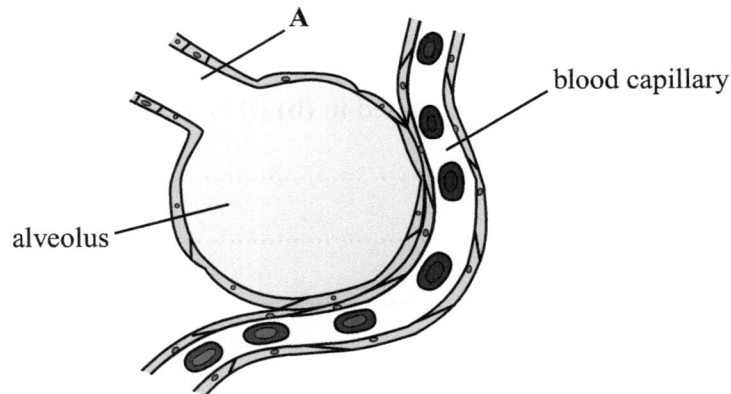

Figure 2

(b) Name the structure labelled **A**.

....

[1]

(c) State **three** features of alveoli, visible in **Figure 2**, that make them efficient
gas exchange surfaces.

1. ....

2. ....

3. ....

[3]

The composition of inspired and expired air is different.

(d) (i) Complete **Table 1** by placing **one** tick in each row to show how the proportion of each gas changes between inspired air and expired air.

Table 1

Name of Gas	Change in Proportion from Inspired to Expired Air	
	Increases	Decreases
carbon dioxide		
oxygen		
water vapour		

[3]

(ii) Explain how oxygen moves from an alveolus into a blood capillary.

....

....

....

....

[3]

[Total 11 marks]

4   The menstrual cycle is an important part of human reproduction.
     Figure 3 shows how the uterus lining changes during one 28-day menstrual cycle.

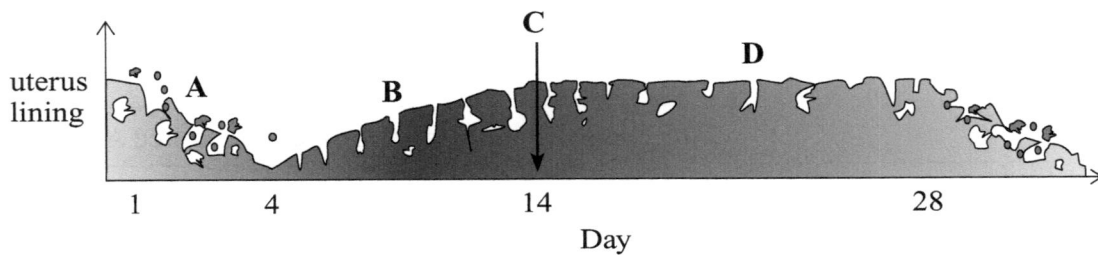

Figure 3

(a) Complete **Table 2** using letters from **Figure 3**. The first one has been done for you.

Table 2

Letter	Stage of the menstrual cycle
C	Ovulation occurs.
	The uterus lining is maintained ready for the implantation of a fertilised egg.
	The uterus lining thickens and grows.
	Menstruation occurs.

[3]

(b) (i)   Name the organ in the female reproductive system that releases an egg during ovulation.

....

[1]

(ii) State **two** adaptations of egg cells to their function in reproduction.

1. ....

2. ....

[2]

(c) Fertilisation takes place in the oviducts of the female reproductive system.

Choose words from the list to complete the sentences about fertilisation.
Each word may be used once, more than once or not at all.

cell division   embryo   gamete   menstruation   ovary   zygote

At fertilisation, one male and one female .... fuse to form

a .... This then undergoes ....

and develops into an ....

[4]

[Total 10 marks]

5 **Figure 4** shows a marine food web found near a hydrothermal vent.

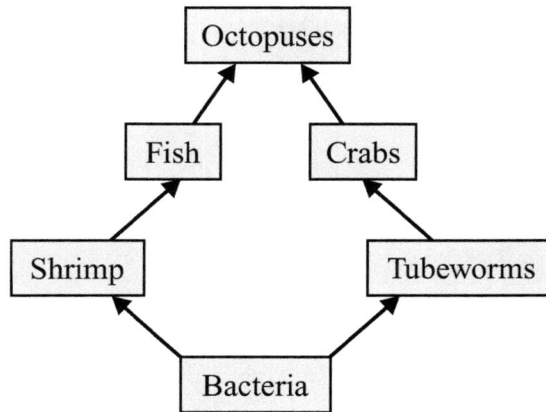

Figure 4

The producers in **Figure 4** are bacteria. They make their own organic nutrients using the energy they get from chemicals released by the hydrothermal vent.

(a) Give **one** similarity and **one** difference between these bacterial producers and typical plant producers.

Similarity: ....

....

Difference: ....

....

[2]

(b) Name **one** primary consumer from the food web.

....

[1]

The organisms in the food web in **Figure 4** are all interdependent.

(c) Suggest and explain how the removal of the population of **tubeworms** could affect the population sizes of:

(i) the crabs,

....

....

....

[2]

(ii) the shrimp.

....

....

....

[2]

[Total 7 marks]

Turn over ▶

6   **Figure 5** shows a photograph of some human blood cells.

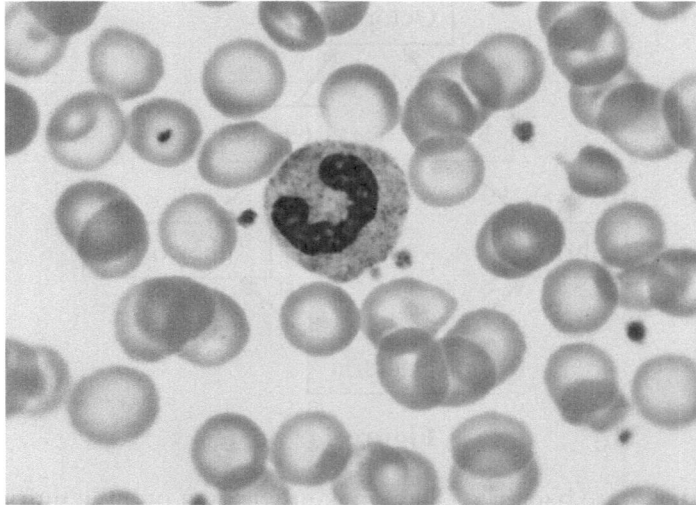

Figure 5

(a) Label a red blood cell and a white blood cell on **Figure 5**.

[1]

(b) (i)   Name **one** component of blood that is responsible for blood clotting.

....

[1]

(ii)   Suggest **one** symptom that a person might suffer from if they do not have enough of the blood component you named in **(b) (i)**.

....

[1]

The function of red blood cells is to carry oxygen from the lungs to all the cells in the body.

(c) Some athletes train in locations high above sea level for several weeks before a race. This increases the number of red blood cells the athletes have.

Suggest how having more red blood cells might increase the amount of energy available for muscle contraction during a race.

....

....

....

[2]

[Total 5 marks]

7 Cystic fibrosis is a genetic disorder caused by a recessive allele.
A couple have a baby boy. The doctor tells them that the baby has inherited cystic fibrosis.
Neither parent shows signs of the disorder.

(a) (i) Complete the diagram below to show how the baby inherited cystic fibrosis.
Use **F** to represent the dominant allele and **f** to represent the recessive allele.

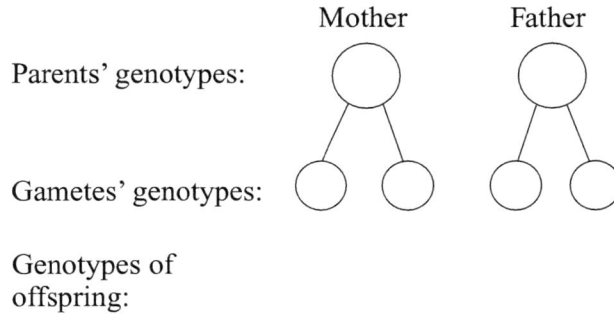

Mother   Father

Parents' genotypes:

Gametes' genotypes:

Genotypes of
offspring:

[3]

(ii) Explain whether the baby is homozygous or heterozygous for this condition.

....

....

[1]

(b) The doctor tells the parents that if they have another child,
the fetus can be tested to see if it will have cystic fibrosis.

State the probability that the couple's next baby will have cystic fibrosis.

....

[1]

The family pedigree in **Figure 6** below shows a family with a history of cystic fibrosis.

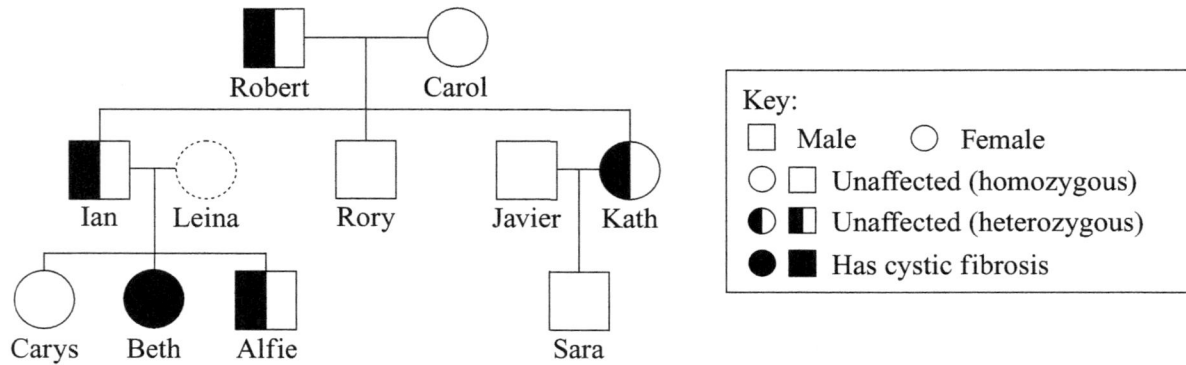

Figure 6

(c) Using the information given above, explain what Leina's genotype must be.

....

....

....

[2]

[Total 7 marks]

8 The peppered moth is an insect that nests on the trunks of trees in Britain.
The moths are prey for birds such as thrushes.
The peppered moth exists in two varieties:

- A light-coloured variety that is better camouflaged on tree trunks in unpolluted areas.
- A dark-coloured variety that is better camouflaged on sooty tree trunks in badly polluted areas.

Figures 7 and **8** show these two varieties of moths on different tree trunks.

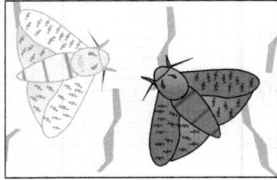 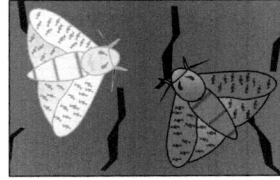

Figure 7   **Figure 8**

The dark variety of the moth was first recorded in the North of England in 1848.
It became increasingly common in polluted areas until the 1960s, when the number of soot-covered trees declined because of the introduction of new laws.

(a) The binomial name of the peppered moth is *Biston betularia*.
State the moth's genus.

....

[1]

(b) (i) State which variety of the moth has a better chance of survival in a soot-polluted area.

....

[1]

(ii) Using the idea of natural selection, explain why the variety of moth given in **(b) (i)** became more common in soot-polluted areas.

....

....

....

....

[3]

Figure 9 shows the percentages of dark- and light-coloured peppered moths in two different towns.

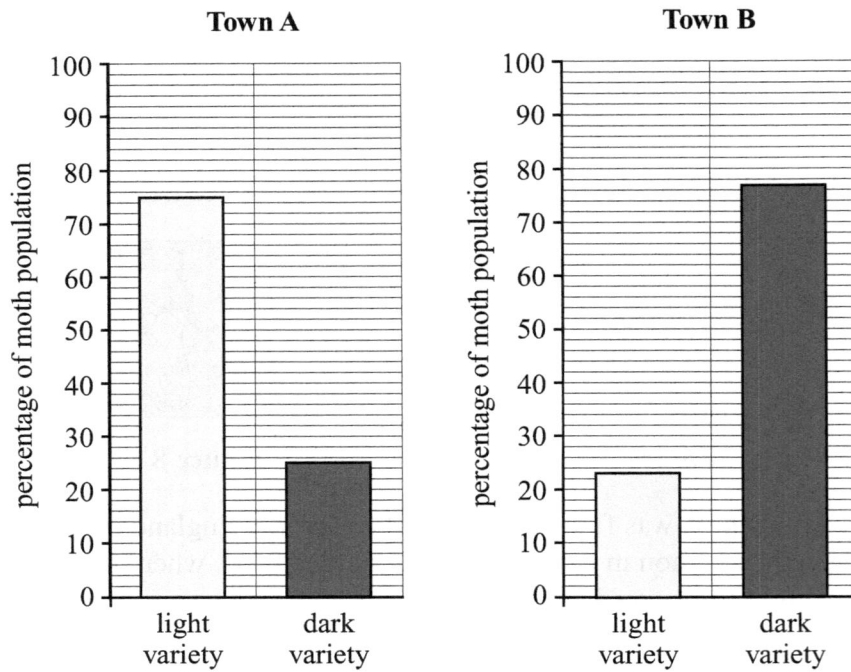

Figure 9

(c) Explain which town, **A** or **B**, is the most polluted.

....

....

[1]

[Total 6 marks]

9 Humans can use genetic modification to produce organisms with desired characteristics.

(a) What is meant by the term genetic modification?

....

....

....

[2]

(b) Bacteria are often genetically modified.
State **two** features of bacteria that make them suitable for this.

1. ....

2. ....

[2]

Selective breeding is also used to produce organisms with desired characteristics.

(c) Describe the process of selective breeding.

....

....

....

....

[3]

(d) Describe **one** way in which selective breeding of crop plants might be used to increase the human food supply.

....

....

....

[2]
[Total 9 marks]

10 **Figure 10** shows the carbon cycle.

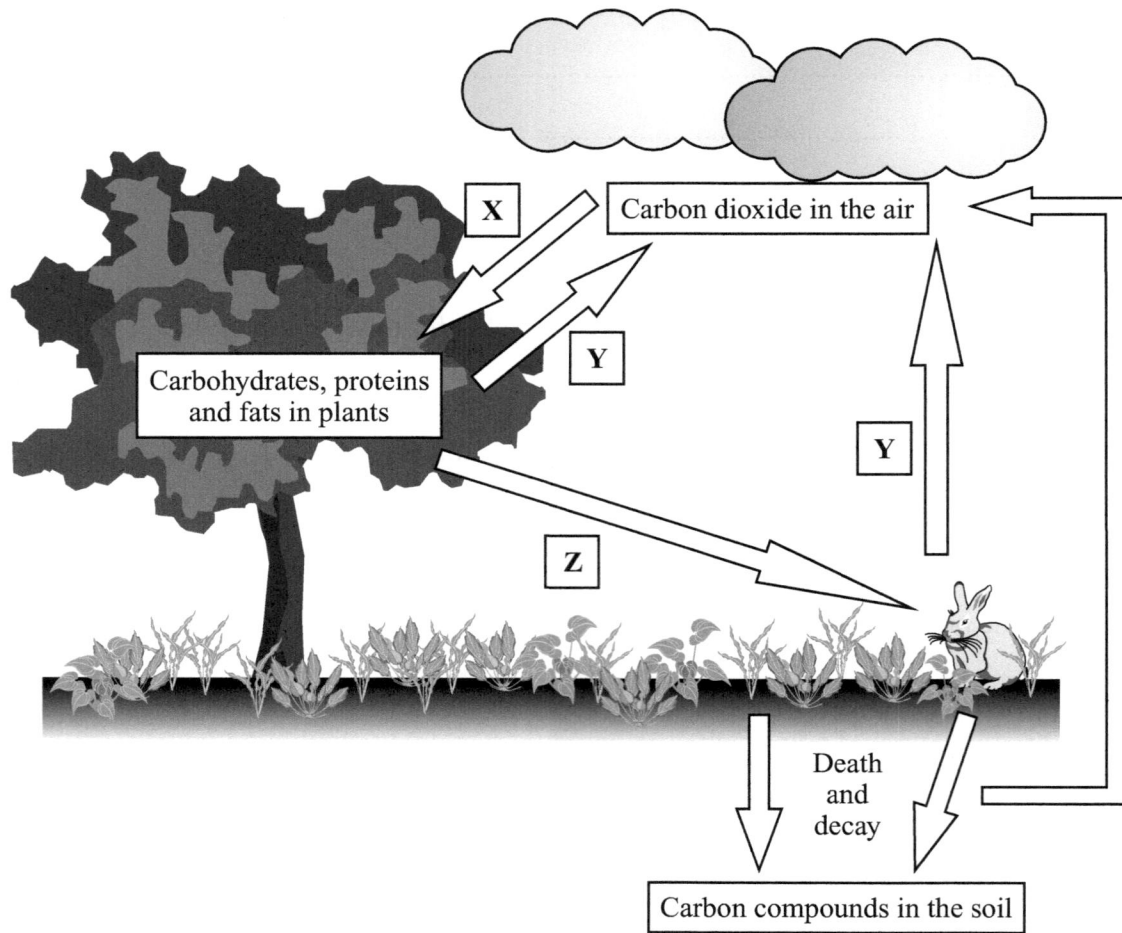

Figure 10

(a) Describe the movement of carbon occurring during processes marked **X**, **Y** and **Z** in **Figure 10**.

X ....

....

Y ....

....

Z ....

....

[3]

Human activities are causing an increase in carbon dioxide in the atmosphere.
A scientist was examining some data to see if there is a link between the global human population and the carbon dioxide concentration in the atmosphere.

Figure 11 shows the two graphs that the scientist examined.

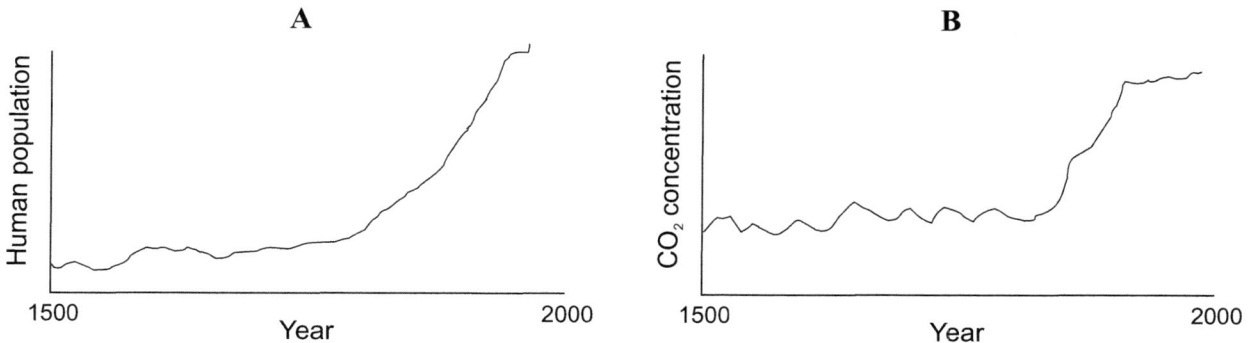

Figure 11

(b) Describe the relationship between the two graphs in **Figure 11**.

....

....

[1]

(c) On their own, the graphs in **Figure 11** do not prove that the increased human population caused the increased carbon dioxide concentration. Give **two** reasons why not.

1. ....

....

2. ....

....

[2]

(d) Give **two** examples of human activities that increase the amount of carbon dioxide in the atmosphere.

1. ....

2. ....

[2]

[Total 8 marks]

END OF QUESTIONS

Cambridge International GCSE Biology

Paper 4 Theory (Extended)

In addition to this paper you should have:
- A pen and pencil.
- A ruler.
- A calculator.

Centre name					
Centre number					
Candidate number					

Time allowed:
- 1 hour 15 minutes

Candidate name
Candidate signature

Instructions to candidates
- Write your name and other details in the spaces provided above.
- Use blue or black ink to write your answers.
- Answer all questions in the spaces provided.
- Do all rough work on the paper.
- Cross out any work you do not want to be marked.
- In calculations, show clearly how you worked out your answers.

Information for candidates
- The marks available are given in brackets at the end of each question part.
- There are 80 marks available for this paper.

1   Blood flows around the body in arteries, veins and capillaries.

(a) **Table 1** shows some of the features of these three different types of blood vessel.
    Complete the table by writing in the name of each type of blood vessel.

Table 1

	Type of blood vessel		
Walls	Thick, muscular	Very thin	Thin
Presence of valves	No	No	Yes
Pressure of blood in vessels	High	Low	Low

[2]

Figure 1 shows a human heart.

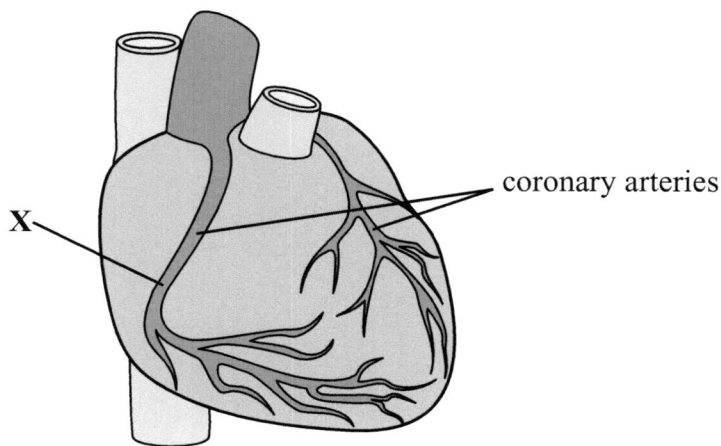

Figure 1

(b) Explain what would happen if the coronary artery was blocked at the point labelled **X**.

....

....

....

[2]

A patient has fatty deposits in the walls of one of his coronary arteries.
The patient's doctor recommends that the patient makes changes to his diet.

(c) (i) Suggest **one** change the patient could make to his diet to reduce the risk of further fatty deposits developing. Give **one** reason this change would be beneficial.

Change: ....

Reason: ....

....

[2]

(ii) Suggest **one** other change the patient could make to his lifestyle to reduce the risk of further fatty deposits developing.

....

[1]

[Total 7 marks]

2   **Figure 2** shows the structure of a DNA double helix.
The two strands are held together by bonds between their bases.

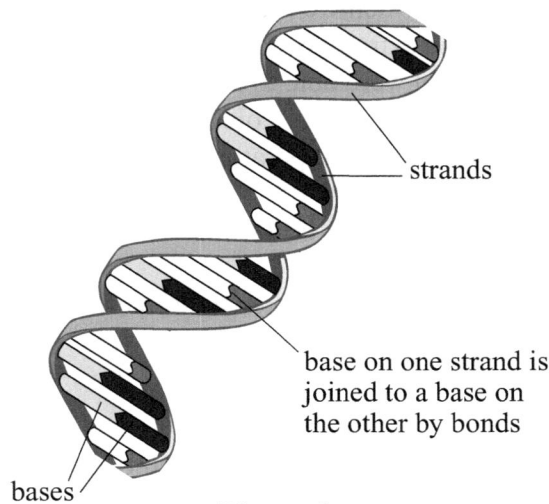

Figure 2

(a) Explain why there will always be equal amounts of bases A and T in a molecule of DNA.

....

....
[1]

(b) Name the part of a cell where strands of human DNA are found.

....
[1]

(c) Genes are lengths of DNA that code for a protein.
Exposure to some chemicals increases the rate of gene mutations.

(i)   Describe what is meant by the term gene mutation.

....
[1]

(ii) Give **one** other factor, besides exposure to certain chemicals,
that can increase the rate of mutation in DNA.

....
[1]

(iii) Enzymes are proteins. Explain why a mutation in a gene that codes for an enzyme could
negatively affect the function of the enzyme.

....

....

....

....
[3]

[Total 7 marks]

Turn over ▶

3   **Figure 3** is an extract from a report by a lifeboat crew member.

> "We were very concerned when we received news of a man lost overboard tonight because the sea is extremely cold at this time of year. Fortunately, we found him quickly and were able to rescue him before he suffered any serious ill effects. His skin was very cold when we picked him up, but his internal body temperature was normal."

Figure 3

(a) State the term given to the maintenance of a constant internal environment.

....
[1]

(b) Describe how the brain obtains information about the internal temperature of the body.

....

....
[1]

(c) (i)   Explain how the man's blood vessels may have helped prevent his internal temperature from falling whilst he was in the sea.

....

....

....
[2]

  (ii) Explain how the man's muscles may have helped prevent his internal temperature from falling whilst he was in the sea.

....

....

....

....
[3]

[Total 7 marks]

4   **Figure 4** shows the amount of energy contained within an area of plants.
    It shows how much energy from the plants is transferred to each trophic level in a food chain.

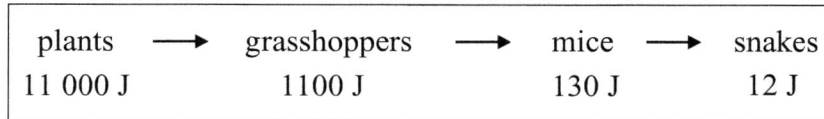

plants	→	grasshoppers	→	mice	→	snakes
11 000 J		1100 J		130 J		12 J

Figure 4

(a) (i)   State how much energy is available to the tertiary consumers in this food chain.

....

[1]

   (ii) Describe how the plants in this food chain obtain their energy.

....

....

....

[2]

   (iii) Calculate the percentage of energy in the grasshoppers that is transferred to the mice.
         Show your working.

.... %

[2]

Figure 5 shows four pyramids of biomass.

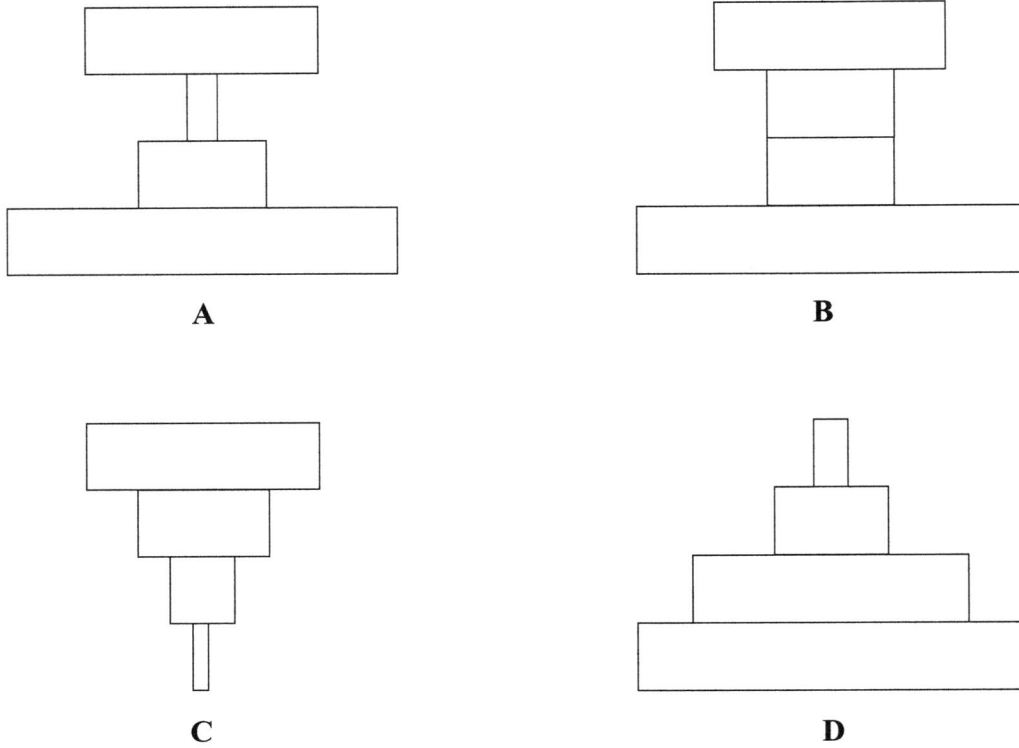

Figure 5

(b) Explain which pyramid of biomass (**A**, **B**, **C** or **D**) represents the food chain shown in **Figure 4**.

....

....

....

[2]

[Total 7 marks]

5   A student grew three plants in a windowsill tray.
    She then put the plants in a cardboard box with a cut-out hole.

    Figure 6 shows the same plants before and after three days in the cardboard box.

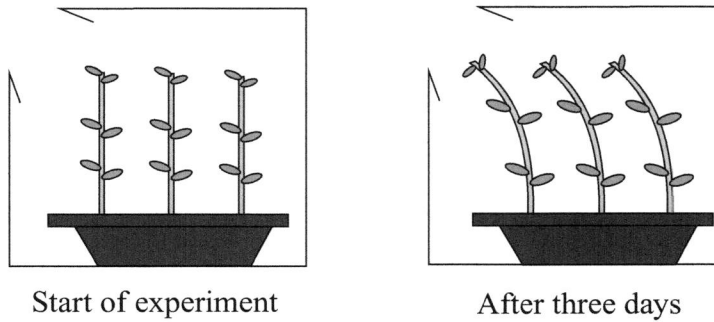

Start of experiment   After three days

Figure 6

(a) (i)   Explain what caused the plants' response.

....

....

....

....

....
                                                                                            [3]

    (ii) Name the response shown by the plants in this experiment.

....
                                                                                            [1]

(b) The plants responded in this way in order to maximise the
    amount of light they received for photosynthesis.

    (i)   Complete the balanced chemical equation for photosynthesis.

        .... + ... ⟶ .... + ...

                                                                                            [2]

    (ii) Give **three** uses of the carbohydrates made in photosynthesis.

        1. ....

        2. ....

        3. ....
                                                                                            [3]

(c) The student removed one of the plants from the tray.
She observed that the roots of the plant were growing downwards.

    (i)   Name the stimulus that causes the roots of a plant to grow downwards.

....

[1]

   (ii)   Suggest why it is beneficial for the roots of a plant to grow downwards.

....

....

[1]

[Total 11 marks]

6 A scientist measured the rate of transpiration in two plants over 48 hours.
The results are shown in **Figure 7**.

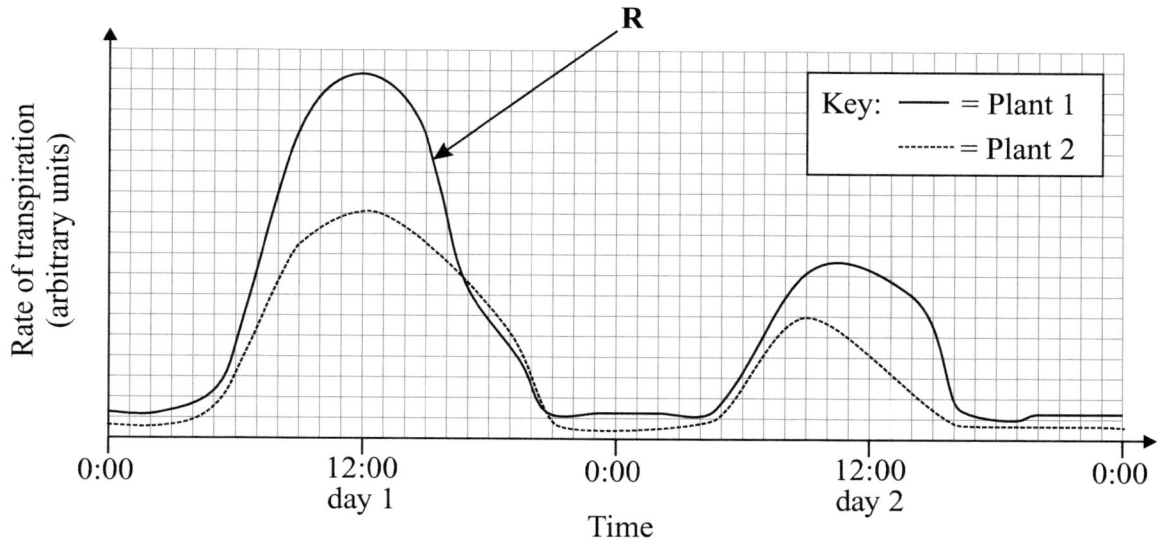

Figure 7

(a) Give the time on **day 2** when the rate of transpiration was highest for **plant 2**.

....

[1]

(b) The rate of transpiration for both plants was slower on **day 2** than on **day 1**.
Suggest **one** explanation for this.

....

....

....

[2]

(c) At time **R** on the graph, **plant 1** was wilting. Suggest **one** explanation for this.

....

....

....

[2]

228

(d) Explain how a transpiration pull moves water through a plant.

....

....

....

....

....

....

[4]

[Total 9 marks]

7   An example of a reflex action is the response of moving your hand away from a painful stimulus.
     Figure 8 shows the parts of the nervous system involved in this reflex action.

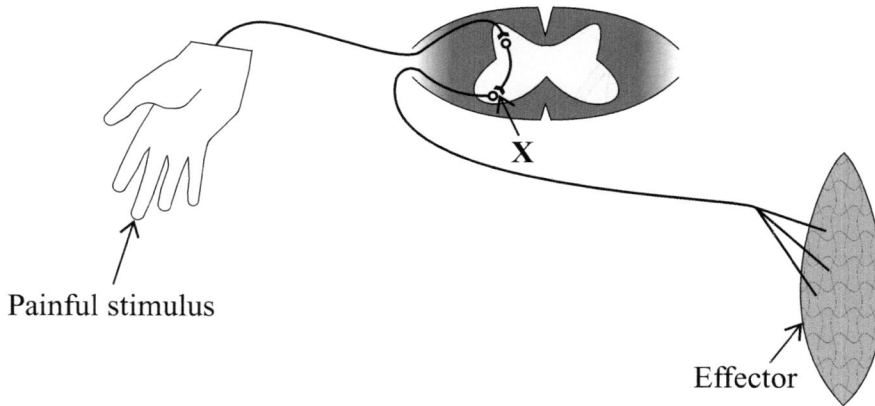

Painful stimulus

Effector

Figure 8

(a) Draw an arrow on **Figure 8** to show the direction in which the
    nerve impulse travels along the **motor neurone**.

                                                                                                    [1]

(b) Explain how the structure labelled **X** ensures that nerve impulses
    only travel in one direction along a reflex arc.

    ....

    ....

    ....

    ....

    ....

    ....
                                                                                                    [4]

(c) Describe the pathway from stimulus to response in this reflex arc.

    ....

    ....

    ....

    ....

    ....

    ....

    ....

    ....
                                                                                                    [6]
                                                                                          [Total 11 marks]

8   The kidneys play a crucial role in filtering the blood.
     Figure 9 shows a kidney nephron and the blood vessels associated with it.

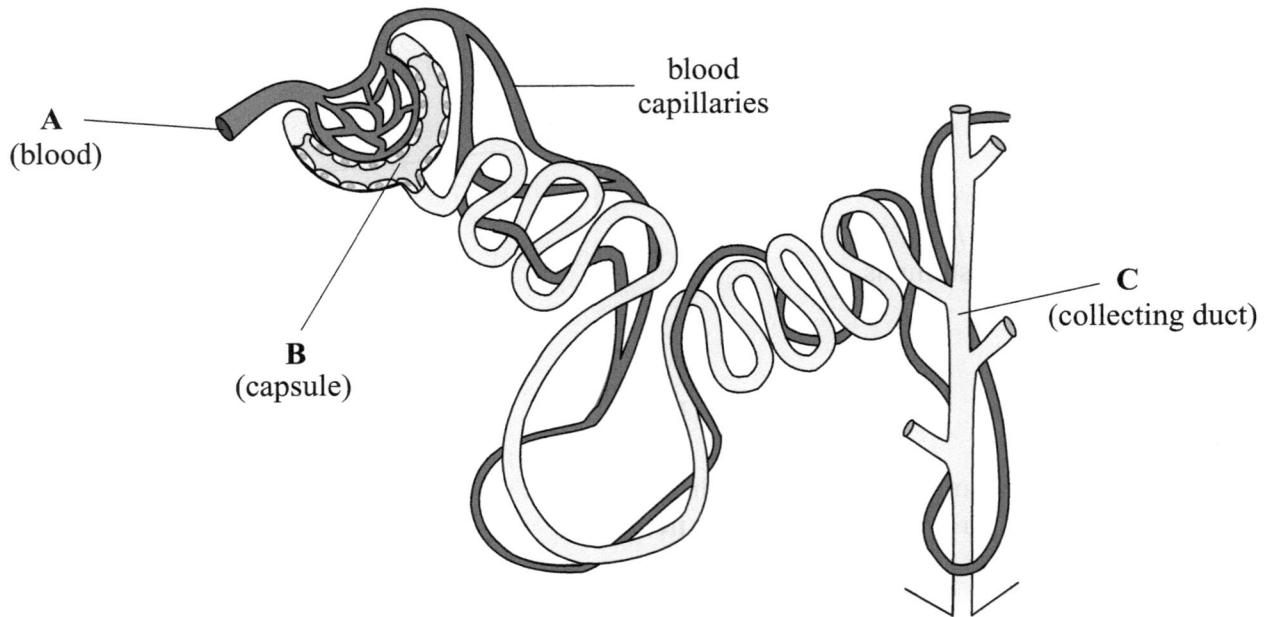

Figure 9

(a) Label the glomerulus on **Figure 9**.

[1]

(b) (i)   The concentration of urea is greatest at point **C**. Explain why.

....

....

[1]

(ii) Explain how the concentration of glucose at point **C** would
      compare to the concentration of glucose at point **B**.

....

....

....

[2]

(c) Name the main blood vessel that delivers blood to part **A**.

....

[1]

[Total 5 marks]

9   It is possible to be vaccinated against the disease measles.
The vaccine contains a weakened version of the measles virus.

Outline how the measles vaccine is likely to provide an individual with immunity to measles.

....

....

....

....

....

....

....

[Total 4 marks]

10 Cows can have alleles for white hair (C^W) and red hair (C^R). A cow with one copy of each allele will have a roan coat — a coat with a mixture of white hairs and red hairs.

(a) Explain why the alleles for white hair and red hair in cows are said to be codominant.

....

....

....

[2]

(b) (i) A roan cow is crossed with a pure-breeding red bull.

Draw a genetic diagram to show the probability of these two cattle producing a calf with a roan coat.

probability of a roan calf: ....

[4]

(ii) Another roan cow is crossed with a roan bull.
Give the ratio of genotypes in the offspring.

.... : .... : ....

[3]

(c) UK dairy cows often suffer from high levels of diseases such as lameness and mastitis. Explain how artificial selection could have led to these diseases being widespread.

....

....

....

....

....

[3]

[Total 12 marks]

END OF QUESTIONS

Practice Paper 5

As part of your assessment, you will take either a practical test (Paper 5) or a written alternative to the practical test (Paper 6). You should check with your teacher which one of those options you'll be taking. Both papers will test your knowledge of experimental skills and investigations. This practice paper is the equivalent of Paper 6 in the exams.

CGP Practice Exam Paper
Cambridge International
GCSE Biology

Cambridge International GCSE Biology

Paper 5 Alternative to Practical

In addition to this paper you should have:
- A pen and pencil.
- A ruler.
- A calculator.

Centre name					
Centre number					
Candidate number					

Time allowed:
- 1 hour

Candidate name
Candidate signature

Instructions to candidates
- Write your name and other details in the spaces provided above.
- Use blue or black ink to write your answers.
- Answer all questions in the spaces provided.
- Do all rough work on the paper.
- Cross out any work you do not want to be marked.
- In calculations, show clearly how you worked out your answers.

Information for candidates
- The marks available are given in brackets at the end of each question part.
- There are 40 marks available for this paper.

1   Water diffuses through partially permeable membranes by osmosis.
    A student carried out an experiment to investigate osmosis using potatoes.
    First, the student cut cylinders out of the potatoes. He then measured and recorded the mass
    of each cylinder before placing them into different concentrations of sugar solution, as shown
    in **Figure 1**.

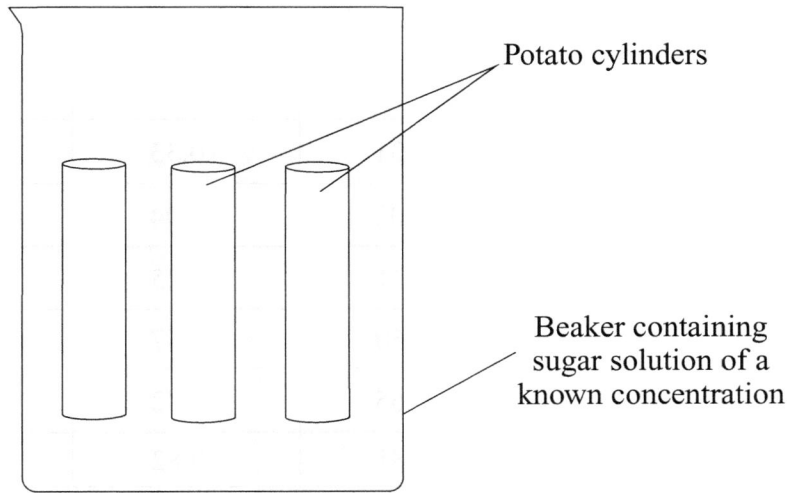

Figure 1

After 20 minutes in the sugar solution, the student dried the cylinders with tissue paper before
weighing them again.

(a) (i)   State **two** variables that the student would have had to keep the same to make the
          experiment a fair test.

          1. ....

          2. ....
                                                                                                              [2]

    (ii) Identify **one** source of error in the student's method and suggest an improvement.

          Error ....

          ....

          Improvement ....

          ....
                                                                                                              [2]

(b) The student's results are shown in **Table 1**.

Table 1

Concentration of sugar solution / M	Change in mass / g			Mean change in mass / g
	Potato cylinder 1	Potato cylinder 2	Potato cylinder 3	
0.0	+0.67	+0.65	+0.69	+0.67
0.2	+0.30	+0.31	+0.33	+0.31
0.4	+0.04	−0.02	+0.04	+0.02
0.6	−0.27	−0.31	−0.25	−0.28
0.8	−0.48	−0.50	−0.47	−0.48
1.0	−0.71	−0.65	−0.72	−0.69
1.2	−0.78	−0.81	−0.82	

(i) Complete **Table 1** by calculating the mean change in mass in the 1.2 M sugar solution. Show your working.

[1]

(ii) Explain why the student used three potato cylinders in each concentration of sugar solution, and took a mean of the results.

....

[1]

(c) Draw a graph of the mean change in mass against the concentration of sugar solution on the grid below. Draw a curve of best fit.

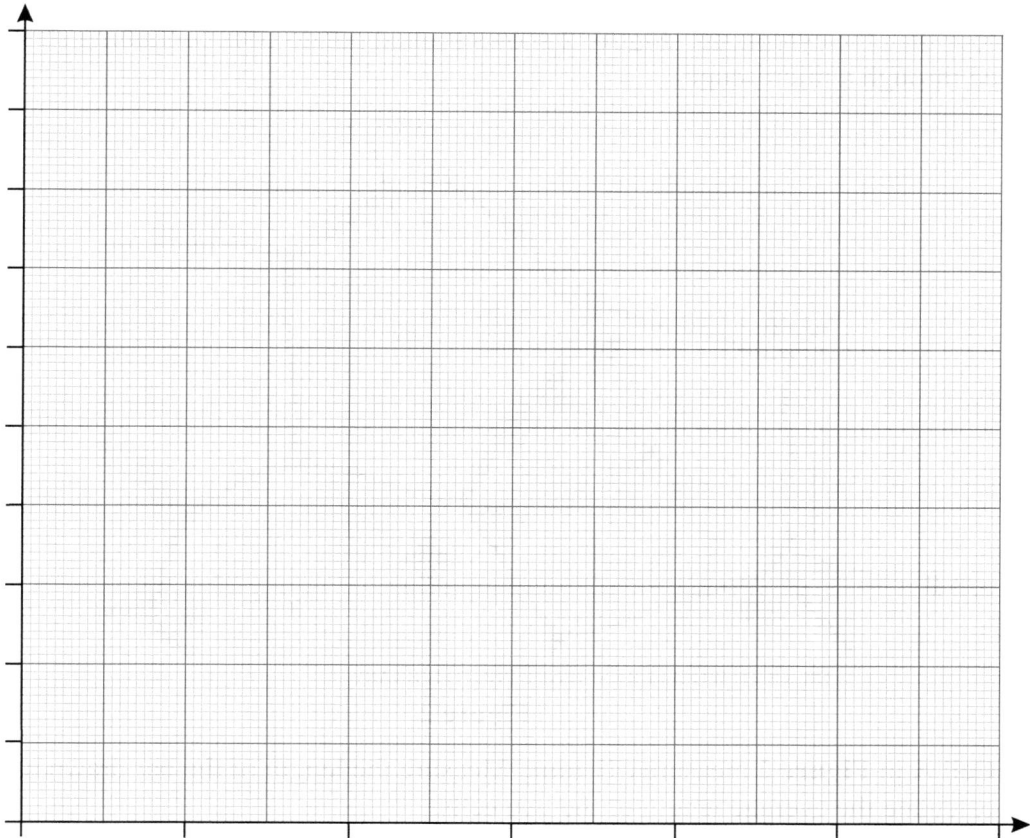

[5]

(d) Another student wanted to repeat the experiment with different concentrations of sugar solution. She was given test tubes containing the following glucose (sugar) concentrations: 0 M, 0.02 M, 0.1 M, 1 M. The test tubes were not labelled, so she was asked to perform tests on samples from the test tubes to determine which test tube contained which glucose solution.

(i) Describe a test she could carry out to try to distinguish between the glucose solutions.

....

....

....

[3]

(ii) **Table 2** shows the substance observed in the samples from the test tubes following the test that the student carried out. Complete the table to show which glucose solution (0 M, 0.02 M, 0.1 M, 1 M) each test tube contained.

Table 2

	Tube 1	Tube 2	Tube 3	Tube 4
substance observed	yellow precipitate	blue solution	red precipitate	green precipitate
glucose concentration / M	....	....	....	....

[1]

(e) Potato plants produce sugars when they photosynthesise. Some of these sugars are converted into starch and stored in structures called starch grains in the plants' cells. Starch grains can be stained. When viewed through a microscope they appear as circular structures and are darker in colour than the cytoplasm. **Figure 2** shows stained potato cells containing starch grains viewed through a microscope.

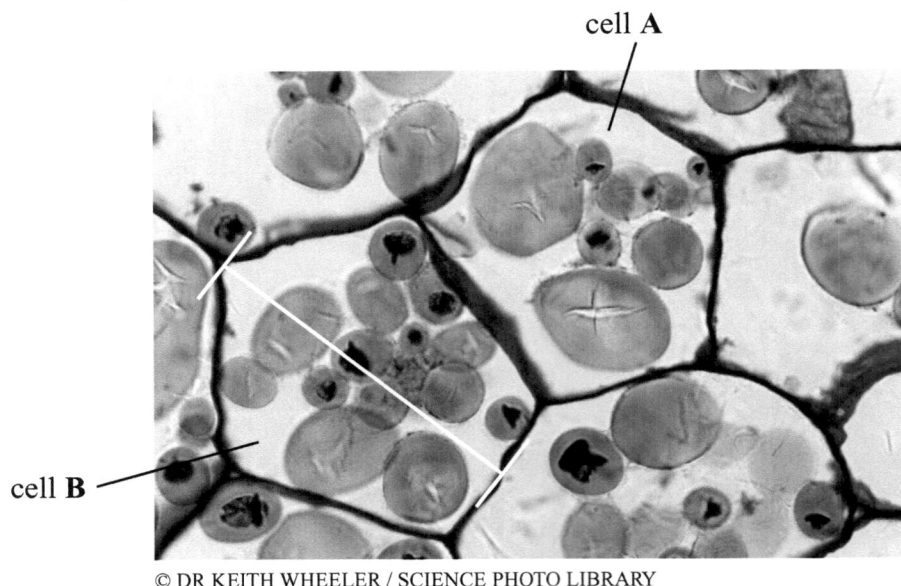

© DR KEITH WHEELER / SCIENCE PHOTO LIBRARY

Figure 2

(i) Cell **A** in **Figure 2** measures 41 mm. Measure the length of the bar drawn on cell **B** and calculate the average length of the two cells.

average length = ... mm

[2]

(ii) Produce a large, labelled drawing of cell **A**.

[4]

[Total 21 marks]

2   A student decided to investigate the effect of light intensity on the rate of photosynthesis in pondweed. The student set up a test tube containing a solution of sodium hydrogencarbonate next to a light source. Sodium hydrogencarbonate dissolves in water and releases carbon dioxide, which plants need to photosynthesise. Next, she took a cutting of the pondweed and placed it into the test tube. She then measured the amount of gas collected in two hours.
She carried out this experiment five times, each time with the light source 10 cm further away from the test tube.
The apparatus that was used for this experiment is shown in **Figure 3**.

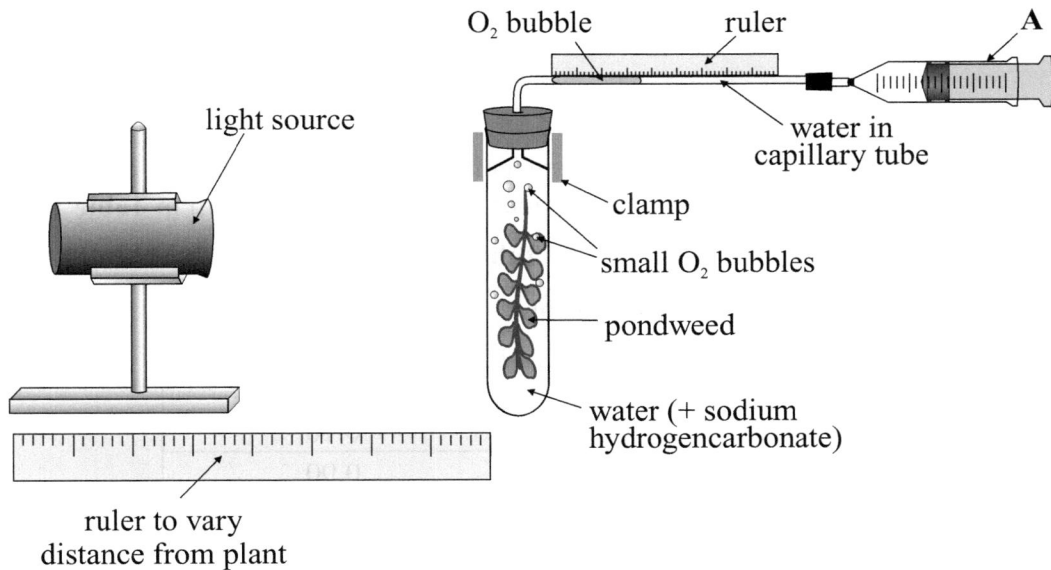

Figure 3

(a) (i)   Name the piece of equipment labelled **A**.

....

[1]

   (ii) Explain why it is important that the student adds the same amount of sodium hydrogencarbonate solution each time.

....

....

[1]

(b) The student started with the test tube 0 cm from the light source.
She repeated the experiment three times at each distance.
Prepare a table to record the results from her experiment.

[3]

(c) Once the experiment was completed the student processed her results and calculated the average rate of gas production at each distance. Her results are shown in **Table 3**.

Table 3

Distance away from light source / cm	Average rate of gas production / cm³/h
0	0.75
10	0.70
20	0.90
30	0.35
40	

(i) The average volume of gas collected when the distance was 40 cm was 0.20 cm³.
Complete **Table 3** by calculating the average rate of gas production at a distance of 40 cm.

[1]

(ii) The student thinks that one of the distances produced an anomalous result.
Suggest which distance this might be. Give a reason for your answer.

....

....

[2]

(iii) Ignoring the anomalous result identified in part **(c) (ii)**, use the results in **Table 3** to describe and explain the effect of the distance from the light source on the rate of gas production in pondweed.

....

....

....

[2]

(iv) Suggest **one** way in which you could increase your confidence in the answer you gave to part **(c) (iii)**.

....

[1]

d) Explain why it is important that the same light source is used each time the experiment is repeated.

....

....

....

[2]

e) After the experiment was conducted, a leaf from the pondweed was tested for starch. The leaf was boiled to stop any chemical reactions happening. The leaf was then heated in ethanol to remove chlorophyll. A few drops of iodine solution were then added.

  (i) Suggest a safety precaution that should be taken when working with substances such as ethanol and iodine solution.

....

....

[1]

  (ii) The leaf tested positive for starch.
  How could the student tell that the leaf contained starch?

....

....

[1]

f) Describe how the student's original experiment could be altered to investigate the effect of temperature on the rate of photosynthesis, rather than light intensity.

....

....

....

....

....

[4]

[Total 19 marks]

END OF QUESTIONS

Answers

Section 1 — Characteristics and Classification of Living Organisms

Pages 9-10
Warm-Up Questions
1) The taking in of substances used for energy, growth and development in organisms.
2) A species is a group of similar organisms that can reproduce to give fertile offspring.
3) Arthropods are invertebrates that have exoskeletons and segmented bodies.

Exam Questions
1 a) Stripes and spots *[1 mark]*
  b) Butterfly F *[1 mark]*
  c) (i) Insects *[1 mark]*
    (ii) Wings / a body that is divided into three parts *[1 mark]*
2 a) Any three from: they feed, which means they require nutrition. / They are sensitive to chemicals in the water, allowing them to detect food. This shows they can respond to changes in their environment. / They are able to travel towards food, showing that they can move. / They reproduce. *[3 marks]*
  b) respiration *[1 mark]*
  c) The removal of metabolic waste products and of substances that are in excess of what the organism needs *[1 mark]*.
  d) E.g. it may be smaller. / It may not be fully developed. *[1 mark]*
  e) *Asterias [1 mark]*
3 a) plants, animals, fungi, prokaryotes and protoctists *[1 mark]*
  b) Any two from: e.g. they are particles/they are not cells / they have a protein coat / they have DNA or RNA as their genetic material *[2 marks]*
4 a) The DNA sequences for the same gene in different organisms can be compared *[1 mark]*. The more similar the sequences are to each other, the more closely related the organisms are *[1 mark]*.
  b) Organism C *[1 mark]* because its DNA sequence has the highest percentage similarity to humans *[1 mark]*.

Section 2 — Organisation of the Organism

Page 17
Warm-Up Questions
1) Similarities — any two from: e.g. both an animal and a plant cell have a cell membrane. / Both an animal and a plant cell have a nucleus. / Both an animal and a plant cell have cytoplasm.
   Differences — any two from: e.g. an animal cell doesn't have a vacuole, but a plant cell does. / An animal cell doesn't have a cell wall, but a plant cell does. / An animal cell doesn't contain chloroplasts, but a plant cell does.
2) nucleus / mitochondria
3) nucleus

Exam Questions
1 a) C *[1 mark]*
  b) They absorb light needed for photosynthesis to make food for the plant *[1 mark]*.
  c) It supports the cell and strengthens it *[1 mark]*.
2 The cell has a hair-like shape, which gives it a large surface area *[1 mark]* to absorb water and mineral ions from the soil *[1 mark]*.
3 a) actual size = image size ÷ magnification *[1 mark]*
   = 7.5 ÷ 100
   = **0.075 mm** *[1 mark]*
  b) 0.075 × 1000 = **75 μm** *[1 mark]*

Section 3 — Movement In and Out of Cells

Page 25
Warm-Up Questions
1) Osmosis is the net movement of water molecules from an area of higher water potential to an area of lower water potential, across a partially permeable membrane.
2) E.g. diffusion is movement from an area of higher concentration to an area of lower concentration, whereas active transport is from an area of lower concentration to higher concentration. / Diffusion is caused by the kinetic energy of randomly moving molecules, but active transport requires additional energy from respiration in order to happen.

Exam Questions
1 a) The potato cylinder in tube D, because this tube contains the most concentrated sugar solution *[1 mark]* so this cylinder will have lost the most water by osmosis *[1 mark]*.
  b) Tube A contained pure water, so some of the water moved by osmosis into the potato cylinder *[1 mark]* from an area of higher water concentration to an area of lower water concentration *[1 mark]*.
2 a) diffusion *[1 mark]*
  b) As the size of the agar jelly cube increases, the time taken for the cube to become yellow increases *[1 mark]*. This is because the bigger cubes have a smaller surface area to volume ratio, which decreases the rate of diffusion *[1 mark]*.

Section 4 — Biological Molecules and Enzymes

Pages 31-32
Warm-Up Questions
1) glucose
2 a) glycerol and fatty acids
  b) amino acids
3) Benedict's solution
4) That starch is present in the sample.
5) Enzymes are proteins that act as biological catalysts in all metabolic reactions.
6) active site
7) An enzyme's active site is complementary in shape to a specific substrate — this means only one substrate is able to bind to the enzyme and usually only one reaction is catalysed.
8) When the temperature is too hot, the bonds holding the enzyme together break. This changes the shape of the enzyme's active site, so the substrate can't fit any more.

Exam Questions
1 A *[1 mark]*
2 A *[1 mark]*
3 E.g. add the sample of egg whites to a test tube containing ethanol *[1 mark]*. Shake the tube for about a minute until the egg whites dissolve *[1 mark]*. Pour the solution into water *[1 mark]*. If any fats are present, they will precipitate out of the liquid and show up as a milky emulsion *[1 mark]*.
4 a) E.g. a dropping pipette *[1 mark]*
  b) 60 °C, as this was the temperature at which the iodine solution stopped turning blue-black first *[1 mark]*, meaning the starch had been broken down the fastest *[1 mark]*.
  c) E.g. the amylase was denatured by the high temperature, so the starch was not broken down *[1 mark]*.
  d) Any two from: e.g. the concentration of starch solution / the concentration of amylase / the volume of starch and amylase solution added to the iodine / the volume of iodine solution in the wells / the pH of the starch and amylase solution *[2 marks]*.
5 DNA has two strands coiled together in the shape of a double helix *[1 mark]*. Each strand contains chemicals called bases *[1 mark]*. The two strands are held together by bonds between them that are formed by pairs of bases *[1 mark]*. The bases always pair up in the same way — it's always A-T and C-G *[1 mark]*.

Section 5 — Plant and Human Nutrition

Pages 40-41
Warm-Up Questions
1) chlorophyll
2) A limiting factor is something present in the environment in such short supply that it restricts life processes.
3) e.g. oxygen production
4) purple
5) To make amino acids and proteins.

Exam Questions
1 a) carbon dioxide + water $\xrightarrow[\text{chlorophyll}]{\text{light}}$ glucose + oxygen *[1 mark]*
  b) A *[1 mark]*
2 delivers water and nutrients to the leaf — E
  helps to reduce water loss by evaporation — A
  where most of the chloroplasts in the leaf are located, to maximise the amount of light they receive — B
  allows carbon dioxide to diffuse directly into the leaf — D
  [1 mark for each correct answer, maximum of 3 marks]
3 a)

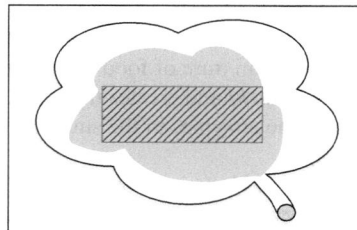

[1 mark]
  b) Plants need both chlorophyll and light to photosynthesise and produce starch — there is only chlorophyll in the green area of the plant *[1 mark]*, and light can only reach parts of the leaf not covered by black paper *[1 mark]*.
4 a) At low light intensities, increasing the CO_2 concentration has no effect *[1 mark]*, but at higher light intensities, increasing the concentration of CO_2 increases the maximum rate of photosynthesis *[1 mark]*.
  b) The rate of photosynthesis does not continue to increase because temperature or the level of carbon dioxide becomes the limiting factor *[1 mark]*.
You don't know if the temperature was kept constant or not, so either the level of carbon dioxide or temperature could have been the limiting factor here — there's no way of knowing.

Page 47

Warm-Up Questions

1) Proteins are needed for growth and the repair of tissue.
2) stomach, pancreas, small intestine
3) gripping and tearing food
4 a) proteases
  b) lipases
5 a) simple reducing sugars
  b) amino acids
  c) glycerol and fatty acids
6) Egestion is when any food that hasn't been digested or absorbed is removed from the body as faeces.
7) Tubes in the villi that absorb digested fats.

Exam Questions

1 a)

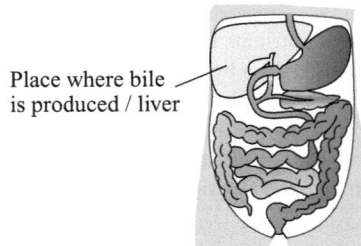

Place where bile is produced / liver

[1 mark]

  b) It neutralises the acidic mixture of food and gastric juices from the stomach *[1 mark]* and creates the alkaline conditions at which the enzymes in the small intestine work best *[1 mark]*.
  c) It emulsifies fats *[1 mark]* to give a much bigger surface area of fat for the enzyme lipase to work on *[1 mark]*.
2 a) amylase *[1 mark]*
  b) E.g. starch is a large, insoluble molecule *[1 mark]*. It must be broken down into smaller, soluble molecules *[1 mark]*, which can pass through the walls of the small intestine and into the blood *[1 mark]*.
3 a) A lack of vitamin C in the diet *[1 mark]*.
  b) E.g. vitamin C is found in things like fresh fruit *[1 mark]*. Fruit does not store well, so on a long trip at sea, sailors might not have had a source of vitamin C in their diet *[1 mark]*.
  c) E.g. the cement and the bone are responsible for holding the tooth in place (and so if these are damaged then the tooth could be lost) *[1 mark]*.

Section 6 — Transport in Plants and Animals

Page 53

Warm-Up Questions

1) Water moves from the root hair cells, through the root cortex cells, then through the xylem vessels and up to the mesophyll cells in the leaves.
2) Transpiration is the loss of water vapour from plant leaves.
3) If there's no water in the soil, a plant starts to wilt because the cells lose water and become flaccid, meaning there is no turgor pressure to support the plant tissues.
4) A source is a part of a plant that releases sucrose or amino acids, and a sink is where they are stored or used in respiration or growth.

Exam Questions

1 a) translocation *[1 mark]*
  b) phloem *[1 mark]*
  c) A *[1 mark]*
2 a) $(10 + 11 + 9) \div 3 = $ **10%** *[2 marks for correct answer, otherwise 1 mark for correct working]*
  b) The plants in Group B are at a higher temperature than those in Group A *[1 mark]*. At higher temperatures, the water particles have more kinetic energy to evaporate and diffuse out of the stomata *[1 mark]*, so the plant loses more mass *[1 mark]*.
  c) E.g. the more humid the air around a leaf, the slower transpiration happens *[1 mark]*. Humid air contains a lot of water, so there's not much of a concentration gradient between the inside and the outside of the leaf *[1 mark]*.

Pages 60-61

Warm-Up Questions

1) A system of blood vessels with a pump and valves to make sure that blood always flows in one direction.
2) E.g. using an ECG, by measuring pulse rate and by listening to the sounds of valves opening and closing.
3) They carry blood back to the heart.
4) They help the blood to clot at a wound.
5) Any three from: e.g. red blood cells / white blood cells / platelets / glucose / amino acids / carbon dioxide / ions / hormones.

Exam Questions

1 a) red blood cell *[1 mark]*
  b) E.g. it has a biconcave disc shape *[1 mark]* to give a large surface area for absorbing oxygen *[1 mark]*. / It contains haemoglobin *[1 mark]*, which can bind to and release oxygen *[1 mark]*. / It doesn't have a nucleus *[1 mark]*, to give more room to carry oxygen *[1 mark]*.
  c) E.g. white blood cell/phagocyte *[1 mark]*. It carries out phagocytosis *[1 mark]*. / White blood cell/lymphocyte *[1 mark]*. / It produces antibodies *[1 mark]*.
  d) E.g. they have permeable walls *[1 mark]*, so substances can diffuse in and out *[1 mark]*. Their walls are usually only one cell thick *[1 mark]*, which increases the rate of diffusion by decreasing the distance over which it occurs *[1 mark]*.

2 a) A disease where the coronary arteries that supply blood to the heart muscle get blocked by layers of fatty material building up *[1 mark]*.
  b) E.g. a high level of saturated fat in the diet increases the blood cholesterol level *[1 mark]*. This increases the risk of coronary heart disease because it increases the risk of fatty deposits forming in the coronary arteries *[1 mark]*.
  c) Any two from: e.g. eating a diet high in salt / high levels of stress / smoking / lack of exercise / the genes you inherit / getting older / being male rather than female *[2 marks]*.

3 a) A is the right atrium. B is the left atrium. C is the septum. *[1 mark]*
  b) Deoxygenated blood enters the right atrium *[1 mark]* through the vena cava *[1 mark]*. The blood moves through to the right ventricle *[1 mark]* which pumps it through the pulmonary artery to the lungs *[1 mark]*.
  c) It needs more muscle because it has to pump blood around the whole body at high pressure *[1 mark]*, whereas the right ventricle only has to pump it to the lungs *[1 mark]*.
  d) They prevent the backflow of blood *[1 mark]*.
  e) E.g. blood can be pumped around the body at a higher pressure. / Blood can be pumped around faster, so more oxygen can be delivered to the cells. *[1 mark]*

4 A *[1 mark]*

5 a) Clotting stops you losing too much blood *[1 mark]* and it stops pathogens from getting in *[1 mark]*.
  b) Fibrinogen is converted to fibrin *[1 mark]*. The fibrin fibres then tangle together to form a mesh in which platelets and red blood cells get trapped, forming a blood clot *[1 mark]*.

Section 7 — Diseases and Immunity

Page 67
Warm-Up Questions

1) A transmissible disease is a disease where the pathogen can be passed from one host to another.
2) The skin acts as a barrier to pathogens. If it gets damaged, blood clots quickly to seal cuts and keep microorganisms out.
3) antigens
4) Passive immunity is the short-term defence against a pathogen by antibodies made by a different organism.

Exam Questions

1 a) Hairs in the nose trap particles from the air that could contain pathogens *[1 mark]*.
  b) E.g. the stomach produces acid, which kills the majority of pathogens that are swallowed (e.g. in food) *[1 mark]*.

2 To prevent the contamination of food by pathogens that may be on the chefs' hands *[1 mark]*.

3 a) The process is called phagocytosis *[1 mark]*. It's where certain white blood cells/phagocytes engulf and digest pathogens *[1 mark]*.
  b) Antibodies are produced by lymphocytes *[1 mark]*. They bind to specific antigens on the surface of a pathogen *[1 mark]* and either directly destroy the pathogen, or mark the pathogen for destruction by other white blood cells/phagocytes *[1 mark]*.

4 When vaccinated, child A was given weakened rubella pathogens *[1 mark]*. These would have had antigens on their surface and so would have caused the child's lymphocytes to start producing antibodies *[1 mark]*. This would have also led to the production of memory cells *[1 mark]*. When child A was exposed to the rubella virus, the memory cells quickly made the specific antibodies against the virus, so child A didn't become ill *[1 mark]*. Child B did not have these memory cells, so when they were infected by the virus they didn't produce antibodies quickly enough and they became ill *[1 mark]*.

246

Section 8 — Gas Exchange and Respiration

Page 71
Warm-Up Questions
1) False
Inspired air has a greater proportion of oxygen than expired air. Expired air has a greater proportion of carbon dioxide and water vapour than inspired air.
2) Ciliated cells waft mucus up to the back of the throat where it can be swallowed.
3) limewater
4) Physical activity leads to an increase in breathing rate.

Exam Questions
1 a) E.g.

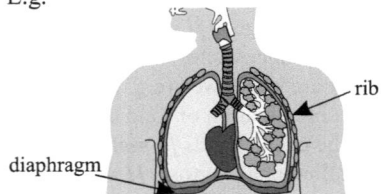

[1 mark for a label pointing to the diaphragm, 1 mark for a label pointing to a rib]
b) bronchus *[1 mark]*
c) the alveoli *[1 mark]*
d) Any two from: e.g. they have a very large surface area *[1 mark]*. / They have a thin surface *[1 mark]*. / They have a good blood supply *[1 mark]*. / They have good ventilation with air *[1 mark]*.
2 C *[1 mark]*

Page 75
Warm-Up Questions
1) Any two from: e.g. for muscle contraction / for protein synthesis / for cell division / for active transport / for growth / for the passage of nerve impulses / to maintain a constant body temperature.
2) carbon dioxide and water
Aerobic respiration is the same in all organisms — it's anaerobic respiration that can be different in different organisms.
3) $C_6H_{12}O_6 + 6O_2 \longrightarrow 6CO_2 + 6H_2O$
4) E.g. by keeping heart rate high / breathing rate/depth high after exercise / by aerobic respiration of lactic acid in the liver.
5) $C_6H_{12}O_6 \longrightarrow 2C_2H_5OH + 2CO_2$

Exam Questions
1 a) To transfer energy (from the breakdown of nutrient molecules) that cells need to do just about everything *[1 mark]*.
b) Any two from: e.g. aerobic respiration uses oxygen, anaerobic respiration does not *[1 mark]*. / Aerobic respiration doesn't produce lactic acid, anaerobic respiration does *[1 mark]*. / Aerobic respiration releases more energy per glucose molecule than anaerobic respiration *[1 mark]*.
c) glucose + oxygen *[1 mark]* → carbon dioxide + water *[1 mark]*
2 a) glucose → lactic acid *[1 mark]*
b) i) aerobic respiration *[1 mark]*
ii) aerobic and anaerobic respiration *[1 mark]*
3 E.g. set up a test tube containing a set amount of yeast and sucrose solution *[1 mark]*. Connect a gas syringe and leave the apparatus in a water bath at a set temperature (e.g. 15 °C) *[1 mark]*. Calculate the rate of respiration of the yeast by measuring the volume of carbon dioxide collected in the gas syringe over a set time *[1 mark]*. Repeat the experiment at different temperatures to measure the effect of temperature on the rate of respiration *[1 mark]*.
4 At lower temperatures, the rate of respiration was slow *[1 mark]*, but increased to a maximum at the optimum temperature *[1 mark]*. As temperature increased beyond the optimum, the rate of respiration decreased until it reached zero *[1 mark]*.

Section 9 — Excretion in Humans

Page 79
Warm-Up Questions
1) the lungs
2) urea, water, ions
3) The liver converts amino acids into proteins.
4) A bundle of capillaries at the start of a kidney nephron.

Exam Questions
1 a) C *[1 mark]*
b) the medulla *[1 mark]*
2 C *[1 mark]*
3 a) Urea is formed in the liver *[1 mark]* by the process of deamination *[1 mark]*, in which the nitrogen-containing portion of amino acids is removed *[1 mark]*.
b) Urea is filtered out of the blood in the glomerulus of a kidney nephron *[1 mark]*. It travels through the nephron, combining with excess water and ions to form urine *[1 mark]*. It then passes out of the nephron, through the ureter and bladder, before being released via the urethra *[1 mark]*.
c) Urea is toxic *[1 mark]* and can harm body cells if it is allowed to build up in the body *[1 mark]*.

Section 10 — Coordination and Response

Page 84
Warm-Up Questions
1)   brain and spinal cord
2)   electrical impulses
3)   e.g. the pupil reflex (in response to bright light)

Exam Questions
1 a)   X: sensory neurone *[1 mark]*
        Y: relay neurone *[1 mark]*
        Z: motor neurone *[1 mark]*
  b)   synaptic gap *[1 mark]*
  c)   The effector is the muscle *[1 mark]* and
        it responds by contracting (which causes
        the man to drop the plate) *[1 mark]*.
2 a)   A: cornea *[1 mark]*
        B: pupil *[1 mark]*
  b)   It controls the diameter of the pupil / the
        amount of light entering the eye *[1 mark]*.
  c) i) rods *[1 mark]*, cones *[1 mark]*
    ii) the fovea *[1 mark]*
  d)   Information is sent using impulses *[1 mark]*,
        via the optic nerve *[1 mark]*.

Page 89
Warm-Up Questions
1)   A chemical produced by a gland and carried
        by the blood, which changes the activity
        of a specific target organ or organs.
2 a)   ovaries
  b)   testes
  c)   adrenal glands
3)   The maintenance of a constant internal environment.

Exam Questions
1 a)   Erector muscles contract when it's cold, which
        makes the hairs stand up *[1 mark]*. This traps
        an insulating layer of air near the surface of the
        skin and so prevents heat loss *[1 mark]*.
  b)   Sweat glands respond by producing very little sweat
        [1 mark], because sweat transfers heat from the body
        to the environment when it evaporates *[1 mark]*.
2   E.g. nervous responses are very fast and hormonal
        responses are slower *[1 mark]*. Nervous
        responses usually act for a short time while
        hormonal responses last for longer *[1 mark]*.
3 a)   Organ A = pancreas *[1 mark]*, Organ B = liver *[1 mark]*
  b)   The pancreas/organ A doesn't produce enough
        insulin *[1 mark]*. This means that the liver/
        organ B is unable to remove glucose from the blood
        for storage *[1 mark]*. So blood glucose is able
        to rise to a dangerously high level *[1 mark]*.
  c)   It makes the liver/organ B turn glycogen into glucose
        increasing blood glucose levels *[1 mark]*.

Page 92
Warm-Up Questions
1)   A response in which parts of a plant grow
        towards or away from a source of light.
2)   auxin
3)   In the shoot tips.
4)   diffusion

Exam Questions
1 a)   phototropism *[1 mark]*
  b)   Shoot B grew straight upwards / did not bend
        [1 mark]. This is because auxin was evenly
        distributed in the shoot tip *[1 mark]* as there was no
        light causing it to accumulate on one side, which
        is needed for phototropism to occur *[1 mark]*.
2 a)   The shoot has grown upwards, away from gravity. /
        The shoot is showing negative gravitropism. *[1 mark]*
  b)   Auxin accumulated on the lower side of the
        shoot *[1 mark]*. This caused the cells on the
        lower side of the shoot to elongate faster,
        so the shoot bent upwards *[1 mark]*.
  c)   The shoots will grow towards the light *[1 mark]*.
        This is because more auxin accumulates on the side that's
        in the shade *[1 mark]*, which stimulates these cells to
        elongate faster causing the shoot to bend towards the light
        [1 mark].

Section 11 — Drugs

Page 95
Warm-Up Questions
1)   A resistant strain could cause a serious infection
        which can't be treated by antibiotics.
2)   e.g. MRSA

Exam Questions
1   C *[1 mark]*
2   Patient B *[1 mark]*
3 a)   Antibiotics don't kill viruses, so prescribing antibiotics
        wouldn't have made the patient well again *[1 mark]*.
  b)   Some of the bacteria may have been resistant to the
        antibiotic prescribed *[1 mark]*. This means that the
        antibiotic would have only killed the non-resistant
        bacteria infecting the patient *[1 mark]*. The resistant
        bacteria would have then gone on to reproduce in
        the patient and maintain the infection *[1 mark]*.
  c)   The patient only has a mild infection for which antibiotics
        aren't really needed *[1 mark]*. Therefore, the doctor does
        not prescribe antibiotics in order to slow down the rate
        at which resistant strains of bacteria develop *[1 mark]*.

Section 12 — Reproduction

Page 101
Warm-Up Questions
1) Sexual reproduction is the process used to produce offspring that are genetically distinct from each other. It involves the fusion of the nuclei of two gametes (fertilisation) to form a zygote.
2) Fertilisation is the fusion of the nuclei of two gametes.
3) Self-pollination is when pollen is transferred from an anther to a stigma on either the same flower or different flower on the same plant.

Exam Questions
1 a) X: Anther *[1 mark]*. It contains the pollen grains *[1 mark]*.
Y: Ovary *[1 mark]*. It contains the female gametes/eggs *[1 mark]*.
b) Flower B because e.g. long filaments hang the anthers outside the flower *[1 mark]*, so that a lot of pollen gets blown away *[1 mark]* / the large, feathery stigmas *[1 mark]* are efficient at catching pollen drifting past in the air *[1 mark]*.
c) Any two from: e.g. brightly coloured petals to attract insects / scented flowers/nectaries to attract insects / large, sticky pollen grains that stick easily to insects / a sticky stigma to collect pollen from insects *[2 marks]*.
2 Because oxygen is needed for germination *[1 mark]* and oxygen was removed from the air in flask A by the sodium pyrogallate solution *[1 mark]*.

Pages 108-109
Warm-Up Questions
1) At the start of the menstrual cycle, menstruation starts and the lining of the uterus breaks down.
2) In the ovaries.

Exam Questions
1 a) X: Sperm duct *[1 mark]*
Y: Urethra *[1 mark]*
b) To produce the liquid that is added to sperm to make semen *[1 mark]*.
c) E.g.

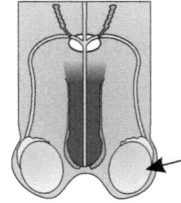

[1 mark for an arrow pointing to either of the testes]
2 a) It allows substances to be exchanged between the mother and the fetus *[1 mark]*.
b) It protects the fetus against knocks/bumps. / It supports the fetus as it grows. / It allows the fetus to move. *[1 mark]*
3 a) testosterone *[1 mark]*
b) Any two from: e.g. extra facial/body hair / development of muscles / enlargement of penis/testes / production of sperm / deepening of voice *[2 marks]*
c) E.g. growth of extra pubic/underarm hair / widening of the hips / development of breasts / start of periods/release of ova *[1 mark]*
4 a) A sexually transmitted infection is an infection that is transmitted through sexual contact *[1 mark]*.
b) HIV is spread via bodily fluids *[1 mark]*. By sharing needles there's a risk of injecting infected bodily fluids/ blood from the previous user of the needle *[1 mark]*.
HIV isn't just spread through sexual contact, although that's a common means of transmission.
c) E.g. abstinence (not having sexual intercourse) / using a condom during sexual intercourse / limiting the number of sexual partners / getting tested for infection after unprotected sex or after contact with several sexual partners / taking medication to reduce the risk of passing the infection on to others *[1 mark]*
5 a) To fertilise an egg. / To carry the male DNA to the female DNA (in the egg). *[1 mark]*
b) E.g. it has a flagellum to enable it to swim to the egg *[1 mark]*. It has lots of mitochondria to provide energy for the flagellum to move *[1 mark]*. The acrosome contains enzymes to help the sperm digest a way through the jelly coat of the egg *[1 mark]*.
6 a) Progesterone inhibits the release of FSH *[1 mark]*.
b) day 14 *[1 mark]*
c) The uterus lining will break down *[1 mark]*.
d) E.g. a high level of progesterone is needed to maintain the lining of the uterus *[1 mark]*.
e) the placenta *[1 mark]*

Section 13 — Inheritance

Page 114
Warm-Up Questions
1)   XY
2)   mitosis

Exam Questions
1 a)   A chromosome is a long length of DNA, which carries genetic information in the form of genes *[1 mark]*.
  b) i)   A diploid nucleus is a nucleus that contains two sets of chromosomes *[1 mark]*.
    ii)   23 *[1 mark]*
2 a)   ribosome(s) *[1 mark]*
  b)   The sequence of bases in the DNA/mRNA *[1 mark]*.
  c)   Cell function is controlled by the production of proteins *[1 mark]*, which is controlled by the genes in DNA *[1 mark]*.
3   B *[1 mark]*

When a cell undergoes meiosis, each new cell ends up with half the number of chromosomes of the original cell.

Page 120
Warm-Up Questions
1)   Inheritance is the transmission of genetic information between generations.
2)   Genotype is the alleles an organism has (its genetic make-up). Phenotype is the observable features of an organism.
3)   on a sex chromosome

Exam Questions
1   Dd *[1 mark]*. Polydactyly is a dominant disorder, so if she was DD all of her children would be affected (and Bissan isn't) *[1 mark]*.

2 a)   E.g.

Genotypes of parents: Rr   Rr

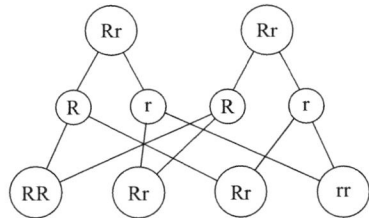

Genotypes of gametes: R   r   R   r

Genotypes of offspring: RR   Rr   Rr   rr

Phenotypes of offspring: red eyes   red eyes   red eyes white eyes

[1 mark for correct genotypes of the parents,
1 mark for correct genotypes of offspring,
1 mark for correct phenotypes of offspring]

You could have drawn a Punnett square instead here, for example:

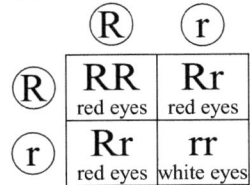

	R	r
R	RR red eyes	Rr red eyes
r	Rr red eyes	rr white eyes

  b)   1 in 4 / 25% *[1 mark]*

3 a) $I^A I^o$ *[1 mark]*
  b) i)

	I^B	I^B
I^A	$I^A I^B$	$I^A I^B$
I^o	$I^B I^o$	$I^B I^o$

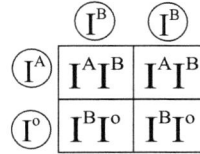

[1 mark for correct alleles in parents,
1 mark for correct genotypes in offspring]
    ii)   0.5 / 50% / 1 in 2 *[1 mark]*
    iii) They will have blood group AB *[1 mark]*, because the I^A and I^B alleles are codominant / neither allele is dominant over the other / both alleles determine phenotype *[1 mark]*.

Section 14 — Variation and Selection

Page 127
Warm-Up Questions
1)   The differences between individuals of the same species.
2)   E.g. pea seed shape / pea seed colour / ABO blood groups.
3)   due to mutations
4)   dry conditions

Exam Questions
1   E.g. the penguin has webbed feet *[1 mark]* to aid swimming *[1 mark]*. / It has a streamlined body *[1 mark]* to reduce drag in water *[1 mark]*. / It has lots of blubber/fat *[1 mark]* to help it stay warm *[1 mark]*.
2   A tall stem plant and a **dwarf** stem plant could be bred together. The offspring with the **highest** grain yield and **highest** resistance to bad weather could then be bred together. Repeating this over several generations means the frequency of the desirable features **increases**. *[1 mark for each word in the correct place, up to a total of 4 marks]*
3   Any two from: e.g. their leaves contain air spaces *[1 mark]* so they can float on the surface of the water and be exposed to the most light *[1 mark]*. / Stomata are usually only present on the upper surface of floating leaves *[1 mark]* to maximise gas exchange *[1 mark]*. / Their stems are flexible *[1 mark]* to prevent damage by currents *[1 mark]*.
4   Ancestors of this stingray showed variation in their appearance *[1 mark]*. These ancestors produced more offspring than could survive *[1 mark]*. Those offspring that looked more like flat rocks were better camouflaged and so less likely to be seen by prey or predators *[1 mark]*. This means they were more likely to survive and reproduce *[1 mark]*. As a result, the alleles that caused the stingrays to look more like flat rocks were more likely to be passed on to the next generation *[1 mark]*. As this process was repeated, the flat rock appearance became more common in the population, until all of the stingrays in the population had this appearance *[1 mark]*.

Section 15 — Organisms and Their Environment

Page 134
Warm-Up Questions
1) a producer
2) A herbivore is an animal that gets its energy by eating plants. A carnivore is an animal that gets its energy by eating other animals.
3) A trophic level is the position an organism occupies in a food chain, food web, or ecological pyramid.
4) So much energy is lost at each trophic level that there's usually not enough left to support more organisms after five stages.

Exam Questions
1 a) E.g. the weevils eat platte thistles so could decrease this population, reducing the food available for honeybees *[1 mark]*. If the honeybee population decreases, the amount of wild honey produced will decrease *[1 mark]*.
   b) decomposers *[1 mark]*
2 a) The concentration of DDT in organisms increases as you go up the trophic levels *[1 mark]*.
   b) $13.8 \div 0.04 =$ **345 times**
      [2 marks for correct answer, otherwise 1 mark for using 13.8 and 0.04 in calculation]
   c) E.g. because DDT is stored in the tissues of animals and a pyramid of biomass represents the mass of the living tissues *[1 mark]*.

Pages 139-140
Warm-Up Questions
1) Lightning makes nitrogen react with oxygen in the air to form nitrates (which plants can take up from the soil and use).
2) Decomposers break down animal and plant proteins and turn them into ammonia — this forms ammonium ions in the soil.
3) A population is a group of organisms of one species, living in the same place, at the same time.
4) An ecosystem is a unit containing a community and its environment, interacting together.

Exam Questions
1 a) i) photosynthesis *[1 mark]*
      ii) carbon dioxide *[1 mark]*
   b) respiration *[1 mark]*
   c) Microorganisms/detritus feeders break down/decompose material from dead organisms *[1 mark]* and return carbon to the air as carbon dioxide through respiration *[1 mark]*.
   d) i) Fossil fuels are formed from dead animals and/or plants which contained carbon *[1 mark]*.
      ii) Carbon is released into the atmosphere as carbon dioxide when fossil fuels are burnt *[1 mark]*.
2 C *[1 mark]*
3 C *[1 mark]*
4 a) i) lag phase *[1 mark]*
      ii) exponential (log) phase *[1 mark]*
      iii) stationary phase *[1 mark]*
   b) E.g. at 12 hours, the population couldn't grow any bigger due to limiting factors (e.g. food, water) *[1 mark]*. At 7 hours, the population size was increasing quickly as the environment had enough resources to support more individuals *[1 mark]*.
   c) E.g. between 16 and 19.5 hours, the population was going through its death phase *[1 mark]*. This happened because the population had used up so many resources that the environment could no longer support it / the population's waste products built up to toxic levels *[1 mark]*.

Section 16 — Human Influences on Ecosystems

Page 145
Warm-Up Questions
1) Any three from: e.g. agricultural machinery / chemical fertilisers / insecticides / herbicides / selective breeding
2) E.g. the animals use less energy moving around and controlling their own body temperature, so they have more energy available for growth, and more meat can be produced.
3) E.g. some people think that making animals live in unnatural/uncomfortable conditions is cruel.
4) Biodiversity is the number of different species that live in an area.

Exam Questions
1 a) i) Any two from: e.g. it's easier to manage / more cost-effective / more profitable *[2 marks]*.
   ii) E.g. the food produced is relatively cheap *[1 mark]*.
   b) E.g. monocultures can require lots of pesticides which can pollute water *[1 mark]*. Monocultures can reduce biodiversity, as they contain fewer plant species than a natural ecosystem. Having fewer plant species means they don't provide habitats for as many organisms *[1 mark]*.
2 a) E.g. to increase the area of land available for crop growth/ livestock production/housing *[1 mark]*. For the extraction of natural resources *[1 mark]*.
   b) Any two from: e.g. loss of soil / flooding / increase of carbon dioxide in the atmosphere *[2 marks]*
   c) E.g. loss of soil — nutrients are lost when soil is washed away, which makes it harder for new trees to grow. / Flooding — flooding can destroy habitats and kill wildlife. / Increase of carbon dioxide in the atmosphere — the carbon dioxide released when trees are burnt contributes to global warming. *[1 mark for each correct explanation, up to a total of 2 marks]*

Page 149
Warm-Up Questions
1) E.g. methane / carbon dioxide
2) Non-biodegradable means can't be broken down through biological decomposition (decomposition by microorganisms).

Exam Questions
1 a) E.g. if organisms eat plastic by mistake they can be poisoned/suffer from intestinal blockages. Organisms can be trapped/entangled/strangled by plastic items. *[2 marks]*
   b) Any two from: e.g. they can take up valuable space in landfills that could be used to feed/house the increasing global population. / They can release toxic gases when they are burnt. / They can release carbon dioxide when they are burnt, which contributes to global warming. / They can release poisons that can enter and contaminate food chains, killing many organisms. *[2 marks]*
2 a) E.g. cattle farming / rice growing *[1 mark]*
   b) Cutting down trees reduces the amount of carbon dioxide removed from the atmosphere during photosynthesis *[1 mark]*. Carbon dioxide is released when trees are burnt to clear land/when dead wood is left to decompose *[1 mark]*.
3 a) E.g. fertilisers *[1 mark]* can leach nitrate ions into waterways (causing eutrophication) *[1 mark]*.
   b) The number of decomposer microorganisms increases downstream of the sewage discharge pipe *[1 mark]*. The sewage provides extra nutrients causing rapid algal growth *[1 mark]*. The algae block out light from plants causing them to die (because they are unable to photosynthesise) *[1 mark]*. The dead plants provide food for decomposer microorganisms, causing the number of decomposer microorganisms to increase *[1 mark]*.

<u>Page 153</u>
<u>Warm-Up Questions</u>
1) A sustainable resource is one which does not run out because it is produced as rapidly as it is removed from the environment.
2) A place where seeds can be stored, with the conditions necessary for keeping them alive for a long time.
3) E.g. to help conserve endangered plant species. / To protect and save plant genetic diversity.

<u>Exam Questions</u>
1 E.g. more offspring will survive to reproduce if the Siberian tigers are bred in captivity, as there is less infant mortality *[1 mark]*. Some of these individuals can then be released into the wild *[1 mark]*.
2 Any three from: e.g. organisms can't adapt to climate change quickly enough. / Habitat destruction reduces the area that an organism can live in. / Animals are killed by hunters. / Species can be affected by pollution in their environment. / Organisms can't defend themselves against or compete with an introduced species. *[3 marks]*
3 B *[1 mark]*
4 a) E.g. it protects a source of food for humans. / It may stop other species (that feed on the fish) from becoming extinct. / It may allow ecosystem functions, like nutrient cycling, to be maintained. *[1 mark]*
   b) Any three from, e.g. legal quotas that put limits on the number and size of fish that can be caught in certain areas *[1 mark]*. / Closed seasons to ban the catching of fish at certain times of year, usually the breeding season *[1 mark]*. / Protected areas, in which certain types of fishing are restricted or banned *[1 mark]*. / Controlled net types and mesh sizes, used to reduce the number of unwanted and discarded fish *[1 mark]*. / Monitoring fish stocks using samples and surveys to help to inform other polices *[1 mark]*. / Education to tell people about the importance of conserving fish stocks/help them make informed choices when shopping for fish *[1 mark]*.

Section 17 — Genetic Modification and Biotechnology

<u>Pages 159-160</u>
<u>Warm-Up Questions</u>
1) E.g. bacteria.
2) Plasmids are used to transfer the desired genes from one organism to another.
3) DNA ligase
4) Any two from: e.g. amylases / proteases / lipases.
5) Any two from: e.g. temperature / pH / oxygen level / nutrient levels / waste products.

<u>Exam Questions</u>
1 a) Genetic modification is the alteration of an organism's genetic material by removing, changing or inserting individual genes *[1 mark]*.
   b) Restriction enzymes *[1 mark]* are used to recognise and cut the desired gene from the organism's DNA *[1 mark]*.
   c) A plasmid is cut open using the same restriction enzyme used to cut out the desired gene *[1 mark]*. The desired gene is then inserted into the plasmid using DNA ligase *[1 mark]*. The recombinant plasmid is then inserted into the target bacterium *[1 mark]*. The modified bacterium multiplies to produce lots of bacteria with the desired characteristics *[1 mark]*.
2 a) Any two from: e.g. bacteria reproduce very quickly in the right conditions. / Bacteria can produce complex molecules. / There aren't many ethical concerns about using bacteria. / Bacteria have plasmids which can be easily modified and transferred. *[2 marks — 1 mark for each correct answer]*
   b) Yeast breaks down sugars to produce ethanol during anaerobic respiration *[1 mark]*. The ethanol is then collected and purified to make biofuel *[1 mark]*.
   c) E.g. enzymes work best at their optimum temperature / if the temperature gets too high, the enzymes will denature *[1 mark]*. So the temperature needs to be controlled to maximise the rate of lactose breakdown *[1 mark]*.
3 a) i) Any one from: e.g. herbicide resistance / insect resistance / a greater nutritional value. *[1 mark]*
      ii) E.g. there would be more maize/food for the growing population to eat, as the yield with herbicide-resistant/insect-resistant plants is usually greater *[1 mark]*. / The maize/food would be better for the growing population as it would provide more nutrients from the same amount of food than the non-genetically modified crops *[1 mark]*.
   b) Any two from: e.g. some people worry that transplanted genes may be passed on to other organisms. / Some people worry that changing an organism's genes could have unforeseen problems that could get passed on to offspring. / Some people worry that genetically modified crops could have a negative impact on food chains/human health. / Genetically modified crops might be expensive. *[2 marks — 1 mark for each correct answer.]*
4 a) E.g. mycoprotein *[1 mark]*
   b) To supply oxygen *[1 mark]* for the fungus to respire aerobically *[1 mark]*.
   c) E.g. to circulate the culture medium inside the fermenter, so the fungus can always access the nutrients needed for growth / to maintain an even temperature/pH inside the fermenter *[1 mark]*. This should increase the yield of penicillin *[1 mark]*.
   d) E.g. nutrients *[1 mark]*.

Paper 1 Multiple Choice (Core)

1   C *[1 mark]*
2   B *[1 mark]*
3   C *[1 mark]*
Image size = magnification × actual size,
so 0.08 mm × 100 = 8 mm.
4   B *[1 mark]*
In the diagram, the concentration of oxygen molecules is higher in the
cell than in the tissue fluid. So the oxygen molecules will move from the
cell to the tissue fluid down the concentration gradient.
5   A *[1 mark]*
6   C *[1 mark]*
7   C *[1 mark]*
8   D *[1 mark]*
9   B *[1 mark]*
10   D *[1 mark]*
11   B *[1 mark]*
12   A *[1 mark]*
13   A *[1 mark]*
14   C *[1 mark]*
15   B *[1 mark]*
16   C *[1 mark]*
17   C *[1 mark]*
18   D *[1 mark]*
19   D *[1 mark]*
20   A *[1 mark]*
21   D *[1 mark]*
22   D *[1 mark]*
23   C *[1 mark]*
24   B *[1 mark]*
25   A *[1 mark]*
26   B *[1 mark]*
27   D *[1 mark]*
You needed to recognise that the flower is
from a wind-pollinated plant.
28   C *[1 mark]*
29   A *[1 mark]*
30   C *[1 mark]*
31   A *[1 mark]*
32   C *[1 mark]*
33   D *[1 mark]*
34   B *[1 mark]*
35   A *[1 mark]*
36   D *[1 mark]*
37   B *[1 mark]*
38   D *[1 mark]*
39   B *[1 mark]*
40   B *[1 mark]*

Paper 2 Multiple Choice (Extended)

1   A *[1 mark]*
2   B *[1 mark]*
3   B *[1 mark]*
4   C *[1 mark]*
Start by converting everything to the same units:
24 mm × 1000 = 24 000 µm.
Magnification = image size ÷ actual size,
so 24 000 µm ÷ 12 µm = 2000.
5   C *[1 mark]*
The rate of diffusion will be faster in beaker A because the temperature
is higher. It will be faster in beaker B because the acid is more
concentrated. It will be faster in D because the surface area to volume
ratio of the agar cubes is larger. The rate of diffusion will be slower in
C because the acid is less concentrated.
6   A *[1 mark]*
7   A *[1 mark]*
8   B *[1 mark]*
9   D *[1 mark]*
10   D *[1 mark]*
11   C *[1 mark]*
12   C *[1 mark]*
13   A *[1 mark]*
14   A *[1 mark]*
15   B *[1 mark]*
16   B *[1 mark]*
17   A *[1 mark]*
18   C *[1 mark]*
19   D *[1 mark]*
20   A *[1 mark]*
21   B *[1 mark]*
22   D *[1 mark]*
23   B *[1 mark]*
24   D *[1 mark]*
25   B *[1 mark]*
26   D *[1 mark]*
27   C *[1 mark]*
28   C *[1 mark]*
29   D *[1 mark]*
30   A *[1 mark]*
31   B *[1 mark]*
32   C *[1 mark]*
8 + 3 = 11% (or 100 − 42 − 47 = 11%). Whichever method you used,
you needed to realise that all the people with blood group B and all the
people with blood group AB have the I^B allele.
33   C *[1 mark]*
34   D *[1 mark]*
35   B *[1 mark]*
36   B *[1 mark]*
37   A *[1 mark]*
38   A *[1 mark]*
39   B *[1 mark]*
40   C *[1 mark]*

Paper 3 Theory (Core)

Pages 202-217

1 a) i) cell membrane *[1 mark]*
   ii) Holds the cell together/controls what enters and leaves the cell *[1 mark]*.
   b) the nucleus *[1 mark]*
   c) The chloroplasts in the cell use light from the Sun *[1 mark]* to produce food/glucose from photosynthesis *[1 mark]*.
   d) i) Any two from: e.g. a plant cell has a cell wall, but an animal cell does not. / A plant cell has chloroplasts, but an animal cell does not. / A plant cell has a vacuole, but an animal cell does not. *[2 marks]*
   ii) E.g. it has a nucleus/cytoplasm/cell membrane/ ribosomes/mitochondria *[1 mark]*.
   e) image size = magnification × actual size
   $$= 150 \times 0.054$$
   $$= \textbf{8.1 mm}$$
   [2 marks for correct answer, otherwise 1 mark for correct working]

2 a) An enzyme is a protein that acts as a biological catalyst in all metabolic reactions *[1 mark]*.
   b) i) E.g. pectinase *[1 mark]*
   ii) E.g. pectinase breaks down pectin in fruit cell walls *[1 mark]* so that the fruit produces juice more easily *[1 mark]*.
   c) i) **glucose → alcohol** + carbon dioxide *[1 mark]*
   ii) E.g. bread making *[1 mark]* and the production of ethanol for biofuels *[1 mark]*.

3 a) A group of different tissues that work together to perform a certain function *[1 mark]*.
   b) bronchiole *[1 mark]*
   c) E.g. alveoli have a large surface area. Alveoli have a thin surface. Alveoli have a good blood supply. *[3 marks]*
   d) i)

	Change in Proportion from Inspired to Expired Air	
Name of Gas	Increases	Decreases
carbon dioxide	✓	
oxygen		✓
water vapour	✓	

   [1 mark for each correct tick]
   ii) There is a higher concentration of oxygen in the alveolus than in the blood capillary *[1 mark]*, so oxygen diffuses *[1 mark]* down its concentration gradient (into the blood capillary) *[1 mark]*.

4 a)

Letter	Stage of the menstrual cycle
C	Ovulation occurs.
D	The uterus lining is maintained ready for the implantation of a fertilised egg.
B	The uterus lining thickens and grows.
A	Menstruation occurs.

   [1 mark for each correct letter]
   b) i) ovary *[1 mark]*
   ii) E.g. they have energy stores in their cytoplasm *[1 mark]*. They have a jelly coating that changes at fertilisation *[1 mark]*.
   c) At fertilisation, one male and one female **gamete** *[1 mark]* fuse to form a **zygote** *[1 mark]*. This then undergoes **cell division** *[1 mark]* and develops into an **embryo** *[1 mark]*.

5 a) Similarity: e.g. both make their own organic nutrients *[1 mark]*. Difference: e.g. the bacteria use the energy from chemicals released by the hydrothermal vent, whereas plants use energy from the Sun *[1 mark]*.
   b) shrimp / tubeworms *[1 mark]*
   c) i) The population of crabs might decrease in size *[1 mark]*, as there would be no tubeworms for them to eat *[1 mark]*.
   ii) The population size of the shrimp could rise *[1 mark]*, as there would be more bacteria for them to eat *[1 mark]*.

6 a) E.g.

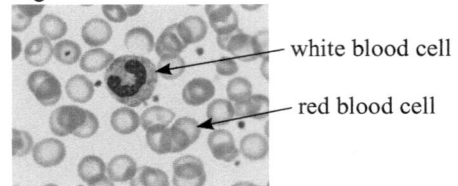

   [1 mark for both a white blood cell and a red blood cell correctly labelled]
   b) i) E.g. platelets *[1 mark]*
   ii) E.g. excessive bleeding/bruising when injured *[1 mark]*
   c) Having more red blood cells means that more oxygen can be carried to the muscles for aerobic respiration *[1 mark]*. This means more energy can be released for muscle contraction *[1 mark]*.

7 a) i) E.g.

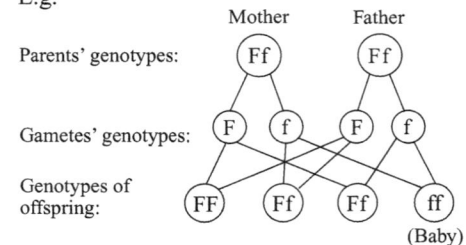

   [1 mark for showing that the parents both have the Ff genotype, 1 mark for showing the gametes' genotypes as F or f, 1 mark for correctly showing all three possible genotypes of the couple's offspring]
   The parents must both have one copy of the recessive allele for cystic fibrosis — so they're both Ff.
   ii) Homozygous, because he has two alleles the same/both of his alleles are recessive *[1 mark]*.

b) 1 in 4 / 25% *[1 mark]*

c) Ff *[1 mark]*. Ian has the genotype Ff, so Leina must also have the genotype Ff in order for her children to inherit the genotypes: FF (Carys), ff (Beth) and Ff (Alfie) *[1 mark]*.

8 a) *Biston [1 mark]*

b) i) the dark variety *[1 mark]*

ii) The dark variety is less likely to be eaten by predators in soot-polluted areas (because they are better camouflaged) *[1 mark]*, so they are more likely to survive to reproduce *[1 mark]*, meaning that the genes for the characteristics that made them successful / genes for dark colouring are more likely to be passed on to the next generation and become more common in the population *[1 mark]*.

c) Town B, because it contains a higher proportion of dark moths *[1 mark]*.

9 a) Genetic modification is the alteration of an organism's genetic material *[1 mark]* by removing, changing or inserting individual genes *[1 mark]*.

b) E.g. bacteria have a rapid reproduction rate *[1 mark]*. Bacteria are able to make complex molecules *[1 mark]*.

c) Organisms with desirable features are selected *[1 mark]*. These organisms are crossed with each other to produce the next generation *[1 mark]*. The offspring with the most desirable features in this generation are then selected and crossed together (so the desirable feature becomes more common in the population) *[1 mark]*.

d) E.g. selective breeding could be used to develop crop plants that grow faster/are disease-resistant *[1 mark]*. This will increase production, creating more food for humans *[1 mark]*.

10a) X — carbon dioxide is being removed from the atmosphere by plants (photosynthesis) *[1 mark]*.
Y — carbon dioxide is being released into the atmosphere by plants and animals (respiration) *[1 mark]*.
Z — carbon compounds in the plants are being transferred to animals as they eat the plants (feeding) *[1 mark]*.

b) E.g. the two sets of data show roughly the same pattern/ a significant increase at the same time *[1 mark]*.

c) Any two from: e.g. the two sets of data may follow similar patterns by chance. / Some other factor may have caused both increases. / The concentration of carbon dioxide varied even when human population was low/fairly constant. *[2 marks]*

d) E.g. deforestation, burning fossil fuels. *[2 marks]*

Paper 4 Theory (Extended)

Pages 218-233

1 a)

	Type of blood vessel		
	Artery	**Capillary**	**Vein**
Walls	Thick, muscular	Very thin	Thin
Presence of valves	No	No	Yes
Pressure of blood in vessels	High	Low	Low

[2 marks for all three correct, otherwise 1 mark for two correct]

b) E.g. the blood supply to the area below the blockage would be cut off/reduced *[1 mark]*. Not enough oxygen would reach this part of the heart muscle, resulting in cells being unable to respire/damage/ death of the muscle tissue/a heart attack *[1 mark]*.

c) i) E.g. Change: reduce the amount of saturated fat in his diet. Reason: this would help to reduce his blood cholesterol level, which would reduce the risk of further fatty deposits forming. / Change: reduce the amount of salt in his diet. Reason: this may help to reduce his blood pressure, which would reduce the risk of further fatty deposits forming. *[1 mark for correct change, 1 mark for correct reason. Maximum 2 marks.]*

ii) E.g. take part in regular exercise *[1 mark]*.

2 a) Because the A and T bases in a DNA molecule always pair up with each other *[1 mark]*.

b) nucleus *[1 mark]*

c) i) A random change in the base sequence of DNA *[1 mark]*.

ii) E.g. exposure to ionising radiation *[1 mark]*.

iii) E.g. a mutation/change in the base sequence of DNA could lead to a change in the amino acid sequence of the enzyme *[1 mark]*. This could alter the shape of the enzyme's active site *[1 mark]*, which could mean it is unable to bind to its substrate and catalyse a reaction (preventing the enzyme from functioning) *[1 mark]*.

3 a) homeostasis *[1 mark]*

b) Receptors monitor the temperature of the blood and the brain coordinates a response based on signals from these receptors *[1 mark]*.

c) i) Arterioles supplying skin capillaries may have constricted / vasoconstriction may have taken place in the arterioles supplying the skin capillaries *[1 mark]*. This would have reduced the amount of heat radiated from his skin to the environment *[1 mark]*.

ii) They may have started to shiver/contract in spasms *[1 mark]*. This would have increased respiration in the muscle cells *[1 mark]*, which would have released more heat to warm the body *[1 mark]*.

256

4 a) i) 130 J *[1 mark]*
Tertiary consumers are the third consumers in a food chain
— so in this case the tertiary consumers are the snakes.

   ii) The plants absorb energy from the Sun
[1 mark] during photosynthesis *[1 mark]*.

   iii) $(130 \div 1100) \times 100\% = $ **12.0%**
[2 marks for correct answer, otherwise 1 mark
for using $130 \div 1100$ in working]

  b) D *[1 mark]*, because the biomass of the organisms
decreases at each trophic level and the bars on this
pyramid get smaller at each trophic level *[1 mark]*.

5 a) i) Light coming through the hole in the box caused
more auxin to accumulate on the shaded sides of the
shoots *[1 mark]*. This made the cells on the shaded
sides of the plants grow/elongate faster *[1 mark]*,
so the shoots bent towards the light *[1 mark]*.

   ii) phototropism *[1 mark]*

  b) i) $6CO_2 + 6H_2O \longrightarrow C_6H_{12}O_6 + 6O_2$
[2 marks for correct answer, otherwise 1 mark for
writing three of the four symbols correctly]

   ii) Any three from: e.g. for respiration / to make cellulose
/ for storage as starch / to make nectar / to make
sucrose for transport in the phloem *[3 marks]*.

  c) i) gravity *[1 mark]*

   ii) E.g. so the roots grow into the soil, where they
can absorb water/mineral ions *[1 mark]*.

6 a) 9:00 a.m. *[1 mark]*

  b) E.g. day 2 was colder, so the water evaporated/diffused
more slowly. / Day 2 was more humid/less windy, so there
was a smaller concentration gradient between the inside
and outside of the leaf so diffusion couldn't happen as
quickly. *[1 mark for reason, 1 mark for explanation]*.

  c) The plant has lost too much water/has lost water faster
than it could be replaced through the roots *[1 mark]*
so its cells have become flaccid/there's not enough
turgor pressure to support the plant *[1 mark]*.

  d) Transpiration/diffusion of water from the stomata
creates a slight shortage of water in the leaf *[1 mark]*.
This draws more water into the leaf, which causes a
column of water molecules to be drawn up through
the plant's xylem vessels *[1 mark]* because water
molecules are held together by forces of attraction
[1 mark]. This in turn means that more water is
drawn up from the roots, and so there's a constant
transpiration pull of water through the plant *[1 mark]*.

7 a) E.g.

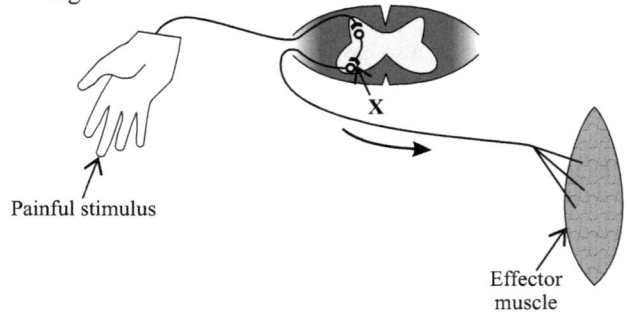

Painful stimulus

Effector
muscle

[1 mark for an arrow anywhere on the neurone
after the X, pointing towards the effector]

  b) When the nerve impulse reaches X/the synaptic gap,
it triggers the release of neurotransmitters *[1 mark]*.
These neurotransmitters diffuse across X/the synaptic
gap to bind with receptor proteins on the membrane of
the next neurone *[1 mark]*, causing the nerve impulse
to continue in the next neurone *[1 mark]*. The receptors
are only on one side of X/the synaptic gap, so the
impulse can only travel in one direction *[1 mark]*.

  c) The stimulus is detected by receptors in the hand *[1 mark]*
and converted into a nerve impulse, which travels along a
sensory neurone *[1 mark]* to a synapse in the CNS/central
nervous system/spinal cord *[1 mark]*. The impulse then
travels along a relay neurone to another synapse *[1 mark]*
before travelling along the motor neurone *[1 mark]* to
the effector muscle, which responds by contracting to
move the hand away from the source of pain *[1 mark]*.

8 a)

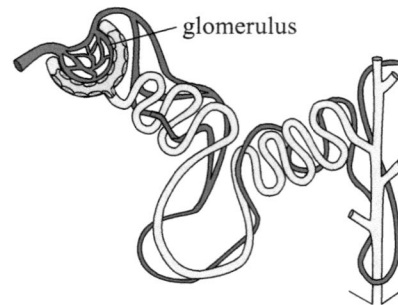

glomerulus

[1 mark]

  b) i) Urea is not reabsorbed into the blood, so its
concentration increases through the nephron
as water is reabsorbed *[1 mark]*.

   ii) The concentration of glucose at point B would
be high and there would be no glucose at point C
[1 mark], as all glucose is reabsorbed back into the
blood in the first part of the nephron *[1 mark]*.

  c) renal artery *[1 mark]*

Answers

9   E.g. the weakened measles virus is injected into the body *[1 mark]*. The antigens on the virus trigger an immune response by lymphocytes *[1 mark]*, which produce antibodies as normal *[1 mark]*. The antigens also trigger the production of memory cells, which give long-term immunity to the measles virus *[1 mark]*.

10a)   The alleles for white hair colour and red hair colour are said to be codominant because they both contribute to the phenotype *[1 mark]* in a heterozygous organism *[1 mark]*.

b) i) E.g.

Bull's gametes

		C^R	C^R
Cow's gametes	C^W	$C^W C^R$	$C^W C^R$
	C^R	$C^R C^R$	$C^R C^R$

Probability of a roan calf = 50% / 0.5 / 1 in 2
[1 mark for the correct genotypes of the bull's gametes, 1 mark for the correct genotype of the cow's gametes, 1 mark for the correct genotypes of the offspring, 1 mark for 50% / 0.5 / 1 in 2. Maximum 4 marks.]

ii) 1 $C^W C^W$ *[1 mark]* : 2 $C^W C^R$ *[1 mark]*: 1 $C^R C^R$ *[1 mark]*

c)   E.g. a population of cows that has undergone artificial selection is likely to be inbred *[1 mark]*. This means that the artificially selected population will have low genetic variation *[1 mark]*, which means they are likely to be susceptible to the same diseases *[1 mark]*.

Paper 5 Alternative to Practical

Pages 234-241

1 a) i) Any two from: e.g. the type of potato used for each cylinder / the size of potato cylinder / the volume of sugar solution / the temperature *[2 marks]*.

ii) E.g. the amount of sugar solution removed when the potato cylinders are dried with tissue paper may vary for each cylinder *[1 mark]*. Make sure the method of drying the potato cylinders is the same each time *[1 mark]*.

b) i) $(-0.78 + -0.81 + -0.82) \div 3 = -2.41 \div 3 = -0.8033...$
= **−0.80 g** (to 2 s.f.) *[1 mark]*

ii) To give more reliable results *[1 mark]*.

c)

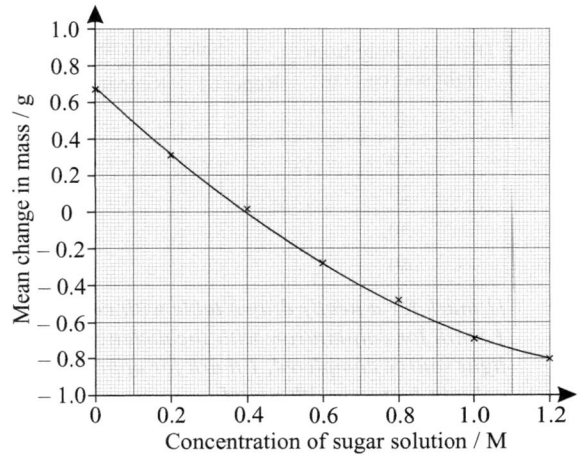

[1 mark for choosing suitable scales, 1 mark for a curve of best fit, 1 mark for having axes labelled correctly with independent variable on the x-axis and dependent variable on the y-axis (with correct units), 2 marks for all points plotted correctly (or 1 mark for at least 5 points plotted correctly). Plotting marks may still be given if an incorrect answer to 1 (b) (i) has been plotted correctly or if variables are on the wrong axes.]

d) i) E.g. she should add Benedict's solution to a sample of solution from each of the test tubes using a pipette *[1 mark]*. She should then place the samples in a water bath set at 80 °C *[1 mark]*. She should look out for a colour change and note the final colour of each solution *[1 mark]*.

ii)

	Tube 1	Tube 2	Tube 3	Tube 4
substance observed	yellow precipitate	blue solution	red precipitate	green precipitate
glucose concentration / M	**0.1**	**0**	**1**	**0.02**

[1 mark]

The higher the concentration of glucose in the solution, the further the colour change goes along the following scale: blue — green — yellow — orange — brick red. If no precipitate forms then there are no reducing sugars in the solution.

e) i)   E.g. $(41 + 47) \div 2 = $ **44 mm**
[2 marks for an answer between 43.5 mm and 44.5 mm, otherwise 1 mark for correct measurement of cell B between 46 mm and 48 mm]

   ii) The drawing should occupy at least half of the available space *[1 mark]*. The drawing should not include any colouring/shading and should be drawn with clear, unbroken lines *[1 mark]*. Structures inside the cell should be drawn in proportion *[1 mark]*. The cytoplasm and starch grains should be labelled using straight, uncrossed lines drawn with a ruler *[1 mark]*.

2 a) i)   gas syringe *[1 mark]*

   ii) E.g. so the same volume of carbon dioxide is released each time *[1 mark]*.

 b)   E.g.

Distance away from light source / cm	Gas collected / cm^3		
	Repeat 1	Repeat 2	Repeat 3
0			
10			
20			
30			
40			

[1 mark for a neatly drawn table with cells for 15 results, 1 mark for column/row with the distances away from light source completed, 1 mark for appropriate row/column headers with units]

 c) i) $0.20 \div 2 = $ **0.10 cm^3/h** *[1 mark]*

   ii) 20 cm *[1 mark]*. The volume of gas collected is higher than that for 10 cm *[1 mark]*.

   iii) As the distance from the light source increases, the rate of gas production decreases *[1 mark]*. This is because the intensity of the light reaching the plant decreases as the light source is placed further away *[1 mark]*.

   iv) E.g. by repeating the experiment at a greater distance from the light source *[1 mark]*.

 d)   E.g. different light sources may produce different intensities of light *[1 mark]*, so using the same light source helps to ensure that the distance between the light source and the test tube is the only thing affecting the light intensity *[1 mark]*.

 e) i)   E.g. wear gloves / a lab coat / safety goggles / keep away from naked flames *[1 mark]*.

   ii) The leaf will have turned blue-black *[1 mark]*.

 f)   E.g. the student could carry out the experiment as described, but instead of varying the distance, the student should keep the light source at the same distance from the test tube throughout the experiment *[1 mark]*. She should instead vary the temperature, by carrying out the experiment at a range of different temperatures, e.g. 10 °C, 20 °C, 30 °C, 40 °C *[1 mark]*. To vary the temperature she should put the test tube in a water bath set to a constant temperature *[1 mark]* and monitor the temperature using a thermometer *[1 mark]*.

Glossary

absorption	The movement of nutrients through the wall of the intestine into the blood.
active immunity	The defence against a pathogen by the production of antibodies in the body.
active site	The part of an enzyme where the substrate binds.
active transport	The movement of particles across a cell membrane from an area of lower concentration to an area of higher concentration using energy from respiration.
adaptation (process of)	The process by which populations become more suited to their environment over several generations. It happens as a result of natural selection.
adaptive feature	A characteristic that an organism inherits, which helps it to survive and reproduce in its environment.
aerobic respiration	The series of chemical reactions in cells that uses oxygen to break down nutrient molecules to release energy.
allele	An alternative version of a gene.
anaerobic respiration	The series of chemical reactions in cells that breaks down nutrient molecules to release energy without using oxygen.
antibody	A protein produced by white blood cells to help to destroy pathogens.
antigen	A molecule on the surface of a cell, e.g. a pathogen, that can cause a response from white blood cells.
asexual reproduction	The process used to produce genetically identical offspring from one parent.
assimilation	The movement of nutrients into the cells of the body where they are used, becoming part of the cells.
balanced diet	A diet that gives you all the essential nutrients you need in the right proportions.
binomial system	An internationally agreed system to scientifically name organisms using their genus and species.
biodiversity	The number of different species that live in a particular area.
biotechnology	The manipulation of living things and biological processes to produce a useful product.
carnivore	An animal that gets its energy by eating other animals.
catalyst	A substance which increases the rate of a reaction, without being changed or used up in the reaction.
cell	Microscopic building block of all life. All living things are made up of cells.
chemical digestion	The breakdown of larger, insoluble molecules into smaller, soluble molecules.
cholera	A disease caused by a bacterium that is transmitted through contaminated water. It causes diarrhoea, dehydration and loss of ions from the blood.

Glossary

chromosome	A long length of DNA, which carries genetic information in the form of genes.
circulatory system	A system of blood vessels with a pump (the heart) and valves to make sure that blood always flows in one direction.
codominance	When both of the alleles in a heterozygous organism are expressed and so both determine the organism's phenotype.
community	All the populations of different species living in an ecosystem.
consumer	An organism that gets its energy by feeding on other organisms.
cross-pollination	When pollen is transferred from the anther of a flower to the stigma on a flower from a different plant of the same species.
deamination	The removal of the nitrogen-containing portion of amino acids to produce urea.
decomposer	An organism that gets its energy from breaking down dead material and waste.
diffusion	The net movement of particles from an area of higher concentration to an area of lower concentration as a result of their random movement.
diploid nucleus	A nucleus that contains two sets of chromosomes.
DNA	A molecule that carries the genetic information necessary to make proteins in a cell.
dominant allele	An allele that is always expressed if it is present.
drug	Any substance that when taken into the body will affect or change chemical reactions in the body.
ecosystem	A unit containing a community and its environment, interacting together.
egestion	The passing out of food that has not been digested or absorbed, as faeces, through the anus.
enzyme	A protein that acts as a biological catalyst in metabolic reactions.
excretion	The removal of metabolic waste products and of substances that are in excess of what the organism needs.
fertilisation	The fusion of the nuclei of two gametes.
flaccid cell	A plant cell that is limp and wilted due to loss of water.
food chain	A diagram showing the transfer of energy between organisms, starting with a producer.
food web	A network of interconnected food chains.
gamete	A sex cell, e.g. a sperm or an egg cell.
gene	A section of DNA that codes for a protein.

Glossary

gene mutation	A random change in the base sequence of DNA.
genetic modification	The alteration of an organism's genetic material by removing, changing or inserting individual genes.
genotype	The alleles an organism has (its genetic make-up).
gravitropism	A response in which parts of a plant grow towards or away from gravity.
growth	The process by which the size and dry mass of an organism increases permanently.
haploid nucleus	A nucleus that contains a single set of chromosomes.
herbivore	An animal that gets its energy by eating plants.
heterozygous	Having two different alleles for a particular gene.
homeostasis	The maintenance of a constant internal environment.
homozygous	Having two identical alleles for a particular gene.
hormone	A chemical produced by glands and carried by the blood, which changes the activity of a specific target organ or organs.
ingestion	The taking of substances (e.g. food and drink) into the body through the mouth.
inheritance	The transmission of genetic information (DNA) between generations.
limiting factor	Something present in the environment in such short supply that it restricts life processes.
meiosis	A reduction division, which halves the chromosome number from diploid to haploid, resulting in four genetically different cells.
metabolism	All of the chemical reactions that happen in cells, including respiration.
mitosis	Nuclear division that results in two genetically identical cells.
movement	An action made by an organism or parts of an organism which results in a change of place or position.
mutation	Genetic change.
natural selection	The process that results in organisms that are better adapted to their environment being more likely to survive and reproduce.
nutrition	The taking in of substances used for energy, growth and development in organisms.
organ	A group of different tissues that work together to perform specific functions.
organ system	A group of organs working together to perform body functions.

Glossary

organism	A living thing. All organisms share the same basic characteristics — movement, respiration, sensitivity, growth, reproduction, excretion and nutrition.
osmosis	(Core) The diffusion of water molecules through a partially permeable membrane. (Extended) The net movement of water molecules from an area of higher water potential to an area of lower water potential, across a partially permeable membrane.
passive immunity	The short-term defence against a pathogen by antibodies made by a different organism.
pathogen	Any organism that causes disease.
phenotype	The observable features of an organism.
photosynthesis	The process that plants use to synthesise carbohydrates (glucose) from raw materials (carbon dioxide and water) using energy from light.
phototropism	A response in which parts of a plant grow towards or away from a source of light.
physical digestion	The breakdown of food into smaller pieces without the food molecules undergoing a chemical change.
plasmolysis	When the cytoplasm inside a plant cell starts to shrink and the membrane pulls away from the cell wall because the cell is short of water.
pollination	The transfer of pollen from the anther of a flower to a stigma.
population	A group of organisms of one species living in the same place at the same time.
producer	An organism that makes its own organic nutrients (food), usually using energy from the Sun during photosynthesis.
recessive allele	An allele that is only expressed when the dominant version of the allele is not present in the organism's genotype.
reflex action	A rapid, automatic response to a certain stimulus that doesn't involve the conscious part of the brain.
reproduction	The processes that produce more of the same type of organism.
respiration	The chemical reactions that happen in cells to break down nutrient molecules and release the energy needed for metabolism.
selective breeding	When humans artificially select the plants or animals that are going to breed so that the frequency of the alleles for desired characteristics increases in a population.
self-pollination	When pollen is transferred from the anther of a flower to the stigma on either the same flower or a different flower on the same plant.
sense organ	A group of receptor cells that respond to a specific type of stimulus (e.g. light, sound, touch, temperature and chemicals).
sensitivity	The ability of an organism to detect and respond to changes in its internal or external environment.

Glossary

sex-linked characteristic	A feature that is coded for by a gene located on a sex chromosome, making it more common in one sex than in the other.
sexual reproduction	The process used to produce offspring that are genetically distinct from each other. It involves the fusion of the nuclei of two gametes (fertilisation) to form a zygote.
sexually transmitted infection (STI)	An infection that is transmitted through sexual contact.
sink	Any part of a plant where sucrose or amino acids are stored or used up.
source	Any part of a plant that releases sucrose or amino acids.
species	A group of similar organisms that can reproduce to give fertile offspring.
stem cell	An unspecialised cell that divides by mitosis to produce identical daughter cells that can become specialised for specific functions.
stimulus	A change in an organism's environment.
sustainable resource	A resource which does not run out because it is made as rapidly as it is removed from the environment.
synapse	A junction between two neurones.
tissue	A group of similar cells that work together to carry out a shared function.
translocation	The movement of sucrose and amino acids through the phloem from a source to a sink.
transmissible disease	A disease where the pathogen can be passed from one host to another.
transpiration	The loss of water vapour from plant leaves.
trophic level	The position an organism occupies in a food chain, food web or ecological pyramid.
turgid cell	A plant cell that is plump and swollen.
turgor pressure	The pressure of water against an inelastic plant cell wall.
variation	The differences between individuals of the same species.
water potential	The likelihood of water molecules to diffuse out of or into a solution.
zygote	A fertilised egg cell.

Index

Index

Index

Index

Index